Diagnosis and Intervention in Behavior Therapy and Behavioral Medicine

Volume 1

Diagnosis and Intervention in Behavior Therapy and Behavioral Medicine

Volume 1

Reid J. Daitzman, Ph.D.
Editor

SPRINGER PUBLISHING COMPANY
New York

For Paula, Sarah, and Brian
and in memory of
Larry Cohen, 1977–1980

Springer Publisher Company, Inc.
200 Park Avenue South
New York, New York 10003

83 84 85 86 87 / 10 9 8 7 6 5 4 3 2 1

Library of Congress Cataloging in Publication Data

Main entry under title:

Diagnosis and intervention in behavior therapy and behavioral medicine.
Includes bibliographies and index.
1. Behavior therapy. 2. Psychology, Pathological. 3. Medicine, Psychosomatic. I. Daitzman, Reid J.
[DNLM: 1. Behavior therapy. WM 425 D536]
RC489.B4D5 1983 616.08 82-16737
ISBN 0-8261-4040-8 (v. 1)

Printed in the United States of America

Contents

Editor and Contributors

Editor

Reid J. Daitzman, Ph.D., received his doctorate from the University of Delaware, an M.S. from Virginia Commonwealth University, and a B.A. from Rutgers University. Formerly, he was an Assistant Professor of Psychiatry and Assistant Director of the Adult Psychiatry Clinic at the University of Virginia School of Medicine. Presently, he is in independent practice in Stamford, Connecticut, and affiliated with the Center for Behavioral and Psychosomatic Medicine, New Haven.

Contributors

James E. Byassee, Ph.D.
Duke University Medical Center
Department of Psychiatry
Durham, North Carolina

Stephen P. Farr, Ph.D.
Texas Tech University
School of Medicine
Lubbock, Texas

Bruce Heller, Ph.D.
University of California
School of Medicine
Langley Porter Institute
San Francisco, California

Jeffrey Klein, Ph.D.
The Sheppard and Enoch
Pratt Hospital
Baltimore, Maryland

Matisyohu Weisenberg, Ph.D.
Bar-Ilan University
Ramat-Gan, Israel

James P. Curran, Ph.D.
Veterans Administration Medical
Center at Davis Park
Providence, Rhode Island

Mario Fischetti, Ph.D.
Veterans Administration Medical
Center at Davis Park
Providence, Rhode Island

William G. Johnson, Ph.D.
University of Mississippi
Medical Center
Jackson, Mississippi

Lydia Temoshok, Ph.D.
University of California
School of Medicine
Langley Porter Institute
San Francisco, California

Acknowledgments

All publications are a collaboration, although the author receives most of the credit. In this case I would like to give recognition to those professional colleagues who gave me the opportunity to grow, to share ideas and frustrations, and who provided a supportive environment to give me the energy to pursue writing. Among these colleagues are Ward McFarland, Jr., Remo Fabbri, Jr., Bill Sherman, Fred Sheftell, Alan Rapoport, and Irwin Zucker. Their accessibility makes my life easier.

I would also like to thank Bernie Mazel for believing in my abilities and channeling my energies, and Ursula Springer for the opportunity to publish this book. Finally, I want to thank my clients. By helping them help themselves, I become wiser every day. I hope the process never ends.

R.J.D.

Introduction

As a practicing clinical psychologist, I am sometimes overwhelmed by the variety of disorders and aberrant lifestyles, attitudes, and symptoms presented to me in my private practice. As a researcher I am overwhelmed by the variety of resources, number of journals, bibliographic data bases, and conflicting theoretical positions advocated by "experts" and respected academicians. Accordingly, the purpose of this volume and subsequent volumes was selfishness and enlightenment: selfishness because I needed a single resource to help me in my clinical practice and enlightenment because I would be given the opportunity to set priorities, establish relevant chapter outlines, and subsequently edit manuscripts that were strictly organized, timely, and practical in the fields of behavior therapy and behavioral medicine. During this process I presumably would become a more effective clinician and researcher and, more important, other readers of the final product would similarly become more effective clinicians, teachers, and researchers. Only you, the reader, will be able to determine whether these noble goals have been achieved.

Outstanding clinicians and researchers were requested to submit specially formated chapters that were cross-referenced with the then DSM-II, and now DSM-III. In turn, Advisory Editors reviewed each contribution for completeness, clarity, and quality.

The previous two volumes of this multi-volume work were published by Garland Publishing Company and were entitled *Clinical Behavior Therapy and Behavior Modification*. (Daitzman, 1980, 1981). In those two volumes, chapter topics included obsessive-compulsive disorders, enuresis, seizure disorders, drug abuse, alcoholism, depression, erectile dysfunction, marital problems, and headache. The present volume, which is part of a multi-volume work to be published by Springer Publishing Company, includes chapters on heterosexual-social anxiety, essentially hypertension, pain and pain control, obesity, encopresis, and hysteria.

Heterosexual-social Anxiety

Heterosexual-social anxiety is a major concern to a significant number of individuals engaged in dating encounters. It is one of the more frequent complaints raised by undergraduate populations utilizing college counseling centers.

The experience and effects of heterosexual-social anxiety, however, are not limited to undergraduates or the undergraduate years. They also appear to have implications for a number of other populations and for later social functioning and various psychiatric disorders.

Essential Hypertension

Essential hypertension is a major health problem throughout the world. For example, this disorder affects well over 20 million persons in the United States alone. Hypertension is associated with reduced life expectancy due to an increase in the frequency of heart attack, stroke, and heart and kidney failure, and it is considered to be a major cause of death.

Between 90 and 95 percent of all hypertension cases can be diagnosed as essential hypertension, which usually is defined by exclusion after ruling out other antecedent organic pathology. The criterion for a diagnosis of hypertension is somewhat arbitrary, with most investigators accepting a lower limit of approximately 140 mm Hg systolic and 90 mm Hg diastolic. Many factors, such as race, heredity, weight, age, diet, salt intake, kidney problems, and hormonal factors, may influence the recorded pressure. Further, the regulation of blood pressure is exceedingly complex and is affected by numerous different physiological systems and feedback loops. This has tended to obscure further complete understanding of the disease.

It has also been well established that lowering blood pressure by pharmacotherapy dramatically reduces these risks. A complication has been the health service delivery difficulties of screening, side effects of antihypertensive drugs, and lack of patient compliance with prescribed treatment.

Pain

Pain is a complex phenomenon that includes both sensory and motivational-emotional components. Pain is not synonymous with nociceptive stimulation or injury. The pain patient may present with absence of clear physiologically defined problems and with little of the classically defined psychopathological symptoms. Yet the patient seems to be suffering greatly. Psychologists have been able to contribute a great deal to the alleviation of patient suffering by the application of behavioral techniques and strategies. Some of these techniques are designed to deal with anxiety; others to deal with depression and helplessness.

At present, most psychologists have learned how to treat pain patients based upon their own clinical experiences. Most graduate programs have not developed training programs to prepare psychologists to deal with problems of pain as well as with many other problems having a significant physical component. Routine clinical assessment is often not adequate for the pain patient. Greater standardization of appropriate assessment procedures would greatly benefit patient care.

Obesity

Obesity is now recognized as a major public health problem in the United States. Individuals who are more than 20 percent in excess of an ideal weight are at risk for the development of a variety of diseases and a shortened life span. Conditions frequently associated with overweight include a number of cardiovascular and kidney diseases, diabetes, and cancer, to name a few. Evidence is now accumulating that risk for the development of these diseases and perhaps mortality can be decreased as a consequence of weight reduction.

Encopresis

Encopresis is a disorder which involves difficulty in the control of fecal expulsion. Some professionals view inappropriate fecal elimination as dysfunctional and problematic when it occurs in a child over two years of age, while some feel that the lack of control over fecal expulsion becomes problematic beyond the age of four. In addition, the number of soiling incidents that must occur before the behavior is labeled "encopresis" is not well specified in most accounts of the problem.

Three separate groups of encopretic children can be delineated: (1) feebleminded or untrained children; (2) children who have a nervous-system or anatomical defect from such disorders as Hirschsprung's disease; and (3) children whose encopresis stems from psychological and behavioral variables. Behavioral interventions may be especially appropriate for the treatment of encopresis.

Hysteria

In its 4,000 year history, "hysteria" has been one of the most active and perplexing concepts challenging human description and understanding. Massive diagnostic revisions in the American Psychiatric Association's *Diagnostic and Statistical Manual,* especially in the third edition (DSM-III), have had a huge impact on the categorization of hysteria. Hysterical personality became Histrionic Personality Disorder, the name change reflecting the syndrome's defining characteristic. The conversion type of hysterical neurosis was split into symptomatically and behaviorally defined categories under the rubric of Somatoform Disorders. A new category, Factitious Disorders, was distinguished from Malingering in terms of the nature of the goals pursued. The dissociative type of hysterical neurosis was similarly split into distinct diagnoses under a separate heading, Dissociative Disorders. The old designation "hysterical psychosis" was officially resurrected under the category Brief Reactive Psychosis. Unfortunately, assessment has not kept up with these diagnostic changes.

The Need for Standardized Chapter Formats

A major goal of the present multi-volumed work was to organize and systematize the chapters with a common single outline. These common outlines would guide the individual contributors as to how to conceptualize the chapter topics and guide the reader by allowing him to compare similar sections among *different* chapters.

Two separate contributor chapter outlines are used: one for diagnosis and the other for intervention.

Contributor Chapter Format for Diagnosis Chapters

Each chapter has ten sections:

1. Introduction and scope of diagnostic category
2. Theoretical analysis, both behavioral and nonbehavioral
3. Assessment-projective, objective, behavioral
4. Proven treatment procedures based upon literature search
5. Prototype clinical prescription
6. Sample case report illustrating clinical prescription
7. Ethical and legal issues and need for special equipment/instrumentation

8. Suggestions for future clinical and experimental investigation(s)
9. One-thousand-word summary
10. References and bibliography.

These ten sections outline the following six questions that the reader of a chapter should be able to answer:

1. What specific intervention(s) and strategies are the treatment(s) of choice for the specific disorder?

2. What is the empirical basis of these intervention strategies, and how well designed was the research?

3. How are the intervention strategies best applied, and what further education, supervision, and equipment is needed for best results?

4. How strong is the relationship between assessment(s) and treatment(s)? Is there discriminant and convergent validity of the various dependent assessment/intervention measures?

5. How can the optimal treatment methods be better standardized, and what types of research can be designed in the near future to further refine the necessary and sufficient assessment/intervention variables?

6. What are the legal and ethical considerations and constraints to be considered before, during, and after implementation of the optimal treatment strategies?

Contributor Format for Intervention Chapters

The intervention chapter outline follows eleven major categories and fifteen subcategories. It is suggested that clinicians follow these major categories when planning any intervention in order to help organize their thinking in the area.

I. Intervention:
  A. Name(s) of Intervention, e.g., Covert Sensitization
  B. Selective Reference Articles
    1. Literature review
    2. Theoretical review
    3. Clinical case reports
  C. Treatment Goal
  D. Theoretical Basis of Mechanism(s) of Change
  E. Concurrent Interventions and Priority of Intervention(s)
  F. Course of Therapeutic Intervention
    1. Rationale presented to client
    2. Client variables
    3. Therapeutic environment
    4. Equipment

5. Data gathering
   a. Self-report
   b. Observation
   c. Self-monitoring
   d. Permanent product measures
   e. Physiological measures
6. Within session recordkeeping form(s)
7. Between session recordkeeping form(s)
8. Homework and recordkeeping for client
9. Group Administration
10. Special problems
    a. Compliance
    b. Relapse prevention
    c. Booster sessions
    d. Precautions of implementation
    e. Contraindication(s)
    f. Paraprofessional administration
    g. Self-help guides/books
    h. Ethical issues
    i. Legal issues
11. Criteria for termination of intervention
12. Referral or concurrent treatment to physician or other health professional

G. DSM-III Diagnoses Where Implementation Could Be Applied
H. Suggestions for Future Research
I. 1,000-Word Summary
J. References
K. Suggested Bibliography

The first three volumes of this work (two from Garland Publishing Company and this volume from Springer Publishing Company) have emphasized diagnosis, with the chapters arranged under the ten-section format listed previously. Future volumes will combine diagnosis and intervention, with an emphasis upon intervention cross-referenced with the eighteen diagnosis chapters. For example, one intervention chapter planned for the next volume is "covert sensitization." The question remains: When is covert sensitization the treatment of choice as well as the priority treatment of choice, and which diagnostic categories would best suggest the implementation of this intervention? Covert sensitization is usually applied with disorders of behavioral excess and loss of self-control, like the addictions and sexual deviations. Covert sensitization, like many interventions, is applied concurrently with other techniques. The intervention chapter for covert sensitization would help organize the determinants and priorities of implementation of covert processes and would cross-reference with earlier chapters on drug abuse, alcoholism, smoking, and obesity.

Design Quality Rating

Once a diagnosis is established, the resulting treatment(s) should be empirically based upon well-designed clinical and experimental research. No one publication has systematically measured the design quality of the literature upon which the treatment was based. The contributors were asked to assign a design quality rating (Gurman & Kriskern, 1978) to each investigation in the chapter. Sometimes this proved to be extremely difficult. Not only were individual papers difficult to score, but entire diagnostic areas were hazy as to experimental design. Where the assignment of the DQR scores proved to be virtually impossible, it is assumed that the probable total score would be in the 0–10 range (poor).

The DQR involves the summation of 13 separate scores. In turn, those scores, which have a value of "5," "3," "1," or "½," are totaled for the DQR. A 0–10 is poor; 10½–15 is fair; 15½–20 is good; and 20½–32 is very good. The 13 criteria and their individual scores follow.

1. Controlled assignment to treatment conditions: random assignment, matching of total groups or matching in pairs (5)

2. Pre–post measurement of change (5)

3. No contamination of major independent variables, e.g., therapists' experience levels, number of therapists per treatment condition, and relevant therapeutic competence; e.g., a psychoanalyst using behavior therapy for the first time offers a poor test of the power of a behavioral method (5)

4. Appropriate statistical analysis (5)

5. Follow-up: none (0), 1–3 months (½), 3–12 months (1), 13–18 months (3), more than 18 months (5)

6. Treatments equally valued: i.e., tremendous biases are often engendered for both therapist and patients when this criterion is not met (1)

7. Treatment carried out as described or expected: clear evidence (1), presumptive evidence (½)

8. Multiple change indices used (1)

9. Multiple vantage points used in assessing outcome (1)

10. Data on other concurrent treatment: evidence of no treatment, or of such treatment without documentation of amount or equivalence (½)

11. Equal treatment length in comparative studies (1)
12. Outcome assessment allowing for both positive and negative change (1)
13. Therapist–investigator nonequivalence (1).

Prescriptive Behavioral Eclecticism, Behavior Therapy, and Behavioral Medicine

Many diagnoses suggest generalized interventions. Furthermore, results of interventions are diagnostic and suggest more rigorous, planned behavior changes. These planned behavior changes become both more refined and diffuse based upon the needs of the particular client, therapeutic progress, therapeutic rapport, and the theoretical bias of the clinician.

Therapy is an ebb and flow with the components interacting toward a goal. Presumably, this goal is known to both doctor and patient. When these conditions are satisfied, the probability of successful therapy is increased. When the ebb and flow is blocked (through lack of preparation, poor rapport, poor motivation, misdiagnosis, or faulty interventions), the probability of the therapeutic experience being successful is decreased. Planned behavior change must be based upon both the needs of the patient and the skill of the therapist; thus diagnosis and intervention must be prescriptive and eclectic.

The exciting prospects of behavioral medicine and behavior therapy are that the fields are richly diverse and interactive. Although "behavioral medicine" is usually used to define a field of inquiry (interventions in psychophysiological and medical problems), behavior therapy is usually defined as the process of intervention using experimentally derived principles of learning and conditioning. In combination, the terms suggest that experimentally derived principles of learning can be applied to psychophysiological and medical disorders. These applications are relevant to more than pathological clinical entities and symptomatic behaviors and encompass disease prevention, rehabilitation, and the maintenance of disease/symptom-free individuals once the diagnostic-behavioral medicine intervention has been completed.

One problem with diagnosis and intervention in behavioral medicine and behavior therapy is that the fields, because of their interactive complexity, have become aprofessional: an individual's degree no longer accurately defines areas of intervention or diagnosis, and nurses, psychologists, physicians, and counselors are competing to implement a system of health treatment that is impossible to reduce to a professional degree. Obviously, the answer to this problem is team treatment.

One aspect of this volume will be to delineate those areas of diagnosis and intervention that are most appropriately treated by different members of the health care team, that is, if a team exists. An individual psychologist or psychiatrist in a solo private practice must assume a greater share of responsibility for all aspects of patient care than the well-staffed and -equipped physician–psychologist–nurse team in a large teaching hospital. It is because behavioral medicine interventions are increasingly data based, integrative, and dependent upon expensive equipment and interdisciplinary training that *Clinical Behavior Therapy and Behavior Modification*, Volumes I and II, and *Diagnosis and Intervention in Behavior Therapy and Behavioral Medicine*, Volume 1, were initiated. In the absence of other coordinating influences, it is the special purpose of this series to guide the solo or small practice clinician and researcher in those diagnostic and clinical areas that may be more normally and appropriately covered by separate personnel who have in-depth training and experience in narrow areas of health care. Until psychologists are required to complete medical courses and physicians are required to complete doctoral core curriculums, these role and professional conflicts will impede the sophistication of the fields, with the client being the ultimate loser.

More generally, this multi-volume work is for all scientists and practitioners who deal with real people with real problems, whether your degree is in medicine, nursing, counseling, physical rehabilitation, or social work. *Diagnosis and Intervention in Behavior Therapy and Behavioral Medicine* is organized and planned to provide optimal diagnostic and treatment methods and rigorous scientific reviews related to maximizing the efficiency and effectiveness of health care. This book also encourages planned intervention based upon empirical evidence, comprehensive assessments related to treatment implementation, and knowledge of behavioral techniques that would allow for *sophisticated* interventions. Finally, the interface of those areas of medicine and psychology related to the prevention of disease, the treatment of disease, and the maintenance of wellness are outlined into rigorous chapter formats in order to maximize the utilization of the information presented.

Reid J. Daitzman, Ph.D.

References

Daitzman, R.J. *Clinical behavior therapy and behavior modification (Vol. 1)*. New York: Garland Publishing Co., 1980

Daitzman, R.J. *Clinical behavior therapy and behavior modification (Vol. 2).* New York: Garland Publishing Co., 1981

Gurman, A.S., & Kriskern, D.P. Research on marital and family therapy: Progress perspective and prospect. In S. Garfield and A. Bergen (Eds.) *Handbook of psychotherapy and behavior change* (2nd ed.) New York: John Wiley, 1978.

1

Heterosexual-social Anxiety

James P. Curran and
Mario Fischetti

Introduction

Heterosexual-social anxiety appears to be a major concern for college students. Martinson and Zerface (1970) reported that problems in dating relationships were the most frequent complaints voiced by an undergraduate population utilizing a college counseling center. In a two-year survey conducted at the University of Iowa, Borkovec, Stone, O'Brien, and Kaloupek (1974) found that approximately 15 percent of the males and 11 percent of the females reported some fear of being with members of the opposite sex, and 32 percent of the males and approximately 38 percent of the females felt some fear when meeting someone for the first time. In another survey cited in Glass, Gottman, and Shumrak (1976), undergraduates were asked to rate various social situations with respect to difficulty. Fifty-four percent of the males and 42 percent of the females rated dating situations as difficult. In a study examining the extent of shyness in an undergraduate population, Pilkonis (1977) reported that 41 percent of the undergraduates surveyed reported being shy, especially in dating situations.

The experience and effects of heterosexual-social anxiety, however, are not limited to undergraduates or the undergraduate years. They also appear to have implications for a number of other populations and for later social functioning. In a factor-analytic study, Landy and Gaupp (1971) found that an interpersonal anxiety factor accounted for most of the variance in responses to a Fear Survey Schedule by both in- and outpatient psychiatric populations. In a survey of socially inadequate

*This section on treatment approaches is based in part on a previous review by Curran, J.P., Skills training as an approach to the treatment of heterosexual-social anxiety: A review. *Psychological Bulletin*, 1977, *84*, 140–157.

psychiatric outpatients, Bryant, Trower, Yardley, Urbieta, and Letemendia (1976) reported that socially inadequate patients were likely to have a history of poor mixing with others and a failure in dating. These patients reported considerable difficulty in a wide range of social situations, including starting up friendships, being in a group with the opposite sex, going to parties, and meeting strangers. Socially inadequate psychiatric male outpatients were considerably less likely to be married than socially adequate psychiatric male outpatients.

In addition to our growing appreciation of the importance of social anxiety in varied psychiatric disorders (Argyle & Kendon, 1967), interest in heterosexual-social anxiety has been stimulated because investigators believe it to be a good target behavior for clinical research. Fishman and Nawas (1973) have noted that since heterosexual-social anxiety is such a pervasive, complex, and debilitating type of anxiety reaction, it provides a good target behavior for therapy outcome studies. Since social anxiety is disruptive to daily functioning, and complete avoidance of social stimuli nearly impossible, recruitment of reasonably large numbers of well-motivated subjects for psychotherapy research should be possible. After conducting a study examining the "goodness" of heterosexual-social anxiety as a target behavior for therapy research, Borkovec et al. (1974, p. 573) concluded that:

> Heterosexual-social anxiety, then, appears to be an ideal target behavior for analogue research. A large number of potential subjects exist; the behavior is clinically relevant; unobtrusive, nondeceptive measurement procedures validly discriminate low- and high-anxious subjects; demand effects beyond repeated testing are negligible; and strong physiological arousal is elicited and does not readily habituate.

Although heterosexual-social anxiety appears to be a good target behavior for clinical research, we shall see that its "goodness" is dependent upon many factors, including the care with which subjects are selected for treatment and the assessment methods employed (Curran, 1977).

We shall begin this chapter by examining various hypotheses concerning the development and maintenance of heterosexual-social anxiety. Multiple assessment paradigms will be discussed and the relative merits and limitations of each method will be evaluated. Different treatment strategies will be presented and outcome literature relevant to each strategy will be critically reviewed and suggestions given for future research. An attempt will be made to describe clinical procedures useful in delineating the influence of multiple maintaining factors, and a case study will be presented as an illustration.

Etiological and Maintaining Factors for Heterosexual-Social Anxiety

Curran (1977) labeled the three major hypotheses regarding the etiology and maintenance of heterosexual-social anxiety as the social-skills deficit, conditioned anxiety, and faulty cognitions hypotheses. Heterosexual-social anxiety from the social-skills deficit framework is seen as reactive in nature (Paul & Bernstein, 1973) and due to an inadequate or inappropriate behavioral repertoire. Individuals may never have learned the appropriate behaviors or may have learned inappropriate responses to dating situations. Consequently, because of the lack of requisite skills, an individual does not cope with the demands of the situation adequately and, therefore, often experiences aversive consequences, which elicit anxiety. The anxiety experienced is viewed as a natural response to the aversive consequences resulting from the skills deficit. Heterosexual-social anxiety viewed from the conditioned-anxiety hypothesis results from classically conditioned episodes where the previously neutral cues of heterosexual-social situations are associated with aversive stimuli. These conditioning episodes may occur whether the individual is proficient or deficient with respect to social skills. Conditioning episodes may occur *in vivo* or vicariously. Finally, there are several cognitive explanations regarding the etiology and maintenance of heterosexual-social anxiety. As in the conditioned-anxiety interpretation of heterosexual-social anxiety, anxiety due to cognitive factors can also arise even when the individual possesses the requisite skills for the dating situation. Some cognitive and informational processing factors mentioned by Curran (1977) which may be responsible for heterosexual-social anxiety are unrealistic criteria, misperception of social cues, overly negative evaluation of performance, negative self-statements, insufficient self-reinforcement, etc. Some of these cognitive factors may directly affect skill performance in the dating situation and others may have a more indirect influence. For example, misperception of social cues may actually lead to inadequate performance in the criterion situation, while overly critical negative self-evaluations may result in anxiety that could interfere with subsequent performances in the dating situations.

We do not view these models as mutually exclusive explanations for heterosexual-social anxiety. Heterosexual-social anxiety is viewed as a multidimensional construct with multiple determinants. As Curran (1977, p. 143) has stated:

> It is quite likely that the basis of heterosexual-social anxiety is different for different individuals and that the anxiety experienced by any one individual may be the result of a combination of a skills deficit, conditioned anxiety, and negative self-appraisal system.

ANXIETY	SOCIAL SKILLS: Adequate	SOCIAL SKILLS: Inadequate
Absent	Cell 1 Nonanxious	Cell 3 Nonanxious (Avoidance, faulty cognitive processing)
Present	Cell 2 Conditioned Anxiety Faulty Cognitive Processing	Cell 4 Reactive Anxiety

FIGURE 1.1
Mini-model of Heterosexual-social Anxiety

Figure 1.1 is an illustration of a conceptual model of heterosexual-social anxiety which incorporates the conditioned anxiety, social-skills deficits, and cognitive explanations of heterosexual-social anxiety. We find this model useful for both assessment and treatment even though it is oversimplified. In this 2 × 2 model, the presence or absence of adequate social skills is crossed with the presence or absence of heterosexual-social anxiety. For illustrative purposes, the constructs of anxiety and skill are treated as dichotomous variables, although these constructs are more appropriately viewed as gradients. Likewise, for presentation purposes, we are ignoring the situational specificity of both anxiety reactions and skills deficits. For example, some individuals may be extremely anxious if they are alone with a date, but relatively non-anxious if they are with their date at a party. Similarly, an individual may have the appropriate skills for initial dating encounters but possess an inadequate repertoire for longer, more intimate relationships.

Individuals in Cell 1 and Cell 2 possess the requisite skills demanded in dating situations. Individuals in Cell 1 are relatively nonanxious, accurately perceive social cues, realistically evaluate their own performances, and do not experience conditioned anxiety in dating situations. Individuals in Cell 2, while possessing the requisite skills, are heterosexually-socially anxious. This anxiety does not necessarily interfere with their heterosexual-social performance, but does cause significant distress. Such distress could eventually disrupt performance and/or lead to avoidance of dating situations. For some individuals, this anxiety is the result of classically conditioned episodes. A dramatic scenario of a potential conditioning episode would be the case of a female who has been sexually assaulted on a date. Although no empirical tests exist demonstrating that heterosexual-social anxiety can be classically conditioned, there exists ample evidence (Bandura, 1969) that anxiety responses may be classically conditioned to a wide variety of stimulus targets. Indirect evidence of conditioned heterosexual-social anxiety exists in that counterconditioning procedures such as systematic desensitization have been demonstrated successful in alleviating heterosexual-social anxiety.

Numerous cognitive and information-processing factors may result in heterosexual-social anxiety even when the individual possesses an adequate behavioral repertoire. Clark and Arkowitz (1975) indicated that high-anxious subjects tended to underestimate their performance in simulated dating situations, while low-anxious subjects overestimate their performance. Curran, Wallander, and Fischetti (1977) found that individuals with both high and low social anxiety devalued their performances in simulated dating situations when compared to judges' ratings. Apparently, even low levels of anxiety may not guarantee the absence of cognitive misappraisal. The results from Smith's (1972) study indicated that high socially anxious individuals are greatly concerned with the evaluation of others, are highly motivated to avoid disapproval, and possess a highly generalized need to be liked. Goldfried and Sobocinski (1975) demonstrated an association between irrational beliefs (e.g., the need to be liked by everyone) and social anxiety. O'Banian and Arkowitz (1975) demonstrated that socially anxious individuals have a more accurate memory for negative feedback and a less accurate memory for positive feedback directed at themselves than did low socially anxious subjects. In an experiment by Smith and Sarason (1975), high socially anxious subjects perceived the same feedback as more negative, evoking a more negative emotional response, than did low socially anxious subjects. To summarize, emotional states and cognitive factors may lead to inadequate social performances because they interfere with these performances either directly or indirectly. However, there are cases in which individuals can perform adequately despite experiencing a fair amount of interpersonal distress.

Individuals in Cell 3 do not possess adequate behavioral repertoires for dating situations and yet experience relatively little anxiety. Although appearing to contradict the logic of the social-skills deficit hypothesis, which predicts the development of reactive anxiety in the unskilled individual, the relative absence of anxiety in the presence of a skill deficit can occur for several reasons. First, an individual may avoid these situations altogether, thus avoiding the development of reactive anxiety. Alternatively, the individual may have been fortunate enough to have had dating partners who were especially diplomatic and did not let a lack of social skills lead to an aversive interaction. Other possibilities would be that the dating situation is a failure, but the individual does not perceive the situation as having been a failure, or if he or she does perceive it as a failure (aversive), he or she blames the dating partner for the unpleasant results. It is our impression that those individuals who blame their partner, rather than themselves, for unsuccessful dating experiences are those individuals who in addition to having low rates of socially skilled behavior also have high rates of clearly obnoxious or unpleasant behavior. The same type of cognitive processes (but in a reverse direction) that occur for individuals in Cell 2 could account for the lack of anxiety in individuals of Cell 3. That is, Cell 3 individuals would tend to overevaluate their performance, be less concerned about the evaluation of others, and be less affected by disapproval from others.

Individuals in Cell 4 are experiencing heterosexual-social anxiety as a reaction to their lack of adequate social skills. These individuals either say or do the wrong things or fail to say or do the right things in dating situations and experience anxiety as the result of the negative interpersonal consequences. Studies (Arkowitz, Lichtenstein, McGovern, & Hines, 1975; Borkovec et al., 1974; Twentyman & McFall, 1975) demonstrating differences between low and high heterosexual-socially anxious individuals on global ratings of skill performance in heterosexual-social interactions provide evidence for the reactive anxiety hypothesis. A difficult assessment task is differentiating individuals in Cells 2 and 4. Both sets of individuals are experiencing heterosexual-social anxiety and both may be evidencing poor social-skill performance in dating situations. Individuals in Cell 4 do not possess the behavioral repertoire to perform adequately, and individuals in Cell 2, while possessing the adequate repertoire, are not performing adequately because of either conditioning or cognitive interference mechanisms. This assessment problem will be discussed further in the section on clinical prescription.

Other evidence exists supporting the multiple-determining-factor model of heterosexual-social anxiety presented in this chapter. Curran et al. (1977) demonstrated the relative independence of the constructs of social skills and anxiety on the basis of observers' ratings of male college students in a simulated dating situation. Observers were able to classify the students in a manner corresponding to the 2 × 2 model presented. In the Pilkonis (1977) study on the nature and extent of shyness in an undergraduate population, cluster analyses of the individual's self-report data were performed. Two large clusters were found, and Pilkonis interpreted these clusters as representing two types of shy individuals. The two types were defined as publicly shy people who are primarily concerned with their behavioral difficulties and privately shy people who focused on the quality of internal events such as negative self-evaluation. Greenwald (1977), in a study examining high- and low-frequency dating females, factor analyzed the subjects' self-report data. Three factors were interpreted as representing physiological anxiety, cognitive evaluation, and a skills factor. Although these factors were correlated with each other, the correlations were in the moderate range, suggesting some independence of the factors.

The evidence seems to support the contention that social skills, conditioned anxiety, and cognitive factors all interact in a complex fashion. The resulting interaction of these constructs produces several heterogeneous types of heterosexual-socially anxious individuals. That is, individuals may be described by one of the component hypotheses discussed or a complex interaction among some or all of the components. Thus, heterosexual-socially anxious individuals appear to be a heterogeneous group, and so we must adequately assess all potential components if we are to develop effective individual treatment plans. Given the complexity of the etiological and maintenance factors for heterosexual-social anxiety, assessment should be multimodel and include self-report, observational, and physiological measures.

Assessment of Heterosexual-social Anxiety

In order to assess a construct adequately, it is imperative to define the construct you are attempting to assess. A definition of anxiety that we feel is most compatible with our position was proposed by Paul and Bernstein (1973, p. 2):

> We shall consider anxiety as a short-hand term for a very complex pattern of responses, characterized by subjective feelings of apprehension and tension associated with physiological arousal involving the sympathetic branch of the autonomic nervous system.

It is important to understand that anxiety is a construct that we infer from cognitive, motoric, and physiological responses. Within each of these response categories, numerous indicators may be taken as samples of the anxiety response. No single indicator possesses a perfect one-to-one relationship with the construct of anxiety. Responses from the various modalities often do not covary, not only because of the imprecision with which they are measured, but also because of the different types of error associated with them. In addition, Lang (1968) has indicated that the response systems themselves may be relatively independent.

In our review of the assessment of heterosexual-social anxiety, we will be presenting assessment strategies and not specific instruments per se. Specific instruments will be mentioned only to illustrate various types of assessment strategies. We will also be addressing the assessment of heterosexual-social anxiety without concern for the etiology of the anxiety (conditioned, skill deficits, or cognitive). We will, however, discuss differential specification of the source of anxiety in the section of this chapter labeled Clinical Prescriptions. Parenthetically, it should be noted that certain measurement strategies appear to be more relevant for the assessment of a particular source of anxiety. For example, data relevant to the classically conditioned hypothesis are generally gathered during a clinical interview during which historical data are examined to determine whether vicarious or *in vivo* conditioning episodes may be responsible for the anxiety.

Perhaps because of the difficulties involved in delineating the various sources of heterosexual-social anxiety, it is rare in clinical outcome studies (actually the only examples found are in single case studies) to find such information provided. In other words, the subjects in treatment-outcome studies are generally treated as a homogeneous group of anxious subjects regardless of the etiology of their heterosexual-social anxiety. This causes major problems in interpreting results of many of the treatment-outcome studies (Curran, 1977) and is an example of what Kiesler (1971) has labeled the "uniformity myth." We shall further discuss this problem in a later section of the chapter.

Figure 1.2 presents a conceptual framework for the assessment of heterosexual-social anxiety which we think includes the dimensions most relevant for its assessment. This model makes use of Cone's (1977) distinction between content of the responses (cognitive, motoric, and physiological) and methods of assessment (self-report, others' report, and physiological). In addition, it includes Wiggins' (1973) classification of settings into naturalistic-immediate, naturalistic-retrospective, controlled, and contrived. Wiggins defines these four global settings in the following manner: (1) naturalistic-immediate, where the behavior is observed *in situ* in the absence of artificial constraints and where the observations are preplanned; (2) naturalistic-retrospective, where an observer is called on to recollect an earlier observation made in naturalistic settings without preplanned observations; (3) controlled, where observations of behavior are made in a laboratory setting or under special circumstances created by the observers; (4) contrived, where the observational setting appears natural to the subject when, in fact, it is under control of the observer. We present this model not only to organize

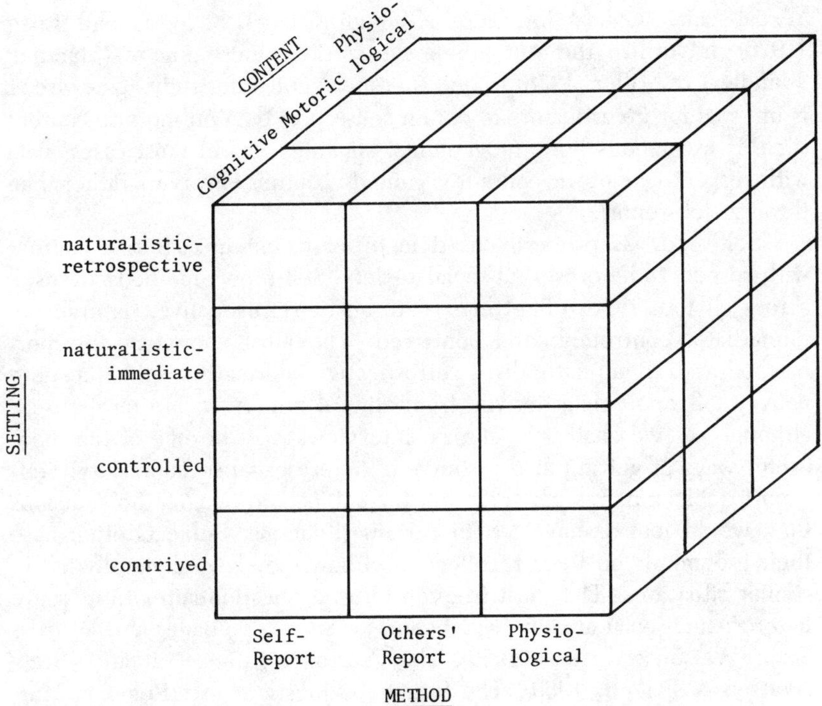

FIGURE 1.2
Schema for the Assessment of Heterosexual-social Anxiety

the various assessment instruments within the heterosexual-social anxiety area, but also to encourage assessment work in some of the cells formed by the matrix which have been neglected. Obviously, it is impossible to obtain assessment data in some of the 36 cells generated by this matrix (e.g., naturalistic-retrospective physiological data of cognitive responses). However, some cells have been underutilized because of the lack of attention paid to the development of appropriate assessment instruments.

Self-report Methods

Self-report measures are the most versatile measures because they can tap all three major response content areas: Were you anxious? (cognitive), Did you stutter? (motoric), and Did you perspire? (physiological). In point of fact, self-report of physiological content is rare in the heterosexual-social anxiety literature although Curran, Gilbert, and Little (1976) did utilize the Autonomic Perception Questionnaire (Mandler, Mandler, & Miller, 1958) in one treatment-outcome study. Likewise, it is unusual for investigators to obtain self-report data on motoric content such as extraneous body movements, shaking, etc. In most cases, data with respect to motoric content is gained via other observers rather than through self-report.

Self-report is primarily used in order to obtain cognitive content with respect to heterosexual-social anxiety. Self-report methods are used across all four types of settings: naturalistic-retrospective, naturalistic-immediate, controlled, and contrived. The most common self-report method used to tap naturalistic-retrospective information is the questionnaire. Self-report data derived from clinical interviews are rarely used, although, as we shall see, clinical interviews may be one of the more useful ways of getting at the source of heterosexual-social anxiety. Self-report questionnaires generally ask the subjects to imagine how anxious they would feel or have felt in certain situations. Subjects often base their judgments on their recollection of how they have generally felt in similar situations. The most frequently used questionnaires to measure heterosexual-social anxiety have been The Social Avoidance and Distress Scale (Watson & Friend, 1969), The Fear of Negative Evaluation Scale (Watson & Friend, 1969), The Situation Questionnaire (Rehm & Marston, 1968), and The Survey of Heterosexual Interaction (Twentyman & McFall, 1975). The Social Avoidance and Distress Scale is a 28-item true–false scale measuring both social anxiety and avoidance behavior in same- and opposite-sex interactions, group and public speaking situations, and interactions with authority figures. Some of the items do not appear to be related to heterosexual-social anxiety per se, and those items that appear more relevant are nonspecific with respect to situational areas of distress. The Fear of Negative Evaluation Scale is a 30-item true–false scale that measures the degree of anxiety one experiences when receiving negative evaluation from others. It, too, contains items that appear to be irrelevant to the measurement of heterosexual-social anxiety. The Situation Questionnaire consists of 30 items, rated on a Likert-type scale. The items are specific to heterosexual-social interactions and were originally developed to be used in a desensitization hierarchy. The Survey of Heterosexual Interaction consists of 20 items specific to heterosexual-social interaction. Subjects rate each item on a 7-point Likert-type scale, a score of 1 indicating "unable to respond" and a score of 7 indicating "able to carry out interaction." Although it does not ask its respondents to evaluate their level of subjective distress, but rather their estimated probability of carrying out an interaction, The Survey of Heterosexual Interaction may have the best psychometric properties of any of the above questionnaires. Twentyman and McFall

(1975) demonstrated that scores on this scale are related to other self-report, self-monitoring, observational, and physiological measures of social anxiety and social skill. Wallander, Conger, Mariotto, Curran, and Farrell (1980) compared the Survey of Heterosexual Interaction, the Social Avoidance and Distress Scale, and the Situation Questionnaire to actual dating experiences and to self- and others' ratings in a simulated social interaction. Of the three self-report questionnaires, the Survey of Heterosexual Interaction consistently had a better relationship with the dating experience information and self- and others' ratings in heterosexual-social interactions.

Subjects in heterosexual-social anxiety studies have often been asked to self-monitor their responses in naturalistic-immediate settings. For example, they have been requested to keep behavioral diaries where they record indirect measures of heterosexual-social anxiety such as the frequency, range, and duration of heterosexual-social interactions during a specific time period (Christensen & Arkowitz, 1974; Christensen, Arkowitz, & Anderson, 1975; Twentyman & McFall, 1975). The frequency, range, and duration of heterosexual-social interactions are indirect measures of the construct heterosexual-social anxiety because these measures are dependent upon numerous other factors not related to the construct. In some cases (Christensen & Arkowitz, 1974), subjects are asked to record their subjective emotional state during these heterosexual-social interactions, and, therefore, they presumably constitute a more direct measure of heterosexual-social anxiety. Although self-monitoring procedures are versatile, they have been demonstrated to be reactive and their accuracy has been questioned (Nelson, 1977). However, in the Twentyman and McFall (1975) study, a partial check on the subjects' self-monitoring was conducted for a prearranged interaction and was found to be accurate.

Self-report measures are frequently taken when subjects are assessed in controlled or contrived settings. These self-report measures are generally overall measures of the subjects' cognitive response system, i.e., subjective feelings of anxiety felt in the situation (e.g., Curran et al., 1976; Twentyman & McFall, 1975), although at times (Curran & Gilbert, 1975) more detailed questions are used. Occasionally, subjects are asked to self-report regarding their physiological state (Curran et al., 1976) in these controlled and contrived situations. We shall discuss the nature of these controlled and contrived assessment settings in the next section on others' report methods.

Others' Report Measures

Either trained or untrained others' reports have been used frequently as dependent measures in the heterosexual-social anxiety literature. Generally, untrained raters are used in naturalistic situations (both immediate and retrospective). Untrained observers are usually asked to report on either indirect measures of heterosexual-social anxiety, such as number of opposite-sex contacts, or asked to infer from the subjects' motoric responses the level of social anxiety experienced by the subjects. For example, in two studies on practice dating (Christensen & Arkowitz, 1974; Christensen et al., 1975), the investigators arranged dates between male and female subjects. After these arranged dates, both the male and female subjects rated each other on a number of scales, including a global measure of social anxiety. Glass et al. (1976) also employed untrained raters in a naturalistic-immediate setting. Male subjects in a minimal dating treatment program were asked to telephone two women during the week in order to practice getting to know them. The female recipients of these telephone calls had all volunteered for a study of telephone conversations. Whether the male subjects called or not was a primary dependent measure, as was the female volunteers' ratings regarding how skillful the male had been and whether she would like to meet him. Two disadvantages in utilizing untrained others' ratings in the naturalistic environment are that (1) the accuracy of their ratings are suspect because the raters are untrained and (2) there is no comparability in the rating process because different individuals are rating different subjects.

Although no one assessment strategy should be regarded as the criterion upon which to validate other assessment strategies, the most popular and implied standard in heterosexual-social anxiety research is trained judges' ratings based on controlled laboratory observations. The process by which these ratings are obtained possesses characteristics that are desirable in many respects. Judges are pretrained by the investigators to an acceptable level of inter-rater reliability. Generally, reliability checks are made during the actual process to see whether it remains at an acceptable level. In most cases at least, a subset of the raters evaluate all the subjects, making for some comparability of ratings across the various subjects. Because the trained judges are not familiar with the subjects, the biases that may occur with peer ratings are diminished. Usually, the subjects' performances in these controlled observations are recorded on either audiotape or videotape. Consequently, such potentially confounding factors such as testing occasion (pre-, post-, and follow-up) and subject group membership (experimental or control) can readily be controlled for by random presentation of the tapes.

For the most part, these controlled laboratory assessments consist of a simulated roleplay, wherein the subject is asked to assume a role in a particular social situation. The simulated laboratory situations can be characterized as one of two types: a discrete type where there is little interaction between the subjects and their partners; and a more extended interaction where there is a continuous interchange between the subjects and their partners. The partners of the subjects in these simulated social interactions are generally trained confederates, or in some cases they are other subjects (Christensen & Arkowitz, 1974). The discrete simulated situations generally take the following form: A narrator describes a particular situation (e.g., Pretend you are in the Student Union. A girl from your psychology class walks up to you and says), followed by a prompt from the confederate (e.g., "What did you think of class today?"). The subject then responds to the confederate. The narration as well as the confederate's prompt have been presented both on audiotape (Rehm & Marston, 1968), and on videotape (Melnick, 1973). Curran (1978) has criticized these discrete situational tests as being nonrepresentative of natural interactions. The give and take of natural conversations are neglected in these discrete tests, and potentially important variables such as the timing and sequencing of responses cannot be assessed. The ability to synchronize social responses with partner behavior has been shown to discriminate socially competent and incompetent individuals (Fischetti, Curran, & Wessberg, 1977).

The more extended interaction simulations by necessity are performed using live confederates. Here, the confederates are preprogrammed by the investigators to behave in similar fashion, although the degree to which confederates actually conform to this role may be a confound in some of these tests. An example of an extended interaction simulation can be found in the work of Curran and his colleagues (Curran, 1975; Curran & Gilbert, 1975; Curran et al., 1976) where subjects were asked to imagine that they had just been to the movies with the confederate on a first date. Subjects were then told to imagine that following the movie they were seated in a pizza parlor with the confederate and were waiting for their pizza and beverages. The subjects were further told that at some point toward the end of their five-minute interaction a light would be turned on, indicating when they were to ask the confederate out for a date the following weekend. The confederates were programmed to give minimal responses (e.g., Subject: How did you like the movie? Confederate: It was pretty good.). In most cases, the design of these extended simulated interactions have been based on the experimenters' judgment about what is a realistic, demanding simulation. Ratings are usually based on the subjective judgments of the raters aided by some general guideline provided by the experimenters. More objective scoring criteria can be more readily developed for the discrete simulated situations because they do not involve a continuous interaction. For example, Glass et al. (1976) used situations in their simulated roleplays that were developed by a behavioral-analytic approach (Goldfried & D'Zurilla, 1969). Here, the situations chosen to be simulated were nominated by groups of college dating students. Scoring keys were based on the generation of potential responses to these situations by dating-age college students and their evaluation of the effectiveness of the responses. Although the extended simulated interactions appear to be more realistic than discrete simulation tests because of their interactive nature, the question always arises as to just how representative these tests are of subjects' behavior in the natural environment.

Assessment of the subjects' heterosexual-social anxiety level in the natural environment presents complex logistical and ethical problems. One alternative would be to assess the subjects in contrived laboratory situations where the subjects are unaware that their performance is being evaluated. Wessberg, Mariotto, Conger, Conger, and Farrell (1979) compared the responses of male undergraduates in two extended simulated dating interactions and in two waiting room situations. During the waiting room situation, the subjects interacted with the same confederates as during the simulated interactions, but were unaware that their performances were being evaluated. The correlations between anxiety ratings derived from the waiting room periods to the simulated situations were almost as high as the correlations between the anxiety ratings obtained in the two simulated situations. Of course, one could still question how representative a waiting room period during a psychological experiment is of naturalistic heterosexual-social situations.

As mentioned previously, when others' ratings are obtained in naturalistic settings, these judgments generally consist of a global rating of anxiety. When trained raters are used to evaluate the heterosexual-social anxiety in subjects in controlled and contrived laboratory situations, both global ratings of anxiety and more specific ratings of anxiety indicators have been used. Specific anxiety indicators are varied and include such dimensions as response latency, speech disfluencies such as stammers, extraneous bodily movements, such as knees trembling, etc. When the same raters are asked to make both specific and global ratings of heterosexual-social anxiety, it is possible that rating a specific behavior will influence the judges' global ratings and vice versa (Curran, 1978). If the judges are just asked to make global ratings, it is unclear what indicators they are using and in what manner they are combining these indicators to come up with a global rating. In a study by Conger, Wallander, Mariotto, and Ward (1980) peer judges, after making global ratings of both social anxiety and social skills, were asked to nominate the cues they used to make these global ratings. The judges nominated many of the same indicators generally used in the literature, although there was more emphasis on verbal content indicators than is generally found. Interestingly enough, some indicators (e.g., eye contact) were used in making the judgments for both social skill and social anxiety. Conger et al. (1980) are now attempting to determine whether these specific indicators are indeed relevant to global anxiety ratings. As Curran (1979) has noted, these narrowly defined specific indicators, while generally more reliable than global ratings, may be so specific as to preclude the possibility of generalizability to criterion behaviors.

One further issue needs to be addressed in our discussion of observational ratings of heterosexual-social anxiety, and that is the difficulty levels of the assessment settings. If the difficulty level of our setting is too high or too low for our population of interest, then it may fail altogether to differentiate anxiety levels within our populations. In an analogous manner, if a test is so difficult that no one can pass it or so simple that everyone can pass it, its predictive utility is nonexistent. The difficulty level of our assessment settings must be relevant to the population of interest.

Psychophysiological Methods

Although physiological responses are regarded as important components of our construct of heterosexual-social anxiety, very little psychophysiological recording has occurred in this area. The Twentyman and McFall (1975) and Christensen et al. (1975) studies are the only two treatment-outcome studies using psychophysiological recordings. Given the difficulties involved in utilizing peripheral psychophysiological measures as indicators of anxiety (Lang, 1968) and the suspiciousness with which these peripheral indicators are viewed as "true" markers of anxiety, it is no wonder that psychophysiological recordings have been largely ignored in this area. However, because psychophysiological components are so central to the construct of anxiety, an attempt should be made to develop sounder psychophysiological indicators in order to assess this important response system.

Concluding Remarks on the Assessment of Heterosexual-Social Anxiety

More research needs to be done on the reliability and validity of the various assessment instruments used to measure heterosexual-social anxiety. Refinement of the existing measures and development of new measures is urged. A review of the literature indicates moderate correlations between anxiety indicators within the same method, but low correlations for instruments across methods (Arkowitz et al., 1975; Bander, Steinke, Allen, & Mosher, 1975; Borkovec et al., 1974; Twentyman & McFall, 1975). In a generalizability study, Farrell, Mariotto, Conger, Curran, and Wallander (1979) obtained self- and observers' ratings of anxiety in two simulated heterosexual-social situations. Three different methods of self-ratings were used. The subjects rated the degree of anxiety they expected to experience in a simulated interaction, rated their anxiety after participating in the simulated social interactions, and rated their appearance of anxiety in those situations when viewing the videotapes of their interactions two weeks after the interactions. Observers' ratings of the subjects' anxiety levels were obtained from two confederates employed during the interactions and from two trained raters who observed the subjects' performances on videotapes. Self-reported anxiety scores employing the three strategies within the self-report domain were only moderately related to each other. There was little relationship between self-reported anxiety scores and judges' ratings of anxiety.

Development of instruments to measure heterosexual-social anxiety should be guided by theoretical and empirical rationales. Attempts to utilize test construction strategies such as the behavioral-analytic approach used by Glass et al. (1976) are encouraged. Further research such as that undertaken by Conger et al. (1980) to delimit the specific behavioral indicators used by judges in evaluating heterosexual-social anxiety should be emulated. More studies such as Wessberg's et al. (1979) evaluating how representative controlled simulated social interactions are of more naturalistic settings should be undertaken. Finally, investigators are urged to develop assessment strategies which, so far, have been largely neglected in the assessment of heterosexual-social anxiety. Drawing upon our 3 × 3 × 4 matrix of potential assessment strategies, we note that many of the cells are not represented in the literature. For example, in the row containing naturalistic-immediate settings, the only assessment strategies employed have been self-monitoring and ratings by untrained observers who do not rate every subject. It may be possible to use trained observers who are familiar with all the subjects, for example, dorm counselors. Likewise, telemetric devices may be utilized in order to obtain psychophysiological recordings in the naturalistic-immediate environment. Because of the complexity of the heterosexual-social anxiety construct, and the lack of agreement across measurement channels, multiple-channel assessment is urged.

Treatment Procedures

Hersen and Barlow (1976) and Mischel (1968, 1973) have stated that one of the most outstanding differences between traditionalists and behaviorists, in general, is the one-to-one relationship between diagnosis and treatment. Rather than attempting to assess the presumed dynamics underlying the problem behaviors and then treating the assessed dynamics, behaviorists attempt to assess the problem behaviors themselves and then treat or modify those varied behaviors. Thus, we would expect treatment procedures in a behavioral approach to heterosexual-social anxiety to follow logically and directly from the results of the assessment strategies described above. In fact, they often do not. Instead, treatments are based on the theoretical interests of the various investigators. Treatment procedures may be categorized by the assumptions made by the investigators regarding the contributions of etiological factors (conditioned anxiety, cognitive misappraisal, and social skills deficits) to the relative levels of anxiety found in a heterosexual-socially anxious individual.

According to Curran (1977), the four major categories of treatment procedures that appear in the literature are (1) response practice approaches; (2) conditioned anxiety reduction approaches; (3) cognitive-restructuring approaches; and, (4) response acquisition approaches. It should be noted that while each approach emphasizes one of the alleged factors responsible for heterosexual-social anxiety, these approaches often include components germane to the other sources of anxiety. The classification of treatment approaches into four basic approaches is based on what seems to be the focal approach of the particular treatment procedure. In the following four subsections, each of the four major approaches to the treatment of heterosexual-social anxiety will be reviewed. Table 1.1 presents a summary of each of the reviewed studies to assist the reader in cross-study comparisons. Contained in Table 1.1 are summary statements regarding several parameters that were judged as affecting the internal and external validity of each of the studies reviewed. The contents of Table 1.1 were taken largely from an earlier paper by the first author (Curran, 1977) with the addition of a Design Quality Rating. The Design Quality Rating system was developed by Gurman et al. (in press). Points are assigned to a study if it meets certain criteria (e.g., inclusion of a follow-up), and points are summed and/or evaluative statements assigned to various point ranges. The inclusion of a Design Quality Rating was an editorial decision and the statements contained therein do not necessarily reflect the evaluation of the authors.

Response Practice Approaches

Studies examining response practice approaches have attempted to evaluate the utility of arranged heterosexual interactions as a method for increasing dating interaction and reducing heterosexual anxiety. This approach assumes that the heterosexual-socially anxious individual possesses the necessary repertoire of social skills and that exposure to heterosexual contacts in and of itself will clear up misconceptions and provide feedback on the appropriateness of the exhibited behavior. Since it is assumed that mere exposure to heterosexual-social encounters will lead to appropriate employment of social skills and a decrease in anxiety, the implicit assumptions of this approach are that the individual has, in general, a relatively high level of skill and a relatively low level of

TABLE 1.1
Treatment Procedures in Studies Reviewed

Authors	Focal Therapy	Subjects Source	Sex*	Selection
Martinson & Zerface (1970)	Response practice	University	M	Dating frequency and fear
Christensen & Arkowitz (1974)	Response practice	University	M and F	Interested in increasing dating frequency, skill, and comfort
Christensen, Arkowitz, & Andersen (1975)	Response practice	University	M and F	Dating frequency and fear
Melnick (1973)	Response acquisition	Psychology class	M	Uncomfortable in dating; no more than 2 dates/week
Curran (1975)	Response acquisition and desensitization	University	M and F	Screening interview and Situation Questionnaire
Curran & Gilbert (1975)	Response acquisition and desensitization	Psychology class	M and F	Screening interview and Situaion Questionnaire
Curran, Gilbert & Little (1976)	Response acquisition and sensitivity training	University	M and F	Screening interview
McGovern, Arkowitz, & Gilmore (1975)	Response acquisition	Psychology class and university	M	Dating frequency and fear; dating discomfort
MacDonald, Lindquist, Kramer, McGrath, & Rhyne (1975)	Response acquisition	University	M	Less than 4 dates in 12 months
Bander, Steinke, Allen & Mosher (1975)	Response acquisition and sensitization training	University	M	Situation Questionnaire; Social Distress and Avoidance Scale; dating frequency
Twentyman & McFall (1975)	Response acquisition	Psychology class	M	Survey of heterosexual interactions; dating frequency
Rehm & Marston (1968)	Cognitive-evaluative	University	M	Dating problems
Glass, Gottman, & Shmurak (1976)	Response acquisition and cognitive evaluative	Residence hall	M	Volunteers for dating skills development

*M = male and F = female

TABLE 1.1 (continued)

Therapist	Controls: Minimal Contact	Controls: Non-Specific	Assessment: Channels	Validity Assessment	Transfer	Follow-up	Design Quality Rating
None	Yes	Yes	Self-report	No	Indirect	No	Very good
None	No	No	Self-report	No	Indirect and direct self-report	No	Fair
None	Yes	No	Self-report, behavioral, physiological	No	Indirect and direct self-report	Just self-report	Fair to good
Principal investigator	Yes	Yes	Self-report, behavioral	No	Indirect	No	Poor to fair
Multiple and crossed	Yes	Yes	Self-report, behavioral	No	No	No	Very good
Multiple and crossed	Yes	No	Self-report, behavioral	No	Indirect	Self-report, behavioral	Very good
Multiple and crossed	No	No	Self-report, behavioral	No	Indirect	No	Good to very good
Principal investigator	Yes	Yes	Self-report	No	Indirect	No	Good
Two investigators	Yes	Yes	Self-report, behavioral	Yes	Indirect	Just self-report	Very good
Two investigators	Yes	Yes	Self-report, behavioral	Yes	Indirect	Just self-report	Very good
Multiple undergraduate assistants	Yes	No	Self-report, behavioral physiological	Yes	Indirect and direct self-report	Just self-report	Very good
Multiple and crossed	Yes	Yes	Self-report, behavioral	Yes	Indirect	Self-report, behavioral	Fair to good
Multiple undergraduate program	Yes	No	Self-report, behavioral	Yes, but failed	Direct	Self-report, behavioral	Very good

anxiety. The anxiety experienced is probably due to cognitive misappraisal and perhaps some mild conditioned anxiety.

Martinson and Zerface (1970) randomly assigned male college subjects to an individual counseling, delayed treatment control, or practice dating program consisting of semistructured, arranged interactions with female volunteers. The practice dating program was reported significantly more effective than the other two groups in reducing dating fear and significantly more effective than the delayed control group in increasing dating frequency. No significant differences between groups were found on a test of general manifest anxiety. All subjects in the study had not dated the previous month and had identified themselves as fearful of dating situations.

Christensen and Arkowitz (1974) studied the effectiveness of a practice dating program that included a feedback exchange from dating partners. There were no comparison groups and no screening procedures were used. The volunteer subjects joined to increase dating comfort, skill, and frequency. Data indicated that the subjects were not low-frequency daters. Subjects reported a significant decrease on two self-report measures of anxiety after treatment, as well as self-reported increases in heterosexual interactions and increases in skill on actual dates.

Christensen et al. (1975) compared practice dating with feedback to practice dating without feedback to a waiting list control. Again, there was no screening of volunteers, who averaged one date per month. Groups were equated using self-report inventories of anxiousness. At post-treatment, self-report, behavioral, and physiological measures were collected. Data from within modes of assessment were combined and the results indicated that both treatment groups were significantly different from the control group on the composite self-report anxiety measures in frequency and range of dating and casual heterosexual interaction, on several discrete behavioral measures (speech latency), and on pulse rate. However, there were no significant differences between groups on observers' and partners' overall ratings of anxiety and skill in the behavioral situations used to obtain the observational measures. A three-month follow-up, which included only the treatment groups and used only self-report measures, indicated significant decreases in self-report of anxiety and increases in skill when compared to pretreatment scores.

Rehm and Marston (1968) used no selection criteria other than accepting volunteers who felt uncomfortable in dating situations. They compared a self-reinforcement group (subjects systematically worked up a hierarchy of *in vivo* heterosexual interactions which they themselves created, they evaluated themselves with respect to their individual goals, and they rewarded themselves for accomplishing each individual goal), a nonspecific therapy control, and a contact control (talking about the problem). No test for equivalency was made at pretest, but pretest, post-test, and follow-up global self-report and behavioral measures were taken. These results favoring the self-reinforcement group over the control groups tended to be self-report in nature. None of the behavioral ratings showed any significant differences between groups. There was some doubt that the self-reinforcement manipulation caused the change in self-report of anxiety since the procedure involving self-reinforcement had other potential therapeutic components such as gradual approach to the feared stimuli.

While the results of these studies are generally positive, design and methodological flaws make any conclusions tenuous. Inadequate screening of subjects casts doubt upon the severity of the volunteers' dating problems. In fact, it appeared the subjects for these studies were, for the most part, skilled individuals with mild levels of discomfort in social situations. There was an overreliance on self-report measures, which generally did show differences from pre- to post-treatment. However, in general, when behavioral measures were used, they showed no significant differences. In a number of studies there were no control groups, and when follow-up was incorporated, it was usually incomplete and consisted primarily of subjective measures. None of the studies attempted to validate their selection procedures. The assumptions behind response practice approaches seem to make them relevant to the treatment of highly skilled, mildly anxious individuals only. These are the type of individuals who wish only to become more comfortable in dating situations. They generally have had some experience with heterosexual interactions and have experienced some success. In the case of heterosexual-socially anxious individuals with higher levels of anxiety, there is always some danger that contact with peers without any preparation will result in a failure experience that could cause increased anxiety.

Conditioned Anxiety Reduction Approaches

The conditioned anxiety reduction approaches assume that heterosexual-social anxiety is the result of *in vivo* or vicarious aversive conditioning experiences in heterosexual-social encounters. As in response practice approaches, the heterosexual-socially anxious individual is assumed to have an adequate repertoire of social skills. In the response practice approaches, however, the individual is assumed to have a general level of anxiety which is low, but bothersome. In the conditioned anxiety reduction approaches, no such assumption is made. In fact, the anxiety experienced may even be severe enough to cause total avoidance of the opposite sex in order to alleviate the anxiety. The role of cognitive-misappraisal in the conditioned anxiety reduction approaches is considered to be minimal. It seems obvious that for highly anxious individuals, direct, prolonged contact with the opposite sex without any preparation, especially if that contact is with untrained peers, would clearly be inappropriate. Counterconditioning procedures are viewed as the treatment of choice to reduce the conditioned anxiety in this type of heterosexual-socially anxious individual. Such approaches emphasize systematic, gradual exposure to the feared or aversive stimuli.

Curran (1975) compared the effect of a replication skills training program, a systematic desensitization program, an attention placebo control (relaxation training only), and a waiting list control group Pre- and postassessments consisted of both self-report inventories and behavioral ratings of both anxiety and skill from a simulated dating interaction. The subjects were selected by dating history criteria and from norms obtained on self-report anxiety inventories, so it appeared that dating, anxious subjects had in fact been obtained. Results indicated that the skills training and systematic desensitization groups demonstrated significant changes over time for both behavioral ratings of anxiety and skill while the control group did not demonstrate such changes.

Curran and Gilbert (1975) compared a replicaton skills training program, a systematic desensitization program, and a waiting list control group on self-report inventories and observational ratings of anxiety and skill pre- and post-treatment, and at six-months follow-up from treatment. Both treatment groups, but not the control group, demonstrated significant decreases in self-report and behavioral anxiety indicators at post-test and follow-up and did not differ significantly from each other. Both treatment groups demonstrated significant increases in dating freqquency (an indirect measure of transfer) both during and after treatment. Behavioral skills ratings were significantly greater for the replication group than the control group at post-test, and significantly different from both the control and desensitization group at follow-up. Subject selection was similar to Curran's (1975) and appeared adequate.

Fishman and Nawas (1973) evaluated the effectiveness of a systematic desensitization program, a placebo control, and a no treatment control on pre- and post-treatment self-report, behavioral, and physiological measures. Despite the authors' possibly truncated systematic desensitization program, the systematic desensitization group significantly differed from both control groups on a number of self-report measures of anxiety as well as on the heart rate dependent measure. Subjects were selected based on their scores on self-report inventories of social avoidance and effectiveness.

Mitchell and Orr (1974), using only pre- and post-test self-report measures, compared a systematic desensitization group, a short-term systematic desensitization group, a relaxation training only control group, and a no treatment control group. They found significant reductions in reported anxiety in both systematic desensitization groups, but not the control groups. Subject selection was based on significant deviations from the norm on self-report inventories of anxiety.

Bander et al. (1975) compared the relative effectiveness of a minimal contact control, a nonspecific therapy, sensitivity training, skills training, and skills training plus systematic desensitiziation groups. Premeasures consisted of self-report of anxiety, biographical data, and interview data. Postmeasures included the premeasures plus behavioral ratings. The three-week follow-up data consisted of self-report anxiety measures. Both the skills training and the skills training plus systematic desensitization groups were, in general, superior to the control groups with regard to self-reported anxiety reductions and judges' ratings of skill improvement at post-test. Self-report data at follow-up showed maintenance of the self-reported anxiety reduction evident at post-test. A lack of increased effectiveness with the addition of the systematic desensitization component to the skills training group was explained by Bander et al. (1975) as due to the hierarchical nature of the skills training, which could have resulted in an *in vivo* desensitization. Since selection procedures involved all the dependent measures associated with pretesting, subject selection is considered adequate.

In summary, the reviewed literature indicates that systematic desensitization treatments do as well as skill training treatments in reducing heterosexual-social anxiety, though skills training programs seem to be superior in skill acquisition at follow-up. More attention has been given to the selection of truly anxious and inhibited subjects in conditioned anxiety reduction studies than was the case in the response practice approaches. This makes sense, since high levels of anxiety are a focal concern with conditioned anxiety reduction approaches. The above studies also fare better than the response practice approach studies in their use of multimodal and follow-up assessments. However, they do not fare much better in the validation of their assessment instruments and in the measurement of transfer to actual dating situations.

Cognitive Restructuring Approaches

Cognitive restructuring approaches, like the response practice approaches and the conditioned anxiety reduction approaches, assume that heterosexual-socially anxious individuals possess a sufficient repertoire of social skills. This approach emphasizes the deleterious effects of anxiety, as does the conditioned anxiety reduction approach, but the source of the anxiety is assumed to be the result primarily of dysfunctional cognitions and not the result of conditioned anxiety. Anxiety experienced because of dysfunctional cognition may be the result of unrealistic criteria for success, misperceptions regarding actual performance, negative evaluations of self, or insufficient self-reinforcement of good performance. Of course, in any individual, any combination of these factors can come into play.

Rehm and Marston (1968) believed that the anxiety experienced by males in heterosexual-social interactions was due to negative self-evaluations and not the result of an inadequate behavioral repertoire. They reasoned that increasing self-reinforcement behavior would lead to a positive change in self-concept with an associated reduction in anxiety and an increase in approach behavior toward females. As the reader may recall, this study was also reviewed under response practice approaches, and the reader is referred to this review. While the focal intent of the project was to investigate the effects of cognitive misappraisal, there was some doubt that the self-reinforcement procedures caused the significant change in self-report of anxiety since the procedures had other potential therapeutic components such as gradual approach to the feared stimuli and an objective restructuring of behavioral goals. Also, the subject selection procedure seemed more appropriate to a response acquisition approach than to a cognitive misappraisal approach, since subjects were selected simply if they felt uncomfortable in dating situations, with no specific screening on cognitive misappraisal variables. Assuming that increasing positive self-statements was one of a number of potent therapeutic components in the Rehm and Marston procedures, the results indicated that the self-reported increase in the self-concept of the subjects did lead to a decrease in self-reported anxiety, but did not produce behavioral changes.

Glass et al. (1976) compared the effectiveness of a waiting list control, a response acquisition approach, a cognitive self-statement modification approach, and a program combining both approaches in the treatment of girl-shy college males. Since the combined treatment program was longer than either the response acquisition and cognitive modification programs alone, two control groups were added which were extended versions of the individual programs and which were equivalent in length to them. The cognitive self-statement modification program was based on the Meichenbaum (1976) training model, which consisted of learning to verbalize negative self-talk, to recognize the negative self-talk as such, and then to produce positive, adaptive self-talk behavior. Glass et al. (1976) used coping models to demonstrate the cognitive self-statement modification techniques. Subjects were simply asked to volunteer for a dating skills development program, thus subject selection was inadequate. Behavioral and dating history data were collected at pretest, post-test, and six months after treatment. Follow-up treatment assessment included a phone call transfer measure. Multiple therapists were used, and crossed-over treatment conditions and groups were equated at pretest. The results at post-treatment and follow-up indicated that all treatment groups performed significantly better than the waiting list control on the behavioral situations included in the treatment. At post-test only the cognitive modification group demonstrated improvement on the untrained behavioral situations, a measure of transfer, and this improvement was maintained at follow-up. No differences were found between the groups on the dating frequency measures. This is not surprising, since no differences in skill ratings were found between the experimental group and a group of men picked by sorority women as being dating competent. In other words, the subjects appeared not to be low-frequency daters. In summary, the results seem to imply that response acquisition training can effectively teach individuals appropriate responses for specific situations but that this training did not transfer to new situations without some direct cognitive modification. (It is appropriate to note here that cognitive modification is often informally a part of many response acquisition programs.) In addition to the above findings, the authors note that treatment effects were not independent of subject characteristics. Those subjects higher in anxiety and lower in social skills benefited most from the program. Subjects who, in a relative sense, were low-frequency daters benefited most from the cognitive modification approach. These results emphasize the importance of the interaction of subject characteristics with treatment effects and strengthen the argument that adequate subject selection and pretreatment assessment are crucial to the research in this area.

The shortcomings of the Rehm and Marston (1968) study have been touched upon previously. Subject selection procedures were inadequate; no test for equivalency was made for the groups at pretest; a proportionate change score was inappropriately used as a dependent measure when there was a significant correlation between pre-scores and difference scores; follow-up was incomplete; and there were no measures of transfer. In contrast, the Glass et al. (1976) study was a well-controlled study except for the very inadequate subject selection procedures, which paid little attention to selecting subjects along dimensions relevant to the focal therapy: negative self-statements and cognitive misappraisal. Both of the studies reviewed employing cognitive approaches did use multimodal dependent measures. While there is little outcome research demonstrating the effectiveness of cognitive approaches in the treatment of heterosexual-socially anxious individuals, evidence presented in the theoretical analysis section (Clark & Arkowitz, 1975; Smith, 1972; Smith & Sarason, 1975) argues plausibly that many socially anxious individuals have faulty cognitive appraisal systems and some kind of cognitive restructuring appears appropriate for these individuals.

Response Acquisition Approaches

The primary assumption of response acquisition approaches (Bandura, 1969) is that the source of the anxiety experienced by heterosexual-socially anxious individuals is partially, if not mostly, reactive in nature (Kanfer & Phillips, 1970) and due to an inadequate or inappropriate behavioral repertoire (Curran & Gilbert, 1975). An individual may never have learned the appropriate behavior, he may not have learned it sufficiently for skillful application, or he may have learned inappropriate behavior. Thus, response acquisition approaches differ from the previous three approaches in their focus on training requisite skills. Response acquisition programs (skills training) generally incorporate to varying degrees such techniques as information dissemination, discussion, video and/or *in vivo* modeling, behavioral rehearsal, coaching, video and/or group feedback, and *in vivo* homework assignments (Curran & Gilbert, 1975). These techniques have been employed to teach a variety of social skills. Content areas in skill acquisition programs generally include components such as the giving and receiving of compliments, nonverbal methods of communication, positive and negative assertion, the expression of positive and negative feelings, handling periods of silence, training in asking for dates, speaking fluently on the telephone, methods of handling criticism, ways of enhancing physical attractiveness, approaches to physical intimacy problems, listening skills, etc. (Curran, 1977).

McGovern, Arkowitz, and Gilmore (1975) compared a waiting list control, a discussion group, a behavioral rehearsal group (rehearsals in an office), and a second behavior rehearsal group (rehearsals in the natural environment). Subjects were college males who had less than three dates in the previous month and who stated they were anxious in social situations, desired to date more, and needed improvement in their social skills. Pre- and post-treatment measures were exclusively self-report. In general, the experimental groups reported significant decreases in anxiety as compared to the control group but did not differ from each other. The questionable selection criteria, the total reliance on self-report, lack of follow-up, and the lack of data on subjects' characteristics (degree of anxiety and/or skill deficit) make interpretation of this study difficult.

Melnick (1973) compared a minimal contact control, an insight-oriented individual therapy control, and four experimental groups (vicarious learning, vicarious learning plus participant modeling, vicarious learning plus participant modeling plus videotape observation, and vicarious learning plus participant modeling plus self-observation plus therapist reinforcement). Subjects were college students reporting discomfort on dates who dated less than twice a week. Pre- and postprogram measures consisted of an adjective checklist and two behavioral assessment tasks. Because of the small number of subjects in each group, the author combined the control groups, the two groups without benefit of self-observation feedback, and the two groups with the self-observation feedback. In general, the data derived from the behavioral tasks showed the self-observation feedback condition to be superior to the experimental group without feedback, which was in turn superior to the control groups. Melnick concluded that participant modeling plus self-observation was useful in inducing behavioral change while participant modeling alone was not beneficial. This conclusion is suspect because of inadequate subject selection, confounding of therapists across conditions, lack of follow-up, and a less-than-satisfactory rationale for combining groups.

Curran (1975) and Curran and Gilbert (1975) were reviewed under conditioned anxiety approaches, and the reader is referred to that section of the chapter for a more detailed discussion. Both of the Curran studies, in general, supported the efficacy of a skills acquisition approach in increasing behavioral ratings of skills in heterosexual-socially anxious subjects. In another study, Curran et al. (1976) compared the effectiveness of a replication skills training procedure to a sensitivity training procedure using pre- and post-treatment self-report and behavioral measures as well as an indirect measure of transfer (dating frequency). Again, as in other Curran studies, subject selection was stringent. The results indicated that while there was no significant difference between groups on general measures of self-reported anxiety, the replication skills training group demonstrated significant treatment effects over the sensitivity group on specific behavioral and self-report measures of anxiety and on the indirect transfer measure (date frequency). The major weaknesses in the Curran studies are the lack of validity data for some of their assessment instruments, the lack of direct measure of transfer, and no physiological indicators of anxiety. The three Curran studies taken as a unit, however, provide support for the effectiveness of the response acquisition approach to heterosexual-social anxiety.

MacDonald, Lindquist, Kramer, McGrath, and Rhyne (1975) selected subjects based on self-report measures of anxiety and on dating history using reasonably stringent criteria. Subjects were randomly assigned to a behavioral rehearsal, a behavioral rehearsal plus extrasession assignments, an attention-placebo control, and a waiting list control group. Therapists were crossed over groups and pretreatment equivalency of groups was established. Pre- and postassessment included self-report and behavioral ratings of anxiety and skill. A six-month follow-up was conducted on dating behavior. Results indicated a significant improvement over controls for the behavior rehearsal groups on some self-report measures of anxiety and on a number of behavioral ratings of anxiety and skill. The placebo group and the rehearsal group with extra-session assignments showed a significant increase in dating behavior at follow-up. The study can be taken as support for response acquisition approaches, having been limited only by an incomplete follow-up (self-report only) and no physiological measures.

Bander et al. (1975) was reviewed in this chapter in the section on conditioned anxiety reduction procedures. In brief, the results were generally in agreement with Curran et al. (1976) in demonstrating the superiority of specific replication training procedures over sensitivity training for specific target behaviors. Subject selection procedures were adequate, therapists were crossed over conditions, and all groups were equated on premeasures. However, follow-up was short term and included only self-report measures, the behavioral measures were only obtained at post-treatment, the principle authors served as therapists, and no validity data were provided for the dependent measures (even though a validation procedure was mentioned).

Twentyman and McFall (1975) used a contrasted group strategy to obtain construct validity for their assessment measures in comparing a behavioral skills training treatment to an assessment-only control. Subject selection procedures were adequate and included dating frequency and normative data on self-report inventories of anxiety. Pre- and post-measures included self-report, behavioral, and physiological measures. A six-month follow-up included only self-report data. Results indicated significant group differences in favor of behavioral training on a number of measures in all three response modalities. Self-report differences reported at post-test were not maintained at follow-up. In general, except for a somewhat limited follow-up (self-report only) and a lack of control for nonspecific therapy factors, this study was well-designed and supports the skills training approach to heterosexual-social anxiety.

Glass et al. (1976) was reviewed under cognitive approaches and the reader is referred to that review for a more detailed exposition. In a generally well-designed study, these authors found a response acquisition approach, a cognitive modification approach, and a combination approach to be superior to a waiting list control on behavioral measures of improvement at post-test and at a six-month follow-up. Improvement failed to transfer at follow-up for the skills acquisition group but did for the cognitive modification groups. The authors concluded that while response acquisition approaches can effectively teach skills in specific situations, cognitive modification was needed to facilitate transfer of learning to untrained situations.

Clinical Prescription

Responsible clinical application of treatment procedures for heterosexual-social anxiety necessitates good clinical assessment. Whether the focal treatment of choice will be response practice, response acquisition, conditioned anxiety reduction, cognitive modification, or a combination of some or all of these approaches will depend upon a thorough assessment of the subject. Of course, while comprehensive initial assessment of the client is important, the treatment program decided upon should remain flexible and open to ongoing assessment, potentially changing the course of that treatment (Hersen & Barlow, 1976). For example, there is a good deal of individual difference with respect to the type of social situations that elicit anxiety in individuals who are dating anxious. Since it is difficult to ferret out all of these idiosyncracies during the initial assessment, some will be discovered during the course of treatment.

During initial and ongoing assessment of the client, utilization of multiple channel measures is highly desirable (cognitive, behavioral, physiological). Since physiological measures require the most expensive equipment, assessment of both cognitive and behavioral response channels is about all that can be realistically expected of therapists in most applied clinical settings. Of course, when physiological assessment is possible, it should be used. Cognitive, behavioral, and physiological assessments should be aimed at obtaining such information as the degree of heterosexual-social anxiety as well as the relative contributions of cognitive misappraisals, conditioned anxiety, and behavioral skills deficits factors to the individual's level of anxiety. More specific questions can be generated from the broader questions, for example, in the case of cognitive factors, what is the degree and the direction (overestimation or underestimation) of the misappraisal and what are the specific accompanying irrational thoughts, beliefs, or assumptions that underly the misappraisal? Is the misappraisal more acute in some social situations than in others? In the case of behavioral skills deficits, what are the specific components comprising the skills deficits and to what extent are these specific skills components generalized across situations?

Farrell et al. (1979), in a generalizability study of self- and judges' ratings of heterosexual-social anxiety and skill, provide a good model for the assessment of some of the variables to be considered in heterosexual-social anxiety. The subjects in this study were asked to roleplay in two simulated social situations. In the first situation, subjects were asked to maintain a conversation with two female confederates (subjects were males) for five minutes, imagining that they were in a pizza parlor following a double date in which the other male had to leave early. The second simulated social situation resembled the popular television program "The Dating Game." In both situations, subjects were asked to evaluate themselves in a number of ways. First, subjects were asked to rate the level of anxiety they anticipated feeling and the level of skill they anticipated they would demonstrate before the roleplay began. Then the subjects rated the level of anxiety they felt and the level of skill they demonstrated immediately after participating in the roleplays. Finally, two weeks later, subjects were asked to rate a videotape of the roleplays with regard to how anxious and how skilled they appeared. In addition to the self-ratings, the confederates participating in the roleplays rated the subjects on appearance of anxiety and skill. Also, a separate set of judges rated videotapes of the roleplays for appearance of anxiety and skill in the subjects. Anxiety and skill ratings were given on 11-point Likert scales for each attribute.

By comparing the anxiety and skill ratings across measurement modes (self- vs. judge), across method of observation (anticipatory, participatory, and retrospective self-ratings and participatory and nonparticipatory judges' ratings), and across situations (two roleplays), a great deal of information can be obtained. For example, such variables as cognitive evaluation, degree of anxiety, degree of skill, and the generalizability (or specificity) of these across situations can be evaluated. The situations investigated can be tailored to an individual subject's needs, so that any number of different roleplays might be utilized for each individual being assessed. The results of the Farrell et al. (1979) study amply demonstrate the richness of information that can be obtained from such procedures. For example, significant level differences in anxiety were found within modes (self- vs. judges') and methods (anticipatory, participatory, or retrospective). These significant differences could help differentially diagnose not only an individual's degree of cognitive misappraisal, but also its nature, namely anticipatory, participatory, or retrospective, and the situational specificity of the anxiety reaction.

The situational specificity of the anxiety reaction can be important in determining the etiology of the anxiety, especially when the task is to differentially diagnose conditioned anxiety or anxiety caused by faulty cognitive processing from reactive anxiety. In roleplay situations, an individual may perform unskillfully either because he does not have a repertoire of skills or because his high level of anxiety is suppressing skills that exist. Carefully selected heterosexual-social situations chosen along a threatening-nonthreatening dimension could help clarify whether a repertoire of skills indeed exists. For example, heterosexual-socially anxious individuals might be asked to roleplay situations with an opposite sex partner *in vivo* or on videotape, or simply respond to the hypothetical situations using paper and pencil. Alternatively, *in vivo* confederates could be trained to roleplay nonresponsive, minimally responsive, and highly responsive dating partners. Subject performance in each situation would then be compared multimodally. Once it is established that the etiology of an individual's heterosexual-social anxiety is basically caused by cognitive misappraisal or conditioned anxiety and not a skills deficit, further differentiation as to the cause of the anxiety can be made, if necessary, by taking a careful heterosexual-social history and by administering inventories of irrational beliefs.

Once adequate assessment has been accomplished, an intervention program should be constructed so as to be maximally effective. The presence of skills deficits generally necessitates a response acquisition program incorporating some combination of the techniques and content areas mentioned under Response Acquisition Approaches. Many response acquisition approaches contain elements that appear pertinent to the treatment of conditioned anxiety and, to a lesser extent, cognitive misappraisal. Conditioned anxiety components of basically a skills deficit problem might be efficaciously handled with the addition of systematic desensitization to the response acquisition program. Cognitive-evaluative misappraisal could be treated in a structured fashion using the cognitive modification program discussed under Cognitive Restructuring Approaches.

With respect to response acquisition approaches, it is our contention that the treatment of heterosexual-social anxiety is most therapeutically potent and cost effective in a group rather than an individual therapy setting. We should stress that this contention is based on our own biased observations and not on empirical evidence. Individual approaches cannot readily provide the breadth of discussion and variety of problems that is often possible in a group setting. Groups share information, and group experiences are in and of themselves social situations. Groups provide an opportunity for socially anxious males and females to get together and be exposed to one another. This decreases the tendency of one sex to consider the other sex an "alien race" by facilitating discovery of common interests and fears. Having a sexual balance in the group also helps with modeling and rehearsal procedures. The realism provided in roleplays in which the opposite sex is actually present is invaluable. We think that having the opposite sex participate in the behavioral rehearsals is important enough that when there is a lack of female or male subjects in a group, this lack should be corrected with appropriate-sex confederates who have had some minimal amount of training.

Ideally, groups should be led by two leaders of the opposite sex. Opposite-sex group leaders have different perceptions regarding certain problems and are often able to complement one another. Two leaders can work as a team, one concerning him- or herself with running the structured program, the other concerning him- or herself with group dynamics and cohesiveness. There is a tendency for training groups to drift into lengthy discussions without engaging in actual rehearsal and practice, and the presence of two leaders helps avoid this pitfall.

Since there is little or no evidence regarding the effective components of social skills treatment programs, we recommend using as many components of the treatment as possible: information dissemination, discussion, video and/or *in vivo* modeling, behavioral rehearsal, coaching, video and/or group feedback, and *in vivo* homework assignments. Discussions should emphasize the following: everyone occasionally experiences anxiety in heterosexual-social interactions, and, therefore, the subjects in the group are not "deviant"; the group is constructed to have a nonthreatening atmosphere in which mistakes can be made without any significant consequences and where learning can occur; social behavior is a skill that can be learned and improved with practice; anxiety often results from erroneous thinking, which will be corrected during the training as it appears. These points probably need to be repeated many times at opportune moments during the training to encourage a relaxed group atmosphere. Mechanical application of the training, without sensitivity to possible feelings of embarrassment or abnormality, would be detrimental to the participants.

It is generally advisable for group leaders in the social anxiety area to have at least some experience with more traditional forms of group approaches. Modeling tapes should have both positive and negative models and should incorporate failures occasionally (e.g., lack of goal attainment) even when the model is skillful. The reason for this is to make the point that skill does not guarantee success, it just increases the probability of success. To promote generalization of learning, every group member should interact with every other group member in roleplays as much as possible. Subjects should have the videotaping procedures fully explained to them and should see themselves on videotape before their first actual roleplay so that they may concentrate on their skill production and not on the novelty of the filming situation. Feedback after roleplays must be given in such a way as not to rub the client's inadequacy in his or her face. Roleplays should be redone after feedback to give the subject a chance to incorporate the feedback he or she receives. Since the second performances are usually better than the first, the subjects' confrontations with his or her inadequacy is lessened by the success of the second roleplay. Group members, rather than the leaders themselves, should be encouraged to provide as much of the feedback to subjects as is possible. Forcing subjects to analyze the strengths and deficits of other subjects is good social skills training in and of itself. Finally, constructive pressure should be constantly applied to those subjects who avoid the *in vivo* homework assignments outside of the sessions, as this may be crucial to transfer of skills in their environment.

Sessions should be held one or two times a week, enough time to allow *in vivo* homework assignments to be completed without disrupting the continuity of the group. A group size of about six to eight members is ideal. This size group usually provides enough problem heterogeneity to promote fruitful group discussion while allowing everyone in the group the opportunity for individual attention through roleplays.

A Case Report

Mr. A was a 28-year-old Vietnam veteran who had a ten-year history of alcohol abuse. He began his drinking while serving in Vietnam. He drank up to a quart of hard liquor every day in addition to guzzling cans of beer. Since his return from Vietnam, he had been in state hospitals six times for detoxification and had been arrested for public intoxication many more times. Mr. A reported that the longest period he did not drink was about three weeks, some two years prior to the treatment about to be described. Other attempts at staying sober had lasted approximately one to four days. Mr. A was a patient of the second author.

Mr. A did not have a drinking problem until he joined the service at the age of 18 to escape what he considered an intolerable home situation. Mr. A's father was about 60 years old when he married for the first time. During Mr. A's childbirth, Mr. A's mother suffered spinal injury due to her advanced age. The injury left her with a crooked posture which made embulation possible, but difficult. Mr. A reported that both of his parents rarely went out or had company in their home, preferring to live alone. He thought his mother to be cold, distant, somewhat domineering, and overprotective. He reported that he had a good relationship with his father. Mr. A's father spent time talking with him and protected him from his mother's domineering style. When Mr. A was 16 years old, his father died, making life at home with mother intolerable. She would not allow him to have friends, insisting that he stay home at all times. She constantly talked about how evil women were and strictly forbade dating. When Mr. A turned 18, he immediately joined the service. Mr. A's first few attempts at developing relationships with women failed. He reportedly asked one woman to marry him on the second date. Despondent, Mr. A began to drink, and in Vietnam, began seeing prostitutes, a number of whom he also asked to marry him. Mr. A continued to go out with prostitutes until about a year before treatment, at which time he stopped seeing prostitutes because "sex without a relationship began to be more depressing than no sex at all."

In the month of August, Mr. A entered the Day Hospital treatment program at a VA hospital. Mr. A was referred from the Inpatient Ward where he had been detoxified two weeks before. He reported it was the first time he had received follow-up treatment of any kind after detoxification. After a few sessions of therapy, Mr. A admitted that he drank because he felt lonely and thought himself incapable of ever having a long-term relationship with a woman. Mr. A's treatment plan was developed and included Antabuse therapy, group and individual therapy, activity therapy, family therapy, and an intensive social skills training program. Mr. A agreed to record on a daily basis the intensity of his impulses to drink. He was asked to rate the intensity of his strongest impulse on any particular day on a scale of 1 to 10, with 1 indicating very little impulse and 10 indicating that the impulse was so strong that he actually had taken a drink. Mr. A kept a record of his daily drinking impulses from the end of August, when he began his treatment, until the following May, when his treatment coordinator, the second author, left the section of the country where Mr. A resided.

Mr. A's initial assessment on self-report measures of social anxiety revealed high levels of anxiety. In addition, in a number of roleplayed social situations with female confederates, he was rated by judges to be highly anxious and moderately low in social skills. In roleplays with male confederates, Mr. A's anxiety was rated by judges as markedly decreased and his amount of social skills was rated as moderate to moderately high. Mr. A himself rated his own anxiety and skill levels with male and female confederates at approximately the same level as the judges. The data seem to indicate that Mr. A's heterosexual-social anxiety was mostly reactive in nature, probably due to an almost total lack of exposure to heterosexual-social situations. Some conditioned anxiety and cognitive factors also appeared to be present. High skill levels with males made prognosis good.

Mr. A was given response acquisition training including all the techniques and content areas mentioned under response acquisition approaches. Sessions lasted 90 minutes and were conducted five days a week for four weeks. The group had a male and a female leader, who did most of the behavioral rehearsals, and three other veterans besides Mr. A. Mr. A was very conscientious about doing his *in vivo* homework assignments and was an active and enthusiastic participant in the program. As a result, he learned quickly.

At post-test, Mr. A's anxiety and skills ratings by judges in roleplays identical to pretest roleplays indicated a significant decrease in anxiety and an increase in skill. Nontrained social situations, different from the pretest situations (a measure of transfer) were also handled well by Mr. A. Mr. A's own ratings were consistent with the judges', indicating his ability for accurate appraisal and his increased confidence in himself. Toward the end of the training he reported initiating a few short conversations with women on the bus, something he had never done before. Despite his newfound confidence, however, Mr. A still had doubts that he could handle himself in an interaction with a woman which lasted more than 20 minutes, about the length of time of the longest roleplay during his social skills training.

An addition to the treatment program was devised which made use of a response practice approach. Two simulated dates, separated by four weeks, were arranged with college-age women who had experience as confederates in social skills training but did not know Mr. A. The dates took place at the Day Hospital in the recreation room. They lasted three hours each and were double dates in which Mr. A and another veteran from his social skills group spent time with two women. The two women were not the same for each date. The dates were structured around games such as Monopoly and Risk. The participants brought nonalcoholic refreshments and snacks. Mr. A and his friend rated their anticipated levels of anxiety and skill before the dates. In addition to the anticipatory self-ratings, Mr. A and his friend rated themselves on general levels of anxiety and skill and on verbal and nonverbal behavioral indicators at the end of every hour during the date. The verbal behaviors rated were: timing, generating talk, maintaining talk, prompting, checking reception, avoiding heavy topics, listening skills, using feeling talk, giving and receiving compliments. Nonverbal rated behaviors were: posturing, eye contact, head nods, smiling, laughing, body movements, hand gestures, and personal space observance. The female confederates also rated Mr. A and his friend on the same variables at the end of every hour during the date. No communication about the ratings was allowed between confederates and subjects.

Mr. A's anticipatory anxiety was extremely high before the first date. During the date his ratings were low and agreed with the female confederate's ratings of his anxiety. His ratings on the skill measures were moderately high and also agreed with the ratings of the female confederates, who were asked to use their own extensive experience with men in judging the subject's overall level of skill and anxiety. Interestingly, while Mr. A's evaluation of his performance agreed with the female confederate's during the date, 24 hours later he was convinced he had actually done terribly. The data from the first date was presented to him to help disconfirm his retrospective misappraisal. On the second date, Mr. A showed little anticipatory or retrospective anxiety, indicating that the first simulated date had had some effect. His ratings of skill and anxiety during the second date were similar to those of the first date and once again agreed with the female confederate's rating of him. Mr. A was generally being judged by the female confederates as having low anxiety and moderately high skill even when compared with a number of other men they had dated in their lives.

After the first simulated date, Mr. A was released from the Day Hospital. He arranged to start college in January. Having been released from the Day Hospital in early November, the months of November and early December were difficult for him. He attributed the difficulty to the lost support of the Day Hospital program. In December, Mr. A was fired from the job he had recently acquired, which resulted in one day's return to drinking. This was the only time that Mr. A drank. After this incident, Mr. A decided to start spending time on the college campus he was about to attend. Once Mr. A began doing so, he made friends immediately and actually started dating women around the middle of December. At this time, his drinking impulses dropped dramatically. By January, Mr. A was dating women regularly, and by February, he was living with a woman. Just prior to the beginning of his relationship with this woman, Mr. A's confidence in his ability to control his drinking impulses was such that he discontinued the Antabuse therapy. Despite having great difficulties with his schoolwork through the spring semester, Mr. A's drinking impulses stayed under control. In May, Mr. A announced that he was engaged to be married. At this time, he had successfully controlled his drinking and had very low drinking impulses for a period of $5\frac{1}{2}$ months. This $5\frac{1}{2}$-month period of low drinking impulses corresponded exactly with the beginning of the development of his male and female friendship network. Prior to this time, his drinking impulses had been consistently in the middle to high range. The drinking impulse data supported Mr. A's contention that he drank primarily out of loneliness.

Legal and Ethical Considerations

One of the advantages of the treatment approaches reviewed in the area of heterosexual-social anxiety is that they involve few, if any, legal or ethical problems. As has been stated in the behavioral treatment and clinical prescription sections, careful assessment of a patient is requisite before an appropriate treatment strategy can be designed. Comprehensive assessment will have important implications for the pace of therapy and the type of experiences to which the subject is exposed. These considerations are important from an ethical standpoint since the strategies involve exposure to the feared stimuli. For example, it would clearly be inappropriate to use a response practice approach with peers if the patient has relatively high levels of anxiety and poor social skills. The possibility for a failure experience causing increased anxiety under these conditions are greatly enhanced. It should be noted here that such was the situation in the case report provided above. The response practice section of the patient's therapy involved trained confederates because it was crucial at that point in therapy for the subject not to have an aversive experience.

Above and beyond careful consideration of the pace and content of training approaches, there are legal and ethical considerations involved in assessing generalization of the effects of treatment. Measurement of generalization (transfer of training) has been attempted by assessing performance in roleplays of trained and untrained situations. Kazdin (1977), however, has argued that a better test of generalization is assessment by a measure methodologically distant from the previous training method. Extra-laboratory measures to detect generalization have often involved deception, such as telephone follow-ups in which the subject does not realize he is being assessed (McFall & Twentyman, 1973). McFall and Twentyman suggest that subjects be informed that they will be monitored unobtrusively post-treatment. This appears to be a good solution for the deception problem. Finally, it appears clear that patients have the right to be fully informed of the procedures to be employed and that they have the right to reject any component of the training program that they so choose. The use of confederates will necessitate making confidentiality issues clear to them.

Suggestions for Clinical and Experimental Research

Many of the deficiencies outlined by Curran (1977) in the area of heterosexual-social anxiety treatment research are still pertinent today. The major problem still involves the development of reliable and valid measures of heterosexual-social anxiety. Since we have discussed those problems in an earlier section of our chapter, we need not dwell on them here except to note that we must not only be able to assess the presence of heterosexual-social anxiety, but also to assess the etiological basis of the response. In our discussion of theoretical considerations, we talked about three primary hypotheses regarding the etiology and maintenance of heterosexual-social anxiety: classical conditioning, skills deficit, and cognitive factors. From a theoretical perspective, it is hypothesized that the various factors responsible for the maintenance of heterosexual-social anxiety would interact with various treatment strategies and components within various treatment strategies. For example, those subjects who possess good requisite skills but perform poorly in heterosexual-social situations because of cognitive interference mechanisms would theoretically improve most with a cognitive treatment strategy. In addition to the suggestion regarding the refinement and development of assessment techniques for clarification of the etiology of heterosexual-social anxiety, the following additional suggestions are made:

1. Examination of active treatment components. As was seen in our review of treatment outcome studies, different types of strategies including cognitive, counterconditioning, and skills acquisition techniques have been utilized in the treatment of heterosexual-social anxiety. Within each type of treatment strategy, treatment programs differ along many dimensions. For example, within the skills acquisition approach,

some programs seem to emphasize the teaching of individual behaviors while others seem to focus on the teaching of interpersonal strategies. Components within the treatment package differ, some utilizing modeling procedures while others do not. Some programs stress *in vivo* practice, while others put less emphasis on homework assignments. Some skill acquisition programs conduct behavioral rehearsals until mastery is achieved, while others have a set number of rehearsal trials. Various components within each treatment strategy need to be evaluated with respect to their relative effectiveness. In fact, differences within treatment programs within each type of treatment approach may actually be more important than differences between the various treatment approaches. For example, some treatment programs are individually based, while others are group based. Some treatment programs include both male and female subjects, while others exclude members of the opposite sex. If, for example, the group context (especially groups consisting of opposite-sex members) is extremely important for therapeutic success, then differences in treatment strategies may be more due to these parameters rather than their alleged treatment ingredients.

2. Development of adequate subject selection procedures. As Curran (1977) noted in his review, if investigators are interested in the construct of heterosexual-social anxiety, then it behooves them to select subjects on this basis. This is clearly not always the case, and as Curran (1977, p. 153) has stated,

> Suspicions about the degree of anxiety actually experienced by subjects should be generated by studies that involve inappropriate, inadequate, incomplete, or non-existing screening criteria, the payment of subjects either with experiential credit or money, the selection of a fairly large proportion of subjects from a given subject pool, recruitment of subjects for purposes other than anxiety relief (e.g., to improve dating skills), and the like.

Screening should involve multiple channels using reliable and valid instruments with appropriate norms.

3. Implementation of appropriate experimental controls. Our review of treatment outcome studies in this chapter indicates a number of potential experimental confounds in these studies. Such confounds include lack of equivalency of treatment and control groups at pretest, lack of adequate controls for repeated assessment, passage of time, subjects' expectancy, therapist and experimenter bias, nonequivalency and biases in the raters, and inappropriate statistical analyses.

4. Inclusion of follow-up assessment. Most of the studies reviewed in this chapter have not included a follow-up assessment. Those studies that did include a follow-up did so on considerably fewer subjects because of attrition and generally did not assess the subject on all the dependent measures used at pre- and post-treatment testing. The longest follow-up examining the maintenance of treatment gains was conducted by Curran and Gilbert (1975), and that was only a six-month follow-up. Because of the lack of long-term follow-up data, it is still unclear whether treatment gains demonstrated post-treatment are maintained for extended periods of time.

5. Assessment within the natural environment. Although it is difficult to measure a subject's heterosexual-social anxiety in the natural environment, it is imperative that we make the attempt. It has often been demonstrated (Hersen & Bellack, 1976) that behaviors learned in a laboratory do not readily transfer to the natural environment. Strategies that were discussed in the assessment section such as peer ratings, behavioral diaries, and so on, should be utilized, although they do possess flaws. Other more ingenious methods with fewer methodological problems must be devised. We could be more confident of our simulated laboratory assessment if we showed that ratings from these situations did generalize well to different kinds of contrived situations as in the Wessberg et al. (1979) study or to naturalistic situations.

Conclusion

It is evident from this review that heterosexual-social anxiety is a problem for a significant number of individuals in dating encounters and that it appears to have ramifications for later social functioning. The nature of dating anxiety is an ideal target behavior for analog research if subjects are appropriately selected. Three primary and nonmutually exclusive hypotheses (conditioned anxiety, faulty cognitions, and skills deficits) concerning the etiology and maintenance of heterosexual-social anxiety attest to its complexity. Multimodal assessment with valid instruments is required to determine the nature of the anxiety response and the suitability of various treatment approaches. We think that the development and refinement of reliable and valid assessment instruments is the most critical problem facing investigators and clinicians working with heterosexual-social anxiety.

A review of the literature indicates that the approaches employed (Response Practice, Cognitive, Conditioned Anxiety Reduction, and Response Acquisition Approaches) in the treatment of heterosexual-social anxiety have demonstrated some promise. However, methodological problems (inadequate screening of subjects, lack of long-term follow-up, inappropriate or nonexistent controls, absence of measurement of transfer to the natural environment, use of nonvalidated assessment instruments) prevent us from making strong conclusions regarding the relative effectiveness of each of these treatment approaches. In addition, as we have tried to stress, the treatment of choice must be determined by a thorough assessment of the etiological and maintaining factors of the anxiety response. Careful attention to the above methodological problems in future research should produce data that will allow for more efficacious clinical treatment.

Summary

Heterosexual-social anxiety is a major concern to a significant number of individuals engaged in dating encounters. It is one of the more frequent complaints raised by undergraduate populations utilizing college counseling centers. Heterosexual-social anxiety also seems to be associated with later social functioning and various psychiatric disorders.

Research interest in heterosexual-social anxiety has been prompted because it appears to possess characteristics that make it an ideal target behavior for therapy analog research. It is a pervasive and clinically relevant problem, fairly large numbers of subjects can be recruited, measurement procedures can discriminate low- and high-anxious subjects, strong physiological arousal is elicited and does not readily habituate, and demand effects beyond repeated testing are negligible. However, the "goodness" of heterosexual-social anxiety as a target behavior for analog research is affected by many factors, including, most notably, the careful screening of subjects.

There are three primary hypotheses regarding the etiology and maintenance of heterosexual-social anxiety; skills deficits, conditioned anxiety, and faulty cognitive processes. Heterosexual-social anxiety from the skills deficit framework is seen as reactive in nature and as a result of an inadequate or inappropriate behavioral repertoire. Because of the lack of requisite skills, an individual does not cope with the demands of dating situations adequately and, therefore, often experiences aversive consequences, which elicit anxiety. Heterosexual-social anxiety as interpreted from the conditioned anxiety hypothesis is viewed as the result of classically conditioned episodes where the previously neutral cues of dating situations are associated with aversive stimuli regardless of the individual's skill level. There are a number of variations of the faulty-cognitive-process interpretation of heterosexual-social anxiety including unrealistic criteria, misperception of social cues, and overly negative evaluation of performance, among others. Direct and circumstantial evidence exists to support each of these hypotheses. These hypotheses should not be seen as mutually exclusive; rather, heterosexual-social anxiety should be viewed as multiply determined in origin. A conceptual model which we find useful for both assessment and treatment, incorporating all three hypothoses, is presented in this chapter. Since treatment intervention should be guided by the etiology of components of the anxiety response, data relevant to all three hypotheses should be collected during assessment.

A 3 × 3 × 4 conceptual framework for the classification of heterosexual-social anxiety assessment strategies is presented. The facets include the content of the response (cognitive, motoric, and physiological), the method of assessment (self-report, others' report, and physiological), and the assessment setting (naturalistic-immediate, naturalistic-retrospective, controlled, and contrived). Self-report methods have been primarily used to obtain cognitive responses (e.g., subjective level of anxiety) in all four assessment settings. Others' report methods focus on the motoric responses of the subject. Generally, untrained observers are used in naturalistic settings while trained observers are used in controlled and contrived settings. Although no one assessment strategy should be regarded as the sole criterion on which to validate other assessment strategies, the most popular standard in heterosexual-social anxiety research appears to be trained observers ratings in controlled laboratory settings. Although this assessment strategy possesses many desirable characteristics, data are lacking regarding the representativeness of the subjects' behavior in these settings to their behavior in the natural environment. Physiological methods have been used rarely in heterosexual-social anxiety research, although it is an extremely important component of the anxiety response. Data relevant to the reliability and validity of existing instruments and the development of instruments representing strategies so far neglected in the literature are badly needed.

The four major categories of treatment approaches that appear in the literature are: (1) Response Practice, (2) Cognitive, (3) Conditioned Anxiety Reduction, and (4) Response Acquisition. The first three approaches assume that the patient possesses adequate skills for coping with heterosexual-social encounters, while the Response Acquisition strategy does not make this assumption. The Response Practice approach consists of arranged heterosexual interactions. It is assumed that exposure to heterosexual-social interactions will lead to appropriate skills employment and a decrease in anxiety. Cognitive approaches attempt to clear up faulty misconceptions, change unrealistic criteria, decrease negative self-statement, and increase positive self-statements and positive self-reinforcement. Conditioned anxiety reduction of heterosexual-social anxiety has consisted primarily of systematic desensitization. Here, patients are gradually exposed to the feared situation (first in imagery and later *in vivo*) and taught a coping response (e.g., relaxation) to the situations. Response Acquisition approaches attempt to train patients in the requisite skills needed for dating encounters. Response Acquisition approaches incorporate to varying degrees such techniques as information dissemination, discussion, modeling, behavioral rehearsal, coaching and feedback, and *in vivo* homework assignments.

Evidence supporting each of these approaches is presented, although at times the data are difficult to interpret because of methodological flaws. In point of fact, each of these four approaches appears to incorporate some components of the other approaches and the relative effectiveness of the approaches may be determined by procedural components not as yet systematically studied. Clinical prescriptions regarding assessment and treatment are offered and a case study provided as an illustration.

The major problem for both treatment of and research on heterosexual-social anxiety is the development of reliable and valid assessment procedures. It appears essential to evaluate the relative contributions of skills deficits, cognitive, and conditioned anxiety factors in the development and maintenance of heterosexual-social anxiety. In the treatment outcome studies reviewed, subjects have been treated as a etiologically homogeneous group even though they appear to be heterogeneous. Theoretically, presently undetected differences in the relative contributions of the various etiological factors could interact with the various treatment strategies, thus confounding interpretations. Other methodological shortcomings found in the treatment outcome literature include the lack of adequate control groups, lack of assessment of transfer to the natural environment, and lack of long-term follow-up. These methodological problems need to be rectified in order to provide more efficacious treatment of heterosexual-social anxiety.

References

Argyle, M., & Kendon, A. The experimental analysis of social performance. In L. Berkowitz (Ed.), *Advances in experimental social psychology* (Vol. 3). New York: Academic Press, 1967.

Arkowitz, H., Lichtenstein, E., McGovern, K., & Hines, P. The behavioral assessment of social competence in males. *Behavior Therapy*, 1975, *6*, 3–13.

Bander, K.W., Steinke, G.V., Allen, G.J., & Mosher, D.L. Evaluation of three dating-specific treatment approaches for heterosexual dating anxiety. *Journal of Consulting and Clinical Psychology*, 1975, *43*, 259–265.

Bandura, A. *Principles of behavior modification*. New York: Holt, Rinehart, & Winston, 1969.

Borkovee, T.D., Stone, N., O'Brien, G., & Kaloupek, D. Identification and measurement of a clinically relevant target behavior for analogue outcome research. *Behavior Therapy*, 1974, *5*, 503–513.

Bryant, B., Trower, P., Yardley, K., Urbieta, K., & Letemendia, F.J. A survey of social inadequacy among psychiatric patients. *Psychological Medicine*, 1976, *6*, 101–112.

Christensen, A., & Arkowitz, H. Preliminary report on practice dating and feedback as treatment for college dating problems. *Journal of Counseling Psychology*, 1974, *21*, 92–95.

Christensen, A., Arkowitz, H., & Anderson, J. Beaus for cupid's errors: Practice dating and feedback for college dating inhibitions. *Behavior Research and Therapy*, 1975, *13*, 321–331.

Clark, J.V., & Arkowitz, H. Social anxiety and self-evaluation of interpersonal performance. *Psychological Reports*, 1975, *36*, 211–221.

Cone, J.D. The relevance of reliability and validity for behavior assessment. *Behavior Therapy*, 1977 *8*, 411–426.

Conger, A.J., Wallander, J.L., Mariotto, M.J., & Ward, D. Peer judgments of heterosexual-social anxiety and skill: What do they pay attention to anyhow? *Behavioral Assessment*, 1980.

Curran, J.P. An evaluation of a skills training program and a systematic desensitization program in reducing dating anxiety. *Behavior Research and Therapy*, 1975, *13*, 65–68.

Curran, J.P. Skills training as an approach to the treatment of heterosexual-social anxiety: A review. *Psychological Bulletin*, 1977, *84*, 140–157.

Curran, J.P. Comment on Bellack, Hersen, & Turner's paper on the validity of roleplay tests. *Behavior Therapy*, 1978, *9*, 462–468.

Curran, J.P. Pandora's box reopened. The assessment of social skills. *Journal of Behavioral Assessment*, 1979, *1*, 55–71.

Curran, J.P., & Gilbert, F.S. A test of the relative effectiveness of a systematic desensitization program and an interpersonal skills training program with date anxious subjects. *Behavior Therapy*, 1975, *6*, 510–521.

Curran, J.P., Gilbert, F.S., & Little, L.M. A comparison between behavioral training and sensitivity training approaches to heterosexual dating anxiety, *Journal of Counseling Psychology*, 1976, *23*, 190–196.

Curran, J.P., Wallander, J.L., & Fischetti, M. The importance of behavioral and cognitive factors in heterosexual-social anxiety. Paper presented at the Midwestern Psychological Association Convention, Chicago, 1977.

Farrell, A.D., Mariotto, M.J., Conger, A.J., Curran, J.P., & Wallander, J.L. Self-ratings and judges' ratings of heterosexual-social anxiety and skill: A generalizability study. *Journal of Consulting and Clinical Psychology*, 1979, *47*, 164–175.

Fischetti, M., Curran, J.P., & Wessberg, H.W. Sense of timing: A skill deficit in heterosexual-socially anxious males. *Behavior Modification*, 1977, *1*, 179–194.

Fishman, S., & Nawas, M. Treatment of polysomatic or global problems by systematic desensitization. In R. Rubin (Ed.), *Advances in behavior therapy*. New York: Academic Press, 1973.

Glass, C.R., Gottman, J.M., & Shmurak, S.H. Response acquisition and cognitive self-statement modification approaches in dating skills training. *Journal of Counseling Psychology*, 1976, *23*, 520–526.

Goldfried, M.R., & D'Zurilla, T.J. A behavioral-analytic model for assessing competence. In C.D. Spielberger (Ed.), *Current topics in clinical comments psychology* (Vol. 1). New York: Academic Press, 1969.

Goldfried, M.R., & Sobocinski, D. Effects of irrational beliefs on emotional arousal. *Journal of Consulting and Clinical Psychology*, 1975, *43*, 504–510.

Greenwald, D.P. The behavioral assessment of differences in social skills and social anxiety in female college students. *Behavior Therapy*, 1977, *8*, 925–937.

Hersen, M., & Barlow, D.H. *Single case experimental designs: Strategies for studying behavior change*. New York: Pergamon Press, 1976.

Hersen, M., & Bellack, A.J. Assessment of social skills. In A.R. Ciminero, K.R. Calhoun, & H.E. Adams (Eds.), *Handbook of behavioral assessment*. New York: Wiley, 1976.

Kanfer, J.H., & Phillips, J.S. *Learning foundations of behavior therapy*. New York: Wiley, 1970.

Kazdin, A.E. Assessing the clinical or applied importance of behavior change through social validation. *Behavior Modification*, 1977, *1*, 427–452.

Kiesler, D.J. Experimental design in psychotherapy research. In A.E. Bergin & S.L. Garfield (Eds.), *Handbook of psychotherapy and behavior change: An empirical analysis*. New York: Wiley, 1971.

Landy, F.J., & Gaupp, L.A. A factor analysis of the Fear Survey Schedule—III. *Behavior Research and Therapy*, 1971, 9, 89–94.

Lang, P.J. Fear reduction and fear behavior: Problems in treating a construct. In J.M. Schliem (Ed.), *Research in psychotherapy* (Vol. III). Washington, D.C.: American Psychological Association, 1968, pp. 90–102.

MacDonald, M.L., Lindquist, C.U., Kramer, J.A., McGrath, R.A., & Rhyne, L.D. Social skills training: Behavior rehearsal in groups and dating skills. *Journal of Counseling Psychology*, 1975, *22*, 224–230.

Mandler, G., Mandler, J.M., & Miller, E.T. Autonomic feedback: The perception of autonomic activity. *Journal of Abnormal and Social Psychology*, 1958, *56*, 367–373.

Martinson, W.D., & Zerface, J.P. Comparison of individual counseling and a social program with nondaters. *Journal of Counseling Psychology*, 1970, *17*, 36–40.

McFall, R.M., & Twentyman, C.T. Four experiments on the relative contributions of rehearsal, modeling, and coaching to assertion training. *Journal of Abnormal Psychology*, 1973, *81*, 199–215.

McGovern, K., Arkowitz, H., & Gilmore, S. Evaluation of social skills training programs for college-dating inhibitions. *Journal of Counseling Psychology*, 1975, *22*, 505–512.

Meichenbaum, D. A cognitive behavior modification approach to assessment. In M. Hersen & A. Bellock (Eds.), *Behavioral assessment: A practical handbook*. New York: Pergamon, 1976.

Melnick, J. A comparison of replication techniques in the modification of minimal dating behavior. *Journal of Abnormal Psychology*, 1973, *81*, 51–59.

Mischel, W. *Personality and assessment*. New York: Wiley, 1968.

Mischel, W. Toward a cognitive social learning reconceptualization of personality. *Psychological Review*, 1973, *80*, 252–283.

Mitchell, K.R., & Orr, T.E. Note on treatment of heterosexual anxiety using short-term massed desensitization. *Psychological Reports*, 1974, *35*, 1093–1094.

Nelson, R.O. Methodological issues in assessment via self-monitoring. In J.D.

Cone & R.P. Hawkins (Eds.), *Behavior assessment: New directions in clinical psychology*. New York: Brunner/Mazel, 1977.

O'Banian, K., & Arkowitz, H. Social anxiety and selective memory for affective information about the self. Unpublished manuscript, University of Denver, 1975.

Paul, G.L., & Bernstein, D.A. Anxiety and clinical problems: Systematic desensitization and related techniques. Morristown, N.J.: General Learning Co., 1973.

Pilkonis, P.A. Shyness public and private and its relationship to other measures of social behavior. *Journal of Personality*, 1977, *45*, 585–595.

Rehm, L.P., & Marston, A.R. Reduction of social anxiety through modification of self-reinforcement: An instigation therapy technique. *Journal of Consulting and Clinical Psychology*, 1968, *32*, 565–574.

Smith, R.E. Social anxiety as a moderator variable in the attitude similarity-attraction relationship. *Journal of Experimental Research in Personality*, 1972, *6*, 22–28.

Smith, R.E., & Sarason, I.G. Social anxiety and the evaluation of negative interpersonal feedback. *Journal of Consulting and Clinical Psychology*, 1975, *43*, 429.

Twentyman, C.T., & McFall, R.M. Behavioral training of social skills in shy males. *Journal of Consulting and Clinical Psychology*, 1975, *43*, 384–395.

Wallander, J.L., Conger, A.J., Mariotto, M.J., Curran, J.P., & Farrell, A.D. Comparability of selection instrument in studies of heterosexual-social problem behaviors. Behavior Therapy, 1980, *11*, 548–560.

Watson, D., & Friend, R. Measurement of social-evaluative anxiety. *Journal of Consulting and Clinical Psychology*, 1969, *33*, 448–457.

Wessberg, H.W., Mariotto, M.J., Conger, A.J., Conger, J.C., & Farrell, A.D. Ecological validity of roleplays for assessing heterosocial anxiety and skill of male college students. *Journal of Consulting and Clinical Psychology*, 1979, *47*, 525–535.

Wiggins, J.S. Personality and prediction: Principles of personality assessment. Reading, Mass.: Addison-Wesley Publishing Co., 1973.

Suggested Readings

Characteristics of Target Problems of Heterosexual-Social Anxiety

Borkovec, T. D., Stone, N., O'Brien, G., & Kaloupek, D. Identification and measurement of a clinically relevant target behavior for analogue outcome research. *Behavior Therapy*, 1974, *5*, 503–513.

Greenwald, D. P. The behavioral assessment of differences in social skills and social anxiety in female college students. *Behavior Therapy*, 1977, *8*, 925–937.

Pilkonis, P. A. Shyness public and private and its relationship to other measures of social behavior. *Journal of Personality*, 1977, *45*, 585–595.

Etiology and Maintenance

Curran, J. P. Social skills: Methodological issues and future directions. In A. S. Bellack & M. Hersen (Eds.), *Research and practice in social skills training*. New York: Plenum Press, 1979.

Glass, C. R., Gottman, J. M., & Shmurak, S. H. Response acquisition and cognitive self-statement modification approaches in dating skills training. *Journal of Counseling Psychology*, 1976, *23*, 520–526.

Assessment

Bellack, A. S. Behavioral assessment of social skills. In A. S. Bellack & M. Hersen (Eds.), *Research and practice in social skills training*. New York: Plenum Press, 1979.

Curran, J. P. & Mariotto, M. J. A conceptual structure for the assessment of social skills. In M. Hersen, D. Eisler, & P. Miller (Eds.), *Progress in behavior modification*. New York: Academic Press, 1980.

Curran, J. P. & Wessberg, H. W. The assessment of social inadequacy. In D. Barlow (Ed.), *Behavioral assessment of adult disorders*. New York: Guilford Press, 1981.

Treatment Strategies, Components, and Procedures

Bander, K. W., Steinke, G. V., Allen, G. J., & Mosher, D. L. Evaluation of three dating-specific treatment approaches for heterosexual dating anxiety. *Journal of Consulting and Clinical Psychology*, 1975, *43*, 259–265.

Christensen, A., Arkowitz, H., & Anderson, J. Beaus for cupid's errors: Practice dating and feedback for college dating inhibitions. *Behavior Research and Therapy*, 1975, *13*, 321–331.

Curran, J. P. & Gilbert, F. S. A test of the relative effectiveness of a systematic desensitization program and an interpersonal skills training program with date anxious subjects. *Behavior Therapy*, 1975, *6*, 510–521.

Glass, C. R., Gottman, J. M., & Shmurak, S. H. Response acquisition and cognitive self-statement modification approaches in dating skills training. *Journal of Counseling Psychology*, 1976, *23*, 520–526.

Evaluation of Treatment Effectiveness

Curran, J. P. Skills training as an approach to the treatment of heterosexual-social anxiety: A review. *Psychological Bulletin*, 1977, *84*, 140–157.

2

Essential Hypertension

James E. Byassee and Stephen P. Farr

Essential hypertension is a major health problem throughout the world. For example, this disorder affects well over 20 million persons in the United States alone. Hypertension is associated with reduced life expectancy due to an increase in the frequency of heart attack, stroke, and heart and kidney failure, and it is considered to be a major death-causing agent (Galton, 1973).

Between 90 and 95 percent of all hypertension cases can be diagnosed as essential hypertension, which usually is defined by exclusion after ruling out other antecedent organic pathology. The criterion for a diagnosis of hypertension is somewhat arbitrary, with most investigators accepting a lower limit of approximately 140 mm. Hg systolic, and 90 mm. Hg diastolic (Byassee, 1977). Many factors, such as race, heredity, weight, age, diet, salt intake, kidney problems, and hormonal factors may influence the recorded pressure. Further, the regulation of blood pressure is exceedingly complex and is affected by numerous different physiological systems and feedback loops (Anokhin, 1961). This has tended to further obscure complete understanding of the disease.

The notion has been offered that essential hypertension is a recognizable entity with a pronounced hereditary influence (Platt, 1959, 1963, 1964). However, most physicians presently agree that there is no clear distinction between normal and abnormal pressures, apart from the arbitrary statistical division of stating that a given blood pressure is markedly deviant from the population samples (Sleight, 1971). Genetic factors do appear to account for a major portion of the variance in blood pressure readings, but other factors seem to account for the greatest proportion (Miall, 1971).

As indicated previously, essential hypertension is a potent source of cardiovascular mortality and morbidity. The Framingham studies showed persons with hypertension to be at dramatically increased risk of death from myocardial infarction, congestive heart failure, stroke, and other conplications, as well as at risk from changes in morbidity and mortality associated with the accelerated atherosclerosis and renal and vascular changes that occur with sustained hypertension (Dawber, Kannel, Revotskie, & Kazan, 1962). However, it has also been well established that lowering blood pressure by pharmacotherapy dramatically reduces these risks (Veterans Administration Cooperative Study Group, 1967, 1970). A complication has been the health service delivery difficulties of screening, side effects of antihypertensive drugs, and lack of patient compliance with prescribed treatment (Patel, 1977).

Theoretical Analysis

Nonbehavioral

Despite the fact that essential hypertension is regarded as being without organic cause, research has continually been directed to organic etiologies. It has been suggested that malfunction of the kidney or certain endocrine glands whose hormones influence kidney function may cause hypertension, although the kidney's abnormal balance of water, sodium, and other electrolytes often found in hypertensives may be a consequence of the disorder rather than a cause (Ledingham, 1971). Animal studies have shown that trace quantities of cadmium in drinking water from birth can induce hypertension which is reversible when the cadmium is treated so that it can be easily excreted from the kidneys. Autopsies have indicated that the kidneys of patients victim to hypertension and its complications usually contain higher cadmium concentrations than those of patients with normal blood pressure. However, the cause and effect relationships here are also unclear (Galton, 1973).

Psychodynamic theorists posit that the hypertensive patient experiences conflicts between passive dependent longings and aggressive competitive impulses, or conflict between chronic anger and a need to repress angry feelings because of fear of loss of love and esteem (Ostfield, 1973). Although there appears to be no clear "hypertensive personality," there does seem to be a similar perception as to how hypertensives view their way of life or their attitudes and values (Wolf, 1977). Problems with the validity of diagnosis, reliability of blood pressure measurement, and traditional difficulties in personality research continue to obscure the findings in this area (Byassee, 1975).

Most investigators agree, however, that the disease is significantly exacerbated by stress or that stress is a main etiological factor. The cardiovascular system in response to stress is characterized by an increase in heart rate and vascular output, a widespread constriction of arterial vessels, and a subsequent increase in blood pressure. Prolonged experience of stress events may eventually lead to an "upward resetting" of the regulatory mechanisms, such as the carotid sinus and other baroreceptors, and blood pressure remains permanently elevated (Patel, 1977; Wallace & Benson, 1972). Although it is not clear whether or not there are innate characteristics that lead to the development of essential hypertension directly, there is evidence that hypertensives tend to inhibit aggression or overreact with inhibited rage or a suppressed rage response (Buss, 1966; Meyer, 1968; Harrell, 1980). Further, it appears to be generally accepted that this vulnerability or general susceptability to stress is in part due to genetic or constitutional factors.

Behavioral

Basic research with animals, normotensive humans, and hypertensive patients has literally mushroomed in recent years (Patel, 1977; Schwartz & Shapiro, 1973; Shapiro, Mainardi, & Surwit, 1977a) along with the theoretical and applied work in the area of biofeedback and self-control generally (Barber, 1971a, 1971b; Dicara, Barber, Kamiya, Miller, Shapiro, & Stoyva, 1975; Farr, Smith, & Meyer, 1975; Hendrix & Meyer, 1974; Miller, Barber, Dicara, Kamiya, Shapiro, & Stoyvar, 1974; Seer, 1979; Shapiro, Barber, DiCara, Kamiya, Miller, & Stoyva, 1975; Stoyva, Barber, DiCara, Kamiya, Miller, & Shapiro, 1972; Williamson & Blanchard, 1979). Although hereditary influences probably interact with environmental factors to cause hypertension, environmental stimuli affecting the learning history of the organism are important and potentially modifiable contributors. There is strong evidence that emotional stressors have a direct impact on transient increases in blood pressure. There is also some dispute as to the relationship between transient increases and permanent hypertension (Buss, 1966; Harrell, 1980). As indicated previously, prolonged experience of stress events may eventually lead to a resetting of blood pressure regulatory mechanisms, thus permanently elevating the blood pressure (Wallace & Benson, 1972; Patel, 1977; Schwartz & Shapiro, 1973).

As Patel (1977) and others have suggested, a behavioral approach to hypertension would then involve an "unlearning" of maladaptive behaviors elicited during the individual's response to stress. This would occur by teaching hypertensives to reduce sympathetic activity in situations involving aggression and anxiety. In the context of a broader social learning model (e.g., Bandura, 1969), patients should also be taught to recognize anger–fear situations, to express their feelings in an adaptive and physiologically effective fashion, and to avoid such situations or operate on the environment to reduce their likelihood. A similar broad-based approach has been developed for cardiac patients as well as those with a "coronary-prone personality" (Suinn, 1974, 1977).

Assessment

The diagnosis of essential hypertension is a medical procedure. Epidemiological studies indicate that mortality is directly related to the height of either the systolic or the diastolic blood pressure. Yet many of these studies are based on an isolated reading of blood pressure taken at one point in time. Also, some individuals even with sustained high blood pressure live out a normal life span (Freis, 1971), and a number of studies indicate that borderline or labile hypertension is associated with less cardiovascular disease than is persistently elevated hypertension (Smirk, 1957). Freis points out that commonly accepted treatment criteria are diastolic pressures of 100 mm Hg, with the understanding that the value represents an average value obtained during at least two clinic visits other than the initial visit, or via home blood pressure recordings. He also states that patients with borderline readings will sometimes have their hypertension subside, and that considerations such as age, family history, and evidence of organic involvement should contribute to medical judgment as to treatment planning. On this basis, active treatment is usually indicated if the readings are both severe and fixed.

Once basal blood pressure has been found to be elevated, and possible organic causes ruled out by appropriate procedures, the physician may elect not to treat, to treat with chemotherapy, or in borderline cases especially to counsel the patient with respect to losing weight, salt intake, and "taking it easy." Because of the patient compliance problem, however, the utility of these recommendations cannot be firmly stated.

Preliminary professional research as well as material from the popular press have indicated that various biofeedback and/or self-control methods might be useful in the control of hypertension. Partly because of the publicity and patients' requests for advice and "nonmedical" treatment, physicians may choose to recommend a course in transcendental meditation (Yogi, 1975), biofeedback, or relaxation training (e.g., Benson, 1975). Developing a treatment plan using learning theory principles and behavioral/biofeedback methodology, however, cannot be rigorously defended at this time based on the data available, although many reviews point to the potential utility of such procedures (Byassee, 1977; Frumkin, Nathan, Prout, & Cohen, 1978; Shapiro, Schwartz, Ferguson, Redmond, & Weiss, 1977a). At this point, we view self-control methods as ancillary to chemotherapy approaches or of possible use in borderline conditions with proper medical monitoring.

Treatment Procedures

The presence of undesirable side effects represents a persistent problem for physicians treating labile or borderline conditions with chemotherapy. This is also a major issue relevant to patient compliance to the prescribed regimen. Under these circumstances, Patel (1977) notes that asking patients with symptomless hypertension to submit to possible lifelong medication with possible unpleasant side effects is a major difficulty. Chemotherapy side effects (e.g., headache, dizziness, gastrointestinal disturbance, asthenia, etc.; see Gifford, 1974) contribute to physician reluctance to prescribe for borderline conditions.

Although there is no firm experimental evidence to support the contention that psychotherapy by itself reduces hypertension, it appears to be a common psychiatric impression that such therapy may be a useful adjunct to medication. There are some case reports in the literature describing hypotensive results from psychotherapy alone (Lachman, 1972). Shapiro et al. (1977a) reviewed two studies conducted prior to the ready availability of antihypertensive agents in the 1950s, using psychotherapy with hypertensives. They point out that declines in blood pressure of up to 20–40/10–30 mm Hg were achieved in individuals involved in long-term psychotherapy. In addition, the general mechanisms of verbal reassurance, support, and a successful provider–patient relationship are aspects that facilitate the general physician–patient relationship.

Schwartz and Shapiro (1973) have suggested teaching hypertensives how to recognize anger–fear situations (which tend to raise blood pressure) and to express their reactions and feelings in an adaptive manner so as to minimize "fight or flight" responses. They also recommend teaching individuals to adjust their lifestyle in a way that minimizes exposure to stressful life events. This treatment approach, suggested in conjunction with behavioral methods outlined below, has yet to be evaluated experimentally.

In recent years, research has indicated that it is possible for humans to be trained to alter the level of their own arterial blood pressure without the use of antihypertensive drugs. Such training may eventually prove to have considerable benefit either apart from or as an adjunct to current drug regimens, where drug control cannot be obtained, to reduce dosage, or where disturbing side effects exist. These self-control methods have evolved along two paths. The first of these has to do with self-administered relaxation training, and the second is concerned with biofeedback and instrumental conditioning strategies derived from the psychological principles of learning theory.

Relaxation Techniques

Nonpharmacologic interventions aimed at teaching relaxation or lowered states of arousal are far from new. In the Eastern practices of Yoga and Zen, various exercises have been used for thousands of years which allow individuals to develop remarkable control of their physiological systems (Wenger, Bagchi, & Anand, 1961). Hypnosis, of course, also has a long history as a relaxation technique and is still frequently employed in various psychotherapy techniques where states of low arousal or suggestibility are desired by the therapist (Lazarus, 1971; Wolpe, 1969). Riddick and Meyer (1973) define relaxation as a descriptive term for a complex pattern of responses characterized by subjective feelings of peace and calmness associated with lowered physiological arousal, especially in the sympathetic branch of the autonomic nervous system, and a diminution of gross motor movements. Benson (1975) also points out how the many relaxation methods share similar mechanisms: (1) a mental device upon which to focus to shift away from externally oriented thought; (2) a passive or indifferent attitude as to success in achieving the response; (3) reduced gross motor activity resulting in decreased muscle tonus; (4) a quiet environment with minimal external distraction.

Progressive relaxation. Relaxation of muscle fibers, or complete absence of muscle contractions, was seen as the direct physiological opposite of tension and therefore an appropriate treatment for the overly tense or anxious person (Jacobson, 1938). Jacobson discovered that by systematically tensing and relaxing various muscle groups, and by learning to attend to and discriminate the resulting sensations of tension and relaxation, a person may dramatically reduce muscle contractions and experience a feeling of deep relaxation. Jacobson gave his patients very prolonged training, often lasting 50 to 200 sessions, in the treatment of various stress-related disorders (Wolpe & Lazarus, 1966). Wolpe (1958) modified this set of exercises in his development of a technique called reciprocal inhibition or systematic desensitization, which was designed as a treatment for anxiety. Wolpe's modification resulted in a relaxation training program that could be completed in approximately six 20-minute sessions with two 15-minute daily home practice sessions. Patients are taught to relax their muscles and, while relaxing, they are encouraged to confront their anxieties in small graded steps in their visual imagination. As a result of this procedure, the individual gradually learns to control fear and avoidance responses in real life. This technique has been evaluated experimentally by many researchers and has been proven to be a very successful treatment for a variety of fear and anxiety reactions (Paul, 1969a, 1969b). Most of the relaxation approaches currently in use are derivatives of either Wolpe's (1958) or Lazarus' (1971) similar technique. One manual for therapists (Bernstein & Borkovec, 1973) has outlined the procedure in some detail. This approach involves the alternate tensing and relaxing of the hands, forearms, biceps, forehead, facial muscles, chest, shoulders, upper back, abdominal region, thighs, calves, feet, and so on with a focus on the pleasurable feelings that accompany relaxation. As the sessions proceed, an attempt is made to achieve the same levels of deep muscle relaxation without focusing upon all 16 muscle groups; this is achieved by using tensing–relaxing contrasts for seven muscle groups. Focus is then placed upon four muscle groups, and in the final sessions, the patient is taught to elicit the relaxation response by recalling the sensations of relaxation without tensing any particular muscle groups. The entire training is to take approximately ten sessions, and the pace of therapy is set by the patient's gradual mastery of each step of the program.

In addition, Lazarus (1971) recommends using relaxing images (e.g., sunbathing on the beach), or hypnotic suggestions of warmth and heaviness to deepen the individual's relaxation response. Following this model, Bair and Levenberg (1979) report a successful single-case biofeedback treatment intervention with a 24-year-old college-educated white male. This patient was seen for 22 sessions over a five-week period with a "multimodal" assessment and treatment model that incorporated progressive relaxation techniques. These investigators report that while the amount of change per session remained stable, the observed diastolic pressure decreased progressively from the 100–120 mm Hg range to within "normotensive" limits over the course of treatment. Of particular interest was an attempt to follow the patient into his natural environment and monitor progress. Over the course of the study, readings taken on a random basis suggested that the patient had either learned to reduce his blood pressure on command or that he had stabilized at a new normotensive level.

Jabobson (1938, 1939a, 1939b, 1964) has offered evidence that progressive relaxation is useful in the treatment of hypertension. He has argued that his clinical findings support the view that high blood pressure can result in part from habitual tensions in the skeletal musculature, which can be progressively relaxed with a resultant hypotensive effect. He reports a general relationship between decreases in blood pressure and decreases in muscle activity as shown by electromyograms, and stated also that training in progressive relaxation resulted in greater decreases in electromyogram activity than relaxation without training. Blood pressure data were presented on 14 normotensive subjects, nine of whom had been trained in progressive relaxation. Both systolic and diastolic blood pressure were collected after a 15-minute adaptation period during which the subjects rested in a supine position, and again after 45 minutes of relaxation. Although further analysis of Jacobson's data by Blanchard and Young (1973) did reveal statistically significant decreases in both systolic blood pressure (mean = 8.0 mm Hg) and diastolic blood pressure (mean = 7.8 mm Hg), no significant differences existed between the trained and untrained subjects in the degree of reduction achieved.

Redmond, Gazler, & McDonald (1974) administered progressive muscle relaxation to five hypertensive patients for three five-minute sessions and observed a within-session drop that averaged 13.8/5.5 mm Hg. Following home practice sessions, however, patients were unable to reduce blood pressure in the clinic, until they were "instructed" to do so by slowing their heart beat and making their blood vessels less resistant. There was no examination of between-session blood pressure changes.

Steinhaus and Norris (1964) found a significant reduction in systolic blood pressure (8 mm) for their subjects with initial readings above 130 mm Hg systolic who were trained in progressive relaxation. Similar findings for diastolic pressure were found (8.5 mm). These authors also reported no significant decreases in either mode or blood pressure for those subjects with blood pressure readings within the normal range. Several other studies using combined or comparative relaxation procedures have included progressive relaxation; these are reviewed in a later section.

Autogenic training. Autogenic training is a method of autosuggestion by which the individual is given practice in attending to both his physiological sensations and his immediate state of consciousness. The procedure involves daily practice of certain exercises, including muscular relaxation, and concentration on subjective sensations of warmth and heaviness. It has been suggested as an effective method for training individuals to gain control over various aspects of physiological reactivity and has been tentatively reported to be of therapeutic benefit for difficulties such as asthma, ulcers, skin disorders, various cardiovascular problems, anxiety neurosis, and sleep disturbances (Schultz & Luthe, 1959).

The system involves a number of verbal formulas that make up the "standard exercises" and the "meditative exercises." The verbal content of the standard formulas is focused upon the neuromuscular system (heaviness) and the vasomotor system (warmth), on the heart, the respiratory mechanism, warmth in the abdominal area, and cooling of the forehead. The meditative exercises are composed of a series of seven exercises designed primarily for psychotherapy and personal growth and are reserved for trainees who have mastered the standard exercises. Later, as more research and clinical experience accumulated, special exercises also emerged. These complementary exercises were specially designed to produce normalization of specific pathofunctional deviations such as vasomotor, endocrine, and metabolic disorders (Schultz & Luthe, 1969). Autogenic training is said to be based on the reduction of exteroceptive and proprioceptive afferent stimulation, continuous mental repetition of psychophysiologically adapted verbal formulas, and mental activity conceived as "passive concentration" (Schultz & Luthe, 1959). These are the same basic elements crucial to the relaxation response outlined by Benson (Benson, 1975; Benson, Beary, & Carol, 1974a).

Numerous studies are reported that suggest the efficacy of autogenic training in the increase in peripheral circulation, decrease of muscle potentials, changes in EEG patterns and respiratory and cardiac activity, and other autonomic and visceral changes. Interested readers are referred to Luthe and Schultz (1969) and Luthe (1970), although some of this research is disappointing due to the absence of appropriate control, comparison, or placebo subject groups. From a clinical case perspective, Luthe and Schultz (1969) argue that autogenic training appears to be a helpful therapeutic adjunct to hypertensive conditions that are a function of organic disturbance as well as for the treatment of essential hypertension. The vasodilatory and circulatory effects associated with passive concentration on the different standard formulas include a number of desirable variables that participate in lowering elevated blood pressure readings. Generally, autogenic training represents a shift toward a pattern of reactivity and away from the pattern of changes elicited by stress.

Luthe and Schultz (1969) point out that the clinical results in the treatment of hypertension vary between excellent and an apparently complete failure of response, but it is generally agreed that the effectiveness of the autogenic standard exercises increases if the hypertensive condition is due to functional factors. In many cases, they report marked improvement for essential hypertension after four to eight weeks of standard training. Readings taken before and after one set of standard exercises usually show a 5 to 25 percent reduction of systolic values, and a 5 to 12 percent decrease in diastolic blood pressure.

Klumbies and Eberhardt (1966) applied autogenic training to a group of 83 male hypertensives. Of these, 57 dropped out of training. This motivational problem has been reported elsewhere (Schwartz, 1973) and may relate to the fact that many hypertensives suffer no discernible symptoms that they feel need treatment. In spite of this, the remaining 26 subjects demonstrated impressive improvement. Blood pressure readings were taken repeatedly before starting autogenic training and during subsequent periods, for 5 to 15 months. The most significant decrease of systolic and diastolic readings occurred during the first month of autogenic training. Further decreases continued during the second, third, and fourth months, with little or no change occurring during subsequent periods. The authors noted considerable individual variation in response to treatment, particularly with some individuals showing dramatic improvement. Normalization of blood pressure deviations were noted in 22 out of the 26 patients. The authors also suggest that group training (up to ten persons) is helpful and state that in view of the unfavorable side effects experienced by some individuals on antihypertensive medication, autogenic training may be the treatment of choice for many individuals.

Luthe and Schultz (1970), however, found no significant differences in blood pressure readings of normotensives before and after four weeks of "heaviness" training. A number of subjects, in fact, reported that they experienced distinct heaviness in the extremities in spite of the fact that their blood pressure and sometimes heart rate went up slightly (5 to 15 percent) during training. This phenomenon occurred when subjects fell asleep, began snoring, executed minor movements, or were disturbed by unpleasant intruding thoughts during the exercises. In three subjects whose blood pressures were repeatedly determined during passive concentration on heaviness, inconsistent responses were observed (up on some days, down on others, some days no change). Luthe offered no explanation to account for these results, but as noted previously, similar findings for normotensives were reported by Steinhaus and Norris (1964) using progressive relaxation. Luthe (1963) has also offered a very brief report of an uncontrolled study of 79 labile and essential hypertensive patients who undertook autogenic therapy. It was reported that 19 patients responded well and 29 others showed definite improvement. However, there was no improvement in 37 patients in the study.

The use of autogenic training in the treatment of essential hypertension would appear to have possible positive potential based on the above studies, although the absence of appropriate control-comparison groups limits the conclusions that can be drawn. More data are needed on the relative value of autogenic therapy as compared to other relaxation therapies, as well as relative to no-treatment controls.

Yogic and other meditative techniques. Datey, Deshmukh, Dalvi, and Vinekar (1969) combined muscle relaxation with breathing exercises for treating hypertensive subjects. This management approach involved a yogic exercise known as "Shavasan," which the hypertensives practiced for 30 minutes each day. The technique consisted of lying prone on the floor and engaging in slow rhythmic diaphragmatic breathing. After establishing the rhythm, the subject is asked to attend to the sensation at the nostrils, the coolness of the inspired air, and the warmth of the expired air. This procedure is intended to keep the patient inwardly alert but forgetful of his usual thoughts, thus becoming less conscious of the external environment and attaining relaxation. The patient is also asked to relax the muscles so that he is able to feel the heaviness of different parts of the body. Favorable results were reported, not only with patients having essential hypertension, but also with several hypertensives having renal hypertension. None of the arteriosclerotic patients, however, experienced a significant reduction in blood pressure. A statistically significant decrease of 27 mm Hg in average mean blood pressure was reported after training of an unspecified period of time.

The typical training course was described as requiring three weeks of 30-minute daily sessions.

Benson has reported a series of studies using transcendental meditation (TM) to treat hypertension (Benson & Wallace, 1972; Benson, Rosner, & Maryetta, 1973; Benson et al., 1974a; Benson, Rosner, Maryetta, & Klemchuk, 1974b, 1974c). This method is a form of Indian Yoga coming from the Vedic tradition (Benson, 1975) and has achieved widespread popularity in the United States. TM involves systematic but passive concentration upon a word or sound, known as the *mantra*. The trainee is to practice twice a day for a period of 15 to 20 minutes, in a comfortable and quiet position. Preliminary studies showed that statistically significant reductions of both systolic and diastolic pressures of hypertensives occurred after they had begun the practice of TM. Generally, blood pressure reductions in these studies are small both for subjects taking no antihypertensive medication (6.98 mm Hg mean systolic reduction; and 3.86 mm Hg mean diastolic reduction), and for hypertensives who were medicated throughout the training and follow-up (10.6 mm Hg systolic; 4.85 diastolic) (Benson et al., 1974b, 1974c).

Blackwell, Bloomfield, and Gartside (1976) found that meditation reduced blood pressure in patients who monitored their own blood pressures at home, but that the average decrement was far less when the effects of meditation were evaluated in a clinical setting. The absence of a control group limits the conclusions from this study.

Pollack, Weber, Case, and Laragh (1977) found that 20 hypertensive patients participating in a TM training program showed no significant change in blood pressure after a six month study, although there were small reductions in systolic blood pressure and in pulse rate early in the study. The authors noted, however, that 70 percent of the sample planned to continue TM, even though its effect on their blood pressure was minimal.

Hence, the hypotensive effect of TM appears to be a small one that has not been reliably demonstrated. Further research will be needed to clarify this area.

Brady, Luborsky, and Kron (1974) reported on the use of "metronome-conditioned" relaxation (MCR) in the treatment of four male patients with essential hypertension. This technique involves the use of an abbreviated progressive relaxation procedure coupled with more general suggestions of physical and psychological relaxation given while an auditory metronome is beating at 60 beats a minute. The instructions to "let-go" and "re-lax" the muscles of the body are paced with the metronome's beats. The basic notion is that in time, the metronome's beats will function as stimuli conditional to elicit the relaxation response (Brady, 1973).

Three of the four patients in this study showed statistically significant mean reduction changes in blood pressure. Further, two subjects showed a statistically significant further decrease when the MCR procedure was reinstated over an extended period of time. The possibility of expectation, suggestive factors, or placebo influences, of course, cannot be ruled out in this study.

Stone and De Leo (1976) treated 14 hypertensives with a relaxation technique they based on Buddhist meditation exercises. Patients were to sit comfortably and count their breaths subvocally on a continuous basis for 10 to 15 minutes. Patients were to practice twice daily for a period of six months. Reductions of 14 to 30 mm. Hg mean arterial blood pressure occurred in 8 of the 14 patients. Evidence was also provided of biochemical reduction of peripheral adrenergic activity that did not occur in a nonrandomized group (which also showed no significant reduction in pressure). As the authors note, this finding tends to support the notion that psychotherapeutic reduction of blood pressure may result from a decrement of neuronal activity.

Biofeedback Techniques

Biofeedback techniques offer an individual moment-to-moment information about specific physiological processes so that he or she can then modify and perhaps control many functions once regarded as "autonomic, involuntary, or reflexive" (e.g., heart rate, blood pressure, and brain waves). Although considerable research has yet to be done, the list of variables that have thus far been demonstrated to be under the self-control of human subjects is impressive. With respect to clinical applications, promising preliminary results in the treatment of essential hypertension, cardiac arrhythmias, migraine and tension headaches, Raynaud's disease, and abnormal EEG phenomenon have been reported in either research reports or clinical case studies (Schwartz, 1973). Budzynski and Stoyva (1973) have outlined a series of therapeutic biofeedback techniques that can be used in conjunction with other approaches such as systematic desensitization or autogenic training.

Shapiro and his colleagues at Harvard have shown that healthy college students could learn to raise or lower their systolic blood pressure in a single session (Shapiro, Tursky, Gershon, & Stern, 1969; and Shapiro, Tursky, & Schwartz, 1970a). In a later study, subjects were trained to raise and lower their heart rate without similarly affecting their systolic blood pressure (Shapiro, Tursky, & Schwartz, 1970b). Schwartz (1973) has suggested that this research opens the way for the development of teaching patients patterns of responses:

> For example, the desired goal for those hypertensive patients having normal heart rates may be to lower stroke volume and/or peripheral resistance rather than to change heart rate per se. However, in reducing pain

> from angina pectoris, the desired goal may not be to lower just blood pressure, or heart rate, but rather to lower both functions simultaneously, since by decreasing rate and pressure, the heart requires less oxygen, which in turn leads to reduced pain [p. 668].

More recently, this same group of researchers has focused upon self-control of diastolic blood pressure (Shapiro, Tursky, & Schwartz, 1972), the degree of integration and differentiation of the cardiovascular system (Schwartz, 1972), and a general theory of voluntary control of these response patterns (Schwartz, 1974). Much work remains to be done in this area, however, particularly in the application of appropriate control groups, and the exploration of the issues relating to mediation and follow-up data (Blanchard & Young, 1973; Schwartz, 1973).

Other research reports have been concerned with the use of the operant feedback technique developed by the Harvard group in the treatment of hypertensives. Benson, Shapiro, Tursky, and Schwartz (1971) treated a group of seven hypertensive patients for an average of 21 sessions and produced significant decreases in systolic pressures (mean = 22.6 mm Hg). Brener and Kleinman (1970) used a form of proportional visual feedback and took pressure recordings from the left index finger of two groups of five normotensives for two sessions. Results were consistently higher than those recorded by the more conventional arm cuff technique used, for example, by the Harvard group.

Although definitive results from research investigations in this area have not yet been forthcoming (Blanchard & Young, 1973), some case reports and preliminary clinical findings have shown additional promise. Miller (1972), for example, has described in detail a case study of a 33-year-old hypertensive woman who was given several months of training in voluntary control of blood pressure. An impressive reduction in her diastolic pressure developed, which was maintained for 30 days without drugs in her own natural environment; training resulted in a reduction from a pretraining diastolic baseline of 97 mm. Hg to a level of 76 mm Hg. It is possible, however, that other factors (client–therapist relationship, etc.) could account for the improved readings. An additional impressive element of this case was the attempt to control for some of the demand characteristics of the setting by rewarding the patient first for producing small diastolic decreases and then, as soon as she appeared to be reaching an asymptote for that session, rewarding her for producing diastolic pressure increases, but never above the original baseline. Miller pointed out that this had the added benefit of continued reward for the patient, so as to prevent frustration from failed learning trials.

In a subsequent publication, Miller (1972) reports that when the above patient was apparently "overwhelmed" by a series of difficult experiences, she lost her ability for voluntary control and her hypertension returned. Despite this relapse, this case study does indicate that it is possible to train voluntary control of hypertension. Greater generalization and lasting changes might have been obtained by also using therapeutic approaches that teach the better handling of tension-provoking situations or arrangement of environmental factors so as to minimize stress (Schwartz & Shapiro, 1973).

Another implication of this case report is that for severely hypertensive patients, even if voluntary control is achieved, it might be better for the individual to remain on maintenance medication in the event that he or she might face an overwhelming emotional or physical experience that could produce a cardiovascular accident, in lieu of the use of medication. However, for less severe cases, relaxation training alone might prove to be a method of controlling essential hypertension without both the undesirable side effects of some chemotherapy approaches and the need for costly and sometimes complicated biofeedback machinery.

Goldman, Kleinman, Snow, Bidus, and Koros (1975) treated seven hypertensive patients (average baseline of 167/109 mm Hg) not on medication with the constant cuff procedure, and found decreases of 4 and 13 percent, systolic and diastolic, respectively. Feedback was given for systolic pressures, but significant reductions occurred only for diastolic pressures. Goldman et al. (1975) also found concomitant reduction in cognitive dysfunction, an interesting additional area for further research.

Kristt and Engel (1975) showed that patients could be taught to lower their systolic blood pressure as well as to raise it and alternatively to lower and to raise pressure. In addition, their results showed that patients could be taught skills that persisted for at least three months (reductions in pressure of about 10 to 15 percent). Alpha wave activity, breathing rate, and EMG were also monitored during training (three weeks during hospitalization) but showed no significant change, suggesting that the patients did not learn a simple relaxation response, as these measures might reasonably be expected to respond to a relaxation procedure (Wallace, 1970). Another important feature of this study was that patients recorded their own daily pressures and mailed them to the experimenters for seven weeks prior to hospitalization and training. This self-monitoring procedure was seen as particularly valuable by the authors. It is also important to note that some patients had cardiovascular complications such as cardiac arrhythmias, left ventricular hypertrophy, malignant hypertension, diabetes, and cardiomegaly. Biofeedback was shown to be a helpful adjunct to medical management.

Comparative and multimethod studies. Progressive relaxation, autogenic training, meditative methods, and blood pressure feedback have all demonstrated in the above studies to have some promise in the treatment of essential hypertension. More recently, studies have been published which compare various methods or use several methods of self-control strategies in conjunction.

Modifications of the autogenic training approach have also been offered. Some clinicians have combined some of the autogenic phraseology with progressive relaxation (Love, 1972). Others have combined autogenic training with biofeedback techniques and labeled the approach "autogenic feedback training" (Green, Green, & Walters, 1970). This method involved teaching the individual to practice autogenic training at home while also receiving biofeedback treatment in the laboratory for some particular bodily process. Biofeedback involves the use of instruments to provide moment-to-moment information to an individual about a specific physiological process, such as electromyogram potentials (EMG feedback). This autogenic feedback approach has been used by some researchers in the treatment of hypertension. Moeller and Love (1973) and their associates at Nova University provided nine hypertensive subjects with training in autogenic exercises according to a slightly modified standard approach and gave them feedback electromyography using forearm and frontalis muscles during 17 weekly half-hour sessions. The mean blood pressures for the last eight weeks of training were analyzed and were found to be significantly lower than pretreatment readings. However, this study is limited by the absence of control groups to determine the possible effects of placebo phenomena or of habituation to the setting. Also, it is not possible to determine the relative influence of the EMG training and the autogenic exercises as therapeutic factors.

In a second study, Love, Montgomery, and Moeller (1972) treated one group of 20 subjects with two laboratory EMG biofeedback training sessions a week, coupled with tape-recorded relaxation exercises that they were to practice at home twice per day. Blood pressure was recorded at the beginning and end of the training sessions. Another group received one laboratory biofeedback session per week with the same relaxation procedure to be followed at home. The next group received two biofeedback sessions per week, but did not receive the relaxation tapes and "thus did not practice the exercises." The final group simply had their EMG readings monitored for four weeks and served as a control comparison group. After four weeks of training, there were no significant differences among the three treatment groups, and only minor changes existed in the systolic and diastolic pressures of the control group (mean reduction of 2.20 mm Hg systolic and 0.67 mm Hg diastolic). The three treatment groups pooled together showed a mean reduction of 12.67 mm Hg in systolic pressure and a 9.78 mm Hg drop in diastolic pressure. Statistical analysis indicated a significant difference between the pooled treatment groups and control group. In a subsequent paper the authors reported a one-year follow-up of 23 of the original 32 subjects who were treated. The blood pressure readings of this group indicated a total mean decrease of 27.52 mm Hg systolic and a 17.70 mm Hg diastolic, representing continued gains (Montgomery, Love, & Moeller, 1974).

Generally, the above series of reports on the Nova University sample indicate the apparent effectiveness of relaxation training using autogenic relaxation instructions administered by a tape recorder and EMG biofeedback in treating hypertension. It is suggested further that with several months of training, the effects might be persistent and continually therapeutic, at least as long as one year. The use of a group to assess the effects of training in relaxation *without* biofeedback would have been a helpful addition to this study, as well as the use of an attention-placebo manipulation. Shapiro, Myers, Reiser, and Ferris (1954) showed that simply the inclusion of a subject in a special study had a hypotensive effect, and data should be gathered on the magnitude of this effect, which might likely vary depending upon the particular characteristics of the laboratory or setting and the subjects.

Deabler, Fidel, Dillenkoffer, and Elder (1973), for example, treated six hypertensives who were receiving no medication, using both muscular relaxation (Wolpe & Lazarus, 1966) and a hypnotic procedure, and compared this group to a group of six hypertensives who simply had their blood pressures recorded in the same way, with no instructions to relax. An additional group of nine patients, stabilized on individualized antihypertensive medication, also received the muscular relaxation and hypnosis procedures. Significant lowering of both systolic and diastolic pressures were obtained in both the no drug (systolic 17 percent, diastolic 19.5 percent reductions) and drug (systolic 16 percent, diastolic 14 percent reductions) groups receiving treatment, but there was not significant reduction in the no-treatment control group. This study suggests that relaxation or self-control methods can have a positive effect on patients who are on medication as well as those who are not, a result also found for the practice of transcendental meditation. Since all treated patients received both the muscular relaxation and the hypnotic procedure, it is not possible to assess the relative effectiveness of these two treatment techniques. Further, the control group was not told that the procedure would be a treatment for blood pressure, hence expectancy factors were not operative. However, this did allow habituation to the research setting to be ruled out as an operating hypotensive factor.

Elder, Ruiz, Deabler, and Dillenkoffer (1973) reported on an experiment designed to compare two instrumental conditioning strategies for controlling high blood pressure. All patients were hospitalized essential hypertensives and were not medicated, although many were on antidepressants. One group of six subjects received an external signal contingent upon each self-generated reduction in pressure that met a preset criterion. Another group of the same size received both the signal and verbal praise. These results were compared to a control group that received instructions to relax and avoid thinking about personal problems and to try to lower their blood pressure. The treatment group with both the external signal and verbal praise appeared to do better but only for the diastolic readings. The data also suggested that diastolic pressure might be a more suitable dependent variable than systolic blood pressure for this type of instrumental conditioning. Some individual patients were conditioned to lower diastolic pressure by 20 to 30 percent over a period of four days, although definitive follow-up data were not provided.

In a subsequent study, Elder and Eustis (1975) used a similar procedure in the treatment of 22 primarily medicated outpatients who volunteered themselves as essential hypertensives. Although both systolic and diastolic data were collected, positive stimulus feedback and verbal praise only for diastolic reductions were provided to the subjects. Massed training (daily) for ten sessions (20 trial sessions) was provided for four patients, with the balance receiving spaced training. Within the latter group, female patients performed slightly better than did males. Overall results, however, were less impressive than in the hospitalized, definitely diagnosed group of patients in the previous study, a result the authors attributed primarily to the stronger motivation for the hospitalized sample. No follow-up data were provided for this sample.

Shoemaker and Tasto (1975) compared a taped muscle relaxation program, modified from Jacobson's (1938) approach, to a group receiving noncontinuous biofeedback of systolic and diastolic blood pressure. Data from these treatments were compared to a waiting list control group, which apparently received no instructions to relax or to lower their blood pressure but had their pressure monitored. The authors found that muscle relaxation brought about a reduction of both systolic and diastolic blood pressure, while the biofeedback approach brought about a lesser reduction, but only in diastolic readings. A possible reason for this difference, offered by Shoemaker and Tasto, was that the subjects in the biofeedback group attended to biofeedback signals for both the systolic and diastolic pressures and they seemed to be able to concentrate more effectively on the diastolic signal. Elder, Leftwich, and Wilkerson (1974) also have offered some data suggesting such diastolic contingencies to be more effective.

Byasee (1975) compared autogenic training and progressive relaxation in the treatment of essential hypertension. The control group (unstructured self-relaxation) was instructed to practice relaxation at home for equivalent periods as the two treatment groups. A collection of expectancy procedures was used, including a placebo capsule designed to produce a highly credible control comparison group. All three groups showed reductions in systolic pressure (autogenic 6.1 percent, progressive 12.2 percent, self 9.5 percent), although there were no significant between-group differences. This study was specifically designed to be readily transferable to applied settings. Relaxation training was provided for groups of several subjects at once, and acceptable reliability data using routine clinical sphygmomanometers indicated that the sophisticated and complex measurement methods typically used in such research may not be necessary for an acceptable degree of research precision. Treatment gains failed to persist at a four-month follow-up.

Weston (1974) compared the effects of frontalis EMG feedback to blood pressure feedback utilizing the constant cuff method (Shapiro et al., 1969) both with patients receiving additional relaxation practice and with those who did not. Reductions ranging from 13 to 36 mm Hg systolic and 6 to 20 mm. Hg diastolic were found, although the various treatment procedures produced comparable effects, suggesting a possible generalized relaxation process to be in effect. However, the absence of a control group does not rule out the possibility that observed changes were due to nonspecific factors.

Surwit and Shapiro (1976) compared the effects of feedback from the frontalis muscle and the forearm muscle to blood pressure/heart rate feedback and Benson's meditation relaxation procedure (1975). All subjects displayed moderate reductions in blood pressure, and no particular method appeared to be superior. Carryover effects, however, from session to session or in follow-up evaluations were not significant.

In an extended report, Surwit, Shapiro, and Good (1978) compared the separate effects of biofeedback (cardiovascular), EMG feedback, and meditative relaxation. They found no differences between treatments and only moderate reductions in blood pressure, with the treatment effect disappearing at the one-year follow-up.

Hager and Surwit (1978) treated 30 borderline hypertensives with either relaxation or a portable feedback unit and found that there was no significant difference in blood pressure reductions, as well as the fact that reductions were generally small.

Patel (1973) used a collection of relaxation procedures, including autogenic training suggestions, deep breathing exercises, and ongoing galvanic skin response (GSR) feedback, in the treatment of 20 patients with hypertension. Five patients stopped their antihypertensive medication altogether following the three-month, three-times weekly training sessions. Seven other patients were able to reduce their drug requirement by 33 to 60 percent. Although overall blood pressure reductions were not analyzed, Patel did report that 16 patients' average systolic blood pressure fell from 160 to 134 mm Hg and average diastolic fell from 102 to 86 mm Hg. Again, since this was a clinical study and no control groups were used, it is not possible to determine whether the

GSR feedback, the relaxation training, or some combination was the key factor. Another disappointing feature of this report was that the heterogeneous sample included patients with renal hypertension, essential hypertension, and intracranial hypertension, as well as essential hypertension following pregnancy toxemia. Hence, generalization of the results is limited.

In a second study, Patel (1975) compared his treated group from the prior study to a group of matched controls, who also received increased medical attention and repeated clinical measurements of their blood pressure. Similar reductions were not found. In another study, Patel and North (1975) randomly assigned patients to the treatment and control groups. Treatment groups received six weeks of relaxation therapy using yoga relaxation methods with biofeedback (GSR and EMG). The control group received the same number of sessions (one-and-a-half–hour sessions for six weeks) and were asked to relax on the couch but received no specific instructions on how to relax. Both groups of patients were followed up every two weeks for three months. There was a highly significant difference, with blood pressure reductions of 168/100 to 141/84 in the treated group compared to 169/101 to 160/96 in the control group. These results encourage the conclusion that combined relaxation strategies have some utility.

Taylor, Farquhar, Nelson, and Agras (1977) divided a group randomly into three possibilities: (1) relaxation therapy; (2) nonspecific therapy using nondirective principles; and (3) medical treatment only. Blood pressures were measured at a different time and in a different place from the behavioral treatments. The relaxation therapy group showed a significant reduction in blood pressure post-treatment compared with the nonspecific therapy and medical treatment only groups, even when those patients whose medication was increased were excluded from the data analysis. At follow-up six months post-treatment, the relaxation group showed a slight decrement in treatment effects, while both the nonspecific therapy and medical treatment only groups showed continued improvement; thus, there was not a significant difference between groups.

Frankel, Patel, Horwitz, Friedewald, and Gaarder (1978) randomly allocated 22 hypertensives to one of three groups: (1) diastolic blood pressure feedback, EMG feedback, and verbal relaxation; (2) sham blood pressure feedback; or (3) no treatment. For the 14 patients completing active treatment in an initial or crossover period, the average changes in blood pressure were unimpressive. Overall results did not support the usefulness of these techniques as primary therapy for most hypertensives.

Conclusion. Instrumental conditioning strategies, biofeedback training, and relaxation training have achieved success in the treatment of hypertension. Yet the successes lie primarily in the electronic sophistication involved and in the information provided about the psychological relationships between cognitive, somatic, and autonomic variables and learning principles, and in the statistical significance of the studies. Since the ultimate utility of biofeedback will probably be in treating hypertension, it is logical that the major research effort to date has been with hypertensive patients. Because of this, more basic parameters affecting blood pressure control have not been systematically explored. Indeed, Seer (1979), in reporting upon differences in physiological response patterns between different meditative or relaxation techniques, observes that the physiological pattern of response across different techniques is not consistent. Within any one procedure, differences in the number and length of training sessions, the subject population, or even the context in which training takes place can produce a different physiological pattern. An understanding of the variables such as the role of extended training, continuous analog feedback, and knowledge of the correct response, as well as a variety of issues associated with individual differences expected to most directly affect outcome has not been achieved (Williamson & Blanchard, 1979).

Seer (1979), after reviewing 20 recent studies in this area, similarly concludes that a variety of approaches will likely have to be developed and matched to specific patient characteristics before individual differences in psychological and physical responsivity can be accounted for and marginally effective treatment strategies can be developed. This process is unlikely in the immediate future, and a major shift in attitude, both for the general population and the medical profession will be necessary before a substantially modified treatment approach will come about. The situation today remains much the same as in 1973, when Blanchard and Young observed that the clinical impact or applicability of self-control treatments of hypertension had yet to be demonstrated as uniformly or persistently effective.

Clinical Prescription

Although the research at this point does not clearly spell out the rationale for patient selection for self-control methods, it does seem clear that these methods are useful for some hypertensives. Should there be available personnel and time for a patient with hypertension to invest in these techniques, several important ideas are well established regarding the course to take.

As many reviewers have pointed out, close collaboration with medical personnel is crucial for the treatment of hypertension with behavioral/biofeedback methods. Shapiro et al. (1977b) have pointed out that a team approach is best if there is an opportunity for adequate medical back-up and if biofeedback technology, knowledge of behavioral principles, and medical consultation can all be coordinated.

Patients need to have a thorough medical work-up to rule out secondary hypertension, as well as to prescribe and monitor appropriate medication. Biofeedback and behavioral methods can be applied only after a competent medical diagnosis has been made and team members agree upon treatment planning. It is also important for the physician to be able to collaborate with professionals who are familiar with both behavioral and biofeedback methodologies.

Once the patient's suitability for treatment via chemotherapy is assessed, then assessment issues relevant to developing a treatment plan using social learning and behavioral/biofeedback methodology can be developed. Particularly in cases in which patient compliance is of question in terms of medical procedures, this may also be a problem for biofeedback procedures. Self-control methods are seen as adjunctive to chemotherapy or of possible use in borderline conditions with proper medical monitoring. If the patient is taking antihypertensive medicine, it is important that he not reduce his medicine without consultation with the physician.

Once the decision is made by the clinical team to use self-regulatory strategies, it is important to keep in mind a number of variables relevant to traditional psychotherapy and compliance to prescribed regimens in traditional settings and techniques.

Baselining is an important part of self-regulatory methods in treating hypertension. Just as it is crucial for precise diagnosis, an adequate baseline helps obviate the "regression to the mean effect" or an habituation effect that can erroneously or spuriously appear to be a treatment effect. Patients may respond to initial sessions with higher readings, and as they adjust to the assessment and treatment scheme, pressures decline.

In addition to this difficulty is the general placebo effect. Miller (1975) has pointed out that large placebo effects have been reported in the literature with hypertensives, which can contribute to spurious conclusions as well. Mechanic (1972) has argued that the placebo effect varies according to the sophistication of the patient as to awareness of medicinal effects. Patel (1977) has suggested that placebo-produced reductions are unlikely to be persistent, which points out the importance of careful follow-up procedures. In applied settings the placebo effect could be cultivated to facilitate continued improvement, although it remains as a confounding factor in research applications (O'Leary & Borkovec, 1978).

Because of the multitude of various biofeedback and behavioral interventions that have been used in the treatment of essential hypertension and the continued lack of solid data on the specific aspects of therapy that can be expected to lead to positive outcomes, it is not possible at this time to present with certainty the preferred techniques, length and frequency of sessions to use, and specifics of patient selection that can be expected to lead to favorable outcome. However, many important issues have been identified and should be considered by the practicing clinician as he or she attempts to treat a specific patient.

In addition to the necessary baselining procedure in the clinic, it would be helpful for the clinician to obtain baseline data in a setting other than the treatment setting (e.g., Kristt & Engel, 1975) as well as using measurements from that setting for treatment efficacy and follow-up data. This will help ensure the transfer value of the reduced hypertensive functioning. It is useful, for example, for patients to maintain regular records of their own pressures, learn to take their blood pressure at home, and learn to be more aware of how stress events affect their lives on a moment-to-moment basis. Where follow-up procedures have encouraged continued practice of relaxation techniques, treatment gains are more likely to persist.

Unfortunately, patient-selection variables are not clear from available research. Patient dimensions need further investigation to be precise, but tailoring specific therapeutic procedures to specific patients and their personalities, always an important part of psychotherapy, is becoming more important as the therapies develop further specificity. Cox, Freundlich, and Meyer (1975) point out how extreme obsessive-compulsive characteristics may interfere with biofeedback techniques. In this instance, other self-control methods, such as verbal relaxation training, may be more appropriate. The question "What sort of . . . technique is effective with what sort of people with what sort of problems in conjunction with what other procedures?" (Coursey, 1975), cannot be currently answered with certainty. At present, Seer (1979) does suggest that relaxation or meditation techniques may be more reliable than blood pressure biofeedback procedures in producing small but relatively reliable changes in blood pressure. At any rate, as patients in applied settings begin to respond less favorably to standard procedures outlined in this chapter, the clinician will need to modify his prescribed regimen to account for the patient's current needs and adjustment.

Case Report

Within the context of a case report, Rappaport and Cammer (1977) illustrate the validity of using broad-spectrum behavior techniques in conjunction with medical support. Mr W was a 71-year-old, married, retired, personnel counselor who was referred for chronic essential hypertension and periodic fibrillation. He had been hypertensive for five years and had been treated by an internist with chemotherapy, although prescribed medications had been ineffective or not tolerated by him. History revealed a cerebral thrombrosis in 1962 and periodic angina pectoris for several years. Psychological evaluation suggested compulsive and perfectionistic tendencies, as well as tension and anxiety. Initial blood pressure recordings were "consistently 170/100."

The patient was instructed in the relationship between tension and essential hypertension and was offered nine sessions in relaxation and stress control. Breath meditation, similar to the Benson (1975) technique, was taught, and the patient was instructed to practice twice daily. At the time of discharge (ten sessions), the patient had readings of 140/100. He was also encouraged to modify his perfectionistic tendencies. Follow-up results showed that the patient continued practicing, and physician records after eight months showed stabilization at 135/90.

In many ways this represents a typical case report in the literature (see, for example, Bloom & Cantrell, 1978). Although no lengthy baseline was established, it was noted that the patient had chronic hypertension for five years with associated cardiovascular problems. Although placebo and nonspecific factors may have played a role, as noted previously, these factors should be groomed and cultivated to facilitate therapy outcome. For example, the supportive and nurturant aspects of therapy, the expectation of favorable outcome, and other nonspecific factors are just as important as they could be in any form of psychotherapy.

Ethical and Legal Issues

With regard to biofeedback and behavioral interventions for essential hypertension, patients with known diseases who are seeking therapies to improve their disease state should be encouraged to receive services from licensed practitioners. Medical monitoring should occur in conjunction with a hypertensive "taking a class" in relaxation training or in transcendental meditation. However, only trained and licensed or supervised practitioners should attempt to "treat" any stress-related disorder, and collaborative physician consultation is crucial.

Biofeedback equipment represents a somewhat different set of legal/ethical requirements due to the electronic sophistication needed and the interdisciplinary nature of the practice. Not only are medical collaborations indicated and conservative claims for possible outcome important (e.g., Fuller, 1978), a thorough working knowledge of techniques and instrumentation is essential.

An excellent review of legal and regulatory issues and standards in this area is offered by Schwitzgebel (1978), who points out that with some medical disorders, such as in essential hypertension, the client may prematurely abandon needed medicinals or fail to pursue ongoing medical attention. Medical liaison is needed, not only for these reasons, but also because of the increasing overlap of medicine and psychology in the whole area of behavioral medicine. Biofeedback devices, as well as other equipment such as relaxation tape recordings, measurement instruments, and so on, used in the treatment of various behavioral disorders may be regulated in the future by the Food and Drug Administration as "medical devices" and medical supervision may be required. For nonmedical practitioners, close adherence to extant ethical standards (which includes awareness of legal requirements) as well as maintaining multidisciplinary planning is particularly important.

Suggestions for Clinical and Experimental Research

Instrumental conditioning strategies, biofeedback training, and relaxation have achieved success in the treatment of hypertension. Yet these successes lie primarily in the electronic sophistication involved, in the information gained concerning the relationships of cognitive, somatic, and autonomic variables to learning principles, and in the *statistical* significance of the studies. The *clinical* impact or long-term applicability of self-control treatments to individual hypertensives has yet to be demonstrated as uniformly or persistently effective (Blanchard & Young, 1973; Frumkin et al., 1978; Shapiro et al., 1977a).

Equally important is the problem that for several reasons it is very difficult to compare one study with another. Studies vary in application of treatment modalities, characteristics of patients, length of training, attainment of follow-up data, wide variations in drug regimes, and method of data presentation offered. Some researchers focus upon the reduction of necessary antihypertensive medication as a key dependent variable (e.g., Patel, 1973), others report in percentage of blood pressure reduction above the commonly accepted but somewhat arbitrary cutoff of 140/90 mm. Hg (e.g., Deabler, et al., 1973), while others have used absolute blood pressure readings and percentages (Byassee, 1975). Further, the absence of standard subject selection makes comparisons across studies dubious. Brady et al. (1974), for example, used a group designated "labile hypertensives"; Patel (1973) used several different diagnostic categories of hypertension; and no diagnostic medical corroboration was obtained by Elder and Eustis (1975). Further, data are often based on samples of "borderline" hypertensives, and many researchers have included subjects whose initial pressures were "near normal." If a regression to the mean effect did indeed operate, these subjects would be expected to be less responsive to treatment. Most of these confounding factors are likely due to difficulties in subject recruitment, but they continue to make meaningful conclusions problematic (Table 2.1).

If self-control strategies are ultimately found to be equally effective, there still remains the problem of the optimal delivery mode. Group training appears to have great promise since most relaxation approaches are easily group administered and can be delivered by trained paraprofessionls. Yet only three studies have used group-administered techniques. Klumbies and Eberhardt (1966) used group techniques, but failed to provide information as to how or when blood pressures were recorded, and they failed to employ control groups. In the more optimal design of the Byassee (1975) study, group techniques were used, but treatment gains were equivocal at follow-up and the self-relaxation group achieved success equivalent to that of the progressive relaxation training and autogenic training groups. In the only study to use progressive relaxation by itself in a treatment group (Shoemaker & Tasto, 1975), taped presentations were used. However, taped presentations have been shown to be inferior to personally administered relaxation instructions, though this deficit can be mitigated by the inclusion of response-contingent feedback (a complex and expensive procedure) in a taped presentation (Riddick & Meyer, 1973). Continued efforts to assess delivery mode variables are needed.

Leigh (1978) has recently argued the feasibility of "potentiating" the initial learning stages of biofeedback acquisition through pharmacologic means. In proposing that chronically hypertensive patients do not know how it feels to be normotensive or even hypotensive, these individuals had no reference point or goal in the initial stages of biofeedback training for them to approach. No single medication was found that served as a good potentiator (reducing blood pressure) within this context. However, this investigator reported that if systolic pressure was reduced pharmacologically, then on subsequent nonmedication relaxation training sessions, 11 patients were able to lower systolic pressure to a "far greater degree" than after a non-"potentiated" session. Certainly the idea of pharmacologic potentiation has been inadequately explored and warrants further and more careful investigation.

Often follow-up data have not been collected in self-control of hypertension studies, and in instances where it has, results have been contradictory. In the Byassee (1975) study, pressures were reduced for some subjects at four-month follow-up. This was so despite tentative data indicating that these subjects did continue to practice their exercises, though irregularly. Similar results were reported by Benson and Wallace (1972). While comparisons with other studies are limited by the conditions noted above, the absence of persistence over the four-month period is inconsistent with the findings of Love et al. (1972), who re-

TABLE 2.1
Behavioral and Biofeedback Interventions for Essential Hypertension

Study	Method(s)	No. of Hypertensive Subjects Completing Treatments	No. of Sessions or Length of Training	Reduction of Pressure	Design Quality Rating (Gurman et al., 1978)
Redmond et al. (1974)	Progressive muscle relaxation	5	Three 5-minute sessions	Within session 13.8/5.5 mm Hg	19
Klumbies & Eberhardt (1966)	Autogenic training	26 (83 dropped out)	Unspecified over 4 months	35/18 mm Hg	17
Luthe (1963)	Autogenic training	79*	Unspecified for 6–8 weeks	19 *Ss* "well" 29 *Ss* "improved" 37 *Ss* "no improvement"	19
Datey et al. (1969)	"Shavasan" (muscle relaxation and deep breathing)	10	Unspecified	27 mm Hg reduction in average mean arterial BP	15
Benson et al. (1973)	Transcendental Meditation	30	9 weeks of meditation	15 mm Hg systolic	19.5

*Subject totals do not add up correctly.

TABLE 2.1 (continued)

Benson et al. (1974b)	Transcendental Meditation	22	25 weeks of meditation	6.98/3.86 mm Hg	19
Benson et al. (1974c)	Transcendental Meditation	14	20 weeks of meditation	10.6/4.85 mm Hg	19
Blackwell et al. (1976)	Transcendental Meditation	7	6 months of meditation	13.0/7.3 mm Hg (home) 2.6/4.0 mm Hg (clinic)	22
Pollack et al. (1977)	Transcendental Meditation	20	6 months of meditation	Statistically no significant relation	17
Brady et al. (1974)	Metronome-conditioned relaxation	4	Daily ½ hr for 4 weeks approx.; 20 sessions for 3 Ss, 75 sessions for 1 S	3.4 mm Hg diastolic	20
Stone & De Leo (1976)	Psychologic relaxation	19	Five 20-minute sessions	9/8 mm Hg supine 15/10 mm Hg upright	21
Benson et al. (1971)	Systolic blood pressure biofeedback	7	8 to 34 sessions (30 trials/session)	16 mm Hg systolic	18

(continued)

TABLE 2.1 (continued)

Study	Method(s)	No. of Hypertensive Subjects Completing Treatments	No. of Sessions or Length of Training	Reduction of Pressure	Design Quality Rating (Gurman et al., 1978)
Schwartz & Shapiro (1973)	Diastolic blood pressure biofeedback	7	10 feedback sessions	5 mm Hg within sessions; no reduction between sessions	18
Goldman et al. (1975)	Systolic blood pressure biofeedback	7	9	8/15 mm Hg	20
Kristt & Engel (1975)	Systolic blood pressure biofeedback	5	14 sessions/week for 3 weeks	19/8 mm Hg in home recordings	22
Moeller & Love (1973)	EMG feedback and autogenic training	6	17 weekly ½-hr sessions	12% systolic and diastolic	19
Love et al. (1973)	EMG feedback, autogenic training and relaxation instructions	29	22 *Ss* twice weekly; 7 once weekly for 16 weeks	14.74/12.70 mm Hg	29

TABLE 2.1 (continued)

Deabler et al. (1973)	Progressive relaxation and hypnotic relaxation	9** 15	8-9 in 5 days	25/13 mm Hg** 28/19 mm Hg	24
Elder et al. (1973)	Gp 1: Diastolic blood pressure feedback Gp 2: Diastolic blood pressure feedback and verbal praise	Gp 1: 6 Gp 2: 6	8 weekly sessions	Gp 1: 3 mm Hg increase / 4 mm Hg decrease Gp 2: 23 mm Hg / 21 mm Hg	26
Elder & Eustis (1975)	Diastolic blood pressure feedback	22	10 daily for 4Ss; 9 in 80 days for 18Ss	8/2 mm Hg	17
Shoemaker & Tasto (1975)	Gp 1: Systolic and diastolic blood pressure feedback Gp 2: Taped progressive relaxation	Gp 1: 5 Gp 2: 5	6 sessions in 2 weeks	Gp 1: 1 mm Hg increase / 1 mm Hg decrease Gp 2: 6 mm Hg / 7 mm Hg	23
Byassee (1975)	Gp 1: Group progressive relaxation Gp 2: Group autogenic relaxation Gp 3: Group control	Gp 1: 11 Gp 2: 10 Gp 3: 10	8 sessions in 8 weeks	Gp 1: 12.2%/5.4% Gp 2: 6.1%/7.0% Gp 3: 9.5%/7.5%	27

**9 medicated; 15 non-medicated.

(continued)

TABLE 2.1 (continued)

Study	Method(s)	No. of Hypertensive Subjects Completing Treatments	No. of Sessions or Length of Training	Reduction of Pressure	Design Quality Rating (Gurman et al., 1978)
Weston (1974)	Diastolic blood pressure feedback vs. EMG feedback with and without additional relaxation practice	42	8 weeks	13-36/6-20 mm Hg comparable effects in 2 x 2 study	27
Surwit & Shapiro (1976); Surwit et al. (1978)***	EMG feedback vs. BP; HR feedback vs. meditation	81 group	10 sessions (twice weekly for 5 weeks)	1 mm Hg / 2 mm Hg	29
Hager & Surwit (1978)	Gp 1: Systolic blood pressure feedback Gp 2: Meditation (Benson)	Gp 1: 7 Gp 2: 10	40 training sessions (2/day, 5 days for 4 weeks)	1 mm Hg / 2 mm Hg pooled	26
Patel (1973)	GSR feedback and relaxation instructions	20	3 sessions/week for 3 months	26 mm Hg / 16 mm Hg	20

*** Extended report of Surwit & Shapiro (1976).

TABLE 2.1 (continued)

Patel & North (1975)	GSR feedback and verbal relaxation instructions	34 (17 controls)	12 sessions (Twice weekly for 6 weeks)	Tx 26.1/ 15.2 mm Hg control 8.9/ 4.2 mm Hg	27
Taylor et al. (1977)	Medical tx**** only vs. non-specific tx vs. medical tx and relaxation	11 vs. 10 vs. 10	medical tx vs. 5.5 vs. 5.1 ($\bar{x}$)	1.1/0.3 mm Hg 2.8/1.8 mm Hg 13.6/4.9 mm Hg	29
Frankel et al. (1978)	Diastolic blood pressure, EMG feedback and autogenic training	7 (8 no tx; 7 sham)	20 in 16 weeks	3 mm Hg increase 0 mm Hg	29

**** tx = treatment

ported on one-year follow-up data for 72 percent of the subjects originally treated. These subjects received 16 weeks of both autogenic training (practiced at home and administered by tape) and EMG feedback training during 16 weekly treatment sessions at the clinic. Although control-group data were not collected beyond the first four weeks, subjects did show mean reductions of 14.74 mm Hg systolic and 12.70 mm Hg diastolic during training and *continued* gains from the end of treatment to the one-year follow-up (a total drop of 27.52 systolic and 17.70 diastolic). Despite the fact that information on home practice or possible medication changes was not available, these results are impressive.

It may be that individually administered biofeedback and/or relaxation training is important for long-term results (Hendrix & Meyer, 1974). Perhaps of even greater significance, however, is that longer training may increase the probability that subjects will make needed lifestyle or environmental changes that support their learned lower level of arousal (e.g., changing jobs, work schedules, home routines). Several researchers have clearly indicated that such changes are desirable for hypertensives (e.g., Schwartz, 1973; Schwartz & Shapiro, 1973), and positive preliminary data on the therapeutic applications of such change techniques have been published with cardiac patients (Suinn, 1974).

As noted previously, Miller (1972a, 1972b) discussed one subject in his laboratory who was trained in self-control by blood pressure feedback but lost her cardiovascular control when events "seemed to overwhelm her," not surprising since stress events and even boredom can exacerbate arousal. Indeed, an attempt to teach subjects to relax without also instructing them in the application of such techniques to combat stress events (e.g., Hendrix & Meyer, 1974) is incomplete. In most of the research reported here, subjects were instructed that they could use the relaxation response to combat stress, but typically no specific instructions were offered on how to make such an application. It is not stated in the study by Love et al. (1972) whether such instruction was offered to the subjects whose treatment gains were maintained at follow-up.

In evaluating uncontrolled research, two particular problems noted previously occur as regression and placebo effects. Although hypertensives often experience no discernible physical symptomatology (Schwartz, 1973), they are naturally more likely to seek out treatment when they are most concerned about their condition. Since physiological systems tend to fluctuate between periods of exacerbation and amelioration, it is possible to obtain volunteers whose blood pressures will show reduction simply due to spontaneous fluctuations regressing toward their mean pressure levels. Also, more motivated subjects are likely to remain in training once it has begun, thus accelerating this regression even further.

The placebo effects are likewise of crucial importance in establishing treatment procedures for hypertension. Expectancy of therapeutic gain (Hendrix & Meyer, 1974), demand characteristics of the setting (Meyer, 1968), and a variety of other factors often have a hypotensive effect. Several reasonable hypotheses are available. For one, subjects may be able to reduce their blood pressures in response to the demand characteristics of the setting; that is, they are told that they were participating in effective treatments, and they experience reassurance and anxiety reduction. Second, blood pressures may be reduced as a consequence of nonspecific factors that all therapies have in common, for instance, suggestion, contact with authority sources, group process, expectancy for improvement, and other factors. Third, blood pressures may have been reduced as a result of the active components of therapy.

Ideally, it would be desirable to incorporate a simple "no treatment" baseline group which would have no expectation for improvement as well as a placebo group. However, sample size limitations sometimes do not permit the use of both types of controls. Yet, in order to be definitive, both types of comparison groups are ultimately required.

It is possible to argue that the results are sometimes a consequence of nonspecific factors, that is, a result of credible and potent placebo components. Gains that fail to persist would seem to support this idea, since placebo effects are sometimes known to be transient (Hendrix & Meyer, 1974). However, studies have attested to the power of progressive relaxation and autogenic training, although no comparisons with placebo groups in the treatment of essential hypertension could be located, except for the Byassee (1975) study. These nonspecific factors are also sometimes confounded with specific procedures, for example, instructions to relax at home and record home practice impressions, or with an emphasis on passive concentration. Kanfer (1973) has discussed learning to monitor one's own behavior as an essential prerequisite for the acquisition of self-control. Hence, the requirement that subjects practice at home and provide verification data is an important factor in terms of encouraging subjects to monitor their own behavior. The multitude of placebo group research problems has been thoughtfully reviewed by O'Leary and Borkovec (1978).

In summary, the interaction of Byassee (1975) and Elder and Eustis's (1975) reported sex differences in combination with observations of other relevant subject variables need to be investigated. Further, the role and interaction effects of placebo variables, home practice effects, and the type of treatment that best "fits" a type of individual are still unclear. Additionally, the extension of learned cardiovascular control to more general improved coping skills, as in the context of psychotherapy, needs to be evaluated (Schwartz & Shapiro, 1973).

In terms of convergent theoretical and applied thinking in the hypertension area, several recent papers have offered some important initial theoretical concepts which relate to the importance of the "patient–technique fit" issue and represent exciting new directions for both research purposes and clinical applications. Schwartz (1973, 1974, 1976) has discussed in a series of publications the potential biofeedback and self-control technologies have for use in voluntarily training patients in various *combinations* of visceral, neural, and motor responses based on the particular pattern of disregulation or disease/disorder exhibited. He has suggested that underlying psychobiological mechanisms unique to that individual are responsible for the disregulation of the cardiovascular system and might therefore require a strategy based on an investigation of the pattern of responses involved. Similar thinking relevant to the concept of anxiety has been offered by Davidson (1978).

Schwartz (1976) discusses four stages of biobehavior disregulation in essential hypertension. The first stage involves the nature of environmental demands on the organism. Situational pressures, such as the threat of pain or performance demands of the environment which require behavioral adjustment of the organism, lead to transient increments in blood pressure, which can then become chronic, provided these environmental demands remain persistent and prolonged. In Stage II, alteration in cortical reactivity in response to feedback from other systems in the body operates to innervate the neural system so that the brain can choose to habituate to feedback impulses from the body or to respond to them. If the brain habituates to ongoing chronic stress responses, feedback to the brain from the body, rather than removing the organism from the source of stress or operating on the environment to reduce the source of stress, the system becomes disregulated relative to the health needs of the organism. Hence, the information-processing component of the organism may serve to support hypertensive functioning, as opposed to operating to reduce overreactive visceral and somatic functioning. In Stage III, sustained chronic hypertension can result in end-organ damage, as a result of sustained cardiac output and increased vascular resistance, or the buildup of plaque in the arteries. Hence, disregulation can be encouraged by peripheral requirements for sustained higher levels of cardiovascular reactivity. Finally, in Stage IV, the negative feedback loop to the brain, especially from the baroreceptors, can encourage disregulation by losing the capability of healthy functioning due to sustained firing to maintain the higher pressures required by the organism (due either to Stage III requirements or to demands of the environment).

Schwartz (1976) says that intervention via chemotherapy may be incomplete, since it fails to attend to the contribution of cortical reactivity (Stage II), or the nature of the environmental demands (Stage I). If treatment strategies are aimed at only Stage I or/and Stage II and fail to consider appropriately the possibility of end-organ damage which might require chemotherapy, treatment would also be incomplete.

This general area of theorizing offers greater specificity for both research and clinical applications, and represents a useful model for considering the needs of a particular patient. Applied research following this model has not yet been offered, but appears to be an important future direction.

Several conclusions are clear: (1) The crucial and specific operations for reducing hypertension using self-control methods are not yet known; (2) various forms of relaxation training, instrumental conditioning, and biofeedback can reduce blood pressure for periods of several months, although follow-up data may not always continue to reflect the reductions attained; and finally (3) it is evident that the disorder of essential hypertension cannot be seen as an independent phenomenon represented simply by blood pressure readings. The particular reading gathered on any given day is a response determined by situational and diurnal variations and the complex physiology and personality characteristics of that individual, as well as the particular environmental context. All of these factors need careful research consideration if definitive conclusions about essential hypertension are to be reached.

Summary

Essential hypertension is a major health problem. Recent research has suggested that biofeedback and behavioral self-control methods are potentially effective treatment strategies for this disorder, either as primary intervention procedures or as ancillary techniques to chemotherapy.

A number of relaxation and meditation procedures have been studied regarding their effectiveness in reducing blood pressure. Progressive relaxation, autogenic training, transcendental meditation, and other meditative approaches aimed at achieving the "relaxation response" (Benson, 1975) have generally produced positive results, although there is a multitude of methodological problems and issues that render generalizations regarding treatment effectiveness from the majority of these studies as potential rather than actualized.

Biofeedback techniques, in which patients are given moment-to-moment information about their systolic or diastolic blood pressures, or for various other physiological responses such as electromyogram potentials, have also shown some promise. Because of the complexities of the syndrome of essential hypertension, design problems of various studies, and problems in attempting to compare diverse and sometimes complex treatment methods, conclusions remain tentative.

A number of research areas continue to complicate the development of precise research findings. The importance of establishing a reasonable baseline measurement period for blood pressure readings of patients who volunteer for such treatment approaches outweighs the potential confounding effects of habituation to the clinical treatment setting. There is also a need for assessing transfer value (obtaining baseline and post-treatment measures in a setting different from the actual treatment setting). Problems with effective control and placebo research procedures remain. Finally, adequate follow-up procedures are also essential to determine whether treatment gains are maintained.

In spite of the multitude of complications in attempting to study these treatment techniques, the bulk of studies do indicate that various self-control procedures have considerable promise. Future studies, perhaps attempting to design specific approaches for particular types of patients, may offer more striking results. Researchers have discussed the fact that the importance of tailoring the particular clinical treatment tasks to the unique characteristics of the individual patient can sometimes be lost in a study which demands consistency, some rigidity of requirements, and standardized procedures (e.g., Frankel et al., 1978). Impressive clinical case studies continue to support the need for further theorizing and treatment-application studies.

References

Anokhin, P. The physiological basis for the pathogenesis of hypertension. In J. Cort, V. Fence, Z. Hejl, & J. Jirka (Eds.), *Symposium on the pathogenesis of essential hypertension*. Prague: State Medical Publishing House, 1961.

Bair, S. L., & Levenberg, S. B. Multimodal behavioral approach to the treatment and management of essential hypertension. *Psychotherapy, Research and Practice,* 1979, *16*, 310–315.

Bandura, A. *Principles of behavior modification*. New York: Holt, 1969.

Barber, T., DiCara, L., Kamiya, J., Miller, N., Shapiro, D., & Stoyva, J. (Eds.), *Biofeedback and self-control 1970*. Chicago: Aldine, 1971.(a)

Barber, T., DiCara, L., Kamiya, J., Miller, N., Shapiro, D., & Stoyva, J. *Biofeedback and self-control reader*. Chicago: Aldine, 1971.(b)

Benson, H., Shapiro, D., Tursky, B., & Schwartz, G. E. Decreased systolic blood pressure through operant conditioning techniques in patients with essential hypertension. *Science,* 1971, *173,* 740–742.

Benson, H., & Wallace, R. K. Decreased blood pressure in hypertensive subjects who practiced meditation. *Circulation*, 1972, *XLV* & *XLVI*, Supplement II.

Benson, H., Rosner, B. A., & Maryetta, B. R. Decreased systolic blood pressure in hypertensive subjects who practiced meditation. *Journal of Clinical Investigation,* 1973, 52, 8a.

Benson, H., Beary, J.F., & Carol, M.P. The relaxation response. *Psychiatry,* 1974, *37*, 37–46.(a)

Benson, H., Rosner, B.A., Maryetta, B.R., & Klemchuk, H.P. Decreased blood pressure in borderline hypertensive subjects who practiced meditation. *Journal of Chronic Disease*, 1974, *27*, 163–169.(b)

Benson, H., Rosner, B.A., Maryetta, B.R., & Klemchuk, H.P. Decreased blood pressure in pharmacologically treated hypertensive patients who regularly elicited the relaxation response. *The Lancet*, 1974, *12*, 289–291.(c)

Benson, H. *The relaxation response*. New York: Morrow, 1975.

Bernstein, D.A., & Borkovec, T.D. *Progressive relaxation training: A manual for the helping professions*. Champaign, Ill.: Research Press, 1973.

Blackwell, B., Bloomfield, S., & Gartside, P. Transcendental meditation in hypertension. *The Lancet*, 1976, *14*, 223–226.

Blanchard, E.B., & Young, L.D. Self-control of cardiac functioning: A promise as yet unfulfilled. *Psychological Bulletin*, 1973, *79*, 145–163.

Bloom, L.J., & Cantrell, D. Anxiety management training for essential hypertension in pregnancy. *Behavior Therapy*, 1978, *9*, 377–382.

Brady, J.P. Metronome-conditioned relaxation: A new behavioral procedure. *British Journal of Psychiatry*, 1973, *122*, 729–730.

Brady, J.P., Luborsky, L., & Kron, R.E. Blood pressure reduction in patients with essential hypertension through metronome-conditioned relaxation: A preliminary report. *Behavior Therapy*, 1974, *5*, 203–209.

Brener, J., & Kleinman, R.A. Learned control of decreases in systolic blood pressure. *Nature*, 1970, *226*, 1063–1064.

Budzynski, T.H., & Stoyva, J. Biofeedback techniques in behavior therapy. In D. Shapiro, T.X. Barber, L.V. DiCara, J. Kamiya, N.E. Miller, & J. Stoyva (Eds.), *Biofeedback and self-control 1972*. Chicago: Aldine, 1973.

Buss, A.H. *Psychopathology*. New York: Wiley, 1966.

Byassee, J.E. Progressive relaxation and autogenic training in the treatment of essential hypertension. Unpublished doctoral dissertation, University of Louisville, Louisville, Ky., 1975.

Byassee, J.E. Essential hypertension. In R.B. Williams, Jr., & W.D. Gentry (Eds.), *Behavioral approaches to medical treatment*. Cambridge: Ballinger, 1977.

Coursey, R.D. Electromyograph feedback as a relaxation technique. *Journal of Consulting and Clinical Psychology*, 1975, *43*, 825–834.

Cox, D., Freundlich, A., & Meyer, R. Differential effectiveness of EMG feedback, verbal relaxation instructions, and medication placebo with tension headaches. *Journal of Consulting and Clinical Psychology*, 1975, *43*, 892–899.

Datey, K.K., Deshmukh, S.N., Dalvi, C.P., & Vinekar, S.L. "Shavasan": A yogic exercise in the management of hypertension. *Angiology*, 1969, *20*, 325–333.

Davidson, R.J. Specificity and patterning in biobehavioral systems: Implications for behavior change. *American Psychologist*, 1978, *33*, 430–436.

Dawber, T.R., Kannel, W.B., Revotskie, N., & Kazan, A. The epidemiology of coronary heart disease—The Framingham Enquiry. *Proceedings of the Royal Society of Medicine*, 1962, *55*, 265.

Deabler, H.L., Fidel, E., Dillenkoffer, R.L., & Elder, S.T. The use of relaxation and hypnosis in lowering high blood pressure. *The American Journal of Clinical Hypnosis*, 1973, *16*, 75–83.

DiCara, L.V., Barber, T.X., Kamiya, J., Miller, N.E., Shapiro, D., & Stoyva, J. (Eds.), *Biofeedback and self-control 1974*. Chicago: Aldine, 1975.

Elder, S.T., & Eustis, W.K. Instrumental conditioning in out-patient hypertensives. *Behavior Research & Therapy*, 1975, *13*, 185–188.

Elder, S.T., Leftwich, D.A., & Wilkerson, L.A. The role of systolic versus diastolic contingent feedback in blood pressure conditioning. *The Psychological Record*, 1974, *24*, 171–176.

Elder, S.T., Ruiz, R., Deabler, H.L., & Dillenkoffer, R.L. Instrumental conditioning of diastolic blood pressure in essential hypertensive patients. *Journal of Applied Behavior Analysis*, 1973, *6*, 377–382.

Farr, S., Smith, R., & Meyer, R. Promise and problems in biofeedback research. *Psychologia*, 1975, *18*, 212–220.

Frankel, B.L., Patel, D.J., Horwitz, D., Friedewald, W.T., & Gaarder, K.R. Treatment of hypertension with biofeedback and relaxation techniques. *Psychosomatic Medicine*, 1978, *40*, 276–293.

Freis, E.D. The chemotherapy of hypertension. *Journal of the American Medical Association*, 1971, *218*, 7, 1009–1014.

Frumkin, K., Nathan, R.J., Prout, M.F., & Cohen, M.C. Nonpharmacologic control of essential hypertension in man: A critical review of the experimental literature. *Psychosomatic Medicine*, 1978, *40*, 294–320.

Fuller, G.D. Current status of biofeedback in clinical practice. *American Psychologist*, 1978, *1*, 39–48.

Galton, L. *The silent disease: Hypertension*. New York: Crown, 1973.

Gifford, R.W. A practical guide to medical management. In Merck, Sharp & Dohme (Eds.), *The hypertension handbook*. West Point: Merck & Co., Inc., 1974.

Goldman, H., Kleinman, K.M., Snow, M.Y., Bidus, D.R., & Korol, B. Relationship between essential hypertension and cognitive functioning: Effects of biofeedback. *Psychophysiology*, 1975, *12*, 569–573.

Green, E.E., Green, A.M., & Walters, E.D. Voluntary control of internal states: Psychological and physiological. *Journal of Transpersonal Psychology*, 1970, *2*, 26–51.

Gurman, A.S., & Kniskern, D.P. Research on marital and family therapy: Progress, perspective, and prospect. In S.L. Garfield & A.E. Bergin, *Handbook of psychotherapy and behavior change*. New York: Wiley, 1978.

Hager, J.L., & Surwit, R.S. Hypertension self-control with a portable feedback unit or meditation-relaxation. *Biofeedback and Self-Regulation*, 1978, *3*, 269–276.

Harrell, J.P. Psychological factors and hypertension: A status report. *Psychological Bulletin*, 1980, *87*, 482–501.

Hendrix, M., & Meyer, R. Applications of feedback electromyography. *Journal of Bio-Feedback*, 1974, *2*, 12–21.

Jacobson, E. *Progressive relaxation*. Chicago: University of Chicago Press, 1938.

Jacobson, E. Variations in blood pressure with skeletal muscle tension in man. *American Journal of Physiology*, 1939, *126*, 546–547.(a)

Jacobson, E. Variation of blood pressure with skeletal muscle tension and relaxation. *Annals of Internal Medicine*, 1939, *12*, 1194–1212.(b)

Jacobson, E. *Anxiety and tension control: A physiologic approach*. Philadelphia: Lippincott, 1964.

Kanfer, F.H. Self-regulation: Research, issues and speculations. In M.R. Goldfried & M. Merbaum (Eds.), *Behavior change through self control*. New York: Holt, Rinehart & Winston, 1973.

Klumbies, G., & Eberhardt, G. Results of autogenic training in the treatment of hypertension. In J.J. Lopez Ibor (Ed.), *IV World Congress of Psychiatry, Madrid, 5.-11. IX. 1966*. International Congress Series No. 117, 46–47. Amsterdam: Excerpta Medica Foundation, 1966.

Kristt, D.A., & Engel, B.T. Learned control of blood pressure in patients with high blood pressure. *Circulation*, 1975, *51*, 370–378.

Lachman, S.J. *Psychosomatic disorders: A behavioristic interpretation*. New York: Wiley, 1972.

Lazarus, A.A. *Behavior therapy and beyond*. New York: McGraw-Hill, 1971.

Ledingham, J.M. The etiology of hypertension. *The Practitioner*, 1971, *207*, 5–19.

Leigh, H. Self-control, biofeedback, and change in "psychosomatic" approach. *Psychotherapy and Psychosomatics*, 1978, *30*, 130–136.

Love, W.A. Problems in therapeutic application of EMG feedback. Paper presented to the Biofeedback Research Society, Boston, November, 1972.

Love, W.A., Montgomery, D.D., & Moeller, T.A. Working paper number two. Unpublished manuscript, Nova University, 1973.

Love, W.A., Montgomery, D.D., & Moeller, T.A. Working paper number two. Unpublished manuscript, Nova University, 1974.

Luthe, W. Autogenic training: Method, research, and application in medicine. *American Journal of Psychotherapy*, 1963, *17*, 174–195.

Luthe, W. *Autogenic therapy (Vol. IV). Research and theory*. New York: Grune & Stratton, 1970.

Luthe, W., & Schultz, J.H. *Autogenic therapy (Vol. III). Applications in psychotherapy*. New York: Grune & Stratton, 1969.

Luthe, W., & Schultz, J.H. *Autogenic therapy (Vol. II). Medical applications*. New York: Grune & Stratton, 1970.

Mechanic, D. Social psychologic factors affecting presentation of bodily complaints. *New England Journal of Medicine*, 1972, *286*, 1132–1139.

Meyer, R. Chronic high blood pressure, essential hypertension, and the inhibition of aggression. *APA Proceedings*, 1968, *76*, 535–536.

Miall, W.E. Heredity and hypertension. *The Practitioner*, 1971, *207*, 20–27.

Miller, N.E. Learning of glandular and visceral responses: Postscript. In D. Singh, & C.T. Morgan (Eds.), *Current status of physiological psychology: Readings*. Monterey: Brooks-Cole, 1972.

Miller, N.E. Clinical applications of biofeedback: Voluntary control of heart rate, rhythm, and blood pressure. In H.I. Russek (Ed.), *New horizons in cardiovascular practice*. Baltimore: University Park Press, 1975.

Moeller, T.A., & Love, W.A. A method to reduce arterial hypertension through muscular relaxation. Unpublished manuscript, Nova University, 1973.

O'Leary, K.D., & Borkovec, T.D. Conceptual, methodological, and ethical problems of placebo groups in psychotherapy research. *American Psychologist*, 1978, *33*, 821–830.

Ostfield, A.M. What's the payoff in hypertension research? *Psychosomatic Medicine*, 1973, *35*, 1–3.

Patel, C.H. Yoga and biofeedback in the management of hypertension. *The Lancet*, 1973, *13*, 1053–1055.

Patel, C. 12-month follow-up of yoga and biofeedback in the management of hypertension. *The Lancet*, 1975, *1*, 62–65.

Patel, C.H. Biofeedback-aided relaxation and meditation in the management of hypertension. *Biofeedback and Self-Regulation*, 1977, *2*, 1–41.

Patel, C.H., & North, W.R.S. Randomized controlled trial of yoga and biofeedback in management of hypertension. *The Lancet*, 1975, *2*, 93–95.

Paul, G.L. Outcome of systematic desensitization. I: Background, procedures, and uncontrolled reports of individual treatment. In C.M. Franks (Ed.), *Behavior therapy: Appraisal and status*. New York: McGraw-Hill, 1969.(a)

Paul, G.L. Outcome of systematic desensitization. II: Controlled investigations of individual treatment technique variations, and current status. In C.M. Franks (Ed.), *Behavior therapy: Appraisal and status*. New York: McGraw-Hill, 1969.(b)

Pickering, G.W. *High blood pressure*. London: Churchill, 1968.

Platt, R. The nature of essential hypertension. *The Lancet*, 1959, *2*, 55–57.

Platt, R. Heredity in hypertension. *The Lancet*, 1963, *1*, 899–904.

Platt, R. The natural history and epidemiology of essential hypertension. *The Practitioner*, 1964, *193*, 5–13.

Pollack, A.G., Weber, M.A., Case, D.B., & Laragh, J.H. Limitations of transcendental meditation in the treatment of essential hypertension. *The Lancet*, 1977, *1*, 71–73.

Rappaport, A.F., & Cammer, L. Breath meditation in the treatment of essential hypertension. *Behavior Therapy*, 1977, *8*, 269–270.

Redmond, D.P., Gazler, M.S., & McDonald, R.H. Blood pressure and heart rate response to verbal instructions and relaxation in hypertension. *Psychosomatic Medicine*, 1974, *36*, 285–297.

Riddick, C., & Meyer, R. The efficacy of automated relaxation training with response-contingent feedback. *Behavior Therapy*, 1973, *4*, 331–337.

Schultz, J.H., & Luthe, W. *Autogenic training: A psychophysiologic approach in psychotherapy*. New York: Grune & Stratton, 1959.

Schultz, J., & Luthe, W. *Autogenic therapy (Vol. I). Autogenic methods*. New York: Grune & Stratton, 1969.

Schwartz, G.E. Voluntary control of human cardiovascular integration and differentiation through feedback and reward. *Science*, 1972, *175*, 90–93.

Schwartz, G. Biofeedback as therapy: Some theoretical and practical issues. *American Psychologist*, 1973, *28*, 666–673.

Schwartz, G.E. Toward a theory of voluntary control of response patterns in the cardiovascular system. In P.A. Obrist, A.H. Black, & J. Brener (Eds.), *Cardiovascular psychophysiology*. Chicago: Aldine, 1974.

Schwartz, G.E. Biofeedback, patterning and the treatment of essential hypertension. In J.V. Basmajian & J. Stoyva (Eds.), *Biofeedback techniques in clinical practice* (Vol. III). New York: Biomonitoring Applications, Inc., 1976.

Schwartz, G.E., & Shapiro, D. Biofeedback and essential hypertension. Current findings and theoretical concerns. *Seminars in Psychiatry*, 1973, 5, 493–503.

Schwitzegebel, R.K. Suggestions for the uses of psychological devices in accord with legal and ethical standards. *Professional Psychology*, 1978, 9, 478–488.

Seer, P. Psychological control of essential hypertension: Review of the literature and methodological critique. *Psychological Bulletin*, 1979, *86*, 1015–1043.

Shapiro, A.P., Schwartz, G.E., Ferguson, D.C.E., Redmond, D.P., & Weiss, S.M. Behavioral methods in the treatment of hypertension: A review of their clinical status. *Annals of Internal Medicine*, 1977, *86*, 626–636.(a)

Shapiro, D., Barber, T.X., DiCara, L.V., Kamiya, J., Miller, N.E., & Stoyva, J. (Eds.), *Biofeedback and self-control 1974*. Chicago: Aldine, 1975.

Shapiro, D., Mainardi, J.A., & Surwit, R.S. Biofeedback and self-regulation in essential hypertension. In G.E. Schwartz & J. Beatty (Eds.), *Biofeedback: Theory and research*. New York: Academic Press, 1977.(b)

Shapiro, D., Myers, T., Reiser, M.D., & Ferris, E.B., Jr. Blood pressure response to veratrum and doctor. *Psychosomatic Medicine*, 1954, *16*, 478.

Shapiro, D., Tursky, B., Gershon, E., & Stern, M. Effects of feedback and reinforcement on the control of human systolic blood pressure. *Science*, 1969, *163*, 588–589.

Shapiro, D., Tursky, B., & Schwartz, G.E. Control of blood pressure in man by operant conditioning. *Circulation Research*, 1970, *26 (Suppl. 1)*, 27, 1227-I-32.(a)

Shapiro, D., Tursky, B., & Schwartz, G.E. Differentiation of heart rate and blood pressure in man by operant conditioning. *Psychosomatic Medicine*, 1970, *32*, 417–423.(b)

Shapiro, D., Tursky, B., & Schwartz, G.E. Control of diastolic blood pressure in man by feedback and reinforcement. *Psychophysiology*, 1972, 9, 296–304.

Shoemaker, J.E., & Tasto, D.L. The effects of muscle relaxation on blood pressure of essential hypertensives. *Behavior Research & Therapy*, 1975, *13*, 29–43.

Sleight, P. The diagnosis of hypertension. *The Practitioner*, 1971, *207*, 36–42.

Smirk, F.H. *High arterial pressure*. Blackwell: Oxford, 1957.

Steinhaus, A.H., & Norris, J.E. Teaching neuromuscular relaxation. U.S. Office of Education, Cooperative research project No. 1529, George Williams College, 1964.

Stone, R., & De Leo, J. Psychotherapeutic control of hypertension. *New England Journal of Medicine*, 1976, *294*, 80–84.

Stoyva, J., Barber, T., DiCara, L., Kamiya, J., Miller, N.E., & Shapiro, D. (Eds.), *Biofeedback and self-control 1971*. Chicago: Aldine, 1972.

Suinn, R.M. Behavior therapy for cardiac patients. *Behavior Therapy*, 1974, 5, 569–571.

Suinn, R.M. Type A behavior pattern. In R.B. Williams, Jr., & W.D. Gentry (Eds.), *Behavioral approaches to medical treatment*. Cambridge: Ballinger, 1977.

Surwit, R.S., & Shapiro, D. Biofeedback and meditation in the treatment of borderline hypertension. Paper presented at the NATO symposium on biofeedback and behavior. Munich, Germany, 1976.

Surwit, R.S., Shapiro, D., & Good, M.I. Comparison of cardiovascular biofeedback, neuromuscular biofeedback, and meditation in the treatment of borderline essential hypertension. *Journal of Consulting and Clinical Psychology*, 1978, *46*, 252–263.

Taylor, C.B., Farquhar, J.W., Nelson, E., & Agras, S. Relaxation therapy and high blood pressure. *Archives of General Psychiatry*, 1977, *34*, 339–342.

Veterans Administration Cooperative Study Group on Antihypertensive Agents. Effects of treatment on morbidity in hypertension. Results in patients with diastolic blood pressures averaging 115–129 mm Hg. *Journal of the American Medical Association*, 1967, *202*, 116–122.

Veterans Administration Cooperative Study Group on Antihypertensive Agents. Effects of treatment on morbidity in hypertension. Results in patients with diastolic blood pressures averaging 90–114 mm Hg. *Journal of the American Medical Association*, 1970, *213*, 1143–1152.

Wallace, R.K. Physiologic effects of transcendental meditation. *Science*, 1970, *167*, 1751–1754.

Wallace, R.K., & Benson, H. The physiology of meditation. *Scientific American*, 1972, *226*, 84–90.

Wenger, M.A., Bagchi, B.K., & Anand, B.K. Experiments in India on "voluntary" control of the heart and pulse. *Circulation*, 1961, *24*, 1319–1325.

Weston, A. Perception of autonomic processes, social acquiescence, and cognitive development of a sense of self-control in essential hypertensives trained to lower blood pressure using biofeedback procedures. Unpublished doctoral dissertation, Nova University, 1974.

Williamson, D.A., & Blanchard, E.B. Heart rate and blood pressure biofeedback. I. A review of recent experimental literature. *Biofeedback and Self-Regulation*, 1979, *4*, 1–34.

Wolf, S. Cardiovascular disease. In E.O. Wittkower, & H. Warnes (Eds.), *Psychosomatic medicine: Its clinical applications*. New York: Harper & Row, 1977.

Wolpe, J. *Psychotherapy by reciprocal inhibition*. Stanford: Stanford University Press, 1958.

Wolpe, J. *The practice of behavior therapy*. New York: Pergamon, 1969.

Wolpe, J., & Lazarus, A.A. *Behavior therapy techniques*. New York: Pergamon, 1966.

Yogi, M.M. *Transcendental Meditation*. New York: New American Library, 1975.

Suggested Readings

Basmajian, J. V., & Stoyva, J. (Eds.), *Biofeedback techniques in clinical practice*. New York: Biomonitoring Applications, Inc., 1976.

Benson, H. *The relaxation response*. New York: Morrow, 1975.

Blanchard, E.B., & Ahales, T.A. Behavioral treatment of psychophysical disorders. *Behavior Modification,* 1979, 3, 518–514.

Garfield, S.L. & Bergin, A.E. (Eds.), *Handbook of psychotherapy and behavior change*. New York: Wiley, 1978.

Holmes, D.S. The use of biofeedback for treating patients with migraine headaches, Raynaud's disease and hypertension: A critical evaluation. In C.K. Prokop, & L.A. Bradley (Eds.), *Medical psychology: Contributions to behavioral medicine*. New York: Academic Press, 1981.

Kaplan, N. (Ed.), *Clinical hypertension*. Baltimore: Williams & Wilkins, 1978.

Leitenberg, H. (Ed.), *Handbook of behavior modification and behavior therapy*. New York: Prentice-Hall, 1978.

Runck, B. *Biofeedback—Issues in treatment assessment*. Rockville, Md: National Institute of Mental Health, 1980.

Russek, H.I. (Ed.), New horizons in cardiovascular practice. Baltimore: University Park Press, 1975.

Schwartz, G.E., & Beatty, J. (Eds.), *Biofeedback: Theory and research*. New York: Academic Press, 1977.

Williams, R.B., Jr., & Gentry, W.D. (Eds.), *Behavioral approaches to medical treatment*. Cambridge: Ballinger, 1977.

3

Pain and Pain Control

Matisyohu Weisenberg

Introduction

> No positive medical findings of a physiological nature can be found. The patient appears to be oriented, displays appropriate affect with no evidence of a thought disorder. There is no display of la belle indifference of the classic hysteric. Yet the patient complains of pain, has limited physical activity, consumes countless pills each day, has a reduced social and sexual experience, has not been able to work at his usual job, has sought help from dozens of health care providers, has undergone several surgeries, has spent thousands of dollars for health care and has yet to find relief from pain.

The above example illustrates one of the frustrating problems of pain control with which the medical profession has had limited success. Severing nerve connections does not produce lasting relief, and prescribing medication is not adequate. Psychologists have taken up the challenge and have demonstrated a reasonable degree of success in dealing with pain control by utilizing a variety of behavioral strategies and techniques. This chapter will deal with some of these behavioral approaches.

Pain is a widespread phenomenon commonly associated with disease or tissue damage (cf. Sternbach, 1968; Weisenberg, 1977.) However, pain is a complex phenomenon that involves a great deal more than nociceptive stimulation per se or tissue damage itself. Pain perception involves emotional arousal, motivation, and cognition, including memory of past experience. Pain perception is the result of a great deal of processing from the moment of nociceptive stimulation at the periphery to the point of awareness (cf. Chapman, 1978). Many psychological variables influence the final perception.

Pain reactions often convey a great deal more than a signal that tissue damage is occurring. As Szasz (1957), Zborowski (1969), and others have pointed out in discussing human reactions to pain, communication aspects are frequently overlooked. Pain reactions can mean "Don't hurt me," "Help me," "It's legitimate for me to get out of my daily responsibilities," "Look, I'm being punished," "Hey, look, I am a real man," "I'm still alive." Much of the behavioral approach at pain control developed by Fordyce (1976, 1978) and his colleagues is based upon the meaning of the pain as seen through its behavioral consequences rather than upon the nociceptive stimulation.

Pain and anxiety are usually associated with each other. The general conclusion is that the greater the anxiety, the greater the pain (Sternbach, 1968). Therefore, control and reduction of anxiety can help reduce pain. The exact relationship of pain and anxiety, however, is still not fully understood. Thus, prescribing diazepam or teaching muscular relaxation will not automatically by itself result in the absense of pain.

Although anxiety is prevalent in chronic pain, it is much more apparent in acute pain, that is, pain of recent onset (Sternbach, 1968, 1974, 1978b). Acute pain is associated with autonomic reactions that may be proportional to stimulus intensity. These include increases in heart rate, blood pressure, pupillary diameter, and striated muscle tone. In brief, these are the signs commonly connected with flight or fight reactions and anxiety. Anxiety reduction techniques help a great deal.

Chronic patients with pain of several months' duration seem to show an habituation of autonomic signs. Sternbach (1974, 1978b) has stressed depressive reactions such a disturbance of sleep, appetite, and libido. Use of antidepressive medication or otherwise treating the depression can help reduce the pain (Spear, 1967; Taub, 1975).

Brena (1978) has described the devasting cycle of chronic pain referring to the "Five D's" syndrome. Chronic pain patients are usually involved in a cycle of (1) *drug* misuse. Changes and decreases in physical activity result in (2) *dysfunction*, resulting in (3) *disuse* lesions such as frozen joints. These pain patients as a consequence are (4) *depressed*. Depression, in turn, makes the chronic pain patient more pain prone. The end point becomes (5) *disability*, for which Western societies provide compensation. The compensation in turn reinforces reduced activity, disuse, dysfunction, and drug use ultimately leading to unbearable suffering.

Thus, when examining the reactions to pain and pain control it becomes vital to consider the complexity of the phenomenon. Pain is a sensation, but its perception involves a whole range of motivational, emotional, and cognitive variables. Therefore, psychological intervention can have a great impact upon pain perception. Principles of learning and social influence processes have been applied effectively to pain control. Behavioral techniques include greater use of stress- and anxiety-reducing procedures such as relaxation, desensitization, hypnosis, biofeedback, modeling, and a variety of cognitive strategies. In other instances patients are taught that they can control and contain the influence of pain on their lives even when the sensation of pain itself cannot be eliminated completely. The amount of general anesthesia, surgical intervention, and the number of pills prescribed and consumed for pain and anxiety control have consequently gone down with the use of such behavioral approaches.

Even when pharmacologic means are used to control pain, the psychological status of the patient will often determine their chemical effectiveness. Beecher (1959, 1972) has cited many examples supporting this assertion. The greater the stress, the more effective are placebos. There are certain drugs such as morphine that work for pain of pathological origin (which is usually accompanied by anxiety) but which fail to work for experimentally produced pain (which has little anxiety). "Thus, we can state *a new principle of drug action:* some agents are effective only in the presence of a required mental state" (1972, p. 178).

This chapter will briefly examine some of these phenomena by first looking at theoretical approaches to pain and its measurement. Following this, behavioral intervention strategies will be described. Illustrations will be taken from both acute and chronic pain situations. Many of the controlled studies are a result of laboratory research. Laboratory research has limitations when applied clinically (cf. Beecher, 1959). However, clinical studies lack pain stimulus control and often combine treatments so that the active, essential ingredients are not always known, and most studies do not utilize control groups. It is, therefore, important to examine both laboratory and clinical evidence.

Theoretical Analysis

Nonbehavioral

There are many theories of pain, each of which tries to account for some aspect of this complex phenomenon. Three approaches will be briefly mentioned here: (1) psychophysiological, (2) neurohumoral, and (3) psychiatric. They have been discussed in greater depth elsewhere (Weisenberg 1977, in press-b).

Psychophysiological approaches. The psychophysiological approach builds upon the neurological framework of pain perception. At the periphery are sets of free nerve endings, A-delta and C fibers associated with two qualities of pain—short-latency pricking pain and long-latency burning pain, respectively (Mountcastle, 1974). Temporal and spatial patterns may contribute to what is perceived. There is still some disagreement as to whether or not afferent impulses in these A-delta or C fibers are both necessary and sufficient peripheral input to evoke painful sensations in the human being (cf. Sternbach, 1978a). Pricking pain impulses enter the dorsal spinal cord where they synapse and ascend via the anterolateral system to thalamic centers and from there to somatic sensory areas of the cerebral cortex. Burning pain impules follow a similar course into the anterolateral system but project to different thalamic, hypothalamic, and cortical areas. These latter projections seem to account for the affective, autonomic reaction to pain impulses. The nature, location, and interactions of higher pain centers are still not clearly spelled out (Mountcastle, 1974).

Melzack and Wall (1965, 1970) proposed a theory that is still enmeshed in controversy—the gate-control theory of pain. Conceptually, gate-control theory proposes a dorsal spinal gating mechanism in the substantia gelatinosa that modulates sensory input by the balance of activity of small-diameter (A-delta and C) and large-diameter fibers (A-beta). Activity of large fibers closes the gate and prevents synaptic transmission to centrally projecting T (transmission) cells while small-diameter fibers open the gate and facilitate T-cell activity once a critical level is reached. Small-fiber activity is believed responsible for prolongation of pain and spread to other parts of the body. A central control trigger can also influence the gate. Thus, cognitive processes can either open or close the gate.

The exact gating mechanism as well as the effects of the balance of activity of large and small fibers has been and remains the major source of disagreement concerning the theory (cf. Iggo, 1972). More than with any other theory, however, Melzack and Wall (1970) have emphasized the different aspects of pain perception. Pain has a sensory component similar to other sensory processes. It is discriminable in time, space, and intensity. However, pain also has an essential aversive-cognitive-motivational and emotional component that leads to behavior designed to escape or avoid the stimulus. Different neurophysiological mechanisms have been described for each system. The fibers that project to the ventrobasal thalamus and somatosensory cortex are partly involved in the sensory-discriminative aspects of pain. Fibers that project to the reticular formation, medial intralaminar thalamus, and limbic system are related to the aversive-cognitive-motivational and emotional component of pain that leads to escape behavior. Higher cortical areas are involved in both discriminative and motivational systems influencing reactions on the basis of cognitive evaluation and past experience. More than any other theoretical approach, gate control emphasizes the tremendous role of psychological variables and how they affect the reaction to pain. Especially with chronic pain, successful pain control often involves changing the motivational component while the sensory component remains intact. Hypnosis, anxiety reduction, desensitization, attention, distraction, as well as other behavioral approaches can be effective alternatives and supplements to pharmacology and surgery in the control of pain. Their effects are mostly on the motivational component of pain.

In a more recent statement of gate-control theory, Melzack and Dennis (1978) have emphasized differences between chronic and acute pain. With acute pain there is usually a well-defined cause and a characteristic time course whereby the pain disappears, most often with the occurrence of healing. The rapid onset of pain is referred to as the *phasic* component. The more lasting persistent phase is referred to as the *tonic* component. The tonic component serves as a means of fostering rest, care, and protection of the damaged area so as to promote healing.

With chronic pain, however, the tonic component may continue even after healing has occurred. Melzack and Dennis (1978) refer to low-level abnormal inputs that produce self-sustaining neural activity. These inputs seem to be memory-like mechanisms related to pain. They can occur at any level of the nervous system. Normally, these so-called inputs, referred to as *pattern-generating systems*, are inhibited by a central control biasing system. Where neuronal damage occurs, such as after amputation or after peripheral nerve lesions, the central inhibitory influence is diminished, thus allowing sustained activity to occur even as a result of non-noxious input. Thus, for example, Loeser and Ward (1967) demonstrated abnormal bursts of firing in dorsal horn cells as long as 180 days after the sectioning of dorsal roots in the cat.

Melzack and Dennis (1978) propose that the abnormal, prolonged bursting activity that occurs in deafferented or damaged neuron pools can be modulated by somatic, visual, and autonomic inputs as well as by inputs from emotional and personality mechanisms by means of the activation of descending inhibitory input. Short-acting local blocks of trigger points or intense stimulation by dry-needling cold injection of saline or electrical stimulation can interrupt the abnormal firing and produce relief beyond the duration of the treatment.

On the other hand, memories of prior pain experiences at spinal or supraspinal levels can also trigger abnormal firing patterns. Thus, once the pain is under way the role of neuromas, nerve injury, or other physical damage begins to be of lesser importance. What is needed is therapy to affect the pattern-generating mechanisms. Once the person is free from the influence of the pattern-generating mechanisms even temporarily, he can begin to maintain normal activity, which in turn fosters patterns of activity that inhibit abnormal firing. These abnormal firing mechanisms can be affected by multiple inputs. It is therefore preferable to use simultaneous multiple therapies such as antidepressant drugs, electrical stimulation, anesthetic blocks, and realistic goals for the patient to achieve relief and to make life worth living.

Neurohumoral approaches. Several of the most exciting findings in recent years relate to the discovery of an endogenous neural humoral system of control of pain. There are three major sets of findings. (1) The finding of zones such as the midbrain periaqueductal gray matter from which stimulation-produced analgesia (SPA) can be obtained (Libeskind, Mayer, & Akil, 1974; Libeskind & Paul, 1978; Reynolds, 1969). (2) These same zones seem to be closely associated with the opiate binding sites and mechanisms of action of morphine in the nervous system (Lebeskind, Mayer, & Akil, 1974; Simon & Hiller, 1978). (3) Furthermore, it appears that the body produces its own group of endogenous morphine-like substances called endorphins (Hughes, Smith, Kosterlitz, Fothergill, Morgan, & Morris, 1975; Simon, Hiller & Edelman, 1975).

SPA, as reviewed by Cannon, Libeskind, and Frenk (1978), has been reported to produce blocking of behavioral responses even to intense pinch, tissue-damaging heat, and subcutaneous application of painful chemical substances. Results have been obtained in cats, monkeys, and man for both acute and chronic pain. Pain relief lasts significantly beyond the time of stimulation. Analgesic effects are localized depending upon the brain site stimulated.

SPA seems to share common sites and mechanisms of action with the opiates. As with SPA, strong analgesic effects for opiates are found when injected into the periaqueductal gray matter or in the more caudal or rostral periventricular structures. Both SPA and morphine are blocked by narcotic antagonists such an naloxone. Both SPA and opiate analgesia seem to produce an effect by inhibiting pain in a descending direction to lower centers in the spinal cord in a selective manner. As Cannon et al. (1978) describe it, there is a strong suggestion of an endogenous pain-suppressive system that is activated either by electrical stimulation or by drugs.

The discovery of endogenously produced endorphin has led to a series of studies relating a variety of pain-control strategies to the production of these endogenous substances. Thus, it has been reported that the pain-control effects of acupuncture but not of hypnosis have been blocked by naloxone (Mayer, Price, Barber, & Raffi, 1976). Terenius (1978) reviewed evidence that lumbar cerebrospinal fluid from patients with chronic pain showed lower concentrations of endorphin. In turn, congenital insensitivity to pain may be related to a tonic hyperactivity of an endogenous pain-control system (Dehen & Cambier, 1978). Naloxone has been reported to have no effect (Michic & Binkert, 1978) or a significant effect (Levine, Gordon, & Fields, 1978) in blocking the effects of placebos.

A great deal is still unknown; however, studies dealing with the endogenous pain-control system provide a neurohumoral basis for the behavioral and psychological control of pain. Ultimately, it might be possible to achieve the ideal nonaddicting pain-control strategy, with the fewest side effects and complications, when we will be capable of behaviorally unlocking the body's own endogenous pain-control system.

Psychiatric approach. Psychiatrically oriented theories have been written mainly to account for reactions to chronic pain that have been refractory to routine medical/dental treatment.

Engel (1959) has spoken of "psychogenic" pain and the pain-prone patient based to a large extent upon his experience with atypical facial pain patients. In Engel's view, although pain can require an early stage with the development of a psychic organization for pain perception, the experience of pain no longer requires external stimulation, just as visual or auditory sensation can occur without sensory input. Such pain without external stimulation can be felt in some part of the body, and from the patient's view is no different from pain based on external stimulation. Pain has special interpersonal meaning related to concepts of good and bad and success and failure. Pain is an important way of dealing with guilt.

According to Engel, pain-prone patients may show some or all of the following; (1) conscious or unconcious guilt with pain providing atonement; (2) a background predisposing to use of pain as punishment; (3) a history of suffering, defeat, and intolerance of success, large numbers of painful injuries, operations, and treatment; (4) pain as a replacement for loss, or threat of loss of relationship; (5) a tendency toward a sadomasochistic type of sexual development with pain occurring over sexual conflict; (6) pain location related to unconscious identification with a love object in which the pain either is the one suffered by the love object or is aroused by conflict with the love object; (8) psychiatric diagnoses including either conversion hysteria, depression, hypochondriasis, or occasionally paranoid schizophrenia.

Szasz (1955) speaks of pain as arising as a consequence of threatened loss of or damage to the body or a body part. The communication aspects of the pain are extremely important in understanding reactions to pain. At the first level are the straightforward facts that the clinician requires to evaluate the physical symptom. The second level involves use of the pain complaint as a cry for help. It is tied to the first level. At the third level of communication, pain can be viewed as a symbol of rejection, where the request for help has been frustrated. Pain complaints can become a form of aggression and a means of atoning for guilt.

In a later publication, Szasz (1968) refers to *l'homme douloureux* who has made a career out of his pain. Such individuals give up their former careers as attorneys, businessmen, models, and so on, when they fail or are no longer sustained by these and take on a career of suffering. It is the caretaker's responsibility to recognize such people and refrain from treating them, for the doctor can also help in the creation of a sick man. The career chronic-pain patient does not wish to give up his suffering.

Merskey and Spear (1967) reviewed and evaluted these as well as other psychiatric theories of pain, pointing to the difficulties involved in obtaining evidence to support them. They conclude that each approach has some value but none of them is adequate to explain pain phenomena.

Based upon his own research, Merskey (1968) describes the model psychiatric patient with pain as a lower-class married woman who possibly once was but no longer is pretty, was never keen on sexual intercourse, has a history of repeated negative physical findings, many with conversion symptoms in addition to pain, with a sad tale of a hard life and depression that does not respond to antidepressant drugs.

In Merskey's (1965a, 1965b) studies of psychiatric patients, pain was associated most frequently with neurosis, especially hysteria. It was relatively rare in schizophrenia or endogenous depression. Nearly all the pain patients were married, came from large families, had problems of frigidity and unsatisfactory sex lives, and showed a great deal of resentment toward others. They had an excess of bodily symptoms and a special concern with their bodies.

Pilling, Brannick, and Swenson (1967) suggest that pain functions in place of anxiety and depression. Patients with pain presented less often with depression and anxiety. These patients may use pain or other organic symptoms in place of depression and anxiety.

Four classes of patients have been defined by Sternbach (1974) on the basis of their Minnesota Multiphasic Personality Inventory Profiles (MMPI):

1. The *hypochondriasis* pattern (highest on the Hypochondriasis scale) displays extreme somatic preoccupation. It is more common among somatogenic than psychogenic patients. It is possible that Szasz's *l'homme douloureux* would fit into this group. It should also be noted that hypochondriacal patients were classed as treatment failures in the pain clinic program.

2. *Reactive depression* profiles consist of patients with high Depression scores that are willing to admit that the pain has gotten them down. These patients respond well to antidepressant medication.

3. *Somatization* reaction profiles are associated with patients that present the psychosomatic V. They are high on the Hypochondriasis and Hysteria scales and relatively low on the Depression scale. These patients focus on bodily symptoms to avoid latent depression. This pattern occurs in both psychogenic and somatogenic pain patients. Such patients have adjusted to their pain and derive satisfaction from the sick role. Moderate treatment success has been obtained in this group.

4. *Manipulative reaction* profile patients have clear physical findings. They show an elevated Psychopathic Deviate scale. The patient uses his symptoms deliberately to manipulate others. This pattern was observed in a group of patients who have litigation pending.

To deal with the various and at times ambiguous psychiatric terms used to describe the chronic-pain patient, Pilowsky and Spence (1975, 1976a, 1976b, 1976c) introduced the concept of abnormal illness behavior. Illness behavior refers to the way an individual perceives and reacts to symptoms of all kinds. Psychiatric syndromes such as hypochondriasis, conversion reaction, neurasthenia, malingering, and so on, are all included under the concept of abnormal illness behavior. There is an inappropriate reaction by the patient to his symptoms and to the careful explantion of his doctor. A factor-analytic study of an Illness Behavior Questionaire (IBQ) has yielded main factors.

Chronic-pain patients can be classified according to their responses on the 62 Yes–No item IBQ. Patients with pain that did not respond to conventional treatment were found to be more convinced as to the presence of disease, more somatically preoccupied, and less likely to accept reassurance from the doctor. There was no relationship found between abnormal illness behavior and degree of organic pathology (Pilowsky & Spence, 1976a).

Although none of these theoretical statements concerning pain is complete in and of itself, they all point to factors to be considered in evaluating a patient who presents for treatment. As Chapman (1977) has pointed out, complaints of pain reflect not only tissue damage but a variety of dimensions of human suffering.

There are several major problems in approaches that emphasize personality traits. These problems can best be summarized as lack of replication, use of similar nomenclature but different measures, and often conflicting results. Many of these studies have been reviewed previously (Weisenberg, 1975, 1977).

Behavioral

Behavioral approaches have stressed the consequences of pain as seen in the activities of the individual with pain. Much of the conceptualization has developed as a result of dealing with chronic-pain patients. These conceptualizations do not directly contradict neurophysiological or neurohumoral formulations. Instead, most behavioral approaches view pain phenomena from a different level of analysis.

Clinicians who utilize a behavioral approach differ in terms of how narrow or broad a conceptualization they use. Fordyce (1976, 1978) emphasizes the *observable,* measurable, overt actions of the organism. Underlying internal causality or mental events may be interesting but not really necessary to consider when modifying behavior. By careful analysis of the environmental conditions and by the application of the principles of learning, it is possible to control pain phenomena.

Others, although mindful of the principles of learning and conditioning, merge their behavorial approaches with different conceptualizations as well. Sternbach (1974), for example, greatly emphasizes the impact of the consequences of pain on a patient's behavior. Yet, theoretically, Sternbach does not hesitate to use dynamic formulations. In his discussion of how patients present their cases to the clinic and in his diagnoses of patients' problems, Sternbach also uses a transactional analysis and a more traditional psychiatric nosology for example, hysterical neurosis, conversion type (DSM-II: 300.13).

It is important to keep in mind that a behavioral view of pain phenomena can cover a narrower or broader range of concepts. So, too, when assessing treatment of patients most programs do not rely soley on one type of treatment. Evaluation of treatment effectiveness thus is not a simple matter.

Since Fordyce (1976, 1978) has presented what may be viewed as the most "pure" behavioristic approach, it is essentially his veiwpoint that will be summarized here. Fordyce (1978) uses a variation of the Merskey (1968) and IASP Subcommittee on taxonomy (1979) definition of pain as an unpleasant experience primarily associated with tissue damage or described in such terms, or both associated and described in tissue-damage terms, whose presence is known by some form of *visible or audible behavior*. If there were no pain behaviors resulting, then there would be no pain problem. Pain behavior need not occur as a direct consequence of nociceptive stimulation. A person can perceive an experience ordinarily associated with nociceptive stimulation even without there being a nociceptive stimulus. In turn, the presence of a nociceptive stimulus does not necessarily lead to pain behavior. Suffering is the negative affective response that occurs as a consequence of pain—the unpleasant experience—and is tied to higher nervous centers. It can occur as a consequence of many things: emotional distress, anxiety, depression, loss of loved ones, and the like. It is even further detached from nociceptive stimulation than pain. Suffering that can occur as a result of emotional distress can be mislabeled as pain. Pain behaviors may then occur. These behaviors are erroneously attributed to nociceptive stimulation.

Fordyce lays great stress upon the distinction between acute and chronic pain when looking at pain behaviors. Acute, time-limited pain does lead to a variety of pain behaviors such as grimacing, moaning, or limping. However, because of its short time duration it is more readily tied to its nociceptive stimulus and less subject to learning and conditioning. Acute pain may require some lifestyle changes temporarily, but, it usually does not lead to a lasting change.

Chronic pain, however, persists for an extended period of time. Symptom behaviors continue to occur and are therefore more readily subject to learning and conditioning independent of the nociceptive stimuli that led to their original occurrence. In addition, the chronicity often leads to major, lasting changes in lifestyle, activities, and social relationships. Over time there is more and more rehearsal of sick-behavior and less of well-behavior. Once disability ceases, return to well-behavior may become a formidable task.

In chronic pain Fordyce distinguishes between respondent and operant pain behaviors. Respondent pain behaviors are those that are still tied to antecedent nociceptive stimuli and occur as a consequence of them. These behaviors can be dealt with by a variety of different strategies including medication, occasionally surgery, transcutaneous nerve stimulation, and biofeedback, as well as a variety of cognitive coping strategies.

Operant pain behaviors are those which have existed for an extended period of time in an environment that has provided them with contingent reinforcement. Operant pain behaviors are usually not related to any given bodily site. They develop as a consequence of pain behavior becoming contingent upon reinforcement. Reinforcement can occur directly through such things as the positive consequences of pain medication or the attention of others. Reinforcement can also occur indirectly though the effective avoidance of unpleasant circumstances, such as a job or a difficult social relationship. Reinforcement can also occur as a consequence of the punishment of well-behavior, especially by well-meaning family members who prevent the patient from doing such activity. Through reinforcement, pain behaviors may continue for reasons unrelated to the nociceptive tissue-damaging stimulation.

It should be pointed out that most cases of chronic pain involve a combination of respondent and operant pain behaviors. Fordyce's major treatment description relates, however, mainly to operant pain behaviors. Treatment involves two major elements: (1) the reduction or elimination of pain behaviors and (2) the restoration of well-behaviors. This is done by changing the reinforcement patterns. Contingencies between pain behavior and such things as attention or pain medication are broken. Positive reinforcement is provided for activity as opposed to rest on the part of the patient. Well-behaviors are either reestablished or taught. Generalization of well-behaviors to post-treatment settings is also an integral part of the program.

Before leaving this section, several other comments are in order. It should be made clear that to the extent to which anxiety contributes to pain perception and reactions, any approach that can reduce anxiety will also reduce the reaction to pain. Conceptually, this means that the application of relaxation, desensitization, cognitive coping, and other behavioral techniques is based upon a similar rationale as in any other stress situation. Similar theoretical underpinnings are applicable. The reader is referred to any standard behavioral text (e.g., Bandura, 1969; Wolpe, 1973).

One important behavioral concept that must be singled out is modeling. According to Bandura (1969, 1971), most of our learning takes place through a process of modeling, that is, observing how others react to circumstances in their environment and with what consequences. This concept applies to pain and pain perception as well. Individuals can learn which actions lead to painful experiences, which behaviors are appropriate under such circumstances, and how others in a similar circumstance to themselves with a similar background are capable of coping with the painful situation.

In the pain literature, modeling effects have been demonstrated as a significant part of cultural differences in the reaction to pain (cf. Weisenberg, in press-a), in clinical preparation for surgery (cf. Melamed, 1977), in reducing the pain of treatment of burn patients (cf. Fagerhaugh, 1974), and in a variety of other clinical and laboratory settings (cf. Craig, 1978). Modeling processes can be an effective part of pain control, as will be discussed in later sections.

Assessment

Assessment involves determining the level and type of pain experienced and, when possible, providing an analysis of contributing factors to permit the development of a treatment plan, as well as contributing a baseline to evaluate treatment effectiveness. Assessment, ideally, should provide some indication as to which component of the pain reaction has been affected. This is not easy to do with our present level of knowledge and technology.

In assessing the reaction to pain, Beecher (1959) has spoken of two basic components. There is a reaction based primarily upon the stimulus itself and there is a psychic processing of this reaction. It is not easy to distinguish and sort out the individual components. Clinically, health providers often ask the question, "Is the pain reaction appropriate to the presumed physical damage?" This question infers ability to measure separately individual components of the pain reaction.

In the laboratory, a number of procedures have been developed to separate sensory from motivational components of pain. Tursky (1974, 1976), for example, used electric-shock stimulation. The approach distinguishes between the sensory and reactive components on the basis of the way the shock is rated. Clinical adaptations of the Tursky approach are possible.

To measure the sensory component, a *magnitude estimation* procedure is used in which a standard electric shock of, say, 30 volts is presented and given a numerical rating of 10. Other presentations of shock stimuli above and below the standard are rated by the subject, who provides a numerical estimate in comparison to the standard. Results indicate that with skin impedence anchored at 5,000 ohms, perceived shock intensities yield a power function.

To assess the reactive motivational components of pain, Tursky asks subjects to indicate four levels of intensity as the shock intensity is raised: (1) sensation threshold, (2) discomfort, (3) pain, and (4) tolerance.

Results of these different procedures can be seen in the Sternbach and Tursky (1965) study of ethnic differences in reaction to pain. The reactive measures in which subjects were asked to identify the four gradations of (1) sensation threshold, (2) discomfort, (3) pain, and (4) tolerance did yield ethnic differences. The magnitude estimation approach did not yield ethnic differences, however, thus showing that the sensory evaluation of the shocks did not differ as a function of ethnic grouping.

Recent applications of *signal detection* or *sensory decision* theory to the measurement of pain reactions is another method of sorting out the sensory component (d') from the criterion used to judge the stimulus as painful (Lx) (Chapman, 1978; Clark, 1974). In assessing pain control techniques, it becomes possible to know whether the effects are on the basic sensory component or on the attitudinal-motivational component of pain. The analysis developed to sort signal from noise requires many more stimuli than the magnitude estimation procedure of Tursky and is mainly useful in the laboratory, where the stimulus input is clearly defined. Clark (1974) has hypothesized that pain thresholds raised by placebos, redirection of attention, hyynosis and such represent a response bias based on a reluctance to report pain (Lx) rather than a change in the sensory perception of the pain stimulus (d'). By contrast, a mixture of nitrous oxide administered for a duration sufficient to produce analgesic properties produces a change in the neural activity of the sensory system (d').

Clinically, attitude change can be very important. Beecher (1972) has argued that analgesic drugs work mostly by affecting subject attitude and predisposition to complain about pain. Morphine, for example, is described as not affecting the sensation of pain as much as the reaction to it. The patient may feel the pain but is unconcerned. In chronic-pain treatment, the practitioner may be at a loss regarding his ability to eliminate the patient's pain. Treatment consists of teaching the patient to live and function despite the pain (cf. Fordyce, 1976).

In assessing pain in general, it is important to specify the locus of pain: deep or superficial, localized or radiating, and so on. The quality of the pain sensation may be of diagnostic value. As Sternbach (1978b) points out, pains related to nerve damage are usually described as jabbing, shooting, or lightning-like. Causalgia is usually described as burning. Patients also apply cold as treatment. In both causalgia and neuralgia the skin is often very sensitive to the touch. Vascular pains are often described as throbbing with vasodilation or tight or cramping with vasoconstriction. Muscle pains are often described as aching and are worsened by remaining in one place too long. Visceral pains are often described as deep, having local tenderness, with an aching quality and occasional radiation of sharp pain.

Description of the temporal aspects of pain is also important. Is the pain constant in severity or does it change and with what? What makes the pain better or worse? Pains of short duration but sharp in nature often are related to nerve injury. Constant headaches are usually but not always muscle-contraction in nature. Periodic headaches tend to be vascular. Pains that follow but do not accompany activity are usually of muscular origin.

An important dimension to be considered is the point in time for which assessment can occur: (1) prior to treatment or the experience of pain, (2) while experiencing acute pain, or (3) while experiencing chronic pain (pain of at least six months' duration).

Pretreatment

This phase often is related to anxiety or fear of a specific situation, for instance, fear of dental treatment or fear of surgery. Assessment may include many of the same techniques and measures as used with other phobias.

Weisenberg (in press, b), for example, has used a Fear Inventory (see table 3.1) to permit assessment of the fears patients have regarding dental treatment. The items listed in the inventory contain situations that Gale (1972) found to be sources of dental fear. The inventory can be used to pinpoint specifics of patient fears, to develop a hierarchy of fears, and to assess intervention strategy. Once more the assumption is that reduction of patient fear and anxiety will lead to less pain or at least less suffering during dental treatment.

Other assessment techniques rely upon routine standard instruments. Included might be the MMPI, the State–Trait Anxiety Inventory (STAI) (Spielberger, Gorsuch, & Lushene, 1970), more situationally specific anxiety measures such as Corah's Dental Anxiety Scale (1969), measures of coping style (cf. DeLong, 1970), or any other routinely used questionnaire that might relate to the upcoming stress situation.

TABLE 3.1
The Weisenberg Dental Fear Inventory

The items in this questionnaire refer to things and experiences that may cause fear or other unpleasant feelings in the dental office. Please answer each item with your first impression as it is most likely to be accurate. Remember there are no right or wrong answers.

Name ______________________________ Date ______________

Date of birth ______________________

1. In the past two years, how often have you visited a dentist? Check the statement that most applies to you.

_____A. Not at all
_____B. One time
_____C. Two times
_____D. Three times
_____E. Four times
_____F. More than four times

2. In general, which statement best describes how you feel when you go to the dentist's office? Check only one.

_____A. I look forward to it as a pleasant experience
_____B. I feel a little uncomfortable
_____C. I feel somewhat tense
_____D. I feel moderately anxious
_____E. I feel quite anxious
_____F. I feel very anxious
_____G. I feel absolutely terrified

3. For each item, check the column that describes how much you are disturbed by the event nowadays.

Event	Not at All	A Little	A Fair Amount	Much	Very Much
Dentist tells you he is through					
Dentist asks you to rinse your mouth					
Dentist is cleaning your teeth					
Making another appointment with the nurse					
Dentist squirts water in your mouth					

TABLE 3.1 (continued)

Event	Not at All	A Little	A Fair Amount	Much	Very Much
Dental assistant places a bib on you					
Calling a dentist to make an appointment					
Dentist places cotton in your mouth					
Dentist looks at your chart					
Getting into your car to go to the dentist					
Dentist cleans your teeth with steel probe					
Thinking about going to the dentist					
Dentist is putting in the filling					
Getting into the dentist's chair					
Nurse tells you it is your turn					
Dentist is laying out his instruments					
Sitting in the dentist's waiting room					
Dentist squirts air into a cavity					
Dentist laughs as he looks into your mouth					
Having a probe placed in a cavity					
Dentist is giving you a shot					
Dentist holds a syringe and needle in front of you					
Dentist tells you that you have bad teeth					
Dentist is drilling your tooth					
Dentist is pulling your tooth					

From a behavioral perspective, Fordyce (1976) views scores on an instrument such as MMPI as indicating high- or low-frequency behavior rather than an indication that an individual possesses a given personality. For example, a person complaining of pain scoring high on the Hypochondriasis scale is *not* viewed as having hypochondriasis. From a behavioral point of view such an individual is seen as possessing a readiness to signal pain. Those in the environment of the patient, therefore, are likely to receive repeated signals that the patient is experiencing pain. Elevations on the F scale or Depression scale suggest that the pain has a high emotional cost or that the pain is occurring in someone who already has emotional distress. Scale 4, 9, or both 4 and 9 elevations seem to indicate that the person is restless or energetic, while a K scale elevation together with elevation on scales 2 and 7 suggest that inactivity is not reinforcing but rather has a high emotional cost to the patient.

Laboratory-type tests of pain threshold and tolerance—electric shock, pressure algometer—have also been used to predict future reaction to pain. However, they do not predict well pain tolerance in a specific situation (Parbrook, Steel, & Dalrymple, 1973). Wolff (1971) did isolate a pain-endurance factor that on the basis of a laboratory-type test of pain threshold and tolerance predicted postoperative pain tolerance. However, the meaning of this pain-tolerance factor is still somewhat vague and requires futher research clarification.

Acute Pain

A number of different approaches have been used to assess the patient's reaction to pain. These include: (1) matching techniques in which the patient is stimulated until he indicates that the clinical pain intensity reaches the level of external stimulation; (2) paper and pencil measures have been used with either verbal descriptors or scales describing the pain; and (3) a variety of other assessments related to the pain experience.

Matching approaches. Sternbach (1974) has combined an ischemic pain measure with a verbal rating as part of his routine, clinical assessment of pain patients. The verbal scale asks the patient to rate his or her pain on a scale of 0 to 100, in which 0 is no pain at all and 100 is pain so severe that the patient would commit suicide if he had to endure it for more than a minute or two. Submaximum tourniquet stimulation is used to produce the slowly building-up pain of ischemia (Smith, Egbert, Markowitz, Mosteller, & Beecher, 1966). Ratings are obtained for the point at which the pain equals the patient's current level and for the maximum pain he or she can tolerate. A tourniquet ratio score is computed by dividing the time to reach clinical pain by the time to reach maximum tolerance and multiplying by 100. This score is compared to the verbal rating. Differences between ratings are shown to the patient and used as a part of the therapeutic procedure. A health provider is thus able to say with a little more confidence, "The pain really isn't that bad." Treatment, especially with chronic pain, can sometimes increase the tourniquet pain ratio score by increasing patient activity and reducing drug intake. Yet the verbal rating could indicate successful treatment as the patient learns to accept his pain condition. Timmermans and Sternbach (1976) have demonstrated that the verbal rating scale is associated with the perceived interference of pain with normal daily activities such as sleep and sex. The ischemic measure of pain was found to be related to depression. Recently, Moore, Duncan, Scott, Gregg, and Ghia (1979) suggested several cautions to be observed when applying the submaximal tourniquet test as the pain ratings derived from it are not linearly related to time and are affected by the manner in which the patient performs the exercise. They suggest that elapsed time should be measured from the moment the cuff is inflated rather than at exercise termination. Each grip exercise should be kept for the same duration of time. Exercise grip strength should be assessed as a fixed percentage of the patient's maximum grip strength. Matches to clinical pain that occur at the extremes of the pain ratings may not reflect a psychological response bias but rather be related to the sigmoid shape of the response curve.

Patkin (1970) demonstrated how a simple, modified, cheap, spring-operated kitchen scale could be used in a clinical setting where pressure is found related to reports of pain, for example, abdominal pain. Pressure is applied to a variety of areas. Tenderness is assessed by readings on the scale for patient reports of pain associated with pressure. Several case examples have been described. Of course, this approach does not readily distinguish between the different components of the pain reaction. It does, however, yield some quantification for baseline use that might be clinically helpful.

Paper and pencil measures. Clinically, pain is usually described in verbal terms. Pain can be described as burning, aching, stabbing, splitting, pounding, nagging, cramping, and so on. Pain can also be intolerable, unbearable, distressing, excruciating, severe. To understand the relationships between these different expressions of pain, Melzack and Torgerson (1971) and Melzack (1975) developed a pain scale, the McGill Pain Questionnaire. They categorized 102 pain terms into three classes: (1) sensory quality descriptors in terms of temporal, spatial, pressure, thermal, and other properties, such as pounding, spreading, crushing, burning, aching; (2) affective quality descriptors in terms of tension, fear, and autonomic properties, such as exhausting, awful, nauseating; and (3) evaluative terms that describe the intensity of the total experience, such as agonizing, excruciating, miserable.

Each term was judged by groups of 20 judges to determine the degree of agreement of classification. Intensity relationships within classes were then judged by 140 students, 20 physicians, and 20 patients. Substantial agreement was obtained in classifying the many different terms used to describe pain.

Development of descriptor scales can make meaningful clinical questionnaires possible, using terms that are spaced appropriately. It becomes possible to say a *strong* pain is almost twice as great as a moderate pain while an excruciating pain is more than four times as great (Tursky, 1976). Melzack and Torgerson (1971) and Melzack (1975) suggest that when used with spatial and temporal varibles, it should be possible to reliably categorize distinct pain syndromes as found in the various disease classifications so that more appropriate diagnosis and treatment could be performed. Dubuisson and Melzack (1976) using the McGill Pain Questionnaire, were able to demonstrate differences among constellations of words for eight clinical syndromes. Eight diagnostic categories were developed on the basis of which 77 percent of the patients were correctly classed. When information such as sex, age, spatial location of pain, and analgesic drugs was added to the verbal descriptions, 100 percent of the patients were correctly classed.

A variety of studies have been performed using the McGill Pain Questionnaire or techniques similar to it. Crockett, Prkachin, and Craig (1977) studied low-back pain patients and a group of volunteers. They demonstrated overlap with the three major dimensions of pain found by Melzack and Torgerson (1971). However, Crockett et al. (1977) obtained five dimensions, suggesting a finer breakdown of categories.

Van Buren and Kleinknecht (1979) examined pain reports following oral surgery. The McGill Pain Questionnaire was found to reflect accurately recovery time and increased use of narcotics. Overlap was found among the sensory, evaluative, and affective subscales. State anxiety was found to be more strongly related to the evaluative and sensory subscale than to the affective subscale that was designed to measure pain, tension, and autonomic aspects of the pain experienced.

Studies of the McGill Pain Questionnaire and instruments similar to it are steps in the right direction. Additional research obviously will be required to clarify, sort, and replicate findings. There are, however, those who might argue that use of scales such as the McGill Pain Questionnaire would be most appropriate for patients with good verbal skills but not for those without such skills (cf. Wolff, 1978).

One approach that has been used to overcome language barriers is the visual analog scale. As described by Wolff (1978), a visual analog scale is a straight line whose ends are fixed by a statement of the extreme limits of the sensation to be measured, for example, No Pain–Excrutiating Pain. The visual analog scale has been found to be sensitive to changes in pain as a result of anesthetic. Scott and Huskisson (1976) report that visual analog or graphic rating scales can readily be used by patients without any previous experience. These authors recommend these scales as the best available method for measuring pain or its relief.

Related assessments. Among the other related assessments it is important to have a dependable physical work-up. Even with all the most outstanding psychiatric symptoms, physical problems should not be overlooked. In turn, it does not necessarily follow that finding a definite physiological lesion automatically accounts for the reaction to pain. As was already indicated many other elements must be included.

Of course, it is important to know which medications the patient is taking, both pain and other medications. Patient use of medication can either enhance or curtail an intervention in acute pain. It is extremely important in chronic pain as well (see later section).

Merskey (1974) recommends inclusion of an assessment of patient personality. The MMPI has been the most widely used instrument with pain patients. For the acute-pain situation, the MMPI may require too much time and might not be as valuable as other more situationally specific measures, especially of anxiety, as mentioned in the previous section. Anxiety has been most closely related to acute pain, whereas depression has been more closely related to chronic pain (Sternbach, 1978b).

Chronic Pain

As with acute pain, it is also desirable that the patient be given a thorough physical. A comprehensive patient history should be available. Ideally, psychological assessment should not be separated from the physical but rather should be routinely done as part of a team, comprehensive work-up for all patients. The psychologist who works with chronic-pain patients must be prepared to work hand in hand with a variety of health-care providers. Team effort rather than individual treatment is required.

Many of the same measures referred to earlier such as the MMPI or the Illness Behavior Questionnaire (Pilowsky & Spence, 1976a,b,c) are routinely used as part of the assessment of the chronic-pain patient.

When interviewing the chronic-pain patient, Sternbach (1974) recommends careful observation of the manner in which the patient responds as well as attention to what is said. Does the patient demand, whine, flatter? What emotional response does the patient elicit from the interviewer—sympathy, irritation? Major areas of information that are useful in understanding the role of the pain in the patient's life and secondary gain related to the pain include: (1) evaluation of the patient's work environment, (2) a careful assessment of the patient's medication history, (3) involvement of litigation, and (4) an evaluation of how the patient would live if he did not have the pain.

Fordyce (1976, 1978) attempts to assess to what extent pain is respondent in nature, that is, related to antecedent, nociceptive stimuli, or to what extent pain is related to environmental consequences and operant in nature. Often pain behavior is both operant and respondent.

The major assessment described by Fordyce deals with the establishment of the operant–respondent distinction, with the treatment program geared mainly toward operant pain behavior. Great emphasis is placed upon changes in behavior related to pain. Major questions to be answered are: (1) What good things happen when pain behavior occurs? (2) What bad things do not happen when pain behavior occurs?

To assess the patient, Fordyce seeks evidence of systematic and direct positive reinforcement of pain behavior, indirect reinforcement through avoidance, or punishment or failure to reinforce patient well-behavior. Assessment should also include a determination of reinforcers to be used in treatment, post-treatment well-behavior targets, and the readiness of the patient's family and environment to support change.

Fordyce starts his patient interview by asking for a description of a typical day from awakening until the patient goes to sleep at night. The emphasis is upon estimating activity including moving, sitting, and reclining.

The patient is asked to describe the time sequence of pain. The clinician attempts thereby to look for systematic relationships to antecedent events and/or to the environment. Sleep-pattern assessment can also provide valuable information. Respondent pain will often feel worse at night when distracting stimulation is at a minimum. What happens when the patient awakens in the middle of the night? Does it lead to medication or awakening of the spouse, or does the patient quietly take care of himself? Sometimes awakening occurs not because of the pain but because of the medication.

To assess the reactions of others to the pain, the patient is asked, "How do people around you know you are in pain? "What do other people do when you have pain?" "When you have pain and you try to do things, what do others around you do?" Discouragement of activity or taking over the patient's activity by others is a common occurrence.

What things make the pain better and what things make the pain worse? "Is the reinforcement for the pain behavior high or low?" is another way of looking at the question. Included among the pain activators would be activities such as housework, routine job, and excercise. Among the pain diminishers are rest and pain medication. The major issue with medication is habituation or addiction, apparently a quite common occurrence with chronic pain.

Other areas of consideration include changes in activity as a result of pain. How has the patient's and his family's life changed as a consequence of the pain? What was done and is no longer being done, and what would be done in the future if pain were not a condition?

Among the reinforcers that must be considered is compensation for injury. A patient who receives compensation for injury or a patient who has litigation pending has less incentive for reducing pain behaviors. Brena (1978), Sternbach (1978b), and Neal (1978) have discussed at length the effects of compensation on fostering pain behavior.

In addition to the interview, Fordyce requires his patients to maintain a diary on which is recorded medication and activity on an hour-by-hour basis. Weekly uptime of less than 80 hours indicates that the patient has considerable functional impairment and that rest is an effective reinforcer. Consistent time-spacing for medication might indicate habituation or addiction.

When selecting patients for contingency management treatment, Fordyce attempts to summarize the information obtained on the patient: (1) What pain behaviors are to be decreased? (2) Which behaviors are to be increased by the patient, spouse, or others? (3) Which reinforcers might be effective in treatment? (4) Which post-treatment activities are reasonable to expect from the patient and spouse? Does the patient or spouse have these behaviors in his repertoire? (5) Are the spouse and the family willing to participate in treatment?

Brena (1978) developed the *Emory Pain Estimate Model*. Three sets of data used are: (1) measures of tissue pathology, (2) measures of pain behavior, and (3) measures of the relationship between tissue pathology and behavior. Tissue pathology is graphed linearly on a scale of 1 to 10 and bisected by pain behaviors that are vertically graphed on a scale of 0 to 10, yielding four quadrants and four classes of patients. Class I patients display pain behavior in excess of demonstrable organic disease. Classes II and III are both pain-disabled and need behavior-modification therapy and functional education. Class IV patients exhibit minimal pain behavior despite considerable organic disease.

Known Treatment Procedures

The basic set of treatment strategies to be discussed can be seen in Table 3.2. It should be pointed out that accurate assessment of effectiveness of any given strategy is not always possible based upon the existing literature. Much of the evidence has been gathered in the laboratory setting. Beecher (1959, 1963), for example, is of the opinion that it is not possible to generalize from the laboratory to the clinic situation. In the clinic, anxiety is much higher. There is the threat of disfigurement or death. The subject also cannot as easily decide to leave in the middle of a treatment such as surgery. In the laboratory, long-term effects also cannot be assessed easily. However, the other side of the argument is that the clinic setting does not provide the controls that are available in

TABLE 3.2
Summary Table of Treatment Strategies

TYPE OF INTERVENTION	SITUATION WHERE APPROPRIATE
COGNITIVE STRATEGIES	Where anxiety is a major contributing factor to the pain reaction and where patient is capable of learning to cope using his own skills and positive expectancies
Placebo and Suggestion	Can be used in preparation for anticipated pain and to cope with episodic acute pain, e.g., MPD syndrome
Hypnosis	Can be used with both advanced preparation and experience of both acute and chronic pain. More effective with pain having a clear organic cause, e.g., cancer
Stress-inoculation Training	Effective with advanced preparation and for experience of acute pain, e.g., prior to or during surgery
Perceived Control	Partially effective prior to and during acute and chronic pain, e.g., pain of muscle contraction
Advanced Preparation for Surgery	Effective prior to pain stimulation, e.g., prior to surgery
MODELING	Has been used for advance preparation as well as during acute episodes, e.g., burn unit
BIOFEEDBACK AND RELAXATION	Has been used as preparation, during acute pain, with pain of an episodic nature, and with chronic pain. Has shown success with tension and migraine headache
DESENSITIZATION	Mainly used to reduce fear associated with treatment, e.g., dental phobia
COMBINED STRATEGIES EMPHASIZING EXTINCTION OF SICK-BEHAVIORS AND ESTABLISHMENT OF WELL-BEHAVIOR	Used mainly with pain of a chronic nature, and where a significant operant component is apparent, e.g., lower-back pain; depression and helplessness may be present

the laboratory. In the clinic it is not always possible to equate patients for pain intensity or physical condition. It is ethically difficult to deny treatment or use less effective treatment. Most often patients undergo simultaneous multiple treatments that make for great difficulty in untangling cause-and-effect relationships.

It thus seems necessary to assess treatment strategies by examining both laboratory and clinical studies. Design quality ratings (see Table 3.3) must be assessed relative to the setting in which the study occurs. Limitations in our ability to generalize, especially to any given patient, must be kept in mind. In this emerging field the best generalization possible is to say that there is no one treatment that works with all patients under all circumstances. Some procedures seem to be best applied in advance of the pain experience, others during acute pain, while others work best for chronic pain. Some strategies work best where anxiety is a major contributing factor, others where depression and secondary gain are major issues. Some strategies are effective when used individually, others only when combined with additional pain-control approaches.

Placebo and Suggestion Phenomena

Placebo responsiveness has been well documented throughout the literature. Beecher (1962) has shown that 35 percent of patients with pathological pain will obtain pain relief with placebos. The greater the anxiety, the greater is the relief from placebo medications. Placebo relief seems to be based partially on the unwritten contract between doctor and patient that states the doctor is going to do all he can to relieve the patient's suffering. If the doctor believes the treatment will work and the patient leaves with the expectation that it will work, the anxiety is relieved and the patient seems to heal himself.

In a laboratory study, Feather, Chapman, and Fisher (1972) were able to demonstrate that a placebo increased tolerance to the pain of radiant heat. A signal-detection analysis indicated that the major effects of the placebo were not on d', pain sensitivity, but upon Lx, the willingness of the subject to report pain. In the clinic setting and especially where reduced anxiety leads to reduced muscle contraction, it is likely that a placebo would also lead to a change in d', as is probably indicated in myofascial pain dysfunction (MPD) studies.

Evans (1974a) has analyzed placebo treatment data collected by McGlashen, Evans, and Orne (1969) as a function of chronic or state anxiety. Placebo reaction that resulted in increased pain tolerance was associated with state anxiety reduction. This result was especially notable for chronic anxiety subjects. Increased anxiety following the ingestion of the placebo drugs resulted in decreased pain tolerance. In an

TABLE 3.3
Summary of Representative Reports of Treatment Strategies

Author(s)	Date	Type of Study	Number of Subjects	Treatment	Outcome	Follow-up	Special Comments	Design Quality Rating
Beecher	1962	Review of 11 clinical studies	1,082	Placebo	35.2% effective	----	Most effective when anxiety is high	Mixed, but many in good–very good range
Billars	1970	Postoperative pain	30	Suggestion and position change	Effective	----	Conviction of effectiveness important ingredient	Good
McGlashen, Evans, & Orne	1969	Laboratory	24	Hypnosis and placebo	Pain reduced by 20%	----	Hypnosis much more effective than placebo for hypnotizable Ss; placebo effectiveness related to anxiety	Very good
Feather, Chapman, & Fisher	1972	Laboratory	9	Placebo	Increased pain tolerance	----	Tolerance not related to change in sensitivity but to willingness to report pain	Very good
Walike & Meyer	1966	Arthritis patients	29	Placebo	13/29 responded at least as well as to active drug	----	Placebo reactors scored higher on MMPI anxiety and dependency	Very good

TABLE 3.3 (continued)

Goodman, Greene, & Laskin	1976	Dental MPD	25	Placebo equilibration	16/25 obtained complete relief	6-29 months	Placebo need not be only drugs	Good
Hilgard & Hilgard	1975	Review of laboratory and clinical applications	several hundred	Hypnosis	Although exact numbers unavailable, a large proportion of cases can be helped	Up to several months	Strong evidence both from lab and clinic to show effectiveness of hypnosis	Mixed from poor, to very good range
Jacoby	1960	Dental patients	308	Hypnosis	Mostly positive	Unknown	Both personal and recorded instructions were used	Poor
Crasilneck & Hall	1973	Case presentations	4	Hypnosis	Positive	Up to 3 months	Cases chosen include naive child and culturally unaware as well as highly sophisticated adult	Poor
Barber & Hahn	1962	Laboratory	48	Hypnosis or pleasant imagery	Positive	----	Hypnosis did not differ from pleasant imagery	Very good
Meichenbaum & Turk	1976	Laboratory	5	Stress-inoculation training	Positive	----	Ischemic pain tolerance was raised from 17 to 32 mins.; control group did not significantly change	Very good

(continued)

TABLE 3.3 (continued)

Author(s)	Date	Type of Study	Number of Subjects	Treatment	Outcome	Follow-up	Special Comments	Design Quality Rating
Staub, Tursky, & Schwartz	1971	Laboratory	40	Control	Positive	----	Control increases pain tolerance; removing control reduces tolerance	Very good
Corah	1973	Dental patients	24	Control	Mixed	----	Results are not clear cut	Good
Keeri-Szanto	1979	Patients postoperation	34	Control	Positive	75 hrs.	It is possible to allow for greater individualized treatment	Very good
Egbert, Baittit, Welch, & Bartlett	1964	Postoperative pain	97	Presurgical preparation	Positive	5 days	Results appear 24 hours after surgery	Good
Baldwin & Barnes	1966	Tooth extraction	82	Preextraction preparation	Positive	1 mo.	Less stress & greater trust in dentist were achieved	Good
Wolfer & Visintainer	1975	Postoperative recovery	80	Presurgical preparation	Positive	10 days	Children prepared showed less upset and more coopera-tion	Very good

TABLE 3.3 (continued)

Johnson, Rice, Fuller, & Endress	1978	Postoperative recovery	149	Presurgical preparation	Positive and no difference	4 wks.	Major surgery patients showed positive results; minor did not	Very good
Vernon	1974	Presurgery injection	30	Modeling	Positive	----	Realistic modeling most effective	Good
Melamed & Siegel	1975	Presurgical preparation	30	Modeling	Positive	4 wks.	Long-term effects obtained	Very good
Machen & Johnson	1974	Dental restorations	58	Modeling and desensitization	Positive	3 dental visits	Modeling somewhat better than desensitization	Good
Budzynski, Stoyva, Adler, & Mullaney	1973	Tension headache	18	EMG biofeedback	Positive	3 mos.	Patients reduced frequency and intensity	Very good
Philips	1977	Tension headache	15	EMG biofeedback	Mixed	8 wks.	Reduced intensity but not frequency	Very good
Gessel	1975	MPD	23	EMG biofeedback	Mixed	End of treatment	15 out of 23 helped by biofeedback	Poor
Gessel & Alderman	1971	MPD	11	Relaxation	Mixed	End of treatment	6 out of 11 helped	Poor

(continued)

TABLE 3.3 (continued)

Author(s)	Date	Type of Study	Number of Subjects	Treatment	Outcome	Follow-up	Special Comments	Design Quality Rating
Sherman, Gall, & Gormly	1979	Phantom-limb pain	16	Relaxation and biofeedback	Most helped	6 mos. to 3 yrs.	8 achieved complete relief, 4 partial relief	Fair
Ayer	1973	Dental	3	Desensitization	Positive	3 dental visits	Imagery used for relaxation	Poor
Fordyce, Fowler, Lehmann, DeLateur, Sand, & Trieschmann	1973	Mixed chronic pain	36	Combined therapy	Positive	22 mos.	Reduction in pain activity, increase in positive health activity	Fair
Newman, Seres, Yospe, & Garlington	1978	Low-back pain	36	Combined therapy	Positive	80 wks.	Improvement in exercise capability and in coping	Fair
Ignelzi, Sternbach, & Timmermans	1977	Mixed pain	54	Combined therapy	Positive	2-3 yrs.	Surgical patients more likely to be readmitted for pain than nonsurgical patients	Fair

earlier paper Evans (1967) did not find placebo reactors to be associated with personality measures of suggestibility.

Evans (1974b) reports the relative efficiency of placebos to drugs such as morphine, Darvon, or aspirin as .54–.56. That is, a placebo is 56 percent as effective as morphine. The effectiveness of a placebo is directly proportional to the active analgesic agent to which it is being compared. Placebo is usually more effective in relieving severe pain. The properties of the placebo mimic the drug to which it is being compared. Effects of the placebo and the comparison drug usually interact and are additive. Higher placebo dosages are more effective than lower dosages. Injections are more effective when described to patients as a powerful drug than when described as an experimental drug. They are more effective when given by a health provider who is more likely to use drugs.

Laskin and Greene (1972) demonstrated the effectiveness of a placebo capsule dispensed by prescription and enhanced by a suggestive name. Twenty-six out of 50 patients (52 percent) with myofascial pain-dysfunction (MPD) syndrome reported improvement in their condition with symptoms of pain and tenderness affected most. Long-term (six months to eight years) evaluation of patients indicated no difference between those who positively responded to placebo therapy or to other forms of therapy. Only six out of 100 patients followed up for a variety of different therapies reported that their MPD problem was under control (Greene & Laskin, 1974).

The doctor–patient relationship is an important element in the effectiveness of placebo therapy. It is important to realize, however, that placebos do not depend only upon drugs. Goodman, Greene, and Laskin (1976) demonstrated that two mock tooth equilibrations for MPD were effective in producing total or near total remission of symptoms in 16 (64 percent) out of 25 patients. Thirteen of the patients for whom follow-up was possible remained symptom free 6 to 29 months later. Successfully treated patients actually did have a variety of tooth occlusal surface disharmonies that remained untreated. Goodman et al. argue that it is the strong positive suggestion that is likely to be responsible for the success of those who provide routine occlusal therapy for MPD.

That expectations of relief influence outcome was demonstrated in a controlled study of audioanalgesia. Melack, Weisz, and Sprague (1963) were able to demonstrate that auditory stimulation did not abolish cold pressor pain. They compared three groups of subjects. Group 1 received strong auditory stimulation but no suggestion about the purposes of the music and noise. Group 2 received strong auditory stimulation together with strong suggestions of effectiveness. Group 3 received strong suggestion but only a low-frequency hum rather than strong auditory stimulation. Each group served as its own control, having received cold pressor stimulation without any sound prior to group assignment. Group 2 produced a substantial increase in pain tolerance, while neither group 1 nor group 3 did in comparison to their control stimulation periods. What the audio stimulation did was divert attention away from cold pressor pain when accompanied by strong suggestion. Therefore, in the hands of a practitioner who could relate well to his patients, it was effective. For practitioners who could not build up expectations of effectiveness, it did not work.

Stroebel and Glueck (1973) have referred to biofeedback treatment as an ultimate placebo. Placebo is used to mean an approach that reinforces favorable expectations from treatment. The word ultimate is used to mean that through the trial-and-error experience of biofeedback a person can acquire a sense of responsibility for achieving the goal of therapy. Essentially, this sense of responsibility allows the patient to cure himself. As will be seen later, this ingredient is one of the major elements assumed to be needed in successful treatment of chronic pain.

Hypnosis

Traditionally, hypnosis has not been viewed as a behavioral technique. As Kroger and Fezler (1976) have shown, however, hypnosis and behavior modification have a great deal in common with hypnotic techniques that enhance and facilitate behavior change. Hypnosis can be especially effective whenever relaxation, imagery, or rehearsal is a part of a treatment. In pain control, hypnosis has been effectively used to control the pain of cancer, surgery, childbirth, burns, and dentistry as well as in many other clinical situations (cf. Hilgard & Hilgard, 1975). As with other forms of pain control, there is not always a clear-cut explanation as to what hypnosis is and why it is effective. Its worst side effect, however, is that it may not work.

Hilgard and Hilgard (1975) have concluded that hypnosis can be an effective way of reducing pain perception in 93 percent of highly hypnotizable subjects. Only 7 percent of this group could not reduce pain at least partially. Sixty-seven percent were able to reduce pain by one-third or more. For the low hypnotizable subjects, 44 percent were able to reduce pain at least somewhat. Thirteen percent of this latter group were able to reduce pain by one-third or more. Hypnosis by itself does not automatically produce analgesia. It requires either specific suggestions of analgesia or related suggestions such as dissociation, reinterpretation of the stimulus, age regression to a time before the pain, or time distortion. Anxiety reduction may reduce distress, but this is not synonymous with pain reduction. Hypnosis is also capable of producing pain relief beyond that of a simple placebo (McGlashen et al., 1969).

Clinically, a variety of different techniques have been used to produce analgesia (Hilgard & Hilgard, 1975). Direct suggestion of numbness and loss of sensation is sufficient for many patients. For others a two-step procedure is used. Numbness is suggested in one part of the body where it is relatively easy to produce, such as the hand. This numbness is then transferred to the body part having pain. Other techniques include displacing the pain from one part of the body to another where it is more readily tolerated. The pain can also be converted to something else such as a tingling. Dissociation and redirecting of attention have also been used. Sarcedote (1970) has used time distortion, hypnoplasty (changing the aching area into something else), and partial or total amnesia to reduce the future anticipation of pain.

To understand hypnosis, Hilgard (1973) has approached this phenomenon on the basis of different levels of consciousness. There seem to be different systems of cognitive functioning so that even though a pain stimulus is able to reach one level of consciousness it is blocked from the more immediate level of awareness. That is, the person does perceive the pain stimulus at some lower level, as seen by studies in which the "hidden observer" is asked if it is painful. However, the person is capable of keeping the pain from coming to the level of awareness that makes it distressing.

Chaves and Barber (1974a) have stressed that many of the claims of hypnosis are based on a readiness on the part of the individual to accept suggestions and not on some magical trance powers that certain individuals possess to influence others. Many experimental studies of hypnosis do not assess the contributions of the separate variables they use in obtaining effect. There are suggestions that certain physiological effects will occur. Instructions are given to maximize motivation to accept suggestion. Suggestions are given for relaxation. Subjects are asked to close their eyes, and so on. Each of these variables contributes to produce a person who is highly motivated to accept suggestion without postulating that a separate state has been attained. Much of what is done under hypnosis could also be done with the waking individual.

Barber and Hahn (1962) for example, asked subjects to immerse their hands in 2°C water for three minutes. One group received hypnotic induction and suggestions of hand anesthesia. A second group was asked to imagine a pleasant situation. A third group was simply exposed to the painful stimulation, while a fourth group was asked to immerse in water at room temperature. The hypnotic and pleasant imagery groups did not yield differences either on subjective reports of pain or on four physiological measures. Both methods were equally effective in reducing subjective pain reports, respiratory irregularities, and forehand muscle tension compared to the noninstructed controls. However, compared to the room-temperature group, the hypnotic analgesia and pleasant groups reported higher levels of pain and showed elevated levels of skin conductance and faster heart rates.

Although Barber and Chaves have accomplished a great deal in changing hypnosis from the status of magic to science, many investigators disagree with their conclusions and regard hypnosis as something real. Crasilneck and Hall (1973) showed that hypnosis can be used effectively even with naive patients who have had no previous conceptions as to how they are to behave. Orne (1974) has stressed that patients are not simply trying to please the doctor but that hypnosis is a real phenomenon. Interestingly, Orne reports greater success in using hypnosis with patients who have a clear organic problem than with so-called psychogenic pain patients.

There is little doubt that regardless of the theoretical arguments concerning the reality of hypnosis, it is an effective technique to be used for pain control. It has also been shown that many of the individual ingredients used for inducing and maintaining trance can be used as part of pain control strategies without any formal induction of hypnosis. These include such things as careful choice of words and voice tone, relaxation, stimulus reinterpretation, and pleasant imagery. Hypnosis can also be effective in dealing with factors associated with pain reaction increase such as anxiety, depression, insomnia, and loss of appetite.

Stress-inoculation Training

Meichenbaum and Turk (1976) describe a technique that they call stress inoculation training. It is based upon previous studies of cognitive techniques such as attention distraction, focusing, and use of imagery (Blitz & Dinnerstein, 1971; Chaves & Barber, 1974b; Kanfer & Goldfoot, 1966).

In an example of an earlier study, Blitz and Dinnerstein (1971) emphasized that instructions are mediated by attentional factors. They tested three groups of subjects using cold pressor stimulation. Group 1 was asked to focus on the cold, ignoring the pain. Group 2 was asked to reinterpret the cold as pleasant, while groups 3 served as a control. Both instructional groups showed elevated pain thresholds in comparison to the controls. Groups 1 and 2 did not differ from each other. Tolerance scores were not affected.

Chaves and Barber (1974b), as part of a continuing series of studies, compared cognitive strategies of imagining pleasant events or imagining the finger to be insensitive to expectations of a reduction in pain or a control condition for pressure stimulation to the finger. Ratings of the average amount of pain felt were reduced most for the cognitive strategies. The expectation of reduction of pain also showed a smaller but an attenuated rating in comparison to the control subjects.

As Meichenbaum and Turk (1976) point out, however, not all reinterpretive or imagery strategies necessarily lead to reduced pain reactions. Greene and Reyher (1972), for example, found that a hypnotic analgesia plus pleasant imagery condition was not as effective as an analgesia suggestion only in modifying tolerance. When using any strategy it must fit the context as well as the person involved. What is relaxing for one person may produce tension in another.

Stress-inoculation attempts to deal with individual differences by offering subjects a variety of different strategies. Subjects choose those strategies which they feel most capable of using. There is a period of training prior to exposure to the pain situation. Using gate-control concepts, subjects are told of the different components of pain, and subjects are provided with different coping strategies to use for each component. Subjects are taught relaxation and slow breathing. They can choose from such strategies as attention diversion or somatic focusing. Imagery manipulations are taught to change the pain stimulation by reinterpreting what is being experienced. Subjects are taught how to generate self-statements to deal with the different phases, such as preparing for pain, confronting pain, and self-reinforcement for having coped. Examples of such statements are: "What is it you have to do?" (preparation statement). "Just relax, breathe deeply and use one of the strategies" (confrontation statement). "You handled it pretty well" (reinforcing self-statement).

Prior to actual confrontation with the pain stimuli, subjects are given the opportunity to practice using different strategies while imagining they were being stimulated. Subjects are also asked to roleplay giving advice to a new subject. The entire training procedure took one hour. Subjects were then exposed to ischemic pain. Compared to a pretest of 17 minutes, post-training tolerance increased to 32 minutes. Meichenbaum and Turk refer to earlier evidence that 10 mg. of morphine were capable of increasing ischemic pain tolerance by only 10 minutes compared to the 15 minutes obtained here. Control subjects did not show any significant increase.

The stress-inoculation procedure offers an interesting approach to preparing patients to deal with pain of an acute nature. There are many anecdotal reports of successful use of this type of pain control since ancient times. The major drawback is a lack of solid clinical evidence to indicate its effectiveness.

Perceived Control

Numerous laboratory studies have indicated that providing subjects with some degree of control over the pain stimulation can reduce stress and increase pain tolerance. Bowers (1968) has argued that lack of control increases anxiety and hence results in larger pain and stress reactions. Subjects informed prior to shock tolerance measurement that they would be able to avoid electric shock tolerated it at a level of more than twice as high as those who thought shock was random. Post-experimental ratings of shock painfulness did not differ for each group.

Staub, Tursky, and Schwartz (1971) related control to predictability. Uncertainty increases anxiety and results in less pain tolerance, while reduction of uncertainty increases tolerance. Subjects given control over the intensity and timing of shocks tolerated higher levels of shock before rating them as uncomfortable compared to no-control subjects. Loss of control after it had been given to subjects resulted in lower intensities of shock being rated as uncomfortable. No-control sujects produced large heart rate responses at all levels of intensity, while control subjects made more differentiated responses, reacting mainly to the most intense shocks.

Clinically, Keeri-Szanto (1979) has described a technique whereby post-surgical patients are permitted to control the administration of their own narcotic medications. Demand analgesia avoids many of the difficulties that occur in non-demand situations. The required prescription has to be written once the patient indicates a need for pain relief. To accomplish this the nurse must be summoned and convinced the patient "really" is in pain and the drug must be signed out from the locked cabinet. The time it takes for the drug to be absorbed after injection also must be included. By the time all of the above has occurred, the pain level for which relief was originally requested has intensified. In contrast, with a demand system patients are less likely to possibly abuse the amount of drug used. It was also possible to identify approximately 20 percent of the patients who were placebo responders and for whom lesser concentrations of narcotic were indicated. Drug administration can thus be accomplished in a way that leads to greater satisfaction of individual needs without necessarily using the most potent maximal dosages.

Isler (1975) has described how the Keeri-Szanto approach has been used with terminal cancer patients even on an ambulatory basis. Instead of these patients being tied to a bed in a drug-induced semicomatose state, they were allowed freedom of movement and were capable of living out their remaining days as active human beings. Lower dosages of pain medication were needed, pain tolerance increased, and in one case pain medication was discontinued altogether.

The issue of control and predictibility as with many other areas of pain perception is not entirely clear. Corah (1973) tried to replicate a study showing that a control device introduced into the dental operatory would produce more cooperative behavior. Twenty-four children ages six to 11 were provided with a two-button green–red device to use during treatment. The control device group showed less response to high arousal procedures as measured by GSR but slightly more response during low arousal procedures compared to a no-control group. Behavioral ratings of each group did not differ. Regarding the effectiveness of control these results are not entirely clear.

In an analysis of control as a variable, Averill (1973) shows that it has been used to refer to behavioral control, cognitive control, or decisional control. He states that it is difficult to conclude that there is a direct relationship between stress and control. Other factors that must be considered include the presence or absence of feedback that tells the subject how well he is controlling, the subject's ability to tolerate the information necessary for control, and what appears as larger short-term stress reactions but long-term adaptations.

It seems that control is an important variable in pain reduction. However, who should be given the control, patient or health provider, may vary depending upon the goals or circumstances. Long-term gain may require greater immediate arousal, as seen in the literature on preparation for surgery. However, an important ingredient in chronic pain tolerance appears to be a sense of control. Many pain-control centers strive to achieve this goal as part of their treatment strategy. The message is, "You can function and control your pain rather than let it control you." Examples of this approach will be mentioned later.

Advanced Preparation for Surgery

Preparation for surgery has had a number of beneficial effects on outcomes that include less use of pain medication, less distress, fewer postsurgical complications, and earlier hospital discharge. Egbert, Battit, Welch, and Bartlet (1964) prepared one group of patients by a preoperative visit. They were told about the preparation for anesthesia and the time and approximate duration of the operation, and warned that they would wake up in the recovery room. They were also told they would feel pain, how severe it might be, and how long it would last. The patients were reassured that feeling pain was normal after abdominal surgery and that there were ways by which they would be able to cope with the surgery. They were taught relaxation procedures, the use of a trapeze, and how to turn their bodies after surgery. They were also told they could ask for medication if it was needed. Compared to a control group, the specially instructed patients requested significantly less narcotic following surgery and were sent home an average of 2.7 days earlier.

Baldwin and Barnes (1966) studied eight- to 14-year-old patients who had to undergo dental extraction. One group of subjects was given from four to seven days between the time of the announcement of the extraction and the extraction itself, while a second group was not notified until the day of the event itself. While both groups showed a stress reaction as measured by figure-drawing constriction prior to surgery, the waiting-period group showed an increase in figure-drawing size (used to infer reduced stress) postsurgery, while the no-waiting-period group remained constricted and began to show an increase in figure size only in the follow-up period one month later.

A number of studies have been done in the area of preparation for surgery. Janis (1958) has emphasized an optimal relationship between the amount of suffering expected and the amount obtained, which seems conducive to a feeling of mastery of a difficult situation and to speed of recovery. The optimal degree of worry or anxiety prior to the stressful surgery is best reached when the patient receives realistic information and is able to listen to and accept what is being said. This occurs when the patient experiences a moderate level of anxiety. The credibility of the practitioner is enhanced and the patient is helped to prepare for the event. The moderate-fear group in the Janis study had been better informed prior to surgery and felt worried before surgery. Fewer in this group became angry, resentful, or emotionally upset following surgery. They had time to build up psychological defenses prior to surgery. Without the "work of worrying," Janis describes a different sequence of events. There is little anticipatory fear. Thus, there is no mental rehearsal of the impending danger. Lack of rehearsal results in feelings of helplessness when the danger manifests itself. Helplessness results in feelings of disappointment in protective authorities, intense fear, anger, and "victimization"—the sense of deprivation, loss, and suffering from a stressful experience.

Unfortunately, subsequent studies have cast doubt upon Janis' emphasis on fear and anxiety. Cohen and Lazarus (1973) have emphasized the importance of coping strategies in dealing with the stress of surgery. Unlike Janis, they feel that denial would be a beneficial strategy to use when the outcome is expected to be positive. Melamed (1977), in a recent review of the preparation literature, reports some support of the Janis hypothesis, but this support is not unequivocal.

The critical ingredients in preparing for surgery still require greater clarification. A period of advanced notice with prior information and coping techniques, however, does seem to help most patients (Johnson, Dabbs, & Leventhal 1970). The amount of detail, the temporal spacing of information, and the personality disposition of the subject appear to affect the outcome (Andrew, 1970; DeLong, 1970). Copers (those who attempt to deal with stress) and those called nonspecific defenders (those who use both coping and avoiding strategies) seem to be able to accept more detailed information than avoiders (those who try to deny or avoid dealing with stress) (DeLong, 1970).

Information regarding the sensations to be experienced seems to be more effective in reducing distress than information regarding the procedures to be used (Johnson, 1973; Johnson & Leventhal, 1974). For example, Johnson, Kirchoff, and Endress (1975), in a study of cast removal, found that children exposed to a brief tape recording which included the sound of the saw and a description of the sensations of heat, flying chalk, and the like, showed less distress and resistance to the procedure compared to a group only told of the procedure or not told at all.

However, here too the results are not completely clear cut. In a study of 81 cholecystectomy patients Johnson, Rice, Fuller, and Endress (1978) attempted to compare the effects of providing either procedural information, information concerning typical sensory experience of surgery, instructions on coping behavior, the combination of coping instruction and information, or no information at all. Regardless of condition, preoperative fear level was positively associated with postoperative number of analgesic dosages, ambulation, and mood. Coping-instruction patients received fewer analgesics. For low-fear patients the effects of information on mood state were mixed. For high-fear patients sensation information led to increased positive moods, while all the intervention strategies reduced postoperative anger. The combined sensation-information and coping-instruction group yielded the shortest hospital stay, while sensation-information patients ventured forth earlier from their homes. It seems, then, that sensation information or the combination of sensation information and coping instruction led to the fastest recovery.

For a second sample of herniorraphy patients, however, these investigators found that patients who received coping instructions reported higher levels of distress on the first postoperative day than those not so instructed. Other measures did not significantly show differences. There was only a trend for sensation information patients to venture forth from home earlier. Thus, there was little support of the results obtained with the cholecystectomy patients. Johnson et al. speculate that during the first 24 to 36 hours it is too early to see the effects of intervention on surgical patient behavior. Differences require at least 48 hours to appear. The cholecystectomy sample was also predominantly female, while the herniorraphy sample was predominantly male. Perhaps sex differences require different interventions. However, it may be the results concerning type of intervention and postoperative recovery remain somewhat clouded.

Wolfer and Visintainer (1975) used a preparation technique that included both children and their parents. Forty children scheduled for surgery together with their parents were provided accurate information concerning the sequence of events, sensory experiences, role expectations, appropriate responses, previews of procedures through play techniques, and supportive care. Compared to 40 children not so prepared, the experimental group yielded less upset behavior and showed greater cooperation with procedures, less resistance to anesthetic induction, less time to first wording, less parental anxiety, and greater satisfaction with care. An age difference was obtained such that children between three and six years old compared to those seven to 14 years old showed greater upset behavior.

Melamed (1977) has also stressed the need to consider variables such as the patients' age and the timing of the advanced preparation. Less time in advance is desirable for younger children. Reducing parent feelings of anxiety has also been found to have a positive effect on the child patient.

Modeling

Modeling refers to the notion that a person can anticipate the consequences of a behavior without having to experience it personally. Bandura (1971) is of the opinion that most learning occurs via modeling rather than on a trial-and-error basis. Craig (1978) has recently done an extensive analysis of social modeling influences on pain, presenting data both from the laboratory and from the clinical setting. Melamed (1977) has summarized evidence of the potent influence of modeling processes in preparing children for surgery.

From both clinical and experimental literature it is clear that modeling is a potent method for affecting the reaction to pain. It is one way of providing advanced information as to see how someone who is similar to one can cope with the treatment without excess anxiety and stress reaction. Models should have some degree of similarity to the patient and should give a fairly realistic reaction, not supress all response (Vernon, 1974).

The laboratory paradigm can be illustrated by the study of Craig and Weiss (1971). Subjects were asked to rate the intensity of incremental shocks while observing the rating of a confederate model. In one condition, the model tolerated a great deal of shock before labeling it as painful, while in a second condition he tolerated a great deal less before terming it painful. The high-tolerance group of subjects rated as painful shock of mean intensity of 8.65 milliamperes. The control subjects yielded a mean of 6.35 milliamps. The low-tolerance group rated a mean of 2.50 milliamps as painful, some 70 percent less intense than the high-tolerance group.

A number of studies have been done in clinical settings. To prepare children for presurgical injections, Vernon (1974) exposed hospitalized patients ages four to nine years to one of two films. One group saw children receiving injections without experiencing pain or expressing emotion. A second group saw a more realistic film in which children moderately reacted to the injections. A third group did not see any film. Reactions to actual injections were rated in a hospital setting. Those who saw the unrealistic film appeared to experience most pain, while those who saw the realistic film exhibited least pain.

In dentistry several studies have demonstrated how modeling can be effective. Machen and Johnson (1974) demonstrated how preschool children (age 36 to 65 months) who were introduced to dentistry through a modeling procedure, compared to a control group, showed greater cooperative behavior over a series of three appointments that included restorative work. Ghose, Giddon, Shiere, and Fogels (1969) showed that older children can serve as models for younger siblings age four years and older. Treatment included a general oral examination, prophylaxis, radiographs, local anesthetic, and amalgam restoration over two office visits.

In an analysis of a burn-care unit, Fagerhaugh (1974) demonstrated how patients used one another as models to learn appropriate pain-control behavior. A burn-control unit is an intensive care type unit in which patients are in close contact for an extended period of time. Patients suffer excruciating pain both from the original burn and from the treatment.

Desensitization, Relaxation, and Biofeedback

Both desensitization and relaxation procedures have become widely accepted as a means of reducing anxiety and eliminating fear. Desensitization, or systematic desensitization as referred to by Wolpe (1973), involves the pairing of anxiety-arousing stimuli with relaxation or other anxiety-countering procedures. These countering procedures serve to reduce the anxiety arousal. The attempt is to substitute relaxation for arousal, one response for another, and is referred to as counterconditioning. To the extent to which anxiety and pain are related, reducing anxiety also reduces the reaction to pain.

Relaxation has been studied in a variety of laboratory settings. Folkins, Lawson, Opton, and Lazarus (1968) found that both cognitive rehearsal and relaxation were effective in reducing reaction to a stressor. Bobey and Davidson (1970) found that relaxation increased pain tolerance to radiant heat and pressure algometer stimulation.

Clinically, Gessel and Adlerman (1971) have taught relaxation to MPD patients. MPD patients who have facial pain because of overactivity of the masticatory muscles appear to have higher chronic levels of muscle tension. Jacobsonian relaxation was taught in from one to 27 sessions. Six out of 11 patients, those with an absence of depression, showed good results. Patients with depression were not helped.

Sherman, Gall, and Gormly (1979) reported that 14 out of 16 phantom limb patients were either completely or partially relieved from pain following a combined treatment of reassurance, progressive muscle relaxation, and biofeedback from the stump and forehead. Follow-up studies of up to three years indicated that the treatment remained effective.

Relaxation can be an effective procedure for increasing pain tolerance. However, experimental results indicate that it is not *always* an effective procedure (cf. Lehrer, 1972). The conditions under which it should optimally affect pain reaction must still be clarified. A better understanding of how anxiety affects pain will probably also clarify the role of relaxation.

Of course, in desensitization situations it is not necessary to use only relaxation. Ayer (1973), using emotive imagery to counter fear of injection, taught children to picture a yapping dog. Injections were given while children were imagining the yapping dog. Tolerance for injections was thereby increased.

Weisenberg and Epstein (1973) described a variety of fear-reducing techniques used to permit the dentist to treat a 26-month-old girl who had resisted treatment even after receiving high dosages of premedication. Techniques included brief desensitization, forced exposure (child physically placed in chair), reward for staying in the chair, modeling (observing her older sister), and rehearsal (playing dentist at home). Use of these procedures in three brief (15-minute) appointments avoided treatment via general anesthesia, always an added, unnecessary risk.

Biofeedback procedures represent a technological advance that allows for shortening the amount of time necessary to learn relaxation as well as control of other bodily functions. For example, in a laboratory experiment, Green, Walter, Green, and Murphy (1969) found that seven out of 21 subjects were able to achieve a very high level of muscle relaxation in less than 20 minutes of a single session when they were provided with EMG feedback. Budzynski and Stoyva (1969) also found that even in a single session, mean EMG levels for a control group ran 70 percent above those of their experimental group.

Chronic muscle tension is associated with clinical pain. Examples include tension or muscle contraction headache (Budzynski, Stoyva, Adler, & Mullaney, 1973) as well as MPD syndrome (Laskin, 1969). Interestingly, Fowler and Kraft (1973) have demonstrated that patients and normals are not able to estimate levels of muscle tension accurately. Through EMG biofeedback training, patients become aware of their ability to control muscle tension.

Temperative feedback has also been used in the treatment of migraine headache. Patients are taught to influence blood circulation patterns by raising peripheral hand temperature. As a consequence they reduce the frequency of migraine headache episodes even though they cannot abort an attack once it has started (Stroebel & Glueck, 1976).

Budzynski et al. (1973) conducted a controlled long-term study of muscle-contraction headache patients. To establish a baseline all patients charted headaches for two weeks. The 18 patients were divided into three groups. Group A patients received biofeedback training, Group B received pseudofeedback, and Group C patients charted but received no feedback. Sixteen biofeedback training sessions, two per week were provided. Home-training exercises were also given. Patients were followed up for three months. Baseline muscle-tension ratings were found to be double those obtained from nonheadache subjects. Following training Group A patients differed significantly from Group B. Group A produced lower levels of muscle tension. At three-month follow-up these differences remained. Four of six Group A patients showed a significant decline in headache frequency with only one out of six in Group B and none in Group C.

Patients appeared to pass through several stages in training. During stage 1 the patient is unable to prevent or abort a headache. The patient gradually learns to relax somewhat but still cannot abort a headache. With further training the patient becomes increasingly aware of tension and is able to abort light-to-moderate headaches. In the last stage patients seem to relax automatically without a conscious effort. A change in lifestyle is produced.

Philips (1977) was able to support Budzynski et al. (1973) in that biofeedback training lowered muscle tension. However, Philips found that biofeedback produced a decrement in headache intensity but not in frequency. Thus, reducing muscle tension per se may not be adequate to effect a change in headache frequency. Other changes appear to be necessary.

Perhaps Philips' patients did not acquire a sense of control. As Stroebel and Glueck (1973) indicate, this feeling of control may be the most important ingredient in biofeedback. Melzack and Perry (1975) similarily, in a controlled study of chronic-pain patients who were provided alpha training, found that the increase in alpha production alone was not adequate to affect pain levels. What was needed was a sense of control.

Gessel (1975) reported the successful treatment of 15 out of 23 MPD patients using EMG feedback. Surface electrodes were attached over the temporalis and masseter areas on the affected side. Sessions lasted 30 minutes. Those who failed to achieve relief of symptoms via biofeedback were successfully treated with tricyclic antidepressant medication. Although this latter group of patients had been able to continue with their principal day-to-day activities, they had shown some degree of clinical depression.

Biofeedback can be used to teach relaxation to be used during desensitization of phobia, as shown by Weisenberg and Stilwell (1974) with dental phobics. If only imagery is used during desensitization, actual performance with real stimuli should be part of the treatment. As Bandura (1977) has suggested, desensitization via imagery reduces autonomic reactions to imagined threats but less so to real threats. It is only when imagination is followed by actual performance desensitization that the fear is eliminated. Thus, dental treatment following an imagined desensitization procedure would be of the utmost importance in eliminating a dental fear to achieve what Bandura refers to as a sense of self-efficacy, that is, the belief that the patient has the ability to remain calm during the dental procedure.

Combined Strategies

Most inpatient pain units do not rely upon only one technique. In one low-back pain program, emphasis is placed upon providing the patient with a sense of responsibility and control to replace a feeling of helplessness. The program includes use of biofeedback, psychotherapy, assertion training, family and sex counseling, individualized exercise programs, vocational counseling, systematic reinforcement for nondisability behavior, and an overall therapeutic milieu (Arsham, 1975).

In Sternbach's program (1974) a treatment contract is negotiated. The patient is asked if he is willing to work to reduce his pain. If so, realistic pain-free goals are worked out. Specific behavioral tasks are spelled out in the contract for both the patient and the provider. The patient becomes an active partner in the treatment. Attention and praise are provided by staff for goal-directed activities, and pain behaviors are ignored. Analgesics are provided on a time basis rather than demand. Antidepressant and tranquilizer medication is used where appropriate. Group therapy is also provided to permit patients to express their concerns, to provide them feedback, and to create an espirit de corps and a sense of not being alone. The misuse of pain as a weapon is often brought out in group therapy. The surgeon is invited to group therapy sessions. He provides critical input to increase the acceptance of the program by explanation of what surgery can or cannot accomplish. Patients are able to realize that surgery is not the only answer to their problems. The average patient is an inpatient for six weeks.

Fordyce's (1976) program is the one most others have used as a prototype. Techniques such as stimulation or biofeedback are used for respondent pain. Operant techniques are used to extinguish pain behaviors such as moans, requests for medication, or lack of physical activity because of pain. Attention is given for health-related activity; inattention for pain behavior. Well-behaviors including future activities are planned. Medication is managed to reduce or eliminate addiction. A time-contingent rather than complaint-contingent regimen is used in which the active ingredient is masked. The goal is to reduce the amount of active ingredient as treatment progresses. A carefully planned exercise program is initiated. Exercise is viewed as a well-behavior in its own right as well as a building block to future behaviors. Rest and attention are used as reinforcers for meeting exercise quota and are withheld for failure to meet the quota. A variety of graphs and records is kept to provide patients with feedback on progress. The spouse or family members are also trained. They are made aware of how they reinforce pain behaviors and are asked to become partners in reinforcing well-behaviors.

There is great concern attached to generalization of well-behaviors beyond the hospital environment. This is done by teaching the patient self-control and self-reinforcement. The patient's natural environment is also programmed. New behaviors and goals are established. Patients are given passes to go home during treatment so that they can try out newly established behaviors in natural environments. Following inpatient discharge, patients continue to come for treatment on a gradually reduced basis.

Long-term follow-up studies indicate that these combined programs can be effective in dealing with chronic pain (Fordyce, Fowler, Lehmann, DeLateur, Sand, & Trieschmann, 1973; Newman, Seres, Yospe, & Garlington, 1978; Ignelzi, Sternbach, & Timmermans, 1977). What remains unclear in these programs is just what the active ingredients are. Must they be conducted only on an inpatient basis and must they be so long?

Clinical Prescription

The direction of treatment of pain patients is determined by the type of problem involved. Especially important would be the time dimension. Is the patient anticipating future treatment that is painful? Is the patient currently suffering from pain of recent origin? Is the patient suffering from pain of a chronic nature? Choice of treatment would differ depending upon the answers to these questions.

It is desirable to obtain as complete a history and description of the pain problem as is possible. The questions mentioned in the section on assessment would be included here. It is extremely important to have a medical work-up based upon a thorough physical examination for acute-pain patients and especially for pain of a chronic nature. Many patients can be more readily given assurance by the psychologist as to the appropriateness of behavioral intervention once a physician has indicated the limitations of medical intervention. Of course, a more important consideration would be the provision of optimal treatment. It would be a mistake to provide behavioral treatment when medical or surgical treatment is most appropriate. Often, too, medication is used hand in hand with behavioral intervention.

An assessment that is valuable in deciding upon a treatment strategy is determining the nature of the pain reaction. Is the reaction more likely associated with anxiety and therefore best dealt with using an anxiety-relieving strategy or is the pain reaction at a stage where it is more likely characterized by depression and helplessness?

What function does the pain serve? Included here would be an assessment of the extent to which the pain reaction can be characterized as respondent or operant in nature.

The psychologist will have to decide whether treatment must be done on an inpatient basis or whether it can be done as an outpatient. Part of the decision would be based upon factors such as the need for multidisciplinary intervention, for instance, physician, physical, occupational therapist, readiness on the part of family members to assume responsibility, the need of specialized equipment, the need for a therapeutic milieu, and of course insurance or other financial backing.

Much of the equipment that psychologists use would be readily available. Most psychologists easily have access to routine psychological examinations. With a minimal charge it is possible to obtain computerized scoring and interpretation of MMPI records. Relaxation tapes are commercially available, and it requires only a cassette tape recorder to produce a self-made tape that patients can take home for their own use.

Biofeedback equipment has tended to become somewhat more sophisticated and expensive in recent years. Many companies currently conduct training programs to teach the use of their equipment. A psychologist might decide whether or not it is worthwhile to purchase his or her own equipment based upon the number of patients he or she sees. EMG and temperature feedback handle many of the pain problems for which biofeedback is appropriate.

Case Reports

Two brief representative cases will be presented.

Patient A

Hackett (1967) has described the type of treatment that can occur when behavioral intervention and techniques are ignored. It also shows the type of challenge that can be thrown at psychologists.

A man was involved in a motorcycle accident on the way to his wedding in which he sustained damage to his brachial plexis. Shortly after the accident the patient's arm was amputated. The patient began immediately to suffer from phantom limb pain. The patient then underwent a series of operations to deal with his pain. Included were three neurectomies, two rhizotomies, a cardotomy, and a mesencephalic tractotomy. No change occurred in the pain. Other treatments followed including tranquilizers, antidepressants, hypnosis, psychotherapy, electric shock therapy, radiofrequency leucotomy, bilateral lesions in the frontal white matter, and thalamic implants of electrodes, one of which penetrated the midbrain putting the patient in a coma for two weeks. When the patient awoke the pain remained unchanged. Four years later the patient died of an unrelated infection. Hackett speculates and wonders what the patient's life would have been like had treatment been undertaken without resort to all the surgery. Perhaps with a proper therapeutic milieu the patient would have learned to adjust and function despite his pain.

Patient B

In contrast to patient A, Fordyce, Fowler, and DeLateur (1968) describe a different outcome based upon application of their operant approach.

The patient is described as a 37-year-old, married woman with one child complaining of low back pain of 18 years' duration. The pain was described as continuous in nature and was exacerbated by physical activity. The patient was unable to remain active for more than 20 minutes at a time. When pain episodes occurred, the patient ceased all activity, reclined, and cried until the pain became less intense. These episodes produced much solicitous behavior from the patient's husband. The patient had undergone four different surgeries without success. Evaluation revealed no neurologic deficit or root irritation.

The pain was treated as operant in nature. The treatment plan was designed to reduce pain behavior and to increase the patient's general level of activity.The patient's medication regimen was shifted to a time-contingent program. No medication was given for complaints of pain. The medication itself was masked, and over a 40-day period the narcotic content was reduced and then deleted altogether. All treatment staff were unresponsive to complaints of pain and discomfort. Activity other than lying in bed produced a friendly and social response by staff. Daily increases in activity produced staff praise. The patient was given occupational therapy in which rest was used as a reinforcer for work at a loom making close-weave cloth. The activity required a considerable amount of physical activity and especially sitting, a position described as most painful. A program was developed to increase walking behavior where rest, social attention, praise, and the patient's own records were used as reinforcers. The patient's husband was also seen for at least one hour per week. The program was described and his cooperation obtained. The husband was taught how to be nonresponsive to pain behavior and how to reinforce well-behavior. The patient was permitted to visit home on passes. Activities for these passes were planned. The patient was given eight weeks of inpatient care and 23 weeks of outpatient care. At the end of outpatient care, the patient was taking driving lessons and was ready to be independently mobile.

Ethical and Legal Considerations

Pain control can involve several ethical legal considerations. The psychologist most often will have to work hand in hand with the physician.

In terms of treatment strategy, the psychologist might be the team leader. Yet, legally, it often is the physician who is recognized as the authority. This occurs whenever medication is involved and, depending upon the geographical area, for the provision of insurance coverage.

Pain control involves an active role on the part of the patient. There are numerous placebo components to the treatment as well as use of external reinforcers to shape behavior. It is important that patients be informed of the treatment program and agree to it. There is no intention to fool or manipulate the patient without his or her consent. When medications are masked and the contents are changed or if saline injections are used, the patient may not know of the contents of the specific injection, but he or she should know in advance that this might occur.

Several clinicians use pain stimuli as routine measurement of pain intensity. Sternbach (1978b) has pointed out the need to consider carefully the justification of inflicting pain on a person who is already suffering. The patient must also be asked to agree. Sterbach recommends that if pain is to be inflicted that it be for the benefit of the patient and not for the clinical investigator.

In general, the problem of data collection and control groups must be carefully considered. How can patients be assigned to a control situation? When is delaying treatment ethical? Can less than adequate treatment be used to test specific ingredients? These issues are not easily answered.

A societal issue that will need revision will be the use of compensation for injury. Neal (1978) and others have raised the issue of the politics of pain. At present the system rewards patients for adopting sick-behavior. It would be most desirable if compensation would reward patients for efforts at rehabilitation. This would require changes in the law as presently constituted.

Suggestions for Clinical and Experimental Research

The recognition that psychologists have a major contribution to make in pain control is a recent development. There are many areas that require greater clarification and expansion. Psychologists are being asked questions for which they do not have answers based upon solid evidence. They rely mostly upon clinical intuition. One such frequent question is, "Will this patient be helped by surgery or will the patient complain of pain even after the surgery?"

At present most psychologists have learned how to treat pain patients based upon their own clinical experiences. Most graduate programs have not developed training programs to prepare psychologists to deal with problems of pain or with many other problems having a significant physical component. Routine clinical assessment is often not adequate for the pain patient. Greater standardization of appropriate assessment procedures would greatly benefit patient care.

Laboratory study has contributed a great deal to pain control. However, one of its great limitations is the lack of paradigms that are comparable to chronic pain. As work over the past several years has shown, chronic- and acute-pain control are not the same. A laboratory paradigm for chronic pain is badly needed.

Another area that has been almost completely ignored is the organizational arrangement of health care delivery and its influence on pain control. This would include such things as the arrangement of the surgical ward and procedures for scheduling surgery as well as the differences between inpatient and outpatient care of chronic-pain patients. It is also possible to ask questions concerning such things as the optimal arrangement of offices—dentists or services, private versus shared labor rooms.

As indicated earlier, given the body's own built-in pain-control system there is a clear challenge given to psychologists. It should be possible to develop the behavioral techniques to stimulate the body's own built-in pain-control system. Ideally, this would be the best system of pain control. It is up to psychology, however, to demonstrate this.

Summary

Pain is a complex phenomenon that includes both sensory and motivational-emotional components. Pain is not synonymous with nociceptive stimulation or injury. The pain patient may present with absence of clear physiologically defined problems and with few of the classically defined psychopathological symptoms. Yet the patient seems to be suffering greatly. Psychologists have been able to contribute a great deal to the alleviation of patient suffering by the application of behavioral techniques and strategies. Some of these techniques are designed to deal with anxiety, others to deal with depression and helplessness.

Three nonbehavioral approaches have been described theoretically: (1) psychophysiological, (2) neurohumoral, and (3) psychiatric. Psychophysiological theories are based upon the structure of the nervous system. A controversial but most influential recent theory is the gate-control theory of pain (Melzack & Wall, 1965, 1970). The theory proposes a gating mechanism in the spinal cord that is based upon a balance of input from small and large fibers. Small fibers open the gate, whereas large fibers close it and prevent further transmission of the pain stimulus. Central inputs can also open or close the gate. In chronic pain, central inputs take on the more important role in pain perception. Although the exact gating mechanism remains a source of controversy, the basic conceptual divisions into sensory and motivational components have gained widespread acceptance. This theory readily accommodates psychological variables and their effect upon pain perception.

Neurohumoral approaches relate to the recent findings of an endogenous system of pain control, the association of this system with opiate-binding, and the production of the body's own morphine-like substances called endorphins. These studies provide a neurohumoral basis for psychological intervention.

Psychiatrically oriented theories have grown out of more traditional approaches that have tried to account for reactions to chronic pain. Emphasis has been placed upon the interpersonal aspects of pain (Engel, 1959) as well as upon the use of pain as a means of communicating (Szasz, 1955). Each approach has contributed something of value. However, investigators such as Merskey and Spear (1967) have found them to be inadequate to explain pain phenomena even though they add valuable insights.

Pilowsky and Spence (1976a) have developed the concept of abnormal illness behavior as a means of dealing with much of the ambiguity of traditional nosology. For chronic-pain patients who do not respond to conventional treatment, abnormal illness behavior is reflected by the greater conviction of the presence of disease, greater somatic preoccupation, and lesser likelihood of acceptance of reassurance by the doctor.

Behavioral approaches have stressed the consequences of pain as seen in the individual with pain. Especially with chronic pain, patients are placed into a situation that leads to major changes in habits and lifestyle. Sick-behaviors tend to be reinforced and well-behaviors are often discouraged. Habituation or addiction to medication become major hurdles that help perpetuate pain behavior. Behavioral approaches are aimed at extinguishing sick-behaviors and establishing well-behaviors that generalize beyond the treatment setting.

Assessment is an extremely important aspect of pain control. It can provide an indication as to which components of pain reaction must be dealt with as well as a baseline for evaluating effectiveness of the intervention. Several procedures such as magnitude estimation and signal-detection theory have been developed as means of describing the different components of pain.

In assessing patient pain, it is important to describe the locus of the pain, its qualities, its temporal characteristics, and those factors that reduce the pain or make it worse. It is also important to distinguish between the patient who currently is not suffering from pain but is anticipating pain from the patient who is currently suffering from acute pain and from the patient who is suffering from chronic pain of at least six months' duration.

A variety of routine psychological tests, such as the MMPI or STAI, have been used in assessing pain patients. From a behavioral view, scores on personality tests are viewed as describing high- or low-frequency behavior rather than being an indication that an individual possesses a given personality.

A variety of matching techniques and verbal measures have been designed to assess pain. Descriptor scales such as the McGill Pain Questionnaire (Melzack, 1975) categorize pain terms into (1) sensory quality descriptors, (2) affective quality descriptors, and (3) evaluative terms. Visual analog scales have been used in place of verbal scales. They are especially appropriate in places where language presents a barrier.

Behavioral assessments of chronic pain emphasize the extent to which pain reactions are respondent (based upon antecedents) or operant (based upon consequences) in nature. What good things happen and what bad things do not happen when pain behavior occurs? Questions are asked concerning the typical patient day, medications taken, physical activity, and the reactions of others in the patient's environment when he or she is in pain. Pain behavior reinforcers, significant others, and potential well-behavior reinforcers are identified.

A number of intervention strategies have been described to reduce pain. When assessing the variety of procedures, it is important to realize that many of the data supporting their effectiveness are derived from laboratory rather than clinical study. The laboratory offers superior opportunity for control. However, it does not permit an assessment of an individual in pathological pain with its implied threat of disfigurement or death. Clinical assessments are made difficult in that treatments often are done in combination, thus making it difficult to separate the vital ingredients that contribute to outcome.

A number of cognitive strategies have been described for reducing pain. These have been shown to be effective for reducing suffering and increasing pain tolerance, especially when anxiety is a major contributor and when the patient is capable of learning to cope. Here most support for effectiveness is laboratory-derived despite the wealth of anecdotal evidence since ancient times.

Placebo and suggestion, as many practitioners know, can be very effective for increasing pain tolerance. Placebos of course need not be thought of only as inert drugs. Some would view as placebo any strategy that produces a positive expectation regarding outcome so that it encourages and permits the patient to act to help himself. Biofeedback is one example.

Hypnosis has strong backing from controlled laboratory assessment. Most clinical reports consist of case histories showing effectiveness rather than controlled outcome studies. Hypnosis has been shown to be more than just a placebo. It appears to be quite effective for hypnotizable subjects with the worst side-effect being that it does not work.

Perceived control has been used to increase pain tolerance. Although the exact definition is somewhat ambiguous, perceived control appears to be an important ingredient in chronic-pain treatment.

Advanced preparation for surgery has been credited with reducing postoperative analgesic requirements and for earlier hospital discharge. Important components of the preparation are the descriptions of the sensations to be experienced as well as some possible coping strategies. Timing of the preparation is important and should allow for differences in age and in ability to utilize the information effectively.

Relaxation, desensitization, and biofeedback have all been used successfully in achieving pain control. Biofeedback represents a technological advance for teaching relaxation. It has been used successfully for shortening the time to teach relaxation, to teach specific muscle relaxation such as in tension headache, and to change peripheral circulation as with migraine patients.

Modeling is an approach for advanced preparation for treatment as well as an approach for teaching social norms regarding pain expression. Modeling has strong support for effectiveness from both laboratory and clinical settings. It can be effective with both children and adults.

Combined strategies have been used mainly in the treatment of chronic pain, especially of an operant nature. Fordyce's (1976) program has been the one most often copied. The program is geared toward extinguishing pain behavior and establishing well-behavior. The major ingredients include lack of attention to pain behaviors and a great deal of attention to positive behaviors such as activity, including walking, planned excercises, and other out-of-bed behaviors. Medications are given on a time basis rather than on demand, with a gradual reduction of narcotic content. Free-time planning of a realistic nature is an important part of treatment. Significant others in the patient's family are also included in the treatment while the patient is in the hospital as well as during a series of planned passes home. Care is taken to assure that generalization of gains continue after the patient returns to his home setting.

Ethically and legally a number of issues have been identified. Included among them would be the need for informed consent on the part of the patient to take part in treatment as well as in clinic research. It appears also that the present system of compensation for disability needs revision so that in the future it will encourage well-behavior rather than the continuation of sick-behavior.

A number of avenues of future research have been identified. These include studies dealing with the effects of the health care delivery system and its organization on pain perception. The recent unlocking of an endogenous pain-control system is an open challenge to psychologists to find behavioral techniques to actuate this powerful system. Ultimately, this could be the preferred method of pain control yielding the fewest side effects.

References

Andrew, J. M. Recovery from surgery with and without preparatory instruction for three coping styles. *Journal of Personality and Social Psychology*, 1970, *15*, 223–226.

Arsham, D. S. *A successful treatment program for chronic backpain patients*. Symposium presented at the meeting of the American Psychological Association, 1975.

Averill, J. R. Personal control over aversive stimuli and its relationship to stress. *Psychological Bulletin*, 1973, *80*, 286–303.

Ayer, W. A. Use of visual imagery in needle phobic children. *Journal of Dentistry for Children*, 1973, *40*, 41–43.

Baldwin, D. C. Jr., & Barnes, M. L. The psychological value of a presurgical waiting period in the preparation of children for dental extraction. *Transactions of the European Orthodontic Society*, 1966, 1–12.

Bandura, A. *Principles of behavior modification*. New York: Holt, Rhinehart & Winston, 1969.

Bandura, A. Analysis of modeling processes. In A. Bandura (Ed.), *Psychological modeling*. Chicago, Ill.: Aldine-Atherton, 1971.

Bandura, A. Self-efficiency: Toward a unifying theory of behavioral change. *Psychological Review*, 1977, *84*, 191–215.

Barber, T. X., & Hahn, K. W. Jr. Physiological and subjective responses to pain producing stimulation under hypnotically-suggested and waking-imaged "analgesia." *Journal of Abnormal and Social Psychology*, 1962, 55, 411–418.

Beecher, H. K. *Measurement of subjective responses: Quantitative effects of drugs*. New York: Oxford University Press, 1959.

Beecher, H. K. Pain, placebos and physicians. *The Practitioner*, 1962, *189*, 141–155.

Beecher, H. K. Quantification of the subjective pain experience. *Proceedings of the American Psychopathological Association*, 1963, *53*, 111–128.

Beecher, H. K. The placebo effects as a non-specific force surrounding disease and the treatment of disease. In R. Jansen, A. D. Keidel, A. Herz, C. Steichele, J. P. Payne, & R. A. P. Burt (Eds.), *Pain: Basic principles, pharmacology, therapy*. Stuttgart: Georg Thieme Publishers, 1972.

Billars, K. S. You have pain? I think this will help. *American Journal of Nursing*, 1970, *70*, 2143–2145.

Blitz, B., & Dinnerstein, A. J. Role of attentional focus in pain perception: Manipulation of response to noxious stimulation by instructions. *Journal of Abnormal Psychology*, 1971, *77*, 42–45.

Bobey, J. J., & Davidson, P. O. Psychological factors affecting pain tolerance.

Journal of Psychosomatic Research, 1970, *14,* 371–376.

Bowers, K. S. Pain, anxiety and perceived control. *Journal of Consulting and Clincal Psychology,* 1968, *32,* 596–602.

Brena, S. F. (Eds.). *Chronic pain: America's hidden epidemic: Behavior modification as an alternative to drugs and surgery*. New York: Atheneum/SMI 1978.

Budzynski, T. H., Stoyva, J. M., Adler, C. S., & Mullaney, D. S. EMG Biofeedback and tension headache: A controlled outcome study. *Psychosomatic Medicine,* 1973, *35,* 484–496.

Budzynski, T. H., Stoyva, J. M., Adler, C. S., & Mullaney, D. S. EMG Biofeedback and tension headache: A controlled outcome study. *Psychosomatic Medicine,* 1973, *35,* 484–496.

Cannon, J. T., Liebeskind, J. C., & Frenk, H. Neural and neurochemical mechanisms of pain inhibition. In R. A. Sternbach (Ed.) *The psychology of pain*. New York: Raven Press, 1978.

Chapman, C. R. Psychological aspects of pain patient treatment. *Archives of Surgery,* 1977, *112,* 767–772.

Chapman, C. R. Pain: The perception of noxious events. In R. A. Sternbach (Ed.), *The psychology of pain*. New York: Raven Press, 1978.

Chaves, J. F., and Barber, T. X. Hypnotism and surgical pain. In T. X. Barber, N. P. Spanos, & J. F. Chaves (Eds.), *Hypnosis, imagination and human potentialities*. New York: Pergamon Press, 1974.(a)

Chaves, J. F., & Barber, T. X. Cognitive strategies, experimenter modeling and expectation in the attenuation of pain. *Journal of Abnormal Psychology,* 1974, *83,* 356–363.(b)

Clark, W. C. Pain sensitivity and the report of pain: An introduction to sensory decision theory. *Anesthesiology,* 1974, *40,* 272–287.

Cohen, F., & Lazarus, R. S. Active coping processes, coping dispositions, and recovery from surgery. *Psychosomatic Medicine,* 1973, *35,* 375–389.

Corah, N. L. Development of a dental anxiety scale. *Journal of Dental Research,* 1969, *48,* 596.

Corah, N. L. Effect of perceived control on stress reduction in pedodontic patients. *Journal of Dental Research,* 1973, *52,* 1261–1264.

Craig, K. D. Social modeling influences on pain. In R. A. Sternbach (Ed.), *The psychological pain*. New York: Raven Presss, 1978.

Craig, K. D., & Weiss, S. M. Vicarious influences on pain-threshold determinations. *Journal of Personality and Social Psychology,* 1971, *19,* 53–59.

Crasilneck, H. B., & Hall, J. A. Clinical hypnosis in problems of pain. *American Journal of Clinical Hypnosis,* 1973, *15,* 153–160.

Crockett, D. J., Prkachin, K. M., & Craig, K. D. Factors of the language of pain in patient and volunteer groups. *Pain,* 1977, *4,* 175–182.

Dehan, H., & Cambier, J. Congenital indifferences to pain and endogenous morphine-like system. *Pain Abstracts: Second World Congress on Pain,* 1978, p. 15.

DeLong, R. D. *Individual differences in patterns of anxiety arousal, stress-relevant information and recovery from surgery*. Unpublished doctoral dissertation, University of California, Los Angeles, 1970.

Dubuisson, D., & Melzack, R. Classification of clinical pain descriptions by multiple group discriminant analysis. *Experimental Neurology*, 1976, *51*, 480–487.

Egbert, L. D., Battit, G. E., Welch, C. E., & Bartlett, M. D. Reduction of postopertive pain by encouragement and instruction of patients. *The New England Journal of Medicine*, 1964, *270*, 825–827.

Engel, G. L. "Psychogenic" pain and the pain-prone patient. *American Journal of Medicine*, 1959, *26*, 899–918.

Evans, F. J. Suggestibility in the normal waking state. *Psychological Bulletin*, 1967, *67*, 114–129.

Evans, F. J. Placebo analgesia: Suggestion, anxiety and the doctor–patient relationship. Paper presented at the annual meeting of the American Psychosomatic Society, Philadelphia, Pa. 1974.(a)

Evans, F. J. The placebo response in pain reduction. In J. J. Bonica (Ed.), *Advances in neurology: International symposium on pain* (Vol. 4). New York: Raven Press, 1974.(b)

Fagerhaugh, S. Y. Pain expression and control on a burn care unit. *Nursing Outlook*, 1974, *22*, 645–650.

Feather, B. W., Chapman, C. R., & Fisher, S. B. The effect of a placebo on the perception of painful radiant heat stimuli. *Psychosomatic Medicine*, 1972, *34*, 290–294.

Folkins, C. H., Lawson, K. D., Opton, E. M. Jr., & Lazarus, R. S. Desensitization and experimental reduction of threat. *Journal of Abnormal Psychology*, 1968, *73*, 100–113.

Fordyce, W. E. *Behavioral methods for chronic pain and illness*. St. Louis: C. V. Mosby, Co., 1976.

Fordyce, W. E. Learning processes in pain. In R. A. Sternbach (Ed.), *The psychology of pain*. New York: Raven Press, 1978.

Fordyce, W. E., Fowler, R. S., & DeLateur, B. An application of behavior modification technique to a problem of chronic pain. *Behavior Research and Therapy*, 1968, *6*, 105–107.

Fordyce, W. E., Fowler, R. S., Lehmann, J. F., DeLateur, B. J., Sand, P. L., & Trieschmann, R. B. Operant conditioning in the treatment of chronic pain. *Archives of Physical Medicine and Rehabilitation*, 1973, *54*, 399–408.

Fowler, R. S., & Kraft, G. H. Tension peception in patients having pain associated with chronic muscle tension. *Archives of Physical Medicine and Rehabilitation*, 1973, *55*, 28–30.

Gale, E. N. Fears of the dental situation. *Journal of Dental Research*, 1972, *51*, 964–966.

Gessel, A. H. Electromyographic biofeedback and tricyclic antidepressants in myofascial pain-dysfunction syndrome: psychological predictors of outcome. *Journal of the American Dental Association*, 1975, *91*, 1048–1052.

Gessel, A. H., & Alderman, M. M. Management of myofascial pain dysfunction syndrome of the temporomandibular joint by tension control training. *Psychosomatics*, 1971, *12*, 302–309.

Ghose, L. J., Giddon, D. B., Shiere, F. R., & Fogels, H. R. Evaluation of sibling support. *Journal of Dentistry for Children*, 1969, *36*, 35–40, 49.

Goodman, P., Greene, C. S., & Laskin, D. M. Response of patients with myofascial pain-dysfunction syndrome to mock equilibration. *Journal of the American Dental Association*, 1976, *92*, 755–758.

Green E. E., Walter, E. D., Green, A. M., & Murphy, G. Feedback technique for deep relaxation. *Psychophysiology*, 1969, *6*, 371–377.

Greene, C. S., & Laskin, D. M. Long-term evaluations of conservative treatment for myofascial pain-dysfunction syndrome. *Journal of the American Dental Association*, 1974, *89*, 1365–1368.

Greene, R. J., & Reyher, J. Pain tolerance in hypnotic analgesia and imagination states. *Journal of Abnormal Psychology*, 1972, *79*, 29–38.

Hackett, T. P. The surgeon and the difficult pain problem. *International Psychiatry Clinics*, 1967, *4*, 179–188.

Hilgard, E. R. A neodissociation interpretation of pain reduction in hypnosis. *Psychological Review*, 1973, *80*, 396–406.

Hilgard, E. R., & Hilgard, J. R. *Hypnosis in the relief of pain*. Los Altos, Calif.: William Kaufman, 1975.

Hughes, J., Smith, T. W., Kosterlitz, H. W., Fothergill, L. A., Morgan, B. A., & Morris, H. R. Identification of two related pentapeptides from the brain with potent opiate agonist activity. *Nature*, 1975, *258*, 577–579.

IASP Subcommittee on Taxonomy. Pain terms: A list with definitions and notes on usage. *Pain*, 1979, *6*, 249–252.

Iggo, A. Critical remarks on the gate control theory. In R. Janzen et al. (Eds.), *Pain: Basic principles, pharmacology, therapy*. Stuttgart: Georg Thieme Publishers, 1972.

Ignelzi, R. J., Sternbach, R. A., & Timmermans, G. The pain ward follow-up analysis. *Pain*, 1977, 277–280.

Isler, C. For severe pain, self-medication on demand. *RN*, 1975, 51–57.

Jacoby, J. D. Statistical report on general practice hypnodontics: Tape-recorder conditioning. *Journal of Clinical and Experimental Hypnosis*, 1960, *8*, 115–119.

Janis, I. L. *Psychological stress*. New York: John Wiley and Sons, 1958.

Johnson, J. E. Effects of accurate expectations about sensations on sensory and distress components of pain. *Journal of Personality and Social Psychology*, 1973, *27*, 261–275.

Johnson, J. E., Dabbs, J. M., & Leventhal, H. Psychosocial factors in the welfare of surgical patients. *Nursing Research*, 1970, *19*, 18–29.

Johnson, J. E., Kirchoff, K. T., & Endress, M. P. Deferring children's distress behavior during orthopedic cast removal. *Nursing Research*, 1975, *75*, 404–410.

Johnson, J. E., & Leventhal, H. Effects of accurate expectations and behavioral instructions on reactions during a noxious medical examination. *Journal of Personality and Social Psychology*, 1974, *29*, 710–718.

Johnson, J. E.. Rice, V. H., Fuller, S. S., & Endress, M. P. Sensory information, instruction in a coping strategy, and recovery from surgery. *Research in Nursing and Health*, 1978, *1*, 4–17.

Kanfer, F., & Goldfoot, D. Self-control and tolerance of noxious stimulation. *Psychological Reports*, 1966, *18*, 79–85.

Keeri-Szanto, M. Drugs or drums: What relieves postoperative pain? *Pain*, 1979, *6*, 217–230.

Kroger, W. S., & Fezler, W. D. *Hypnosis and behavior modification: Imagery conditioning*. Philadelphia: J. B Lippincott, 1976.

Laskin, D. M. Etiology of the pain-dysfunction syndrome. *Journal of the American Dental Association*, 1969, *79*, 147–153.

Laskin, D. M., & Greene, C. S. Influence of the doctor–patient relationship on placebo therapy for patients with myofascial pain-dysfunction (MPD) syndrome. *Journal of the American Dental Association*, 1972, *85*, 892–894.

Lehrer, P. M. Physiological effects of relaxation in a double-blind analogue of desensitization. *Behavioral Therapy*, 1972, *3*, 193–208.

Levine, J. D., Gordon, N. C., & Fields, H. L. Evidence that the analgesic effects of placebo is mediated by endorphins. *Pain Abstracts: Second World Congress on Pain*, 1978, p. 18.

Libeskind, J. C., Mayer, D. J., & Akil, H. Central mechanism of pain inhibition: Studies of analgesia from focal brain stimulation. In J. J. Bonica (Ed.), *Advances in neurology: International symposium on pain* (Vol. 4). New York: Raven Press, 1974.

Libeskind, J. M., & Paul, L. A. Psychological and physiological mechanisms of pain. *Annual Review of Psychology*, 1978, *28*, 41–60.

Loeser, J. D., & Ward, A. A. Jr. Some effects of deafferentation on neurons of the cat spinal cord. *Archives of Neurology* (Chicago), 1967, *17*, 629–636.

Machen, J. R., & Johnson, R. Desensitization, model learning and the dental behavior of children. *Journal of Dental Research*, 1974, *53*, 83–87.

Mayer, D. J., Price, D. D., Barber, J., & Raffi, A. Acupuncture analgesia: Evidence for activation of a pain inhibitory system as a mechanism of action. In J. J. Bonica & D. Albe-Fessard (Eds.), *Advances in pain research and therapy* (Vol. 1). New York: Raven Press, 1976.

McGlashen, T. H., Evans, F. J., & Orne, M. T. The nature of hypnotic analgesia and placebo response to experimental pain. *Psychosomatic Medicine*, 1969, *31*, 227–246.

Meichenbaum, D., & Turk, D. The cognitive-behavioral management of anxiety, anger and pain. In P. O. Davidson (Ed.), *The behavioral management of anxiety, depression and pain*. New York: Brunner/Mazel, 1976.

Melamed, B. G. Psychological preparation for hospitalization. In S. Rachman (Ed.), *Contributions to medical psychology* (Vol. 1). Oxford, England: Pergamon Press, 1977.

Melamed, B. G., & Siegel, L. J. Reduction of anxiety in children facing surgery by modeling. *Journal of Consulting and Clinical Psychology*, 1975, *43*, 511–521.

Melzack, R. The McGill Pain Questionnaire: Major properties and scoring methods. *Pain*, 1975, *1*, 277–299.

Melzack, R., & Dennis, S. G. Neurophysiological foundations of pain. In R. A. Sternbach (Ed.), *The psychology of pain*. New York: Raven Press, 1978.

Melzack, R., & Perry, C. Self-regulation of pain: The use of alpha-feedback and hypnotic training for the control of chronic pain. *Experimental Neurology*, 1975, *46*, 452–469.

Melzack, Z. R., Weisz, A. Z., & Sprague, L. T. Strategems for controlling pain contributions of auditory stimulation and suggestion. *Experimental Neurology*, 1963, *8*, 239.

Melzack, R., & Torgerson, W. S. On the language of pain. *Anesthesiology*, 1971, *34*, 50–59.

Melzack, R., & Wall, P. D. Pain mechanisms: A new theory. *Science*, 1965, *150*, 971–979.

Melzack, R., & Wall, P. D. Psychology of pain. *International Anesthesiology Clinics*, 1970, *8*, 3–34.

Merskey, H. The characteristics of persistent pain in psychological illness. *Journal of Psychosomatic Research*, 1965, *9*, 291–298.(a)

Merskey, H. Psychiatric patients with persistent pain. *Journal of Psychosomatic Research*, 1965, *9*, 299–309.(b)

Merskey, H. Psychological aspects of pain. *Postgraduate Medical Journal*, 1968, *44*, 297–306.

Merskey, H. Assessment of pain. *Physiotherapy*, 1974, *60*, 96–98.

Merskey, H., & Spear, F. G. *Pain: Psychological and psychiatric aspects*. London: Bailliere, Tindall and Cassell, 1967.

Michic, D., & Binkert, E. Is placebo analgesia mediated by morphine? *Pain abstracts: Second World Congress on Pain*, 1978, p.19.

Mountcastle, V. B. Pain and temperature sensibilities. In V. B. Mountcastle (Ed.), *Medical physiology*. St. Louis: C. V. Mosby, 1974.

Moore, P. A., Duncan, G. H., Scott, D. S., Gregg, J. M., & Ghia, J. N. The submaximal effort tourniquet test: Its use in evaluating experimental and chronic pain. *Pain*, 1979, *6*, 375–382.

Neal, H. *The politics of pain*. New York; McGraw-Hill, 1978.

Newman, R. I., Seres, J. L., Yospe, L. P., & Garlington, B. Multidisciplinary treatment of chronic pain: Long-term follow-up of low-back pain patients. *Pain*, 1978, *4*, 283–292.

Orne, M. T. Pain suppression by hypnosis and related phenomena. In J. J. Bonica (Ed.), *Advances in neurology: International symposium on pain* (Vol. 4). New York: Raven Press, 1974.

Parbrook, G. D., Steel, D. F., & Dalrymple, D. G. Factors predisposing to postoperative pain and pulmonary complications. *British Journal of Anesthesia*, 1973, *45*, 21–33.

Patkin, M. Measurement of tenderness with the description of a simple instrument. *The Medical Journal of Australia*, 1970, *1*, 670–672.

Philips, C. Psychological analysis of tension headache. In S. Rachman (Ed.), *Contributions to medical psychology* (Vol. 1). London: Pergamon, 1977.

Pilling, L. F., Brannick, T. L., & Swenson, W. M. Psychologic characteristics of psychiatric patients having pain as a presenting symptom. *Canadian Medical Association Journal*, 1967, *97*, 387–394.

Pilowsky, I., & Spence, N. D. Patterns of illness behavior in patients with intractable pain. *Journal of Psychosomatic Research*, 1975, *19*, 279–287.

Pilowsky, I., & Spence, N. D. Pain and illness behavior: A comparative study. *Journal of Psychosomatic Research*, 1976, *20*, 131–134.(a)

Pilowsky, I., & Spence, N. D. Illness behavior syndromes associated with intractable pain. *Pain, 1976*, *2*, 61–71.(b)

Pilowsky, I., & Spence, N. D. Is illness behavior related to chronicity in patients with intractable pain? *Pain,* 1976, *2,* 167–173.(c)

Reynolds, D. V. Surgery in the rat during electrical analgesia induced by focal brain stimulation, *Science,* 1969, *164,* 444–445.

Sarcedote, P. Theory and practice of pain control in malignancy and other protracted or recurring painfull illnesses. *International Journal of Clinical and Experimental Hypnosis,* 1970, *18,* 160–180.

Scott, J., & Huskisson, E. C. Graphic representation of pain. *Pain,* 1976, *2,* 175–184.

Sherman, R. A., Gall, N., & Gormly, J. Treatment of phantom limb pain with muscular relaxation training to disrupt the pain-anxiety tension cycle. *Pain,* 1979, *6,* 47–55.

Simon, E. J., & Hiller, J. M. The opiate receptors. *Annual Review of Pharmacology and Toxicology,* 1978, *18,* 371–394.

Simon, E. J., Hiller, J. M., & Edelman, I. Solubility of a stereospecific opiate-macromolecular complex from rat brain. *Science,* 1975, *190,* 389–390.

Smith, G. M., Egbert, L. D., Markowitz, R. A., Mosteller, F., & Beecher, H. K. An experimental pain method sensitive to morphine in man. The submaximum effort tourniquet technique. *Journal of Pharmacology and Experimental Therapeutics,* 1966, *154,* 324–332.

Spear, F. G. Pain in psychiatric patients. *Journal of Psychosomatic Research,* 1967 *11,* 187–193.

Spielberger, C. D., Gorsuch, R. L., & Lushene, R. E. *Manual for the State-Trait Anxiety Inventory,* Palo Alto, Calif.: Consulting Psychologists Press, 1970.

Staub, E., Tursky, B., & Schwartz, G. E. Self-control and predictability: Their effects on reactions to aversive stimulation. *Journal of Personality and Social Psychology,* 1971, *18,* 157–162.

Sternbach, R. A. *Pain: A psychophysiological analysis.* New York: Academic Press, 1968.

Sternbach, R. A. *Pain patients: Traits and treatment.* New York: Academic Press, 1974.

Sternbach, R. A. (Ed.). *The psychology of pain.* New York: Raven Press, 1978.(a)

Sternbach, R. A. Clinical aspects of pain. In R. A. Sternbach (Ed.), *The psychology of pain.* New York: Raven Press, 1978.(b)

Sternbach, R. A., & Tursky, B. Ethnic differences among housewives in physical and skin potential responses to electric shock. *Psychophysiology,* 1965, *1,* 241–246.

Stroebel, C. F., & Glueck, B. C. Biofeedback treatment in medicine and psychiatry: An ultimate placebo? *Seminars in Psychiatry,* 1973, *5,* 378–393.

Stroebel, C. F., & Glueck, B. C. Psychophysiological rationale for the application of biofeedback in the alleviation of pain. In M. Weisenberg & B. Tursky (Eds.), *Pain: New perspectives in therapy and research.* New York: Plenum Press, 1976.

Szasz, T. S. The nature of pain. *Archives of Neurology and Psychiatry,* 1955, *74,* 174–181.

Szasz, T. S. *Pain and pleasure.* New York: Basic Books, 1957.

Szasz, T. S. The psychology of persistent pain: A portrait of l'homme douloureux. In A. Soulairac, J. Cahn, & J. Charpentier (Eds.), *Pain: Proceedings of the International Symposium on Pain*. New York: Academic Press, 1968.

Taub, A. Factors in the diagnosis and treatment of chronic pain. *Journal of Autism and Childhood Schizophrenia*, 1975, *5*, 1–12.

Terenius, L. Endogenous peptides and analgesia. *Annual Review of Pharmacology and Toxicology*, 1978, *18*, 189–204.

Timmermans, G., & Sternbach, R. A. Human chronic pain and personality: A canonical correlation analysis. In J. J. Bonica & D. Albe-Fessard (Eds.), *Advances in pain research and therapy* (Vol. 1). New York: Raven Press, 1976.

Tursky, B. Physical, physiological factors that affect pain reaction to electric shock. *Psychophysiology*, 1974, *11*, 95–112.

Tursky, B. The pain perception profile: A psychophysical approach. In M. Weisenberg & B. Tursky (Eds.), *Pain: Therapeutic approaches and research frontiers*. New York: Plenum Press, 1976.

Van Buren, J., & Kleinknecht, R. A. An evaluation of the McGill Pain Questionnaire for use in dental pain assessment. *Pain*, 1979, *6*, 23–33.

Vernon, D. T. A. Modeling and birth order in responses to painful stimuli. *Journal of Personality and Social Psychology*, 1974, *29*, 794–799.

Walike, C., & Meyer, B. Relation between placebo reactivity and selected personality factors. *Nursing Research*, 1966, *15*, 119–123.

Weisenberg, M. (Ed.). *Pain: Clinical and experimental perspectives*. St. Louis: C. V. Mosby, 1975.

Weisenberg, M. Pain and pain control. *Psychological Bulletin*, 1977, *84*, 1008–1044.

Weisenberg, M. Cultural and racial reactions to pain. In M. Weisenberg (Ed.), *The control of pain*. New York: Psychological Dimensions, Inc., in press.(a)

Weisenberg, M. Understanding pain phenomena. In S. Rachman (Ed.), *Contributions to medical psychology*. New York: Pergamon Press, in press.(b)

Weisenberg, M., & Epstein, D. Patient training as an alternative to general anesthesia. *New York State Dental Journal*, 1973, *39*, 610–613.

Weisenberg, M., & Stilwell, N. The use of biofeedback in the treament of dental phobia. Paper presented at the annual meeting of the Eastern Psychological Association, Philadelphia, 1974.

Wolfer, J. A., & Visintainer, M. A. Pediatric surgical patients' and parents' stress responses and adjustment. *Nursing Research*, 1975, *24*, 244–255.

Wolff, B. B. Factor analysis of human responses: Pain endurance as a specific pain factor. *Journal of Abnormal Psychology*, 1971, *78*, 292–298.

Wolff, B. B. Behavioral measurement of human pain. In R. A. Sternbach (Ed.), *The psychology of pain*. New York: Raven Press, 1978.

Wolpe, J. *The practice of behavior therapy*. New York: Pergamon Press, 1973.

Zborowski, M. *People in Pain*. San Francisco: Jossey-Bass, 1969.

Suggested Readings

Bonica, J. J. (Ed.) *Advances in neurology* (Vol. 4). *International symposium on pain*. New York: Raven Press, 1974.

Bonica, J. J., & Albe-Fessard, D. (Eds.). *Advances in pain research and therapy* (Vol. 1). New York: Raven Press, 1976.

Bonica, J. J., & Ventafridda, V. (Eds.). *Advances in pain research and therapy* (Vol. 2). *International symposium on pain of advanced cancer*. New York: Raven Press, 1979.

Brena, S. F. (Ed.). *Chronic pain: America's hidden epidemic: Behavior modification as an alternative to drugs and surgery*. New York: Atheneum/SMI, 1978.

Crue, B. L. Jr. (Ed.). *Pain: Research and treatment*. New York: Academic Press, 1975.

Dalessio, D. J. *Wolff's headache and other head pain* (3rd ed.). New York: Oxford University Press, 1972.

Fordyce, W. E. *Behavioral methods for chronic pain and illness*. Saint Louis: C. V. Mosby, 1976.

Hardy, J. D., Wolff, H. G., & Goodell, H. *Pain sensations and reactions*. New York: Hafner Publishing Co., 1952.

Hilgard, E. R., & Hilgard, J. R. *Hypnosis in the relief of pain*. Los Altos, Calif.: William Kaufman, 1975.

Janzen, R., Keidel, W. D., Herz, A., Steichele, C., Payne, J. P., & Burt, R. A. P. (Eds.). *Pain: Basic principles, pharmacology, therapy*. London: Churchill Livingstone, 1972.

Melzack, R. *The puzzle of pain. New York: Basic Books, 1973*.

Merskey, H., & Spear, F. G. *Pain: Psychological and psychiatric aspects*. London: Bailliere, Tindall and Cassell, 1967.

Neal, H. *The politics of pain*. New York: McGraw-Hill, 1978.

Soulairic, A., Cahn, J., & Charpentier, J. (Eds.). *Pain: Proceedings of the International Symposium on Pain*. New York: Academic Press, 1968.

Sternbach, R. A. *Pain: A psychophysiological analysis*. New York: Academic Press, 1968.

Sternbach, R. A. *Pain patients: Traits and treatment*. New York: Academic Press, 1974.

Sternbach, R. A. (Ed.). *The psychology of pain*. New York: Raven Press, 1978.

Udolf, R. *Handbook of hypnosis for professionals*. New York: Van Nostrand Reinhold, 1981.

Walker, C. E., Hedberg, A., Clement, P. W., & Wright, L. *Clinical procedures for behavior therapy*. Englewood Cliffs, N.J.: Prentice-Hall, 1981.

Weisenberg, M. (Ed.). *Pain: Clinical and experimental perspectives*. St. Louis: C. V. Mosby, 1975.

Weisenberg, M., & Tursky, B. (Eds.). *Pain: New perspectives in therapy and research*. New York: Plenum Press, 1976.

Zborowski, M. *People in pain*. San Francisco: Jossey-Bass, 1969.

4

Obesity

William G. Johnson

Introduction

Measurement and Classification

The most common measure of obesity is body weight, which is then related to height, age, sex, and frame size. Standards relating body weight to these other variables have been published by the Metropolitan Life Insurance Company. The Metropolitan tables are based on desirable weights and indicate for a given height, sex, and frame size an ideal or desirable weight associated with less morbidity and mortality.

The Metropolitan tables provide a quick and easy way to identify an individual's desirable weight. Generally, the standard for defining overweight is taken as *20 percent in excess of a given ideal weight*. The 20 percent value is important as it is at this point and beyond that significant increases in mortality/morbidity occur. The Metropolitan tables, however, are not without their disadvantages. First, the weights are usually obtained in street clothing, which can vary considerably. Second, it is difficult to determine frame size (small, medium, large) as there are no criteria to aid this identification. In actual practice, it is convenient to use the middle value of the "medium frame size" as the desirable weight for a given height and to base the definition of overweight as a 20 percent increase over this value.

A trend in the weight-reduction literature has also been an incorporation of other measures in addition to weight. These measures allow for a more thorough assessment of obesity and treatment influences. For example, constant-pressure calipers to measure *skinfold thickness* provide a more direct estimate of fat content. The most common site used in measuring skinfold thickness is the triceps area, and tables have been published by Seltzer and Mayer (1965) that use the triceps measure for the determination of obesity. The triceps area has been selected becuse of the available normative data and the awkwardness of measuring other sites. As noted by Johnson and Stalonas (1977), however, the measurement of triceps skinfold thickness is not without its difficulty. They note that skinfold thickness should not be used as the final arbiter of weight loss but only as an adjunct to balance-bar weights.

Other measures include so-called risk factors such as cholesterol and triglycerides, which are determined from blood samples. High levels of these measures are unrelated to obesity but are associated with the development of heart and vascular disease.

For the vast majority of patients, it is no secret whether or not they are overweight. Fat has a rather straightforward way of expressing itself. Thus, perhaps the most simple and commonly used method for assessing overweight is the so-called mirror-test. All it requires is for the patient to look in the mirror.

Classification of Obesity

A number of classification schemes for obesity have been proposed but none has proven entirely satisfactory. For example, several years ago, it was convenient to characterize obesity as endogenous or exogenous. Presumably, the endogenous classification referred to internal etiology, whereas the exogenous classification related obesity to factors in the environment. This system has many inadequacies including the fact that there are only a few rare physical diseases that produce obesity; moreover, the role of the environment is much more important than previously thought. It may well be that certain predispositions toward obesity are inherited or otherwise formed in early life but these predispositions interact in some fashion with the environment.

There are two other classification systems that have more merit. One is the *dynamic–static* classification, which merely refers to whether the overweight patient is in the process of gaining weight (dynamic) or whether weight has stabilized at a high level (static). Dynamic obesity appears to be particularly rare, and when present, it may be indicative of a metabolic disorder. For the majority of patients, weight gain is a very slow, insidious process. With repeated dieting, many also display a "yo-yo" effect with weight reductions of up to 30 percent of body weight followed by an increase to the previous weight once the diet is relinquished.

Another convenient classification which may have implications for treatment is based on the *age at onset*. Accordingly, the age at which the patient first became overweight is identified or is classified as childhood, adolescent, or adult. An onset during childhood represents a particular problem, as approximately 80 percent of overweight children go on to become obese as adults (Abraham & Nordseick, 1960; Charney, Goodman, McBride, Lyon, & Pratt, 1976).

Of course, early onset is generally correlated with heavier weights than onset in late adolescence or adulthood. Additionally, as Stunkard and Rush (1974) note, individuals with early onset are less responsive to treatment and are more likely to become depressed during weight loss.

Closely related to the classification based upon age at onset are hyperplastic and hypertropic obesity. Briefly, *hyperplastic* obesity is characterized by an excessive number of fat cells. Available evidence suggests that this form of obesity has an early onset that is related to maternal nutrition during pregnancy and/or early feeding patterns. In contrast, *hypertropic obesity* is more closely related to adult onset and is charaterized by an average number of fat cells but with increased size. As noted, hyperplastic and hypertropic obesity are correlated with early and late onset, respectively. To some extent, the large number of fat cells indicative of hyperplastic obesity provides a tentative explanation of why these individuals have a more difficult response to treatment. Accordingly, it is assumed that the great number of fat cells creates a metabolic demand that makes adherence to reduced caloric intake difficult. When hyperplastic individuals lose weight, the number of fat cells remains constant but they decrease in size.

The evidence supporting hyperplastic and hypertropic classification is not well-established at this time. For example, Ashwell, Priest, and Bondoux (1975) failed to find differences in fat-cell composition of women who had onset of obesity at various stages in life. Brook (1978) also suggests that both hypertropic and hyperplastic obesity may arise at the same point in life and that the number of fat cells laid down in early life is not fixed. In fact, he sites data indicating a progressive increase in fat-cell size during childhood. Obviously, the classification of hyperplastic and hypertropic obesity is not absolute, but it has provided a focal point for research regarding the etiology of obesity with possible implications for treatment.

At this time there is no one classification that is satisfactory. Thus, each individual must be viewed against a particular pattern of life circumstances and developmental experiences. Because of the multitude of genetic and environmental factors that may have an impact on one's weight, it is incorrect to speak of obesity as a unitary disorder of either metabolism, eating, appetite control, or inactivity.

The Prevalence and Health Consequences of Obesity

Several surveys have indicated that obesity is a major health problem in the United States (Society of Actuaries, 1959; Ten-State Nutrition Survey, 1972). Most of these surveys indicate that between 20 and 45 percent of the adult population in the United States is 20 percent over an ideal weight.

Thus, it is now well-recognized that obesity represents a significant health hazard in terms of increased morbidity and mortality. Generally, studies investigating the health consequences of obesity correlate body weight with disease and death. One of the most well-known is the Build and Blood Pressure Study (Society of Actuaries, 1959), which rather convincingly documented that the level of mortality is directly proportional to the degree of overweight. Moreover, this study noted that the increased risk which the overweight experience above that of their normal-size cohorts occurs at weights of approximately 20 percent over the ideal. So, for a 5′4″ woman and a 5′8″ man, weights of 144 and 174 pounds, respectively, would be associated with increased risk for disease and early death. A more recent survey by the Society of Actuaries (1959) has largely confirmed the initial report, with the exception of raising the level at which increased risk occurs from 20 percent to 30 percent over ideal body weight.

As Bray (1978) notes, persons who are 20 percent or more overweight have a 40 to 50 percent greater chance of developing a variety of diseases. They also have a greater than 40 percent chance of dying in any one year when compared to their normal-size cohorts. The specific risks for obesity include development of cardiovascular diseases and hypertension, gall bladder disease, diabetes, cancer, and kidney disease. Of course, there are a wide variety of physiological mechanisms responsible for this increase in morbidity and mortality. Regarding cardiovascular disease, it appears that for approximately every 15 pounds of excess body weight, there is a 2 to 3 mm Hg increase in blood pressure. Likewise, excessive food intake and inactivity over the years results in many metabolic changes, including insulin resistance, which can lead to diabetes.

While these health risks of obesity are unquestioned, until recently it was uncertain whether improved health followed weight reduction. Bray (1976) sites evidence based on a study by Marks (1960) of a group of individuals who were initially overweight and who were subsequently denied the full benefits of insurance coverage. After weight reduction, these policyholders improved their life expectancy to that which was no different from normal-size comparisons who have a standard level of risk for disease. Additionally, several studies (e.g., Reisin, Abel, Modon, Silverberg, Eliahou, & Modan, 1978; Stamler, Stamler, Riedlinger, Algera, & Roberts, 1978) have noted that weight reduction decreases persistent hypertension. Also, it is generally accepted that individuals with adult-onset diabetes can alleviate many of their diabetic symptoms and the need for exogenous administration of insulin by losing weight.

In addition to these health risks, the *psychosocial implications* of obesity may be profound. The obese are stigmatized, are actively discriminated against in work settings, and appear to be significantly more maladjusted than their normal-size counterparts (Allon, 1973; Dwyer & Mayer, 1973; Hirsch, 1973).

Theoretical Analysis

Nonbehavioral Treatments

The nonbehavioral treatments for obesity can be conveniently arranged in the categories of caloric and dietary restriction, including liquid-protien diets; anorectic drugs; and surgery.

Caloric and dietary restriction. The most common form of weight reduction is the low-calorie diet. Typically, the patient is prescribed an 800-1,000 Kcal diet. Extreme forms of caloric restriction can involve hospitalization with an almost total starvation regimen. Experience with caloric reduction per se is uniformly poor. This ineffectiveness could be related to the monotony of calorie counting and the difficulty involved in calculating the calorie content of portions. Also, the fact that the dieter is still eating food but restricting amounts can exert a constant pressure to relinquish the diet. Additionally, drastic caloric reductions such as starvation are frequently associated with severe depression and even psychotic reactions (Robinson & Winnik, 1973; Stunkard & Rush, 1974).

Dietary restrictions indirectly reduce caloric intake by advocating the consumption of specific foods and limiting the consumption of others. These diets contain a list of "shoulds" and "should nots" that are often organized around the four food groups (dairy, meats, fruits, grains) and that conform to restrictions on the intake of protein, carbohydrate, and fats. Many of these diets offer contradictory advice (e.g., low fat vs. high fat), often make little nutritional sense, and in fact, may be dangerous.

Many of these diets promise quick weight loss and involve a reduction of carbohydrates. Low-carbohydrate diets result in initial weight loss over the first three weeks, which is primarily related to water and electrolyte loss.

Regardless, there is no systematic evidence evaluating the effectiveness of dietary restrictions. Moreover, the American Dietetic Association among others recommends that all individuals embarking on a weight-reduction program eat a balanced combination of carbohydrates, proteins, and fat. Currently, the recommended values of daily intake are carbohydrates, 45 percent, fats, 35 percent; and proteins, 20 percent.

One of the more recent developments in dietary restrictions have been the so-called liquid-protein diets. These include both prescription and over-the-counter preparations. Liquid-protein diets contain supplemental protein to avoid the loss of protein that normally occurs during weight loss. Results with these diets have been mixed. Patients who adhere to Optifast, a preparation that can be obtained only from a physician, lose 3 to 5 pounds per week, and one report notes that over 60 percent of the patients lost more than 40 pounds (Genuth, Castro, & Vertes, 1974). In contrast, Millar, Innes, and Munro (1978) report on 55 patients who were on a regimen of Carnation Slender. Most of these patients could not tolerate the Slender for more than six weeks. Those patients who adhered strictly to the Slender for 12 weeks had a weight loss of approximately 9 pounds. However, as noted, most of the patients could not tolerate this regimen. The efficacy of Slender and other such liquid diets appears to be in the short run. Whether individuals can maintain themselves on such restrictive regimens is questionable. Additionally, there is no information as to how these patients fare when they return to eating. We would expect, of course, that if they maintained old eating habits and patterns of inactivity, they would regain their weight.

Coupled with this limited effectiveness, recent data indicate several rather severe side effects including death that have occurred as a result of liquid-protein diets. A recent FDA Drug Bulletin (1978) reports 58 deaths associated with low-calorie protein diets in women. In these cases, there was no evidence of underlying medical problems, and, thus, the general consensus is that they occurred as a direct result of the restricted dietary intake. It is highly advisable, therefore, that these diets be undertaken only under the close supervision of a responsible physician.

In summary, caloric and dietary restriction involve sharply reduced caloric intake (1,000 Kcal) and/or a shift to foods that may represent dramatic changes from preferred foods. Although there is no direct evidence, the proliferation of diets attests to their ineffectiveness. Adherence to such diets is a typically discrete phenomenon. One is either dieting or not and the breakdown in dietary adherence may be due to the program of "should" and "should nots." As Marlatt and Gordon (1979) have stated, once the abstinence cycle has been broken with the person partaking of the "forbidden fruit," the diet is relinquished.

Drug treatment. The drugs used for the treatment of obesity are referred to as anorectics as they tend to induce a disinterest in food. The majority of anorectics are amphetamines or compounds related to them. They reduce voluntary food intake in laboratory animals and change the hunger ratings of human subjects. The current medical position regarding anorectics is that they should be used only as *adjunctive agents* in the treatment of obesity, combined with diet, exercise, and other forms of treatment.

The rationale for the use of anorectics for obesity is twofold. In general, it is thought that these drugs (1) influence the central nervous system and thereby decrease hunger sensations or (2) may have some peripheral, metabolic effects such as an alteration in glucose tolerance or insulin response. In summarizing the available literature, Bulundell and Rogers (1978) state that the major action of anorectic drugs appears to be on the central nervous system and, in particular, on the neurotransmitters of norepinephrine, dopamine, and perhaps serotonin.

A recent extensive evaluation of anorectic therapy for obesity, provided in the report by Scoville (1976), consisted of over 350 studies in which an anorectic was compared with a placebo or where two active compounds were compared with one another. The survey revealed that patients on an anorectic compound lost approximately one-half pound a week more than those on a placebo. There appeared to be little if any differences among the various drugs in terms of their efficacy to induce weight loss. Thus, the effectiveness of anorectic drugs compared to placebos is relatively minor when the amount of weight that must be lost is considered. Additionally, Johnson and Hughes (1979) have noted many deficiencies in the design of studies evaluating anorectic compounds. More specifically, these deficiencies include nonspecific blinding procedures, the relative influence of dietary restrictions versus the anorectic drug, estimates of the subjects' compliance with the drug regimen, and the paucity of follow-up data. There have been several studies, which will be reviewed in a later section, that have compared anorectic drugs with other forms of therapy such as behavior therapy.

Currently, anorectic durgs are recommended for no more than six weeks. This is related to their limited efficacy and the fact that they are associated with a high incidence of side effects, including dizziness, dry mouth, nausea, and insomnia, among others. So the FDA and the AMA Council of Drugs have generally concluded that the compounds are of little use by themselves. As the AMA (1973) notes:

> All anorectic drugs are of limited use and their use for prolonged periods in the treatment of obesity can lead to drug dependence and abuse and must be avoided. The natural history of obesity is measured in years, whereas none of the drug studies have been longer than a few months in duration; thus, the total impact of drug-induced weight loss over that of diet alone must be considered clinically small. The limited usefulness of these agents must be measured against any possible risk factors inherent in their use [p. 369].

Surgical treatments for obesity. An increasingly prominent treatment for the massively obese patient is surgery. The *intestinal bypass* was first decribed by Payne, DeWind, and Commons (1963), who reported on 11 cases. The bypass operation involves short-circuiting the intestinal tract, causing food to pass more quickly through the intestines. The operation is designed to create a "malabsorption syndrome" due to the restricted length of the intestines.

Bray, Greenway, Barry, Benfield, Fiser, Dahms, Atkinson, and

Schwartz (1977) note that weight loss following surgery is related both to the degree of initial weight and to the time since the operation. Thus, the heavier the individual, the greater weight loss resulting after surgery. Also, the most rapid period of weight reduction occurs during the first six months after the operation. Bray (1976) also reports that weight loss during the first six months averages approximately 100 pounds and tapers off to about 30 to 40 pounds in the next year.

Interestingly, Bray et al. (1977) followed the caloric intake of eight patients both before and after surgery. Prior to surgery, the intake averaged 6,700 Kcal per day. During the period of rapid weight loss in the first six months after surgery, the caloric intake was reduced by approximately 80% of this initial level or roughly 1,000 Kcal per day. However, with the passing of time the caloric intake of these patients rose to approximately 3,700 Kcal per day. Over the next several years, caloric intake of these patients rose still further and closely approximated 5,000 Kcal per day. As Bray notes, most patients lost between 30 and 50 percent of their initial body weight, but it was during the period of severe caloric reduction in the first six months after the operation that the weight was lost. Moreover, an analysis of fecal samples indicated that the malabsorption syndrome per se could not possibly count for the dramatic weight loss. Rather, the severe reduction in calories during the first six months following surgery is responsible for the rapid weight loss.

There are many side effects to intestinal bypass surgery, including chronic diarrhea, liver complications, arthritis, hair loss, vitamin deficiencies, renal failure, and liver disease. The fatality rate according to Bray et al. (1977) averages approximately 3 percent, but it has been reported to be as high as 15 percent. Because of these complications, it is recommended that this procedure be used only in the most massively obese individuals who are under threat of significant morbidity unless they lose weight quickly. It is also obvious from Bray's data that these patients must change their eating habits in order to achieve maximum benefits from the surgery.

A more recently developed surgical technique is referred to as the *gastric fold* or *stapling* procedure, in which the stomach is actually folded over. This operation reduces the volume of the stomach to a capacity of only 4 to 6 ounces. Currently, reports of the efficacy of the gastric procedure are limited, but it does appear to have fewer side effects than the intestinal bypass (Halmi, 1980).

Behavioral Approaches to Weight Reduction

There have been two phases in behavioral research on weight reduction. The first phase focused on the efficacy of specific self-control procedures, and the more recent phase is concerned with clinical efficacy. An article by Ferster and co-workers (1962) provided the impetus for a series of investigations which, on one hand, were aimed at weight reduction, but also investigated basic self-control processes. In this article, Ferster and his colleagues outlined a behavioral approach to the control of eating. The basic assumption was that obesity represented a failure in the "self-control" of eating. The behavioral analysis suggested by Ferster including teaching self-control through specific behavioral strategies includes stimulus control, controlling the consequences of eating, and altering eating behavior per se. Almost all subsequent behavioral approaches to weight reduction have been based upon the techniques outlined by Ferster.

Examples of these behavioral strategies include the following:

stimulus control—eating should be restricted to specific locations and times and divorced from other non-eating activities such as watching televison

manipulating the consequences—making the immediate consequences of overeating less positive and the long-term aversive consequences of overeating more immediate

chaining—breaking eating behavior into specific components to slow down the rate of eating and to focus on the enjoyment of food

As noted, weight reduction research was oriented not only toward exploring effective procedures that would produce reliable weight loss but also to self-control processes. In fact, weight reduction provided a convenient arena for studying the efficacy of various self-control strategies. Therefore, the initial phase of research on weight reduction was concerned with weight loss and also with the development and refinement of self-control techniques, which include self-monitoring, aversive conditioning, covert sensitization, internal and external reinforcement, and punishment, among others. Unfortunately, the initial effectiveness of behavioral approaches to weight reduction promulgated many incorrect conclusions regarding the etiology of obesity. For example, it was assumed that obesity is a learned disorder of excessive caloric intake (Mahoney, 1975). While this pattern may be true in some cases, it is an overly simplistic formulation, as it ignores the input of genetic, metabolic, and other psychological mechanisms.

As previously noted, Ferster's work lies at the basis of a great deal of current research. In addition to this seminal article, the application of behavioral analysis of eating to the clinic was prompted by a rather extraordinary and dramatic report of Stuart (1967) on eight obese women.

Stuart noted a mean weight loss over a one-year period of 37 pounds, which was dramatic when compared to previous reports of the time. Stuart's article served to stimulate behavioral treatments of obesity.

Following Stuart, recent attempts at behavior weight reduction are more comprehensive and oriented to increasing appropriate nutrition and exercise in addition to eating-habit change. Moreover, this contemporary approach uses a broader spectrum of behavioral techniques, including cognitive procedures and the use of social support systems such as community groups, family, and friends.

The focus of current weight-reduction programs, then, includes an emphasis on changing eating behavior, promoting proper nutrition, and developing a more active, engaging lifestyle. Although there is some evidence to the contrary, most of the data suggest that overweight adults do not eat differently from those of normal size. Also, both overweight and normal-weight adults eat a balanced diet. However, overweight children have a different eating style with bigger bites, less chewing, and a faster pace.

While there may be no difference in the eating styles of normal and obese adults, eating may be triggered more frequently and by a greater variety of stimuli in the latter. Thus, the emphasis on eating-habit change in the obese is important. They must be made aware of their caloric input and the conditions under which they eat.

Regarding activity, the overweight are considerably less active and more likely to be entrenched in a sedentary lifestyle. In a review of studies on the influence of exercise on weight, Epstein and Wing (1980) found that overweight subjects who exercised regularly lost more weight and body fat than those who did not exercise.

Assessment

Assessment in behavior therapy for weight reduction focuses almost exclusively on behaviors and cognitions relevant for weight loss. There is nothing to be gained from projective techniques, and, as yet, objective psychological tests have provided little in the way of assistance for treatment.

Assessment for weight reduction is essentially a two-step process. Initially, each patient should undergo a thorough screening prior to acceptance in a program. Information gathered from this screening can be evaluated against specific inclusion/exclusion criteria to determine whether the patient is acceptable. The second stage commences once the individual is accepted into a program. This stage consists of an ongoing evaluation, not only of weight loss, but specific behavior changes. In fact, during the initial weeks of a behavioral regimen, the assessment of changes in eating habits and exercise patterns is much more important than weight loss per se.

Screening

What are the specific behaviors that require assessment, and how can they be evaluated? It should come as no surprise that physical condition, eating and activity patterns, and weight and dietary history are important to evaluate. One handy guide is a self-report questionnaire called the Health-Habit Survey, which is routinely used in the Substance Abuse Clinic at the University of Mississippi Medical Center (Johnson, 1979). This questionnaire provides a fast and efficient method for collecting information relevant to weight reduction. Together with a thorough interview and perhaps a week of self-monitoring, the questionnaire gives the therapist the information needed to develop a profile of behaviors that are relevant to weight reduction.

The profile for each patient should be as specific as the data can provide. Information regarding the patient's physical condition is important to determine whether there is any existing illness that may contraindicate weight reduction and/or exercise. Patients who have not had a physical examination within the past six months are routinely referred for such or advised to consult their physician. The Health-Habit Survey also reveals highly relevant information regarding frequency of food intake, its temporal distribution, the content of regular meals and snacks, and the extent to which food intake is controlled by internal versus external influences.

Activity and *exercise* are as important as changes in eating behavior for successful weight loss and long-term maintenance. In fact, the majority of overweight patients describe themselves as being very inactive. It appears that an adult onset of overweight is more directly attributed to a reduction in energy output rather than an increase in caloric intake. So the therapist should be aware of the general activity patterns of each patient including those associated with job and leisure activities.

Personal adjustment is another area that should be evaluated. If an individual experiences persistent difficulties in management of day-to-day functions and interpersonal relationships, the therapist must decide whether these difficulties will jeopardize progress toward weight reduction. Certainly, it is legitimate to refer such patients for psychotherapy prior to weight reduction.

Data on weight and dietary history also provide information regarding the onset of overweight and the stability of weight over time. As noted earlier, childhood onset is correlated with heavier weights, more difficulty losing weight, and an emotional reaction such as depression to weight reduction. In contrast, adult onset of overweight is more likely to result from a combination of decreased activity over the years while maintaining the same or even increased levels of food intake. Furthermore, the stability of weight over the past six months is important. A stable pattern indicates a relatively constant energy balance. Increasing weight suggests that energy expenditure has decreased and/or food intake has increased. Given a relatively constant level of activity, dramatic increases in weight may indicate the presence of some metabolic disorder. While these diseases are rare, it is important to note such dramatic changes in weight and make appropriate referrals to a physician.

The therapist should not automatically accept all patients who apply for weight reduction. Accordingly, the information given during the assessment should be used to develop a profile of relevant behaviors that can then be evaluated against specific inclusion/exclusion criteria. These inclusion criteria might include age, weight, available time, and perhaps reading level. The majority of individuals who apply for treatment are adults, and it is advisable that they be mature and at least 15 years of age. Additionally, the participants should weigh between 20 and 100 percent over a desirable weight. The minimum of 20 percent is chosen because there is an incremental increase in morbidity/mortality at that level. The upper limit of 100 percent is equally important. Behavioral programs for weight reduction typically produce weight loss of between 1 and 2 pounds per week. So after a 10- to 18-week program, the average patient will lose between 10 and 36 pounds. For an individual who weighs 100 percent over an ideal weight, this loss may be considered meager in spite of its clinical importance in reducing risk.

Those individuals who are 100 percent over an ideal weight may be considered for behavioral treatment in conjunction with a partial liquid-diet formula. Currently, such a program is employed at the University of Mississippi Medical Center, which includes standard behavioral treatment with exercise.

The partial formula diet is instituted during the sixth week of a structured program following a schedule which alternates one 60-Kcal packet of formula for breakfast or lunch with three 60-Kcal packets divided between breakfast and lunch. According to this regimen, the patients eat two balanced meals every other day with the liquid serving as a convenient way to keep caloric intake between 800 and 1,000 Kcal and avoid the temptation of overeating.

Most comprehensive behavioral programs involve changes in eating, exercise, and general activity. These changes require *time* to effect, so, in order to be successful, participants must have the time to devote to the program, which may require 30 minutes to an hour per day. During screening, the therapist must ascertain whether the patient has the time and is willing to put forth the effort. In cases where there is doubt, the patient can keep a log of activities for a week.

Last, most behavioral programs include written material describing key components with instructions for implementation. It is important to insure that the patients have a reading level commensurate with the material they will receive.

In addition to these inclusion criteria, there are several exclusion criteria including the following: physical condition, presence of psychological dysfunction, and the source of motivation for weight loss. In general, most overweight patients are healthy; development of disease and premature death awaits them in the future. However, it is strongly advised that all prospective participants have a physical examination prior to commencing the program. Occasionally, some patients present with heart conditions or endocrine problems, which exclude them from participation. It is more common for a patient to have some condition such as hypertension or diabetes which has resulted from their excessive weight or is exacerbated by it. In these cases, a successful weight-reduction program can be tailored to their physical condition, but this requires continual medical consultation.

Regarding personal maladjustment, individuals with frequent and/or recent psychiatric hospitalizations or other evidence of significant adjustment problems will have difficulty losing weight. This does not mean that all patients with adjustment problems are excluded. In many cases, the difficulties in psychosocial function such as depression and social withdrawal are a result of being overweight. Individuals with these problems are generally acceptable, for the behavioral program can encourage the development of more adaptive behavior, which will combat depression and isolation. Another alternative is to consider referral for short-term therapy. In our experience, however, collateral psychotherapy during a weight-reduction program has not proven to be beneficial.

The last exclusion criteria concerns the source of motivation for weight reduction. To be acceptable, participants should have an internal rather than an external interest in losing weight. That is, the patient should want to lose weight not just to please a spouse or comply with the request of others. Generally, patients with an external orientation rapidly lose interest when they confront the demands of a weight-reduction program. In contrast, those who want to lose weight primarily for their own self-enhancement, and perhaps secondarily for others, are much more successful.

Behavior Therapy in Weight Reduction

Behavioral techniques for weight reduction rely upon several classes of self-control procedures including monitoring, stimulus control, various reinforcement manipulations, and aversive procedures such as covert sensitization. In order to increase the efficacy of behavioral treatment, its scope has been expanded to incorporate other components such as exercise, the use of spouses and partners, and booster sessions. The following review will not be an exhaustive survey of the literature. Rather, the most important and representative studies will be discussed. These and other studies are presented in Table 4.1 with their design quality ratings (DQR).

Behavioral Techniques

Self-monitoring. Practically all behavioral programs for weight loss involve some form of self-monitoring. Participants are routinely instructed to record their eating, exercise, caloric intake, general activity, and other situational variables which may influence these behaviors. Romanczyk (1974) found that self-monitoring of weight and caloric intake was as effective as instructions in behavioral management. However, the study is limited because of its brief, four-week duration. In a more extensive evaluation, Bellack, Rozensky, and Schwartz (1974) compared instructions to record food intake prior to eating and after eating, with a nonmonitoring control condition. As expected, the monitoring of food intake prior to eating was most effective in yielding weight loss. The importance of self-monitoring appears to be several-fold. Keeping records of behavior not only provides feedback regarding relevant progress but also serves as a prompt and constant reminder to engage in prescribed behaviors.

Stimulus control. Stimulus control, within the context of weight reduction, refers to the manipulation of antecedent conditions intended to decrease the probability of inappropriate eating behavior. Typically, participants are instructed to confine their eating to specific times and situations during the day, and perhaps to avoid those situations which may increase the probability of inappropriate eating and snacking. For example, McReynolds, Lutz, Paulsen, and Kohrs (1976) compared a standard weight-reduction procedure that included contingency management, shaping, and stimulus control with one based almost entirely on stimulus-control procedures. In addition to instructions on the situational control of eating, the stimulus-control group was also instructed in how to buy groceries, prepare meals, and store food. After 15 weeks of treatment, there was no difference in the two groups. However, the stimulus-control treatment emerged as more successful at the three- and six-month follow-ups. Certainly, training in stimulus control as shown in this and other studies is an effective procedure and must be considered as an active and therefore necessary ingredient in a behavioral weight-reduction program.

Contingency management. Contingency management refers to

TABLE 4.1
Behavioral Research on Weight Reduction

Author(s)	Design Quality Rating Score	Journal
Wollersheim	24.5	Journal of Abnormal Psychology, 1970, 76, 462-474
Penick, Filion, Fox, & Stunkard	15	Psychosomatic Medicine, 1971, 33, 49-55
Janda & Rimm	22.5	Journal of Abnormal Psychology, 1972, 80, 37-42
Harris & Hallbauer	15	Behaviour Research and Therapy, 1973, 11, 523-529
Mahoney, Moura, & Wade	25.5	Journal of Consulting and Clinical Psychology, 1973, 40, 404-407
Bellack, Rozensky, & Schwartz	20	Behavior Therapy, 1974, 5, 523-530
Mahoney	25	Behavior Therapy, 1974, 5, 48-57
Romanczyk	24.5	Behavior Therapy, 1974, 5, 531-540
Diament & Wilson	19.5	Behavior Therapy, 1975, 6, 499-509
Bellack	24.5	Behavior Therapy, 1976, 7, 68-75
McReynolds, Lutz, Paulsen, & Kohrs	19	Behavior Therapy, 1976, 7, 283-291
Öst & Götestam	15.5	Addictive Behaviors, 1976, 1, 331-338
Kingsley & Wilson	19.5	Journal of Consulting and Clinical Psychology, 1977, 45, 288-298
Dahms, Molitch, Bray, Greenway, Atkinson, & Hamilton	18	American Journal of Clinical Nutrition, 1978, 31, 774-778
Stalonas, Johnson, & Christ	24.5	Journal of Consulting and Clinical Psychology, 1978, 46, 463-469

TABLE 4.1 (continued)

Author(s)	Design Quality Rating Score	Journal
Wilson & Brownell	24	Behavior Therapy, 1978, 9, 943-945
Zitter & Fremouw	19	Behavior Therapy, 1978, 9, 808-813
Johnson & Hughes	27	Addictive Behaviors, 1979, 4, 237-244
O'Neil, Currey, Hirsh, Riddle, Taylor, Malcolm, & Sexauer	20	Addictive Behaviors, 1979, 4, 167-177
Hall, Bass, & Monroe	19	Addictive Behaviors, 1978, 3, 139-147
Ashby & Wilson	26	Behaviour Research and Therapy, 1977, 15, 451-483
Peace, LeBow, & Achord	25	Journal of Consulting and Clinical Psychology, 1981, 49, 236-244

either the patient or the therapist providing reinforcement or punishment contingent upon behavior change and/or weight loss. For example, adult participants might deposit an amount of money and receive refunds contingent on weight loss or behavior change. In a study of contingency management, Mahoney, Moura, and Wade (1973) compared the effects of self-reward, self-punishment, a combination of the two, self-monitoring, and a control condition. The self-reward group was instructed to administer portions of a deposit contingent on weight loss and other desirable behaviors while the self-punishment group was instructed to fine themselves. Mahoney et al. found that self-reward for appropriate eating was more effective than punishment for inappropriate eating or the monitoring of eating urges. Unfortunately, the impact of the self-punishment procedure is not appropriately evaluated because there are no data on how often the subjects punished or fined themselves. In a refined study, Mahoney (1974) compared self-monitoring with self-reward for weight loss, self-reward for changing eating habits, and a control condition. Mahoney found that self-reward for changing eating habits was much more effective than the monitoring or reward for weight change.

Bellack (1976) also demonstrated the effectiveness of self-reinforcement and its superiority when compared to self-monitoring. In this particular study, subjects either monitored their efforts at caloric reduction and stimulus control, or monitored and evaluated their behavior by assigning themselves a letter grade (A,B,C, etc.). After seven weeks of treatment, those subjects who self-reinforced lost more weight than those who merely monitored, and these effects were maintained at a seven-week follow-up. These studies indicate the efficacy and importance of contingency management in successful weight reduction in the short run. While the relative impact of self-reward may be greater following several weeks of treatment, according to McReynolds et al. (1976) the influence of stimulus control is more durable and apparent at longer term follow-up.

Covert sensitization. Many weight-reduction programs include an optional sensitization procedure whereby images of specific foods are paired with aversive stimuli to induce a feeling of nausea. The covert sensitization procedure is based on the rationale that when the participant encounters the selected foods in the natural environment, he or she will experience aversion, and thus not eat the "forbidden fruit." There are several studies evaluating the efficacy of covert sensitization and generally they are not convincing. Janda and Rimm (1972) found no difference between covert sensitization, attention-placebo, and no-contact control groups. Elliott and Denney (1975) found the sensitization procedure to be no more effective than a placebo group.

In a well-designed study, Diament and Wilson (1975) compared a covert sensitization group with a placebo control. However, in this particular study Diament and Wilson used other dependent measures such as the amount of food eaten in a simulated situation and salivary output. According to the rationale of covert sensitization, these latter two measures should be reduced. To the contrary, Diament and Wilson found no difference between the covert sensitization and the attention-placebo or other control conditions on any of the measures. These data indicate that covert sensitization is of doubtful effectiveness in and of itself, although it may be used to supplement or augment other treatments.

Exercise. Mayer (1968) has indicated that inactivity is a major factor in the development of obesity, and so increasing activity has become an important component of weight-reduction programs. Activity not only increases caloric expenditure and the metabolism of fat, but it also may aid in cardiovascular conditioning, decrease appetite, and generally promote a sense of well-being (Bjorntorp, 1976; Horton, 1973). In spite of the appeal of exercise, only a few studies have studied its impact on weight reduction. Harris and Hallbauer (1973) found no difference at the termination of a 12-week program between controlled eating and controlled eating plus exercise groups. However, the exercise group lost significantly more weight at a seven-month follow-up. In a more extensive study, Stalonas, Johnson, and Christ (1978) compared contingency management and exercise in a factoral design with a one-year follow-up. There were four groups in this particular study: one group receiving a basic program which emphasized monitoring and stimulus control, another group receiving this basic program plus exercise, a third group receiving the basic program plus contingency management, and the remaining group receiving the program and a combination of exercise and contingency management. After ten weeks of treatment, all four groups lost significant amounts of weight, and they maintained the losses at a three-month follow-up. At one year, only those subjects exposed to exercise or contingency management maintained the weight loss or continued to lose. While the contingency management and exercise groups did not differ on any of the earlier comparisons, there was a tendency for the exercise group to be significantly different at the one-year follow-up.

Cognitions. The important role of cognitive procedures in implementing behavioral changes is well-recognized, and the procedures have become part and parcel of behavior therapy. In a problem as perplexing as obesity, misinformation, myths, factual distortions, and premature conclusions abound. For example, mistaken beliefs regarding the etiology of obesity, the determinants of eating behavior, nutrition, and exercise among others are common. Also, during the course of treatment, participants often develop negative thoughts regarding their progress. Proper attention to these preexisting beliefs and those which develop during a program are necessary to insure long-term habit change and weight loss.

Empirical support for the inclusion of these procedures is provided by Dunkel and Glaros (1978), who found that training participants to identify negative thoughts and then to challenge them with positive thoughts significantly augmented a standard behavioral program. Johnson and Stalonas (1981) have catalogued the cognitions displayed by participants in a weight-control program. Included are negative thoughts about the progress of weight loss, reasons for not exercising, and difficulties encountered in controlling snacking and changing eating habits.

Each of those participating was challenged by positive thoughts such as: (negative thought) "I look terrible, I will never be able to lose all this weight." *vs.* (positive thought) "Why don't I just concentrate on losing the first 10 pounds?"; (negative thought) "Exercise, Oh, I'll do it later." *vs.* (positive thought) "When I've put it off in the past it wasn't done at all" (p. 112–113).

Long-term efficacy. There have been several attempts to increase the durability of behavioral treatments. These have included booster sessions during the follow-up process as well as the inclusion of spouses and other partners in the effort toward weight reduction. Regarding *booster sessions*, Kingsley and Wilson (1977) evaluated the influence by having participants receive a $25 refund from their deposit for attendance at seven of eight treatment sessions and three out of four booster sessions. The refunds were based entirely on attendance and not weight loss. Participants were exposed to either social pressure with 1,200 Kcal/day diet or two forms of standard behavioral treatment—group and individual. In a sense, the booster sessions were an extension of the treatment, as the participants followed the same format during the sessions. Booster sessions were scheduled two weeks after the last treatment session, and subsequently after three months, after another month, and the final session five weeks later. As expected, the results supported the superiority of the behavioral treatment when compared to social pressure, with the group condition being better than the individual. The booster condition was significantly different from the nonbooster condition at the three- and six-month follow-up but not evident at the final two meetings.

To a great extent, the failure of the booster sessions to produce an enduring effect is congruent with other studies. In an extension of this study, Ashby and Wilson (1977) found that neither the frequency of sessions nor their nature (behavioral vs. nonspecific) affected weight loss.

There have been several studies that investigated the influence of spouses and partners on weight reduction. Wilson and Brownell (1978) studied the effects of both booster sessions and family members in the treatment process. Overweight women participated in an eight-week behavioral self-control program in which there was a family member present or absent. The family members were acquainted with the principles of behavior change and the philosophy of the program, and were instructed to cease negative statements and to increase positive statements for improved habit change. Following the treatment, booster sessions were conducted at monthly intervals, whereas those in the no-booster condition merely attended a weigh-in at three and nine months following treatment. Surprisingly, the addition of family members did not lead to more significant weight loss during the treatment or at follow-up. Also, in contrast to Kingsley and Wilson (1977), Wilson and Brownell (1978) found no effect of booster sessions on weight loss.

A more recent study of spouse inducement by Pearce, LeBow, and Archard (1981) is more supportive and sheds some light on the nature of the spouse effect. These investigations compared wives with a cooperative spouse, women without a spouse, wives with spouses instructed not to sabotage their wives' efforts, and an alternate, nonspecific treatment. Immediately following treatment, no differences between the groups were evident. However, at the 12-month follow-up, the cooperative spouse condition was superior in weight loss to the nonspecific and the wives alone conditions but not to the condition in which spouses were instructed to be detached and noninvolved.

Zitter and Fremouw (1978) contrasted pairs of overweight friends working together on a weight-reduction program with another group of individuals who worked alone. In the partner condition, participants earned a dollar of their deposit for each pound lost and an additional dollar when their partner lost a pound. Those subjects working on their own received $2 for each pound lost. At the end of six weeks of treatment, both groups had lost significant amounts of weight and did not differ from one another. At a six-week follow-up, there was tendency for the individual group to have lost more weight than the partner group. At the six month follow-up, the individual group was clearly superior to the partners. So the evidence supplied by Zitter and Fremouw indicates that, rather than facilitate weight reduction, the partners actually reinforced one another for deviating from the requested behaviors.

Behavior Therapy in Comparison with Other Treatments

It is now generally accepted that effective weight-reduction programs cannot rely on only one component but must include a combination of various techniques in an integrated fashion. There have been several studies that have compared such a comprehensive package of treatment techniques with other forms of therapy.

Behavior therapy compared with psychotherapy. Two major studies compared a behavioral approach to weight reduction with traditional psychotherapy. In a now classic study, Wollersheim (1970) assigned 79 overweight females to one of four conditions: positive expectation with social pressure, nonspecific therapy, focal therapy based on behavioral principles, and a no-treatment control. The subjects were exposed to ten sessions over a 12-week period. The positive expectation-social pressure group was designed to be similar to that of popular self-help groups. The nonspecific therapy was modeled to portray an insight orientation, and its members focused on the discovery of unconscious motivation and personality characteristics which were responsible for their weight. In contrast, the focal therapy or behavioral group was designed to take an explicit approach to inappropriate eating. Wollersheim found that the behavioral group was clearly superior to the other treatments both at treatment termination and at an eight-week follow-up.

Another study compared a behavioral approach and traditional group therapy with 32 obese patients (Penick, Filion, Fox, & Stunkard, 1971). Again the results of this comparison after a three-month period were quite dramatically in favor of behavioral therapy. After the treatment, the behavioral approach was clearly superior to the control therapy group. Fifty-three percent of those in the behavioral group had lost more than 20 pounds, 33 percent more than 30 pounds, and 13 percent more than 40 pounds. In contrast, only 24 percent of the control group lost more than 20 pounds and none lost over 30 pounds. Additionally, there was a continuing influence of treatment at both three- and six-month follow-ups. A five-year follow-up of this group by Stunkard and Penick (1979) found no difference between the two groups. From these and other reports it is clear that comprehensive behavioral treatments are far superior to other forms of therapy, be they traditional psychotherapy, nutritional counseling, or the like, at least for a period of one year.

Comparison to drug treatment. Öst and Götestam (1976) conducted the first formal comparison of drug and behavioral treatments. The behavioral treatment was based primarily on Stuart's program and included changes in eating behavior, dieting, and exercise over 20 sessions. Those on the drug received fenfluramine up to 60 mg two times a day. At the end of treatment the behavioral group had lost 20 pounds, the fenfluramine group slightly over 12 pounds, and the control group 7.7 pounds. At this time, the behavioral group showed no other differences reaching a significant level. In fact, the drug group did not differ from those on the control condition.

At a one-month follow-up, the behavioral group maintained significantly lower weights, while subjects in the other two groups did not. Moreover, the gains made by the behavioral group continued at a one-year follow-up, while subjects in the drug and control groups had gone back to their pretreatment weights.

In a more recent study, Dahms, Molitch, Bray, Greenway, Atkinson, and Hamilton (1978) compared the effectiveness of Sanorex (mazindol), Tepanil (diethylproprion), and behavioral treatment with a placebo control. The behavioral group was conducted by a dietician with sessions lasting one hour, and there was emphasis on an analysis and change of eating and exercise habits. At the end of treatment, participants in each class lost weight with no differences among the various groups.

In summarizing their report, Dahms et al. comment on many of the advantages of the behavioral group, including the lower cost and efficacy. In this case, behavior therapy produced weight loss with more efficient use of professional time.

Although not a formal comparison of drug and behavioral group treatments, a report by Johnson and Hughes (1979) is consistent with the above findings. They found that mazindol did yield significantly more weight loss when compared to a placebo condition. However, subjects in a no-drug control condition who were exposed merely to lectures on behavioral techniques lost as much weight as those in the drug group. In this study (Johnson and Hughes, 1979), subjects in the drug group and in the no-drug group were exposed to the identical lectures on behavioral control of eating and exercise.

Applications of Behavioral Approaches in the Clinic

There are several reports of the application of behavioral principles to clinical populations incuding the programs of Musante (1976), Currey, Malcolm, Riddle, and Schacte (1977), Jeffrey, Wing, and Stunkard (1978) at the Stanford Eating Disorders Clinic, and Johnson, Stalonas, Christ, and Pock (1979) in Mississippi.

As described by Musante, the program at Duke required participants to live in a dormitory and eat all their meals in a common dining room. The participants were given a 700 Kcal diet and exposed to lectures on behavior modification and instructions on changing their eating. Musante noted that the average patient stayed approximately ten weeks and that nearly half of the 229 patients described in the report lost more than 20 pounds, with one-fourth losing 40 or more pounds. He also found that length of treatment was correlated with increased weight loss. Thus, of those patients who remained in treatment for over six months, 85 percent lost 20 or more pounds and 61 percent lost 40 or more pounds. However, it must be recognized that this program is costly and intensive, and given this degree of effort, the weight loss is not impressive.

The report by Currey et al. (1977) is even less encouraging. The patients in this program completed 10, 20, 30, and up to 40 weeks of treatment. Of the 56 patients whom Currey followed for one year, 70 percent regressed to their pretreatment weight, 10 percent were able to maintain their weight loss, and only 20 percent continued to lose weight during the year. Jeffrey et al. (1978) followed 125 patients in the Stanford Eating Disorders Clinic. Treatment was conducted in groups led by two therapists meeting for ten weeks or 20 weeks. These sessions involved a variety of behavioral procedures including self-monitoring, stimulus control, slowing the rate of the eating, dietary planning, and exercise. The average weight loss was 11 pounds, and at the follow-up many clients reported being able to maintain the weight loss but they were not able to lose additional weight. As in other programs, weight loss was highly variable and ranged from 40 pounds lost to an almost 50 pound weight gain. In all, approximately 40 percent of the subjects lost weight during the follow-up period and 55 percent gained.

Johnson, Stalonas, Christ, and Pock (1979) describe the development and clinical application of a comprehensive program that integrates nutrition, exercise, and behavioral techniques—all oriented toward weight loss and a more active lifestyle. Data are presented on 54 patients who averaged 35 years of age and approximately 185 pounds and who were 48 percent overweight. The 54 participants lost 9.6 pounds at program termination, which represented a reduction of almost 8 percent of excess weight over the ten-week period.

The 13 patients completing the program in 1976 averaged 9.3 pounds of weight loss, and they progressed to 15.5 pounds lost at the one-year follow-up. Thirty-one percent of individuals in this group lost between 21 and 30 pounds, and one individual lost 34 pounds. While a majority (62 percent) of the participants in this subgroup continued to lose weight, their pattern of weight loss was not characteristic of the group as a whole.

Two groups of 11 and eight participants completed the program in 1977. For the first group (1977-1), there was average weight loss of 8.7 pounds at a nine-month follow-up. As many of the patients in this group regained weight which was lost during the program as continued to lose at a one-year follow-up.

In contrast, an additional group of eight patients completing the program in 1977 (1977-2) was more promising. They lost 11.3 pounds at program termination, were down to an average of 16.8 pounds at three-month follow-up, and had continued to lose at the one-year follow-up. As a group, the reduction from 31.8 percent overweight at the termination of the program to 13.7 percent overweight at the one-year follow-up represented a change from a moderately obese category to a designation of only marginally overweight. In this group, one patient has regained the weight loss, one is maintaining the loss, and the remaining six continued to lose.

Johnson et al. (1979) also reported on two groups who completed the program in 1978. The first (1978-1) averaged 10.4 pounds lost at program termination, which was approximately a 7 percent decrease in percent overweight. At the three-month follow-up, this group evidenced further weight loss to 14.4 pounds lost. The final group in 1978 (1978-2) was the heaviest thus far at 58.9 percent overweight. They lost 8.4 pounds after the ten-week program and continued to lose at the three- and nine-month follow-ups, when they were down to 17.4 pounds lost on the average.

It is obvious from this brief review that an approach that integrates nutrition, eating-habit change, and an active lifestyle within a behavioral framework is the most effective weight-reduction treatment for the vast majority of overweight persons. Behavioral treatment is the most efficacious, economical, and least aversive therapy for weight reduction. Due to the wide variability in response to treatment, components of behavioral treatment such as stimulus control or contingency management may be more important for some participants than for others. The evidence of the superiority of behavioral treatment beyond a one-year period is less than encouraging at this point; however, we can expect that better provisions for the maintenance of weight loss will emerge from research in the involvement of family members.

Clinical Prescription

As previously discussed, it is important to conduct a thorough assessment including evaluation against explicit inclusion/exclusion criteria. The therapist will want to have a profile of each patient's eating behavior, activity patterns, and general lifestyle. This information should be communicated to prospective participants, and they should be well aware of what the program involves. Acceptance in a program for weight reduction should be a mutual decision by the therapist and the patient. The therapist has the relevant knowledge of the patient including an evaluation over inclusion/exclusion criteria. Equally important, the patient should be aware of *what the behavioral program entails*. The assessment and the clinical prescription for weight reduction to follow is based on that outlined by Johnson and his associates (Johnson & Stalonas, 1981; Johnson et al. 1979; Stalonas et al., 1978).

Group Treatment of Obesity

Goals. The weight-reduction program should be a systematic attempt to change eating habits and activity patterns and to promote a more active lifestyle. Such a program is outlined by Johnson and Stalonas (1981), presented in ten chapters which specify for the participants what to do and when to do it. Although the program describes specific tasks to be followed, exactly what is done for each participant depends on the initial assessment, so that in all cases the program can be individualized.

Specific instructions are given for changing eating behavior, increasing exercise, and developing a more active lifestyle. Chapters can be completed in a week or more, but they are criterion referenced, so that a participant is expected to complete the tasks in a chapter prior to moving on to the next chapter regardless of time.

Changes in eating behavior include eating three meals a day, stimulus control, and reduced snacking. Likewise, exercise represents a major portion of the program, and step-wise increases in activity begin at utilization of 150 Kcal/day and progress to 400 Kcal/day in the ninth chapter. These increases in activity are sought on an individual basis and in accordance with specific individual interests. Aerobic or rhythmic exercises are recommended rather than static nonaerobic exercises. Thus, the participants in the program are encouraged to walk, jog, and swim—all activities which, if practiced routinely, can improve cardiovascular and general physical fitness. The participants are also requested to engage in at least one community activity. Examples of these activities include joining a bowling league, taking tennis or golf lessons, jogging, or joining other outdoor recreational groups such as the Sierra Club. These activities not only increase energy expenditure but, more important, promote social contacts, and, thus, they further assure that the overweight do not become trapped in the paradox of increasing both social isolation and weight after the program ends.

Treatment techniques. Johnson and Stalonas (1981) rely on the standard array of self-control procedures including monitoring (including graphing), contingency management, chaining, stimulus control, relaxation training, cognitive restructuring, assertive training, and the use of aversive stimuli. Moreover, these interventions are juxtaposed and integrated with proper nutrition and instructions on energy balance, food appreciation, liquid reduction, and goal setting.

Implementation of the Program. The program can be conducted with a group over ten to 15 weekly meetings with booster and follow-up sessions. With eight to 12 participants, each meeting lasts approximately one to two hours and is conducted by a psychologist and a dietician or nurse co-therapist in our clinic. An outline of the specific topics presented in the group sessions is presented in Table 4.2. A dietician or nurse is a crucial member of the treatment team and functions as a resource person on specific nutritional problems encountered with diseases such as diabetes, heart disease, hypoglycemia, and hyperlipidemia, to name a few.

Conducting group sessions. In our experience, sessions are best conducted on a weekly basis. They should be firmly grounded within a behavioral approach to group therapy (Johnson, 1975), so that in addition to an individual review of progress and group discussion, a variety of other behavioral techniques can be utilized to promote therapeutic goals. Participants can roleplay problem areas such as refusing food from others, practice relaxation training as an adjunct to other tactics for avoiding snacking, and engage in group problem solving to deal with other impediments to their progress. Also, at scheduled intervals, the group can visit local restaurants to practice chaining, time-out while eating, and menu ordering in natural, social environments. Each of these procedures is designed to offer the participants a permanent alternative to their current eating and activity patterns.

Groups may vary in size from as few as four to as many as 15 members. Groups of greater than 12 members, however, tend to become unwieldy, with a limited amount of time to attend to each member. With groups greater than six members, a co-leader is necessary to share responsibility.

TABLE 4.2
Outline for Each Behavioral Weight-Reduction Session

1. (a) Introductions of Participants
   (b) Topics Discussed: Role of weight in life--How losing weight will change life; Fat and food--Facts and myths; Focus of program--Eating, exercise, thinking thin, lifestyle
   (c) Review of Chapter 1 in Weight No Longer

2. (a) Individual and Group Review of Progress
   (b) Exercise Demonstrations; Discussion of Aerobic Exercise and Cardiovascular Fitness
   (c) Orientation for Spouses and Other Family Members
   (d) Topic Discussed: Community Activity (bowling leagues, tennis, swimming, etc.)
   (e) Review of Chapter 2

3. (a) Individual and Group Review of Progress
   (b) Exercise Period
   (c) Nutrition Demonstration (balanced meal, food comparisons, etc.)
   (d) Review of Chapter 3

4. (a) Individual and Group Review of Progress
   (b) Exercise Period
   (c) Refusal Training
   (d) Review of Chapter 4

5. (a) Individual and Group Review of Progress
   (b) Exercise Period
   (c) Relaxation Training
   (d) Review of Chapter 5

6. (a) Eat Out in Restaurant
   (b) Individual and Group Review of Progress
   (c) Review of Chapter 6

7. (a) Individual and Group Review of Progress
   (b) Exercise Period
   (c) Topic Discussed: Reducing Calories within Balanced Meal
   (d) Dealing With Problem Areas
   (e) Review of Chapter 7

8. (a) Individual and Group Review of Progress
   (b) Exercise Period
   (c) Review of Chapter 8

9. (a) Individual and Group Review of Progress
   (b) Exercise Period
   (c) Maintaining Progress
   (d) Review of Chapter 9

10. (a) Eat Out in Restaurant
    (b) Individual and Group Review of Progress
    (c) Follow-up Plans
    (d) Review of Chapter 10

Each session commences with a personal weigh-in period, followed by an individual review of progress, and then group discussion and topic presentation. For accurate and reliable measurement, a balanced-bar scale is necessary. Whether the participants reveal their weight loss is an individual decision. Regardless, it should be emphasized that progress during the first five weeks of the program is not so much in terms of weight loss as in behavior change. Thus, short-term weight loss takes a back seat to learning how to eat correctly and be more active.

Prior to the group discussion a private meeting between each participant and a co-leader is held to review progress, check on homework assignments, and attend to matters of importance for that participant. This "individual time" permits the co-leader to tailor the program to meet individual needs. It should not last more than five to seven minutes per member. During this time, the progress of each member on various components of the program is recorded on a progress review sheet which corresponds to the tasks in *Weight No Longer*. Also, this time allows for individual encouragement, prompting, and suggestion. As the progress of each group participant is being reviewed, other group members can review the material in the next chapter.

After the "individual time," the group convenes and the leaders take ten minutes to review the progress of the total group. Afterward, group discussion is oriented toward implementing the progress and solving common problems. Co-leaders can prompt and lead discussions based on the knowledge of each member's performance. In dealing with areas of difficulty, it is initially helpful to have a participant describe his or her problem, followed by others commenting on possible solutions, and finally concluding with a clear statement of how the person intends to deal with the problem over the next week. Appropriate roleplaying is frequently used to establish firmly the required behavior.

After the issues regarding the week's prior assignment have been thoroughly discussed, it is time to introduce the new material. Careful attention should be paid to ensure that each member understands the next steps to follow in the chapter.

A Case Report

The following is a report on a patient (N.J.) who was a participant in our group program. The description includes information gathered during the screening and assessment phase as well as a summary of N.J.'s progress.

Identifying Information

N.J. was, at the time of screening, 28 years old, white, female, 5′4″, and 171 pounds. She was employed as a staff writer for a local newspaper, is a college graduate with a major in journalism, and lived in an apartment by herself.

History/Onset

N.J. recalled being overweight since childhood. She noted that baby pictures and her baby book all reveal the presence of significant overweight throughout her early years and adolescence. However, she did state that she was not exceptionally large at birth. Although she has been overweight all her life, N.J. reported increasing weight gain, which was more noticeable during her late-teens years. For example, she noticed being overweight during high school, with her weight increasing considerably while in college.

N.J. described her mother as of normal size and her father as moderately overweight (15–20 percent). She also noted that she had one sibling who is slightly overweight. There was no significant disease such as diabetes or hypertension in her immediate or remote family.

Eating Patterns

N.J. reported eating three meals a day, which included a light to moderate breakfast, a cheese sandwich and yogurt for lunch, and a dinner of vegetables and cheese. She did report frequent late-night snacks with substantial caloric intake. N.J. had been a strict vegetarian since 1972, which she attributed to an abhorrence of animal meat and slaughter. Analysis of her food intake revealed a well-balanced intake in terms of proteins, carbohydrates, and fats—although sufficient iron may be a problem. Based on her weight, which had increased 20 pounds over the previous nine months, and her reported food intake, it was estimated that she consumed approximately 2,500 Kcals/day.

Surprisingly, N.J. was a disciplined eater in her three meals a day, but her downfall was the frequent, uncontrolled snacking in the evening, which consisted largely of yogurt and fruit.

Activity Patterns

As previously noted, N.J. worked as a newspaper reporter and her job involved travel and activity. However, a good amount of time was also spent at her desk writing and typing. She was never physically active, although she has engaged in yoga.

Physical Condition

N.J. reported regular childhood diseases and one hospitalization for a tonsillectomy. She appeared healthy but had had no physical examination for over three years, and she was referred for such.

Personal Adjustment

N.J. had no history of psychiatric hospitalizations and reported no serious emotional problems throughout her 28 years. She enjoyed her work and the pursuit of a career in professional journalism. N.J. reported satisfactory personal relationships with peers, but noted that she would have been more outgoing if she could lose weight. In fact, in further elaboration of this issue, she noted that her major desire to lose weight was to increase her physical attractiveness. Although she dated occasionally, she had never been involved in a serious romantic relationship, which she attributes to her overweight condition.

Reason for Losing Weight

N.J. reported that weight loss would increase her physical attractiveness and sense of self-esteem. She also stated that she was concerned with the effect that the excess weight would eventually have on her health.

Past Dieting

N.J. had tried a variety of diets, particularly while she was a high school student and in her early college years. These consisted of a Weight Watchers Program and a variety of diets such as Dr. Stillman's. On one occasion she lost 15 pounds but gradually regained it because of poor adherence.

Summary and Disposition

N.J. met all of our inclusion criteria in terms of age, weight, and available time. Additionally, her personal adjustment was adequate beyond some isolation induced by her overweight; her desire for weight reduction was predominantly internal; but the remaining factor before she was accepted was a thorough physical examination.

She was oriented to the program and referred for a physical examination.

Summary of Progress

N.J. reported to the weight-reduction group approximately three weeks after her screening. Her physical examination had been negative and contact with her physician indicated that she was healthy with no condition that would interfere with her ability to participate in the program. Upon entry, her initial weight was 164 pounds, and it was pointed out that she might wish to postpone treatment if she was continuing on a downward trend. N.J. decided to enter the program, for she felt that her weight decrease was more the result of some fluid loss due to her menstrual period.

N.J. lost rather consistently throughout the ten-week program. Her snacking and other forms of uncontrolled eating rapidly diminished. She began exercising regularly, which consisted of jogging for one half hour a day in addition to regular calisthenics. Additionally, N.J. maintained a caloric intake of approximately 1,000–1,200 Kcals, which she felt was sufficient. During the ten weeks of the program, her weight dropped from 164 to 151 pounds. At the first follow-up four weeks after termination, N.J. was down to 145 pounds, and at the second follow-up one month later, her weight decreased further to 139 pounds. Discussion with her at the one-year follow-up revealed that she had reached a goal weight of 115 pounds and three years following treatment she weighed 119 pounds.

In addition to the rather dramatic and substantial weight reduction, N.J. had effectively learned to control her eating behavior and, more important, to increase her activity level. She noted that physical activity and exercise were now a permanent part of her lifestyle. In fact, she jogs regularly and has entered several local "fun runs." Also, N.J. has noticed significant increases in her social activities and began dating on a regular basis.

Of course, N.J. represents the ideal case. She negotiated all aspects of the program very well and responded with weight loss and a change in lifestyle. Therapists should not expect all patients to respond in such a uniform and highly successful fashion.

Professional, Ethical, and Legal Issues in Conducting Weight-Reduction Groups

There are several features that therapists must consider prior to conducting weight-reduction groups including proper state licensure, thorough familiarity with behavioral techniques, supervised experience and/or attendance at a workshop on weight reduction, and a solid background in basic research on eating behavior and metabolism. First and foremost, the therapist should be licensed or properly certified to practice a profession in his or her locale. Additionally, since there is a very heavy emphasis on behavioral principles and techniques, more than a rudimentary knowledge of behavioral therapy is necessary. Also, it is highly recommended that the therapist have specific training in conducting weight-reduction groups and/or attend a workshop. The therapist should have an understanding of the variables influencing eating, normal metabolism, and common diseases such as diabetes and hypertension that will certainly be encountered in practice. Thus, familiarity with behavior therapy per se is *not sufficient* to conduct weight-reduction groups. This is not to say that the therapist need have formal training in endocrinology, internal medicine, or nutrition. Rather, the therapist conducting weight-reduction groups should have an understanding of normal metabolism and the basic diseases associated with obesity, because questions will arise in the course of practice which must be answered. Attendance at weight-reduction workshops, supervised experience, and a careful reading of the Suggested Bibliography at the end of this chapter should provide sufficient preparation.

Equally important is close collaboration with physicians and dieticians. In fact, the major source of referrals for weight reduction come from these professionals. A close working relationship can insure that patients who come for treatment without a recent physical examination can be referred and followed by their physicians. Also, as noted, dieticians can make an important contribution as co-therapists in weight-reduction groups.

Leaders of weight-reduction groups should also have general clinical training such as that provided in APA-approved clinical and counseling psychology Ph.D. programs. Additionally, they should also have the personal characteristics of warmth, empathy, and genuineness which have been found to be important in the conduct of any therapy. And last, the therapist *must* be of normal size. An overweight or otherwise obese therapist has no credibility in the operation of a weight-reduction group.

Suggestions for Further Research

As is obvious in Table 4.1, the behavioral studies on weight reduction are quite sophisticated in terms of experimental design, adequacy of measures, and control of extraneous variables. Additionally, the behavioral approach appears to be at least on par with and in most cases clearly superior to alternative forms of treatment. However, many problems remain. As outlined by Johnson, Wildman, and O'Brien (1980) these deficiencies include: the brief duration of treatment and follow-up, the use of slightly overweight subjects as opposed to the clinically obese, the meager weight loss which may be statistically but often not clinically significant, and the variability in response to treatment. Also, research assessing the importance of treatment for individuals who are 100 percent overweight is lacking.

Johnson et al. (1980) note a more serious shortcoming in behavioral weight reduction research, namely, that we are not sure what participants do when they implement behavioral programs. Thus, there is a lack of documented behavioral changes that accompany weight-reduction programs. Although participants are instructed to change eating behavior, increase exercise, and engage in a more active lifestyle, exactly what they do is still somewhat of a mystery.

References

Abraham S., & Nordseick, M. Relationship of excess weight in children and adults. *Public Health Reports,* 1960, *75,* 263–273.

Allon, N. The stigma of overweight in everyday life. In G. A. Bray (Ed.), *Obesity in perspective*. Washington, D.C.: U. S. Government Printing Office, 1973.

American Medical Association. *Drug evaluation*. Acton, Mass.: Publishing Sciences Group, 1973, p. 369.

Ashby, W. A., & Wilson, G. T. Behavior therapy for obesity: Booster sessions and long-term maintenance of weight loss. *Behaviour Research and Therapy,* 1977, *15,* 451–463.

Ashwell, M., Priest, P., & Bondoux, M. In A. N. Howard (Ed.), *Recent Advances in Obesity Research: I*. London: Newman, 1975, p. 74.

Bellack, A. S. A comparison of self-reinforcement and self-monitoring in a weight reduction program. *Behavior Therapy,* 1976, *7,* 68–75.

Bellack, A. S., Rozensky, R., & Schwartz, J. A comparison of two forms of self-monitoring in a behavioral weight reduction program. *Behavior Therapy,* 1974, *5,* 523–530.

Bjorntorp, P. Exercise in the treatment of obesity. In M. J. Albrin (Ed.), *Clinics in endocrinology and metabolism*. Philadelphia: W. B. Saunders, 1976.

Blundell, J. E., & Rogers, P. J. Pharmacologic approaches to the understanding of obesity. *The Psychiatric Clinics of North America,* 1978, *1,* 629–650.

Bray, G. A. *The obese patient*. Philadelphia: W. B. Saunders, 1976.

Bray, G. A. To treat or not to treat—that is the question? In G. A. Bray (Ed.), *Recent advances in obesity research: II*. London: Newman, 1978.

Bray, G. A., Greenway, F. L., Barry, R. E., Benfield, J. R., Fiser, R. L., Dahms, W. T., Atkinson, R. L., & Schwartz, A. A. Surgical treatment of obesity: A review of our experience and an analysis of published reports. *International Journal of Obesity,* 1977, *1,* 331–367.

Brook, C. D. G. Fat cells and infant feeding. In G. A. Bray (Ed.), *Recent advances in obesity research: II*. London: Newman, 1978, 196–199.

Charney, E., Goodman, H. C., McBride, M., Lyon, B., & Pratt, R. Childhood antecedents of adult obesity. *New England Journal of Medicine,* 1976, *295,* 6–9.

Currey, H., Malcolm, R., Riddle, E., & Schacte, M. Behavioral treatment of obesity: Limitations and results with the chronically obese. *Journal of the American Medical Association,* 1977, *237,* 2829–2831.

Dahms, W. T., Molitch, M., Bray, G. A., Greenway, F. L., Atkinson, R. L., &

Hamilton, K. Treatment of obesity: Cost-benefit assessment of behavioral therapy, placebo, and two anorectic drugs. *American Journal of Clinical Nutrition*, 1978, *31*, 774–778.

Diament, C., & Wilson, G. T. An experimental investigation of the effects of covert sensitization in an analogue eating situation. *Behavior Therapy*, 1975, *6*, 499–509.

Dunkel, L. D., & Glaros, A. Comparison of self-instruction and stimulus control treatments for obesity. *Cognitive Therapy and Research*, 1978, *2*, 75–78.

Dwyer, J., & Mayer, J. The dismal condition: Problems faced by obese adolescent girls in American society. In G. A. Bray (Ed.), *Obesity in perspective*. Washington, D.C.: U. S. Government Printing Office, 1973.

Elliot, C. H., & Denney, D. R. Weight control through covert sensitization and false feedback. *Journal of Consulting and Clinical Psychology*, 1975, *43*, 842–850.

Epstein, L. H., & Wing, R. Aerobic exercise and weight. *Addictive Behavior*, 1980, *6*.

Ferster, C. B., Nurnberger, J. I., & Levitt, E. B. The control of eating. *Journal of Mathetics*, 1962, *1*, 87–109.

Food and Drug Administration Bulletin. May–June, 1978.

Genuth, S. M., Castro, J. H., & Vertes, V. Weight reduction in obesity by outpatient semi-starvation. *Journal of the American Medical Association*, 1974, *230*, 987–991.

Hall, S. M., Bass, A., & Monroe, J. Continued contact and monitoring as follow-up strategies: A long-term study of obesity treatment. *Addictive Behaviors*, 1978, *3*, 139–147.

Halmi, K. Gastric bypass for massive obesity. In A. J. Stunkard (Ed.), *Obesity*. Philadelphia: W. B. Saunders, 1980.

Harris, M. B., & Hallbauer, E. S. Self-directed weight control through eating and exercise. *Behaviour Research and Therapy*, 1973, *11*, 523–529.

Hirsch, J. The psychological consequences of obesity. In G. A. Bray (Ed.), *Obesity in perspective*. Washington, D.C.: U. S. Government Printing Office, 1973.

Horton, E. S. The role of exercise in the prevention and treatment of obesity. In G. A. Bray (Ed.), *Obesity in perspective*. Washington, D.C.: U. S. Government Printing Office, 1973.

Janda, L. H., & Rimm, D. C. Covert sensitization in the treatment of obesity. *Journal of Abnormal Psychology*, 1972, *80*, 37–42.

Jeffery, R. W., Wing, R. R., & Stunkard, A. J. Behavioral treatment of obesity: The state of the art, 1976. *Behavior Therapy*, 1978, *9*, 189–199.

Johnson, W. G. Group therapy: A behavioral perspective. *Behavior Therapy*, 1975, *6*, 30–38.

Johnson, W. G. Health Habit Survey. University of Mississippi Medical Center, unpublished document, 1979.

Johnson, W. G. *Professional Manual to Accompany "Weight No Longer: The Psychologists' Guide to Lasting Weight Loss."* Jackson: University of Mississippi Medical Center, 1979.

Johnson, W. G., & Hughes, J. R. Mazindol: Its efficacy and mode of action in generating weight loss. *Addictive Behaviors*, 1979, *4*, 237–244.

Johnson, W. G., & Stalonas, P. Measuring skinfold thickness: A cautionary note. *Addictive Behaviors, 1977, 2,* 105–107.

Johnson, W. G., & Stalonas, P. *Weight no longer*. Gretna, La.: Pelican, 1981.

Johnson, W. G., Stalonas, P. M., Christ, M., & Polk, S. R. The development and induction of behavioral weight-reduction program. *International Journal of Obesity*, 1979, *3*, 229–238.

Johnson, W. G., Wildman, H. E., & O'Brien, T. The assessment of program adherence: The Achilles' heel of behavioral weight reduction?, 1980.

Kingsley, R. G., & Wilson, G. T. Behavior therapy for obesity: A comparative investigation of long-term efficacy. *Journal of Consulting and Clinical Psychology*, 1977, *45*, 288–298.

Mahoney, M. J. Self-reward and self-monitoring techniques for weight control. *Behavior Therapy*, 1974, *5*, 48–57.

Mahoney, M. J. Fat fiction. *Behavior Therapy*, 1975, *6*, 416–418.

Mahoney, M. J., Moura, N. G. M., & Wade, T. C. Relative efficacy of self-reward, self-punishment, and self-monitoring techniques for weight loss. *Journal of Consulting and Clinical Psychology*, 1973, *40*, 404–407.

Marks, H. H. Influence of obesity in morbidity and mortality. *Bulletin of the New York Academy of Sciences*, 1960, *36*, 296–312.

Marlatt, G. A., & Gordon, J. R. Determinants of relapse: Implications for the maintenance of behavior change. In P. Davidson (Ed.), *Behavioral Medicine: Changing health life styles*. New York: Bruner-Mazel, 1979.

Mayer, J. *Overweight: Causes, cost, and control*. Englewood Cliffs, N. J.: Prentice-Hall, 1968.

McReynolds, W. T., Lutz, R. N., Paulsen, B. K., & Kohrs, M. B. Weight loss resulting from two behavior modification procedures with nutritionists as therapist. *Behavior Therapy*, 1976, *7*, 283–291.

Millar, J. W., Innes, J. A., & Munro, J. F. An evaluation of the efficacy and acceptability of "Slender" in refractory obesity. *International Journal of Obesity*, 1978, *2*, 53–58.

Musante, G. J. The Dietary Rehabilitation Clinic: Evaluative report of a behavioral and dietary treatment of obesity. *Behavior Therapy*, 1976, *7*, 198–204.

O'Neil, P. M., Currey, H. S., Hirsh, A. A., Riddle, F. F., Taylor, C. I., Malcolm R. J., & Sexauer, J. D. Effects of sex of subject and spouse involvement on weight loss in a behavioral treatment program: A retrospective investigation. *Addictive Behaviors*, 1979, *4*, 167–177.

Öst, L. G. & Götestam, K. G. Behavioral and pharmacological treatments for obesity: An experimental comparison. *Addictive Behaviors*, 1976, *1*, 331–338.

Payne, H. J., DeWind, L. T., & Commons, R. R. Metabolic observations on patients with jejunocolic shunts. *American Journal of Surgery*, 1963, *106*, 273–289.

Peace, J. W., LeBow, M. D., & Archard, J. Role of spouse inducement in the behavioral treatment of overweight women. *Journal of Consulting and Clinical Psychology*, 1981, *49*, 236–244.

Penick, S. B., Filion, R., Fox, S., & Stunkard, A. J. Behavior modification in the treatment of obesity. *Psychosomatic Medicine*, 1971, *33*, 49–55.

Reisin, E., Abel, R., Modon, M., Silverberg, D. S., Eliahou, H. E., & Modan,

B. Effect of weight loss without salt restriction on the reduction of blood pressure in overweight hypertensive patients. *New England Journal of Medicine*, 1978, *298*, 1–5.

Robinson, S., & Winnick, H. Z. Severe psychotic disturbances following crash diet weight loss. *Archives of General Psychiatry*, 1973, 29, 559–562.

Romanczyk, R. G. Self-monitoring in the treatment of obesity: Parameters of reactivity. *Behavior Therapy*, 1974, 5, 531–540.

Scoville, B. A. Review of amphetamine-like drugs by the Food and Drug Administration. In G. A. Bray (Ed.), *Obesity in perspective*. Washington, D.C.: U.S. Government Printing Office, 1976, 441–443.

Seltzer, C. C., & Mayer, J. A simple criterion of obesity. *Postgraduate Medicine*, 1965, *38*, A101–A107. Cited in R. B. Stuart & B. Davis, *Slim chance in a fat world: Behavioral control of obesity*. Champaign, Ill.: Research Press, 1972, p. 11.

Society of Actuaries. *Build and blood pressure study*. Chicago: Society of Actuaries, 1959.

Stalonas, P. M., Johnson, W. G., & Christ, M. Behavior modification for obesity: The evaluation of exercise, contingency management, and program adherence. *Journal of Consulting and Clinical Psychology*, 1978, *46*, 463–469.

Stamler, R., Stamler, J., Riedlinger, W. F., Algera, G., & Roberts, R. H. Weight and blood pressure. *Journal of the American Medical Association*, 1978, *240*, 1607–1610.

Stuart, R. B. Behavioral control of overeating. *Behavior Research and Therapy*, 1967, *5*, 357–365.

Stunkard, A. J., & Rush, J. Dieting and depression reexamined: A critical review of reports of untoward responses during weight reduction for obesity. *Annals of Internal Medicine*, 1974, *81*, 526–533.

Stunkard, A. J., & Penick, S. B. Behavior modification in the treatment of obesity. *Archives of General Psychiatry*, 1979, *36*, 801–806.

Ten-State Nutrition Survey, 1968–1970. DHEW Publication No. (HSM) 72-8131, 1972.

Wilson, G. T., & Brownell, K. Behavior therapy for obesity: Including family members in the treatment process. *Behavior Therapy*, 1978, 9, 943–945.

Wollersheim, J. P. Effectiveness of group therapy based upon learning principles in the treatment of overweight women. *Journal of Abnormal Psychology*, 1970, *76*, 462–474.

Zitter, R. E., & Fremouw, W. J. Individual versus partner consequation for weight loss. *Behavior Therapy*, 1978, 9, 808–813

Suggested Readings

Obesity: Basic Research and Treatment

Johnson, W. G., & Stalonas, P. M. *Weight no longer*. Gretna, La.: Pelican, 1981.

Bray, G. A. *The obese patient*. Philadelphia: W. B. Saunders, 1976.

Bray, G. (Ed.). *Recent advances in obesity research: II. Proceedings of the 2nd International Congress on Obesity*. London: Newman Publishing, Ltd., 1978.

Mayer, J. *Overweight: Causes, cost, and control*. Englewood Cliffs, N.J.: Prentice-Hall, 1968.

Research on obesity: A report of the DNSS/MRC group. Compiled by W. P. T. Jones, Department of Health and Social Security. London: Her Majesty's Stationery Office, 1976.

Schachter, S. Some extraordinary facts about obese humans and rats. *American Psychologist*, 1972, *26*, 129–144.

Stuart, R. B. Behavioral control of overeating. *Behaviour Research and Therapy*, 1967, *5*, 357–365.

Stuart, R. B. A three-dimensional program for the treatment of obesity. *Behaviour Research and Therapy*, 1971, *9*, 177–186.

Stuart, R. B., & Davis, B. *Slim chance in a fat world: The behavioral control of obesity*. Champaign, Ill.: Research Press, 1972.

Stunkard, A. New therapies for the eating disorders: Behavior modification of obesity and anorexia nervosa. *Archives of General Psychiatry*, 1972, *26*, 391–398.

Stunkard, A.T. (Ed.). *Obesity*. Philadelphia: W. B. Saunders, 1980

Behavior Modification

Bellack, A. S., & Hersen, M. *Behavior modification: An introductory textbook*. Baltimore: Williams & Wilkins, 1977.

Exercise

Cooper, K. H. *The new aerobics*. New York: Bantam Books, 1970.

Cooper, M., & Cooper, K. H. *Aerobics for women*. New York: Bantam Books, 1972.

Nutrition

Katch, F. I., & McArdle, W. D. *Nutrition, weight control and exercise*. Boston: Houghton Mifflin, 1977.

Kraus, B. *Calories and carbohydrates*. New York: Signet, 1973.

Williams, R. J. *Nutrition in a nutshell*. Garden City, N.Y., Doubleday, 1962.

5

Encopresis

Jeffrey M. Klein

Introduction

Encopresis is a disorder which involves difficulty in the control of fecal expulsion. Three separate groups of encopretic children can be delineated: (1) feebleminded or untrained children; (2) children who have a nervous system or anatomical defect from such disorders as Hirschsprung's disease; and (3) children whose encopresis stems from psychological and behavioral variables. The following discussion will center on encopresis that has a psychogenic origin.

Two important differences between enuresis and encopresis can be observed. In contrast to enuresis, encopresis occurs much less frequently and is generally considered to be a more serious disorder. In addition, unlike enuresis, soiling rarely occurs during sleep. Encopresis, however, may occur together with diurnal enuresis in cases when the child is unable to control these as well as other bodily processes.

There are no clear-cut criteria for deciding when occasional soiling becomes "serious enough" to be seen as "encopresis." Some professionals view inappropriate fecal elimination as dysfunctional and problematic when it occurs in a child over two years of age (e.g., Silber, 1968), while some feel that the lack of control over fecal expulsion becomes problematic beyond the age of four (e.g., Sheinbein, 1975). In addition, the number of soiling incidents which must occur before the behavior is labeled "encopresis" is not well specified in most accounts of the problem. Bellman (1966) cites that the incidence of encopresis is about 1 or 2 percent. However, this figure may be an underestimate of the true incidence, because soiling tends to be seen as so distasteful by most people that the parents and the child are likely to conceal this problem for as long as possible.

Theoretical Analysis

Nonbehavioral Formulations

Prugh (1963) and other psychodynamic writers discuss fecal expulsion in terms of the child's desire to experience the pleasure involved in the stimulation of the anoretic mucosa during bowel movement. Premature or overly strict attempts at toilet training are often implicated in ego-analytic accounts of such fecal retention problems. In addition, most ego-analytic accounts of the disorder emphasize that encopresis is a symptom reflecting the power struggle between a child and his parents for control. The child is seen as unconsciously using these encopretic symptoms as a means of infuriating or tormenting his mother, who cannot possibly enforce total obedience on this issue. However, encopretic children do not seem unusually obstreperous or rebellious in their overall demeanor. On the contrary, Richmond, Eddy, and Gerrard (1954) found that encopretic children are particularly obedient and conforming and are most often neat in all areas except gastrointestinal functioning. Except for their soiling, these children tend to control overt manifestations of aggression and hostility and tend to impress adults quite favorably with their appropriate and generally polite behavior.

Encopresis has also been viewed as symptomatic of some other problem areas as well. For example, Chapman (1965) states that very withdrawn children who are deeply enmeshed in their own fantasy world may also exhibit encopresis. In these cases, the encopretic behaviors serve to further alienate others from these children because of the negative reaction that most people have to this behavior. Encopresis is also occasionally found to occur in a basically well-functioning child when a new sibling is born into the family. Under these conditions, the encopretic symptom is seen as a means of regressing to a more infantile stage in reaction to the loss of parental attention. The prognosis for encopresis is excellent when it is precipitated by this type of stressor.

Behavioral Formulations

Unfortunately, many of the case studies and much of the behavioral research on the treatment of encopresis have not directly addressed the theoretical issues related to the behavioral view of the development and maintenance of this dysfunctional behavior.

Neale's (1963) classic study of the behavioral treatment of encopresis discussed defecation in terms of the formation of an S–R connection. Neale states that in healthy individuals when a fecal mass is moved into the rectum, a sensation of fullness is experienced which ultimately leads to the response of proceeding to the toilet and then engaging in the act of defecation. During the process of expulsion, feces is emptied from the colon and descends to the rectum. In individuals with well-functioning bowels, this action requires only a few minutes and becomes a fairly simple reflexive response. However, this defecation process is a long series of coordinated reflexes which can be interrupted by a failure in any part of the entire sequence. Neale suggested that it is the child's fear of toilet-related behaviors that plays a very large part in disrupting this reflex sequence, and he viewed the reduction of this fear as quite important for effective treatment of encopresis.

Since there are clearly both learning factors and environmental contingencies that affect the defecation process, the theoretical framework provided by Neale is too simplistic to explain adequately the complex interaction between the maturational factors involved in gaining control over fecal elimination and the external contingencies that would affect or alter this process. It also should be noted that few theorists after Neale have focused on the role of fear in the development of encopresis.

Several recent behavioral conceptualizations of defecation and encopresis have focused on very different aspects of the elimination process. For example, Young (1973) and Ashkenazi (1975) emphasize the importance of the child's developing a better awareness of the physiological sensations that precede a bowel movement. However, O'Leary and Wilson (1975) have quite a different conceptualization of encopresis which involves two separate phases, a constipation or stool-holding phase which alternates with persistent soiling. Most current treatment programs for encopresis tend to focus on the macroscopic, externally observable behaviors related to defecation rather than the actual physiological elimination process as such. From all of these varied conceptualizations, it would seem that a comprehensive behavioral model of encopresis should account for the physiological, maturational, and environmental factors that affect the development and maintenance of encopretic behavior.

Assessment

Projective Data

Projective data would be likely to include many themes of power and control as delineated above. The person's response style would also be likely to vary erratically between being quite meticulous and compulsive, and being vague and messy. In addition, the testing protocol may show instances of anal content and elimination concerns, for example, "colon" or "rectum" responses on the Rorschach. However, Barling (1976) states that projective data are not particularly useful in planning or implementing a treatment intervention, and he advocates the use of direct, ongoing observation instead of the use of traditional assessment data.

Objective Data

For encopresis, there has been relatively little emphasis on the use of objective assessment measures, because the target behaviors involved in soiling can so easily be collected from direct observation.

Behavioral

Assessment issues. An assessment procedure for encopretic children similar to the framework developed for enuretics by Ciminero and Doleys (1976) can be delineated. Before undertaking the treatment of an encopretic child, the child should have a complete medical examination to rule out any organic etiology for the fecal incontinence, for organically caused encopresis may need very different treatment procedures, usually including a surgical intervention (Wright & Walker, 1978).

Specific details concerning the problematic behavior are gathered during the initial assessment period, most often by means of a family interview. Some important areas of exploration include: (1) the history of the child's soiling and withholding-feces behavior, including the frequency of these target behaviors and any obvious environmental contingencies that precede or follow the behavior in question; (2) the amount of bowel control the child had prior to the onset of the present problem; (3) other behavioral or medical problems that might contribute to the encopretic behavior; and (4) family issues that may affect the child's encopretic behavior, including follow-through with the parents' willingness or ability to cooperate with the treatment program.

Implementation issues. Prior to instituting the actual program contingencies, baseline data on target behaviors are often monitored for several days or weeks. These measures are monitored throughout the intervention as an index of the effectiveness of the imposed contingencies on the soiling behavior. Two of the most common target behaviors are the frequency of the soiling behavior and the frequency of the appropriate use of the toilet facilities. Other data that may also be helpful in designing the program contingencies include the specific behaviors that directly precede and directly follow the soiling behavior and when and where the soiling behavior tends to occur.

Although there is considerable variation evident in the current literature as to the length of the monitoring period, it would be reasonable that the monitoring of these variables should continue for at least six weeks after the frequency of the target behavior consistently falls within an acceptable range. Such monitoring facilitates the modification or reimplementation of the program if there is any substantial recurrence of the encopretic behavior.

Treatment Procedures

Prior to the popularization of behavior modification techniques, analytically oriented psychotherapy and medical approaches using laxatives were the most common interventions used to treat encopresis. Analytic interventions have always tended to be quite lengthy and are often relatively ineffective in eliminating the specific problematic target behavior (e.g., Sheinbein, 1975; Yates, 1970). As for the use of laxatives, it has not been well substantiated by research data whether the laxative methods in and of themselves are particularly successful interventions. In addition, most accounts do not clearly specify what types of counseling or adjunct interventions are employed in conjunction with the use of laxatives when this medical approach is used. However, as will be discussed below, laxatives have been used as part of several behavioral interventions, and some of the issues related to combining these two treatment approaches will be examined later.

Behavioral interventions based on an operant paradigm are the most commonly used treatment intervention in much of the recent literature. Behavioral treatment most often focuses on the establishment or reestablishment of appropriate toilet habits, but there is a great deal of variation as to the exact target behaviors that are chosen and the types of rewards that can be earned by the child. Table 5.1 summarizes the treatment outcome studies on encopresis.

Target behaviors. Although most encopresis studies focus on "appropriate defecation in the toilet" as the target behavior, some programs reward two distinct components of this behavior: (1) the child's sitting on the toilet; and (2) the child's actually having a bowel movement while sitting on the toilet (e.g., Bach & Moylan, 1975). In addition, some studies have actually developed some fairly elaborate *training* procedures to shape appropriate toileting response rather than merely reinforcing the target behaviors if and when they occur. For example, Seymour (1976) had the encopretic child taken to the toilet after every main meal and at bedtime, and the child was required to sit on the toilet for five minutes and was rewarded for a "successful trial." In a very intricate and rigorous program devised by Davis, Mitchell, and Marks (1976), the child was taken to the toilet every half hour, and he (or she) stayed there until he eliminated or for 15 minutes if he did not have a bowel movement. Ultimately, the intervals between the trips to the toilet were lengthened and the time that the child remained on the toilet de-

TABLE 5.1
Characteristics of Encopresis Treatment Studies

Author	Number of Subjects (age in years)	Treatment Procedure	Reward	Results	Follow-up	DQR
Neale (1963)	4 (7 1/2-10 3/4)	Operant program for appropriate defecation and for nonsoiling	Food	3 of 4 subjects no soiling	2-6 wks.	2
Gelber & Meyer (1965)	1 (13 3/4)	Operant program for nonsoiling and for appropriate defecation	Hospital privileges	2 soiling incidents	6 mos.	2.5
Pedrini & Pedrini (1971)	1 (11)	Operant program for nonsoiling	Coupons toward book purchases	1 soiling incident	7 mos.	7.5
Edelman (1971)	1 (12)	Operant program using punishment (confinement) and rewards	Less time washing dishes	"Virtually none"	3 mos.	2.5
Young & Goldsmith (1972)	1 (8)	Operant program for appropriate defecation	Matchbox cars; money later	No soiling	1 mo.	2
Young (1973)	24 (5-10)	Conditioning procedure of bowel response	Praise	92% successful	7 mos.-5 yrs.	5
Engel, Nikoomanesh, & Schuster (1974)	7 (6-54)	Operant conditioning of recto-sphincteric responses	Praise polygraph feedback of sphincter responses	4 of 7 subjects no soiling	6 mos.-5 yrs.	2.5
Ashkenazi (1975)	18 (3-12)	Supposi-tories and operant program for elimination	Prize	No soiling	1 mo.	2.5

(continued)

TABLE 5.1 (continued)

Author	Number of Subjects (age in years)	Treatment Procedure	Reward	Results	Follow-up	DQR
Bach & Moylan (1975)	1 (6)	Operant program for appropriate expulsion	Money	No soiling	2 yrs.	6.5
Wright (1975)	14 (3-9)	Enemas, suppositories, and operant program for appropriate defecation and for nonsoiling	Not specified	13 of 14 subjects no soiling	None	6.5
Plachetta (1976)	1 (6)	Operant program for appropriate defecation and for toilet attempt	Money, praise	Not specified	Not specified	0.5
Davis, Mitchell, & Marks (1976)	11 (7-13)	Cleanliness training and operant program for elimination and for nonsoiling	Choice of sweets, access to toys, television privileges	7 of 11 subjects no soiling	Approximately 6 mos.	2.5
Seymour (1976)	12 (3-10)	Tokens for nonsoiling and for appropriate defecation	Tokens for privileges	6 subjects no soiling; 6 subjects 1 - 7 soilings/ week	3-10 mos.	2.5
Butler (1977)	3 (2 1/2-5)	Toilet practice, and nonsoiling, cleanliness training	Praise, food	2 subjects no soiling; 1 subject 1 soiling	6 mos.	2.5
Matson (1977)	1 (16)	Toilet practice and cleanliness training	Praise	No soiling	3 mos.	2.5

TABLE 5.1 (continued)

Author	Number of Subjects (age in years)	Treatment Procedure	Reward	Results	Follow-up	DQR
Davis, Mitchell, & Marks (1977)	11 (7-14)	Operant program for appropriate defecation	Praise, money, food	7 of 11 subjects no soiling	2-7 mos.	2
Doleys, McWhorter, Williams, & Gentry (1976)	3 (8-9)	Cleanliness training and operant program for appropriate toileting and for nonsoiling	Points, rewards	2 subjects no soiling; 1 subject 1 soiling	36 wks.	2
Schaefer (1978)	1 (8)	Enemas, suppositories; reward for nonsoiling and for appropriate defecation; cleanliness training; and "bathtub" confinement for soiling	"Special rewards"	No soiling	6 mos.	2.5

creased. In general, however, this program may be difficult to implement, because the child requires close observation. Since the program entails very frequent trips to the toilet, parents may have difficulty in following the program contingencies.

Rather than focusing on *appropriate fecal elimination*, some programs reinforce the child for remaining clean in addition to or instead of appropriate toilet behaviors. For example, Pedrini and Pedrini (1971) gave a child coupons as a reward for periods of nonsoiling, and these coupons could ultimately be exchanged for concrete rewards. Similarly, Allyon, Simon, and Wildman (1975) used stars as a reward for not soiling, and when the child had accumulated seven stars, she (or he) could go with the therapists for an outing of her choice. Plachetta (1976) used parental praise, self-charting, and stars for nonsoiling and provided monetary rewards when the patient attempted to eliminate in an appropriate manner.

Rewards. Different studies have incorporated many different types of rewards when the child emits the appropriate target behavior. Such studies as those of Neale (1963), Peterson and London (1964), and Madsen (1965) have used food, candy, and money as reinforcers for appropriate bowel elimination. It is often helpful to let the child choose what reward he or she would like best, because this procedure tends to maximize the child's cooperation. Although tangible rewards, such as food or money, are most commonly used as reinforcers, Sheinbein (1975) comments that social reinforcers can be highly effective rewards for appropriate toileting behavior. He states that although such social reinforcers are quite difficult to deliver in a uniform and controlled manner, these reinforcers may have longer effects and may generalize more easily than more concrete rewards.

Use of laxatives as an adjunct intervention. There are various studies that have used laxatives and enemas along with the behavioral approaches described above. The use of these medical adjuncts has been advocated as a means of dealing with several different aspects of the encopresis problem. For example, some researchers feel that encopresis almost always involves constipation or voluntary retention of feces as well as inappropriate defecation. Levin (1975) found that 80 out of 102 cases of nonorganic encopresis were found to have stool impaction accompanying their fecal incontinence, and Fitzgerald (1975) commented that 95 percent of his encopretic patients have shown evidence of their being impacted. Because fecal retention is often a part of encopresis, Wright (1975) feels that laxatives and enemas are an integral part of the intervention, because it guarantees daily defecation that in turn allows the child's distended colon to regain its normal shape and muscle tone.

Ashkenazi (1975) also advocates the use of the suppositories in the treatment of encopresis but suggests quite a different theoretical rationale for its use. She reasons that the child must be aware of rectal distension in order to go to the toilet, and thus, the suppository aids in training the child to be more aware of the sensations connected with rectal distension as a cue for having a bowel movement in the toilet. Unfortunately, there is no research that specifically addresses the incremental utility of employing laxatives as an adjunct to a behavior training program over the use of a straightforward operant approach.

Conditioning procedures. Similar to the rationale given by Ashkenazi (1975), Young (1973) asserts that encopretic children often have no perception of the sphincter reflexes that lead to bowel actions. Rather than relying on suppositories as the means of teaching the child about the internal cues which precede a bowel movement, however, Young devised another type of procedure to achieve this end, and the rationale goes as follows:

After there is food or fluid intake, the entire small intestine manifests increased motility, and this excitation is then transmitted along the intestines. The mass movements of the colon empty the fecal contents from one part of the colon to the next, and frequently such movements produce the desire to defecate. The time interval from the ingestion of food or drink to the occurrence of sensation in the colon is approximately 20 to 30 minutes, and the most common time for the reflex to occur is during the first hour after arising in the morning.

Young's procedure thus uses this sphincteric response to food or fluid intake as part of the training of appropriate toilet behaviors. The patient's parents are told that when the child awakes in the morning, a warm drink or some food is to be given. Twenty to 30 minutes later, the child is taken to the toilet, and bowel action is suggested. The child sits on the toilet for no more than ten minutes. If a bowel action is achieved, then he is shown approval, but if not, a nonchalant attitude is adopted. This procedure can also be repeated after other meals if it is pragmatically possible.

More rigorous conditioning procedures have also been employed to treat encopresis using recent biofeedback techniques. By means of a rectal balloon apparatus, Engel, Nikoomanesh, and Schuster (1974) have trained better bowel control by providing the encopretic individual with instantaneous polygraph feedback of his sphincteric responses. The patient is reminded of the differences between his (or her) responses and normal responses, encouraged to try to modify his responses to make them appear more normal and praised whenever more normal responses result. When the response is poor, the patient is quickly informed of this fact. The verbal reinforcement gradually is diminished as the patient learns what is expected of him and as he demonstrates more normal-appearing sphincteric responses.

These authors identify several factors that appear to be important in the application of operant conditioning to pathophysiological states such as fecal incontinence. One factor is the presence of a well-defined, readily measurable response—in this case, the synchronized sphincteric reflexes. Another factor is the occurrence of a clearly recognizable cue that signals the patient to initiate sphincter control and in this case was caused by the balloon distension. The presence of strong motivation on the part of the patient to bring this response under control is another issue that also greatly affects the treatment outcome.

Mild punishment. Mild punishment has also been used in some treatment programs for encopresis. Sometimes the "punishment" is the withdrawal of affection or attention of the parents or the caretaker. For example, Edelman (1971) uses a 30-minute time-out procedure in which the child was confined to a room by herself. However, many behaviorists feel that reward is generally preferable to punishment, for not only could punishment contribute to a poor self-image, but it does not provide any information about more appropriate behavioral alternatives.

"Cleanliness training" is a somewhat aversive procedure that is being incorporated more often as a part of the behavioral intervention. This cleanliness training requires the child to "clean up his own mess," which may include changing clothes, cleaning soiled clothes, and mopping or cleaning any area that has been inappropriately soiled. Such an expectation is meant to encourage the child to be responsible in dealing with the aftermath of his "accident" as well as intending to increase the likelihood of the child's defecating in an appropriate manner in the future. However, Doleys et al. (1976) state that one possible disadvantage of trying to get the child to follow through on this cleanliness training is that there could be a confrontation between the parent and the child if the child is uncooperative.

Medication. In a recent article Geormaneanu and Voiculescu (1980) discuss treating encopresis with the use of imipramine, an antidepressant. Although little systematic research exists comparing the effectiveness of such a treatment procedure with the other more behavioral approaches more commonly seen in the literature, such a treatment procedure has at times been used in a medical setting or in a physician's private practice. Certainly, more research on the benefits and effectiveness of using an antidepressant as an intervention for encopresis would be useful.

Maintenance. In most studies, the maintenance phase of the behavioral program has been quite haphazard or completely ignored once the desired criterion is reached. Davis et al. (1976) state quite strongly that continuing the program after the child is no longer soiling must be regarded as an essential part of the intervention procedure. The investigators comment that it is all too easy for a mother or a therapist to regard the child as "cured" if he or she has been clean for several weeks and thus discontinue the rewards and the monitoring procedures. These investigators are not certain how long a maintenance program should be continued to maximize the long-lasting effectiveness of the program, but they suggest that it would seem reasonable to maintain the program for at least six weeks after the criterion of nonsoiling is reached.

Training and supervision of program implementors. Although a number of these treatment studies have been executed in institutional settings, some of these programs have been administered by parents under the supervision of trained professionals. Nevertheless, there has been little discussion of the numerous variables involved in the administration and supervision of the program intervention, such as the nature and frequency of the contacts between the professional, the parents, and the child. For example, Wright and Walker (1978) state that for one reason or another, parents often become lax in following the program specifications, and these researchers find that weekly phone contact dramatically increases both consistency and program effectiveness. However, a systematic investigation of the procedures that maximize parental cooperation has not yet been undertaken.

Clinical Prescription

The clinical prescription incorporates many of the different elements outlined above. What becomes fairly clear after examining the multitude of elements in the various programs reported in the literature is that one must balance the desire to have a comprehensive intervention with the need to make the procedures simple and manageable enough so that the parents or the institutional staff can understand the contingencies and comply with the treatment prescriptions.

Before a behavioral intervention is attempted, a medical examination should rule out any possible organic etiology for encopresis. Then a baseline should be taken of the frequency and the location of the soiling behaviors as well as the frequency of appropriate elimination behaviors.

A treatment program for encopresis should include the following elements:

1. Reinforcement of appropriate bowel elimination and toilet behaviors. The child should be given an immediate reward for appropriate toilet behavior. Concrete rewards, such as money or food, are often most useful in this regard; however, the child should have some input about the exact nature of the reward so that he (or she) will be maximally cooperative with the treatment procedures.

2. Reward for nonsoiling behavior. The child's pants should be checked periodically to see whether they are clean. If soiling has occurred, the child should be taken to the toilet, and he should clean himself and his clothes. If he is clean, he should get a star or token which can be exchanged at a later time for a fairly large reward when a criterion number of stars or tokens are accumulated. Because of the large number of rewards that the child could potentially earn, it would not be desirable to use reinforcers that the child would easily tire of. In addition, the use of long-term rewards for nonsoiling and the use of smaller, more immediate reinforcers for appropriate bowel elimination may be more effective than either type of reinforcer alone.

3. Family intervention. The child and his family should meet weekly with the professional to discuss problems connected with the implementation of the program and to discuss the family's reactions to the child's progress or lack of progress in reaching the desired behavioral criteria.

4. Maintenance. The program should continue to be implemented for at least six to eight weeks after the soiling behavior has essentially disappeared.

Of course, the above recommendations are only guidelines that should be modified for the specific contingencies and the exact conditions for each case. Modifications may also have to be made for a large-scale treatment program attempting to deal with many encopretic children at the same time.

A Case Report

The following case study is reported by Schafer (1978). The program was set up for an eight-year-old boy who was soiling himself two to three times a day. The child's parents reported that the soiling started five months previously without any clear precipitating event, and a physician had previously ruled out the possibility of any physical or organic causation of the encopretic behavior. The child was treated on an outpatient basis using the standard program developed by Wright (1975).

Wright's program involves parental administration of behavioral contingencies and cathartics. First, the boy's lower colon was cleaned with an enema, which allowed the distended colon to regain its normal muscle tone and restored sensations in the area. Glycerine suppositories were administered to the child in the morning if the boy did not defecate on his own. If the suppositories were not effective in inducing a bowel movement, an enema was once again administered.

A daily record was kept of the frequency of the soiling. For each successful elimination, the boy earned five points. For each day that the boy went without soiling, he was given an additional five points. The boy was praised for each success, and he was given a special reward for each time he accumulated 30 points. For each soiling episode, the child had to stay in the bathtub for 30 minutes, and he was required to wash out his underwear.

The boy was weaned from the cathartics in the following way: For each week that the child went without soiling, he went off the cathartics for one day of the week. If the boy soiled a day of the week that he was off the program, then another week was added to the schedule.

When the child-sized enema was changed to an adult-sized enema, the soiling quickly diminished, and the boy had only two soiling incidents during the rest of the program. The program was terminated after 16 weeks, since the soiling had disappeared. A six-month follow-up showed no recurrence of the encopresis. In addition, the mother reported that the boy's overall behavior had changed somewhat markedly after treatment and that he was now much more outgoing and more cooperative at home and at school.

This case study is one of a growing number of replications of Wright's (1975) treatment procedure. However, what should be empirically demonstrated in the future is whether this particular set of procedures is actually more effective than other treatment methods, and if so, what elements contribute most to its superior effectiveness.

Ethical and Legal Issues

There are relatively few ethical or legal issues inherent in the behavioral treatment of encopresis. Since intensely aversive techniques are not generally employed, punishment issues are not particularly problematic for this type of intervention. In addition, since soiling is often seen as so distasteful to those who interact with the soiler, any reasonable intervention that can effectively ameliorate this undesirable situation is usually welcomed by everyone involved.

Suggestions for Clinical and Experimental Research

In general, the research on encopresis is quite rudimentary, and most of the treatment studies are methodologically inadequate. The majority of the literature consists of case studies with an *N* of 1 or 2. In the extensive literature search done for the present chapter, no studies were found which attempted to compare the relative effectiveness of different treatments, and no study even attempted to use control groups. Thus, the first order of business for future outcome research is to evaluate the effectiveness of the varying treatment approaches detailed earlier in this chapter.

Other issues which also deserve empirical investigation and exploration include the following:

1. *Process and outcome variables*. As detailed above, a number of treatment procedures have been successful in reducing or eliminating the frequency of soiling episodes. However, which procedure is most useful and what components of the intervention are most responsible for ultimately diminishing the frequency of the soiling behavior have not been adequately addressed. Once these factors are more clearly understood and delineated, it may be possible to develop a treatment program utilizing the most effective combination of elements that both shortens treatment duration and minimizes relapse.

2. *Reinforcement variables*. Many different types of reinforcers have been used in the various studies cited previously including concrete rewards such as food and money, token rewards, and social reinforcers. It is unclear whether the particular type of reward greatly influences the successfulness of the intervention. In addition, the issue of types of reinforcement schedules have been virtually ignored in the encopresis literature. On the basis of the behavioral treatment for other types of behavioral problems including enuresis, an intermittent reinforcement schedule generally yields behavior that is more resistant to extinction. Therefore, in the treatment of encopresis, the relative effectiveness of different reinforcement schedules needs to be examined empirically.

3. *Variables concerning the child and the behavior of the child*. There has been little discussion of whether some treatment procedures are more effective for a particular group of encopretic individuals than

others. For example, several variables which may influence the course of treatment and which could potentially warrant prescribed variations in the approach used include the child's age, the degree of control exhibited prior to the onset of the encopresis, and the presence or absence of other behavioral disturbances.

4. *Parental and family variables.* Many treatment approaches can be administered outside a hospital setting. In these cases the effectiveness of the intervention will depend quite heavily on the cooperation of the parents and in some cases the ability actually to understand and monitor the program contingencies. Therefore, it would be desirable to identify the variables that would promote parental cooperation and maximize the effectiveness of the intervention.

5. *Nonspecific treatment variables.* The research on encopresis has not addressed the most effective way to train someone to implement an intervention program. For example, the number and kinds of contacts the therapist has with the person administering the program contingencies has not been systematically examined for the way it may affect treatment outcome.

6. *The use of laxatives.* Laxatives have been commonly used in the treatment of encopresis by medical practitioners. However, it has been only recently popularized in the behavioral literature by Wright (1975) and Ashkenazi (1975). Future research should examine the effectiveness of the laxative treatment, both when it is used alone within a purely medical context and when it is combined with other behavioral interventions. Another important question surrounding the use of laxatives involves the relationship between stool withholding and soiling in encopresis (e.g., O'Leary & Wilson, 1975); more clearly understanding the relationship between the two fecal behaviors may enable behavioral interventions to treat encopresis most effectively.

Summary

Encopresis is a much less common disorder than enuresis and is most likely to occur while the child is awake. Although psychodynamic theories focus on issues such as the conflicts about control and a passive-aggressiveness that may be expressed by means of the encopretic "symptom," behaviorists focus more clearly on the soiling and nonsoiling behaviors and the frequency and the contingencies of these behaviors. Many of the behavioral interventions focus on decreasing the likelihood of soiling behavior, while some programs more directly shape and train more appropriate toilet practices. In addition to focusing on appropriate elimination as such, different treatment procedures reward the child when he or she remains clean. Rewards have included both concrete reinforcers, such as food and money, and social reinforcers, such as attention and outings with significant others. Cleanliness training has also been used by some researchers, who require that the child "clean up his mess" after soiling occurs. Such training is seen as making the child take responsibility for dealing with the consequences of his behavior, and this training may also increase the likelihood of appropriate toilet behavior in the future.

Some feel that when laxatives are used as part of the behavioral intervention, they teach the child regular daily toilet habits. Others, however, see the use of suppositories as a discriminative stimulus to help the child learn the sensations that precede a bowel movement. Biofeedback techniques have also been employed to increase sphincter control by means of a rectal balloon apparatus and polygraph data, which provide immediate feedback about the adequacy of the sphincter response.

Proper maintenance is considered crucial to the ultimate effectiveness of the intervention, and the program contingencies should not be completely discontinued for a considerable period of time after the soiling is no longer taking place. The cooperation of the family or staff is also important to the success of this type of intervention. Research is needed to compare process and outcome variables of different treatment approaches and to delineate the most effective combination of elements for the treatment of encopresis.

References

Allyon, T., Simon, S. J., & Wildman, R. W. II. Instructions and reinforcement in the elimination of encopresis: A case study. *Journal of Behavioral Therapy and Experimental Psychiatry*, 1975, *6*, 235–238.

Ashkenazi, Z. The treatment of encopresis using a discriminative stimulus. *Journal of Behavior Therapy and Experimental Psychiatry*, 1975, *6*, 155–157.

Bach, R., & Moylan, J. Parents administer behavior therapy for inappropriate urination and encopresis: A case study. *Journal of Behaviour Therapy and Experimental Psychiatry*, 1975, *5*, 239–241.

Barling, J. I. Behavioral treatment of enuresis and encopresis in a young boy. *South African Medical Journal*, 1976, *50*, 1273.

Bellman, M. Studies on encopresis. *Acta Paediatrica Scandinavica*, Suppl. 170, 1966.

Butler, J. F. Treatment of encopresis by overcorrection. *Physiological Reports*, 1977, *40* 639–646.

Chapman, A. H. *Management of emotional problems of children and adolescents*. Philadelphia: Lippincott Co., 1965.

Ciminero, A. R., & Doleys, D. M. Childhood enuresis: Considerations in assessment. *Journal of Pediatric Psychology*, 1976, *4*, 17–20.

Davis, H., Mitchell, W., & Marks, F. A behavioural programme for the modification of encopresis. *Child: Care, Health and Development*, 1976, *2*, 273–282.

Davis, H., Mitchell, W., & Marks, F. A pilot study of encopretic children treated by behaviour modification. *Practitioner*, 1977, *219*, 228–230.

Doleys, D., McWhorter, A., Williams, S., & Gentry, W. Encopresis: Its treatment and relation to nocturnal enuresis. *Behavior Therapy*, 1976, *7*, 77–83.

Edelman, R. I. Operant conditioning treatment of encopresis. *Journal of Behavior Therapy and Experimental Psychiatry*, 1971, *2*, 71–73.

Engel, B., Nikoomanesh, P., & Schuster, M. Operant conditioning of rectosphincteric responses in the treatment of fecal incontinence. *The New England Journal of Medicine*, 1974, *290*, 646–649.

Fitzgerald, J. F. Encopresis, soiling, constipation, what's to be done? *Pediatrics*, 1975, *56*, 348–349.

Gavonski, M. Treatment of nonretentive secondary encopresis with imipramine and psychotherapy. *Canadian Medical Association Journal*, 1971, *104*, 46–48.

Gelber, H., & Meyer, V. Behaviour therapy and encopresis: The complexities involved in treatment. *Behavior Research and Therapy*, 1965, *2*, 227–231.

Geormaneanu, M., & Voiculescu V. Treatment of encopresis with imipramine. *Neurology and Psychiatry*, 1980, *18*, 209–210.

Levin, M. D. Children with encopresis: A descriptive analysis. *Pediatrics*, 1975, *56*, 412.

Madsen, C. H. Positive reinforcement in the toilet training of a normal child. In L. P. Ullman & L. Krasner (Eds.), *Case studies in behavior modification*. New York: Holt, 1965, pp. 305–307.

Matson, J. Simple correction for treating an autistic boy's encopresis. *Psychological Reports*, 1977, *41*, 802.

Neale, D. Behavior therapy and encopresis in children. *Behavior Research and Therapy*, 1963, *1*, 139–149.

O'Leary, K. D., & Wilson, G. T. *Behavior therapy: Application and outcome*. Englewood Cliffs, N. J.: Prentice-Hall, 1975.

Pedrini, B., & Pedrini, D. Reinforcement procedures in the control of encopresis: A case study. *Psychological Reports*, 1971, *28*, 937–938.

Peterson, D. R., & London, P. Neobehavioristic psychotherapy, quasi hypnotic suggestion and multiple reinforcement in the treatment of a case of postinfantile dyscopresis. *Psychological Record*, 1964, *14*, 469–474.

Plachetta, K. Encopresis: A case study utilizing contracting scheduling and selfcharting. *Journal of Behavioral Therapy and Experimental Psychiatry*, 1976, *7*, 195–196.

Prugh, D. G. Towards an understanding of psychosomatic concepts in relation to illness in children. In A. Solnit & S. Province (Eds.), *Modern perspectives in child development*, New York: International University Press, 1963.

Richmond, J., Eddy, E., & Gerrard, S. The syndrome of fecal soiling and megacolon. *American Journal of Orthopsychiatry*, 1954, *24*, 391–402.

Schaefer, C. Treating psychogenic encopresis: A case study. *Psychological Reports*, 1978, *42*, 98.

Seymour, F. The treatment of encopresis using behavior modification. *Australian Paediatric Journal*, 1976, *12*, 326–329.
Sheinbein, M. A triadic-behavioral approach to encopresis. *Journal of Family Counseling*, 1975, *3*, 58–61.
Silber, S. Encopresis: Rectal rebellion and anal anarchy. *Journal of the American Society of Psychosomatic Dentistry and Medicine*, 1968, *15*, 97–106.
Wright, L. Outcome of a standardized program for treating psychogenic encopresis. *Professional Psychology*, 1975, *6*, 453–456.
Wright, L., & Walker, C. E. A simple behavioral treatment program for psychogenic encopresis. *Behaviour Research and Therapy*, 1978, *16*, 209–212.
Yates, A. J. *Behavior therapy*. New York: John Wiley and Sons, 1970.
Young, G. The treatment of childhood encopresis by conditioned gastroileal reflex training. *Behaviour Research and Therapy*, 1973, *11*, 499–503.
Young, I. L., & Goldsmith, A. Treatment of encopresis in a day treatment program. *Psychotherapy: Theory, Research, and Practice*, 1972, *9*, 231–235.

Suggested Readings

Ashkenazi, Z. The treatment of encopresis using a discriminative stimulus. *Journal of Behavior Therapy and Experimental Psychiatry*, 1975, *6*, 155–157.
Azrin, N. H., & Foxx, R. M. A rapid method of toilet training the retarded. *Journal of Applied Behavior Analysis*, 1971, *4*, 89–99.
Doleys, D., McWhorter, A., Williams, S., & Gentry, W. Encopresis: Its treatment and relation to nocturnal enuresis. *Behavior Therapy*, 1976, *7*, 77–83.
Neale, D. Behavior therapy and encopresis in children. *Behaviour Research and Therapy*, 1963, *1*, 139–149.
Wright, L., & Walker, C. E. A simple behavioral treatment program for psychogenic encopresis. *Behaviour Research and Therapy*, 1978, *16*, 209–212.
Young, G. The treatment of childhood encopresis by conditioned gastroileal reflex training. *Behaviour Research and Therapy*, 1973, *11*, 499–503.

6

Hysteria

Lydia Temoshok and Bruce Heller

Scope and Definition of the Problem

"Hysteria" as a diagnostic label is as impressionistic, labile, diffuse, unstable, and superficially appealing as the various phenomena with which it has been associated. Further, the label is almost ubiquitous; as Moebius once said, "everyone is a little hysterical." Part of the problem is that in its 4,000-year history (cf. Veith, 1977), the term has been used to describe myriad behaviors and has accumulated an array of explanatory hypotheses. McDaniel (1978) commented that the only element tying together all the phenomena called "hysteria" is their history. This history constitutes most of the history of psychiatry itself.

Diagnostic definitions have retained some resemblance across their revisions by the American Psychiatric Association from the first edition of the *Diagnostic and Statistical Manual* (DSM-I; APA, 1952) to DSM-II (APA, 1968) to DSM-III (APA, 1980). At the same time, the official psychiatric nomenclature reveals a great deal of controversy and confusion. In Table 6.1, the fates of various uses of the designation "hysteria" are traced from some of their pre-DSM-I origins to their current positions in DSM-III. The shifts in nomenclature and ways of cutting the hypothetical hysterical pie reflect the changing emphasis from psychodynamic formulation to symptomatic description and specifiable diagnostic criteria in DSM-III and, in many cases, revisions of the etiological hypotheses. The categories in Table 6.1 are described and theoretically elaborated in the next section.

We gratefully acknowledge the assistance of Marc Gold in many phases of the preparation of this manuscript.

TABLE 6.1
"Hysteria" (1859–1980)

PRE-DSM-I	DSM-I (1952)		DSM-II (1968)		DSM-III (1980)	
	Superordinate Classification	Category of Hysterical Phenomenon	Superordinate Classification	Category of Hysterical Phenomenon	Superordinate Classification	Category of Hysterical Phenomenon
Hysterical Character (Wittels, 1930; Reich, 1933; Fenichel, 1945)	50.-53. Personality Disorders 51. Personality Trait Disturbance	51.0 Emotionally Unstable Personality	V. Personality Disorders and Other Non-psychotic Mental Disorders 301. Personality Disorders	301.5 Hysterical Personality (Histrionic Personality Disorder)	Axis II: Personality Disorders	301.50 Histrionic Personality Disorder
Hysteria (Briquet, 1859) Convulsive Hysteria Grande Hystérie; also: hystero-epilepsy (Richer, 1881) Hysterical Conversion (Breuer & Freud, 1893-1895)	40. Psychoneurotic Disorders 40. Psychoneurotic Reactions	40.2 Conversion Reaction	IV. Neuroses 300. Neuroses	300.1 Hysterical Neurosis 300.13 Hysterical Neurosis, Conversion Type	Axis I: Clinical Syndromes Somatoform Disorders	300.81 Somatoform Disorder (Briquet's Syndrome) 300.11 Conversion Disorder 307.80 Psychogenic Pain Disorder 300.70 Hypochondriasis
Hypochondriasis				300.7 Hypochondriacal Neurosis		300.71 Atypical Somatoform Disorder

(continued)

TABLE 6.1 (continued)

PRE-DSM-I	DSM-I (1952)		DSM-II (1968)		DSM-III (1980)	
	Superordinate Classification	Category of Hysterical Phenomenon	Superordinate Classification	Category of Hysterical Phenomenon	Superordinate Classification	Category of Hysterical Phenomenon
Ganser's Syndrome Munchausen's Syndrome (Asher, 1951)					Axis I: Clinical Syndromes Factitious Disorders	300.16 Factitious illness with Psychological Symptoms 301.51 Chronic Factitious Disorder with Physical Symptoms 300.19 Atypical Factitious Disorder with Physical Symptoms
Malingering			X. Conditions Without Manifest Psychiatric Disorder	317. Nonspecific Condition	V. Codes for Conditions Not Attributable to a Mental Disorder That Are a Focus of Attention or Treatment	V65.20 Malingering

TABLE 6.1 (continued)

Gilles de la Tourette's Disease (1885)	53. Special Symptom Reaction	53.4 Other	VII. Special Symptoms 306. Special Symptoms Not Elsewhere Classified	306.20 Tic 306.30 Other Psychomotor Disorder	Axis I: Clinical Syndromes Disorders Usually First Evident in Infancy, Childhood, or Adolescence: Stereotyped Movement Disorders	307.21 Transient Tic Disorder 307.22 Chronic Tic Disorder 307.23 Tourette's Disorder 307.20 Atypical Tic Disorder 307.30 Atypical Stereotyped Movement Disorder
Psychological Automatism (Janet, 1889) Hysterical Ambulatory Automatism (Charcot, 1889)	40. Psychoneurotic Disorders 40. Psychoneurotic Reactions	40.1 Dissociative Reaction	IV. Neuroses 300. Neuroses	300.1 Hysterical Neurosis 300.14 Hysterical Neurosis, Dissociative Type	Axis I: Clinical Syndromes Dissociative Disorders	300.12 Psychogenic Amnesia 300.13 Psychogenic Fugue 300.14 Multiple Personality

(continued)

TABLE 6.1 (continued)

PRE-DSM-I	DSM-I (1952)		DSM-II (1968)		DSM-III (1980)	
	Superordinate Classification	Category of Hysterical Phenomenon	Superordinate Classification	Category of Hysterical Phenomenon	Superordinate Classification	Category of Hysterical Phenomenon
Dual Personality, Catalepsy, Somnambulism (Charcot, 1889) Depersonalization in Double Consciousness (Binet, 1889-1890)				300.6 Depersonalization Neurosis	Axis I: Clinical Syndromes Disorders Usually First Evident in Infancy, Childhood, or Adolescence Nonorganic Sleep Disorders	300.60 Depersonalization Disorder 300.15 Atypical Dissociative Disorder 307.46 Sleepwalking Disorder
Hysterical Psychosis (amok, latah, whitico, koro, imu, pibloktoq, and other "exotic psychiatric syndromes")			III. Psychoses not attributable to physical condition listed previously 295. Schizophrenia	295.4 Acute schizophrenic episode	Axis I: Clinical Syndromes Psychotic Disorders not Elsewhere Classified	298.80 Brief Reactive Psychosis

TABLE 6.1 (continued)

Anxiety Hysteria* (Freud, 1909, 1918; Wittels, 1930; Fenichel, 1945)	40. Psychoneurotic Disorders 40. Psychoneurotic Reaction	40.3 Phobic Reaction	IV. Neuroses 300. Neuroses	300.2 Phobic Neurosis	Axis I: Clinical Syndrome: Anxiety Disorders: Phobic Disorders	300.21 Agoraphobia with Panic Attacks 300.22 Agoraphobia without Panic Attacks 300.23 Social Phobia 300.29 Simple Phobia
					Disorders Usually First Evident in Infancy, Childhood, or Adolescence: Anxiety Disorders of Childhood or Adolescence	309.21 Separation Anxiety Phobia

*Anxiety hysteria is included here for its historical interest even though, after 1952, phobic reactions were clearly separated from hysterical conversion and dissociation in the official nomenclature. According to Fenichel, the first neurotic reactions to occur in children have the character of anxiety hysteria. Freud considered it the simplest kind of psychoneurosis; an example is the case of little Hans (Freud, 1909).

Description and Theoretical Analysis

Histrionic Personality Disorder

Behavioral and trait descriptions. While psychoanalytic theories of histrionic (formerly hysterical) personality disorder have been more vociferous and prominent than any other perspective, they have not had much of an impact upon the official nosology. Most of the diagnoses of histrionic personality have consisted of particular clusters of traits and behavioral descriptions. DSM-II (1968) stated:

> These behavior patterns are characterized by excitability, emotional instability, over-reactivity, and self-dramatization. This self-dramatization is always attention-seeking, and often seductive, whether or not the patient is aware of its purpose. These personalities are also immature, self-centered, often vain, and unusually dependent on others [p. 43].

Many of the same terms have been stable across the years and used by various observers of the phenomenon. For example, ten years earlier, Chodoff and Lyons (1958) had focused on the same attributes: the excitable affectivity, sexual provocativeness, dependent demandingness, and dramatic attention-seeking. Slavney (1978) polled all house officers and full-time faculty members at three psychiatric residency programs (N = 101) and asked them to list in rank order the diagnostic importance of eight trait items taken from DSM-II descriptions of hysterical personality disorder, plus the category of conversion symptoms. For the total sample, self-dramatization, attention-seeking, emotional instability, and seductiveness were ranked the most diagnostically important and confidently recognized, while vanity, immaturity, and conversion symptoms were seen as relatively unimportant and less certainly recognized.

Self-dramatization is, of course, the cornerstone and namesake of the DSM-III's Histrionic Personality Disorder. Other diagnostic criteria include: (1) indicators of histrionic behavior: exaggerated emotional expression, and drawing attention to the self to obtain admiration; (2) behavior that is overly reactive and expressed intensely: emotional overexcitability, irrational angry outbursts, manipulative suicidal threats; (3) character disturbances in interpersonal relations: superficially appealing, demanding, inconsiderate, vain, egocentric, self-absorbed, dependent, helpless, and seeking reassurance; and (4) poor sexual adjustment: flirtatiousness or coquetry, sexual naiveté or frigidity, flights of romantic fantasy, behavior caricaturing femininity.

Most of these criteria, which describe an individual's long-term functioning, have been amply described in the literature, with the exception of (2). A history of suicidal gestures was incorporated in Luisada, Peele, and Pittard's (1974) list of behavioral descriptors. Slavney and

McHugh (1974) contrasted a group of inpatients diagnosed as hysterical personality with a control inpatient group and found that a significant feature for the patients with hysterical personality was previous suicide attempts. With regard to some of the other criteria in (2), it may be useful to recall Lazare, Klerman, and Armor's (1966) factor analytic study of 20 trait self-ratings, in which *aggression* had the highest loading, and *oral aggression* the third highest (emotionality was second) on the factor which otherwise represented all the predicted hysterical traits.

Eysenck's Behavioral Neurophysiological Theory. The relationship between temperament and physiology traces its roots back to the honored tradition of Pavlov. Many theories have postulated that the basic dimensions of personality can be derived from the processes of inhibition and excitation and their balance. Explaining the work of Russian experimenters who followed Pavlov, Gray (1964) combined the concepts of inhibition and excitation into a single dimension similar to the Western construct of arousal. Thus, the weaker and more sensitive introverted nervous system is thought to respond to lower intensities of stimulation by developing transmarginal inhibition at these lower levels, in contrast to the more resistant extroverted nervous system, which develops cortical inhibition more easily. In addition to these types of concepts, Eysenck proposed a dimension of Neuroticism, which he regarded as a drive related to overexcitability of particularly the sympathetic branch of the autonomic nervous system, and independent of the Introversion/Extroversion dimension. His aim, developed through a series of works (Eysenck, 1947, 1952, 1953), was to establish objectively a dimensional framework on which to hang the main behavioral observations relevant to psychopathology. In this theory, neurosis is not qualitatively different from normality, but on a continuum with it. Further, different types of psychopathology occupy the poles of continuous variables which are probably orthogonal to each other in this hypothetical space. Thus, Eysenck opposed psychiatric diagnosis, which results in a cluster map—categories of disorders—in favor of a dimensional solution, which gives quantitative estimates of an individual's position on each dimension. In a space demarcated by the orthogonal dimensions of Neuroticism and Introversion/Extroversion, hysterics would be located in the upper right quadrant; that is, a little on the abnormally extroverted side, and a little more on the neuroticism side. "Psychopaths" (antisocial personality disorder) would be in the same quadrant, but considerably more neurotic and rather more extroverted.

Eysenck (1955) was concerned mainly with the I/E dimension in constructing a theory that could account for differences between the hysterics and his psychopathic group, both of which are "extroverted," and the anxious, depressed, and obsessional groups, which fall along the introversion side of the dimension. His point of departure was Hull's Law of Reactive Inhibition, in which any evoked reaction leaves behind in the structure that produced it a state or substance that acts as a primary negative motivation to inhibit the future production of the behavior in question. This hypothetical state or substance is observable only in terms of its effect upon positive reaction potentials. Eysenck then proposed that there are individual differences in the speed of producing and dissipating reactive inhibition, as well as in the strength of the reactive inhibition produced. He thought that individuals susceptible under stress to develop hysterical and psychopathic disorders are characterized by the quick generation of strong reactive inhibition which dissipates slowly. Conversely, anxious, depressed, and obsessive individuals (who are grouped together under the rubric "dysthymics") are those whose susceptibility was prefigured by the generation of weak, slowly developing, and quickly dissipating reactive inhibition.

Eysenck predicted that in Pavlovian and Hullian terms, hysterics, who are imbalanced toward weak excitation and strong inhibition, should be able to form conditioned responses less quickly and less easily and should have less difficulty extinguishing them. He reported an experiment by Franks which confirmed this prediction and also demonstrated that dysthymics have the converse pattern. Still other experiments suggested that the stronger cortical inhibition of hysterics versus dysthymics on learning tasks was paralleled on perceptual tasks in the form of more easily produced satiation.

Eysenck generalized these findings to Mowrer's (1950) theory of the process of *socialization* as the acquisition of a certain set of socially prescribed behaviors, mediated by a process of *conditioning*. According to Mowrer, solutions to social problems involve the autonomic nervous system and organs mediating emotional response, while solutions to individual problems involve the central nervous system and the skeletal musculature. (We would also include conscious cognitive activity.) Classical conditioning, as opposed to instrumental learning, is mediated by the autonomic rather than the central nervous system. Autonomic responses occur as reactions to (1) actual physiological needs, and thus serve homeostatic functions; and (2) conditioned stimuli, and thus act as anticipatory states to *produce* physiological disequilibrium. The disequilibrium is experienced as basically painful emotion whose drive-like quality* imparts to the emotion an important motivational role.

Eysenck viewed the hysteric and psychopathic individual as undersocialized, while dysthymics are oversocialized. While this distinction may be more easily illustrated by the morally transgressing, often criminal psychopathic group and the overscrupulous obsessive-compulsive, it

*Tomkins (1962) would say that emotions are not themselves drives but serve a more important motivational role in *amplifying* the drives.

is more difficult to maintain in the face of years of clinical observation of the hysteric's suggestibility and susceptibility to influence.

Cognitive style theories. Shapiro's (1965) concept of *neurotic style* might appear to develop naturally from Eysenck's dimensional interpretation of individual personality differences, the implication of an ultimate biological basis for these dimensions, and the focus on perceptual and cognitive functioning. Shapiro has paid verbal allegiance, however, to the psychoanalytic character theorists—Freud, Reich, and Abraham—while giving them a twist adapted from the ego theorists—Hartmann, Erikson, and Klein. Shapiro's twist is in tracing the origin of neurotic style to adaptive ego operations rather than to libidinal conflicts. In his view, hysterics demonstrate the defense mechanism of repression (the active process of keeping unacceptable ideas of impulses out of consciousness) as part of their long-established cognitive style, which is global, diffuse, and easily impressed.

Shapiro (1965) states that these consistent, relatively stable modes of functioning which underlie ways of thinking, perceiving, experiencing emotion, and acting have:

> a biologically rooted nucleus of psychological structures that influences characteristic form tendencies of both adaptive and defensive functioning from the beginning, a nucleus around which other forces and influences assert themselves and accumulate [pp. 10–11].

Unfortunately, he did not elaborate on the origin nor the nature of such a hypothetical biologically rooted nucleus, nor did he specify what "other forces" might coalesce around it.

Wolowitz (1972) described the hysteric in terms of the other-directedness of such personalities. He argued that hysteria has been described almost exclusively in women, probably because many of its core features—the emotional reactivity, the interpersonal sensitivity, the dependence—are exaggerations of the prevailing view of women in Western culture. In fact, DSM-III has codified as its final criterion Chodoff and Lyons' (1958) oft-quoted comment that the hysterical personality "is a picture of women in the words of men . . . a caricature of femininity" (p. 739). The question then arises as to whether histrionic personality is found more frequently in women because the diagnosis has been cast *a priori* in terms that bias toward selecting women, or whether histrionic personality is the pathological form of traditionally defined female characteristics. In line with the latter interpretation, obsessive-compulsive or Compulsive Personality Disorder (DSM-III) could be construed as a caricature of certain characteristics found more frequently in middle-class American males: a restricted ability to express warm and tender emotions; preoccupation with matters of rules, order, organization, efficiency, and detail; and excessive devotion to work and productivity, to the exclusion of interpersonal relations. Whatever the basis for the higher frequency of women diagnosed with Histrionic Personality Disorder, still another question remains: Is this difference attributable to cultural conditioning, or wholly or in part to innate sex differences (e.g., Shapiro's biologically rooted nucleus) that set the stage for later development?

Psychoanalytic theory. Most psychoanalytic theories of histrionic/hysterical personality are rooted in Freud's (1905b) notions about the development of infantile sexuality and in his structural theory (1923). With these theoretical developments, it was possible to distinguish a hysterical character that was not dependent on and defined solely by the presence of conversion symptoms. Libido, the energy of sexual drive, is progressively displaced from one zone of sexual excitement to the next; each primary pleasure zone becomes the erogenous center for, respectively, the oral, anal, and phallic phases. With the culmination of infantile sexuality in the Oedipus Complex, the normal resolution is for the child to sublimate the sexual energy until puberty, renounce the opposite-sex parent as a sexual object choice, and identify with the same-sex parent. Frustration of drives in adult life may precipitate regression or the reinvestment of psychic energy into a phase of earlier gratification which had never been fully abandoned. In psychoanalytic theory, a *fixation* of abnormal amounts of psychic energy at lower developmental levels indicates a structural weak spot. This may predispose a person to neurosis when the tendency to seek libidinal gratification conflicts with ego instincts for reality concerns. The type of character or neurosis will be influenced by the structural weak spot; thus, an obsessive-compulsive neurotic has regressed to the conflicts and gratifications characteristic of the anal phase of psychosexual development, while the hysterical character is associated with the phallic–Oedipal phase, where fixation had occurred.

In the 1920s Freud developed more clearly his notion of repression as the type of defense most characteristic of hysteria. In repression, three things may be separately or in combination actively excluded from consciousness: the affectively charged idea, the idea itself, or the affect itself. The hysteric is prone to forget or not recognize unacceptable thoughts, wishes, or memories.

The major theorist after Freud to uphold the dynamic interpretation of hysterical character that emphasized fixation at the phallic–Oedipal level was Reich (1933). Marmor (1953) questioned the stereotyped Oedipal formulation and the accepted observation of a relatively mature level of object relations in hysterics. Drawing upon Wittels' (1930) comments on the pregenital development factors in hysterics, he suggested that pre-Oedipal conflicts played a prominent role in hysteria. Other psychoanalysts emphasized the importance of aggressive as well as sexual urges, and mentioned maternal deprivation as important in hysterical etiology. Easser and Lesser (1965) argued for a separation from the group of patients with hysterical personality those *hysteroid* patients who exhibited more extreme hysterical mannerisms, more ambivalent object relations, and a more disturbed family history in the context of an infantile or borderline personality structure. Zetzel's (1968) description of the "so-called good hysteric," who is unlike the "true good hysteric" in not responding well to analytic treatment, and Abse's (1974) label of the "hysteriform borderline personality" correspond to Easser and Lesser's pre-Oedipally conflicted hysteroid group. Recently, Baumbacher and Amini (1980–81) provided a psychodynamic formulation that proposed *three* subgroups among the hysterical character disorders: (1) hysterical character neurosis, which is associated with the classical triadic Oedipal issues; (2) hysterical personality disorder, which derives from the initial phallic phase and is thus concerned more with dyadic (child–mother) issues; and (3) a borderline personality organization with hysterical features, which utilizes more primitive defenses characteristic of more pre-Oedipal phases and is more fragilely organized. Such diagnostic subtleties may be able to be better captured by DSM-III's multiaxial system.

Somatoform Disorders

DSM-III marks the official birth of at least 12 separate disorders that had been classified together under DSM-II's rubric, "Hysterical Neurosis, Conversion Type." Not only were the conversion and dissociative forms of what had been called Hysterical Neurosis separated from each other, but some symptoms that had been part of the classical definition of conversion hysteria were now elevated to the status of separate diagnostic entities. Their official names, with the exception of Conversion Disorder, give no hint of their lineage. Part of this psychiatric house cleaning reflects the previous confusion involving conversion symptoms, which can occur across a spectrum of diagnoses from Histrionic Personality Disorder to catatonic schizophrenia. DSM-III has taken a firm stand on this diagnostic quicksand by elevating to official status a group of somatoform disorders which all have as their *essential* feature the presence of a physical symptom suggesting physical disorder in the absence of demonstrable organic explanation.

Somatization disorder or Briquet's Syndrome: Behavioral description. This diagnosis is named after Briquet, who published in 1859 a systematic study of hysteria based on 430 cases. He defined hysteria as a neurosis of the brain and linked its origins to a disturbance of the expression of emotion, chiefly violent passion, sorrow, and frustrated love.

Denying the view that sexual frustrations were etiological in hysteria, Briquet thought hereditary factors were more important in predisposing impressionable women to be hypersensitive in certain situations. Further, he found hysteria more frequently in the lower than in the higher social strata, and more often in the country than in the city (Ellenberger, 1970).

While the diagnostic category of Somatoform Disorder has retained some of the flavor of Briquet's description, it has absorbed most of its substance from the criteria first established by Perley and Guze (1962) and pursued in a series of studies by a group in the Department of Psychiatry in the Washington School of Medicine in St. Louis (e.g., Woodruff, Clayton, & Guze, 1971). The main differences are that the St. Louis group specified that at least 25 medically unexplained symptoms for a "definite" diagnosis and 20 to 24 for a "probable" diagnosis were necessary in at least 9 or 10 symptom clusters, while DSM-III requires a minimum of 14 reported symptoms (out of a possible total of 37) for women and 12 for men. The 37 possible symptoms fall into seven main groups: (1) *sickly* (the individual believes that he or she has been sickly for most or a good part of his or her life); (2) *conversion or pseudoneurological symptoms* (e.g., difficulty swallowing, loss of voice, deafness, memory loss, trouble walking, paralysis); (3) *gastrointestinal symptoms* (e.g., abdominal pain, vomiting spells); (4) *female reproductive symptoms* (judged by the individual as occurring more frequently or severely than in most women: dysmenorrhea, menstrual irregularity, etc.); (5) *psychosexual symptoms* (sexual indifference, lack of pleasure or presence of pain during intercourse); (6) *pain* (in back, joints, genital area, extremities, on urination, or other pain excluding headaches); (7) cardiopulmonary symptoms (shortness of breath, palpitations, chest pain, dizziness). The revision of requiring fewer complaints for diagnosing men is important because the original criteria featured so many pregnancy and menstrual complaints that it was biased against diagnosing men. Using the strict Feighner criteria, no exclusively heterosexual male with Briquet's Syndrome had been reported as of the study by Kroll, Chamberlain, and Halpern (1979).

The St. Louis group has assiduously avoided allowing any psychodynamic or even personality-trait considerations to creep into their diagnostic system, although DSM-III does state that individuals with this disorder often have Histrionic Personality Disorder or, more rarely, Antisocial Personality Disorder. Groundwork for the latter connection may have been laid by a study by Cloninger and Guze (1975), which found a strong association between hysterical daughters and fathers who are sociopathic (a pre-DSM-II term, equivalent to Antisocial Personality Disorder today). The authors interpreted this as further evidence that "sociopathy and hysteria result from similar aetiological and pathogenic factors," but they did not speculate as to whether these factors might be genetic, psychodynamic, or social.

Psychogenic Pain Disorder and Conversion Disorder. The experience of psychogenic pain in the absence of physical disorder is separated in DSM-III from Conversion Disorder, in which symptoms are expressed as neurological deficits. In contrast to individuals with Conversion Disorder, individuals with Psychogenic Pain Disorder rarely display *la belle indifférence* (a relative lack of concern about the supposedly severe and distressing symptom), or histrionic personality traits. As Bishop and Torch (1979) noted, however, there are few data to support a separate designation of Conversion Disorder and Psychalgia. These authors analyzed retrospectively 91 cases of Conversion Disorder and 80 cases of Psychalgia, both redefined according to the DSM-III operational criteria. No statistical differences were found between the two groups on the MMPI or on the following variables: sex, race, history of dissociation, history of cerebral disease, pathological identification, hysterical personality, passive–aggressive personality, defensive symptoms, expressive symptoms, trauma, secondary gain, youngest sibling, history of hypochondria, history of psychophysiological reactions, hyperventilation syndrome, or other conversion symptom. Conversion Disorder and Psychalgia diverged from a control group of 94 "neurotic" controls on three variables: whether the symptoms are defensive (serve as an assertive or protective communication), are expressive (communicate negative affect), and provide secondary gain (compensation or solicitude). Bishop and Torch have provided a model of the kind of empirical study that needs to be undertaken to assess the validity of the DSM-III diagnostic criteria. Their study suggests that Conversion Disorder and Psychalgia have not been clearly delineated and may not prove to be reliable nor valid diagnostic entities.

Hypochondriasis and differential diagnoses. The differential diagnoses of Conversion Disorder from Hypochondriasis, and of both from Malingering and from Factitious Disorders are discussed under Assessment, below.

Movement disorders. Tic disorders and Tourette's Disorder are included as possible hysterical phenomena in Table 6.1 because they represent physical manifestations that may be psychogenic and which are not attributable to organic pathology. Tourette's Disorder is named after Gilles de la Tourette, who described nine patients who before the age of ten demonstrated various bizarre motor disorders accompanied by ecolalia and coprolalia (Ascher, 1974). According to DSM-III the recurrent, involuntary, repetitive motor tics of the head, torso, and upper and lower limbs are exacerbated by stress and may be accompanied initially by multiple symptoms including coprolalia, various noises, and other motor activity.

These stress-related features as well as the stereotype are reminiscent of the symptoms associated with such "exotic psychiatric disorders" as *latah*, *susto*, *pibloktoq*, and *imu*, which are discussed under Dissociative Disorders below. Ascher (1948) also understood coprolalia as a dissociative phenomenon. Mahler and Rangell (1943) thought that the Gilles de la Tourette syndrome was attributable to a psychodynamic conflict between repression and instinct in persons with weak subcortical structures who were unable to withstand, constitutionally, overwhelming emotional forces. Fenichel (1945) and Cameron (1947) considered tics to be hysterical conversion phenomena to the extent that they expressed meaningful repressed conflicts through bodily sign language. Fenichel (1945) also discussed the psychodynamics of torticollis in terms of the anal retentive tendencies, suppressed rage, and castration anxiety expressed in this symptom. When such pre-Oedipal dynamics are operating, the tic would be classified among the compulsive disorders, according to Fenichel.

Neurophysiological theories of conversion. Rice and Greenfield (1969) attempted to explore the puzzling clinical phenomenon of *la belle indifférence* by operationally defining anxiety in terms of physiological arousal. Nine patients diagnosed as having conversion reaction who also showed *la belle indifférence* were compared with matched controls who had similar complaints, but of a medically documented nature. Compared with controls, the conversion patients demonstrated as great or greater levels of physiological arousal (measured by heart rate, galvanic skin response (GSR), and frontalis electromyogram). Thus, if there *is* a defensive process such as repression, as hypothesized by psychoanalytic theory, which is involved in *la belle indifférence*, it does not prevent the covert physiological correlates of emotion. This study does not, however, clarify the relation between physiological arousal and the possible action of a psychological defense, such as recognition or suppression of that arousal.

Ludwig's (1972) neurobiological theory of hysterical dysfunction related to increased corticofugal inhibition of afferent stimulation has the denominator of *inhibition* in common with Eysenck's theory described above. Ludwig dismissed the psychoanalytic view of symptoms as symbolic expressions of conflict or compromise formations, and embraced, instead, Kretschmer's (1926) theory. He viewed hysterical phenomena as manifestations of two instinctive reaction patterns: (1) the "violent motor reaction," which could be regarded as a defense reaction against threatening stimuli, and (2) the "sham-death" or immobilization reflex, marked by partial loss of reaction to outer stimuli. Specific conversion symptoms that could be related to the violent motor reaction are convulsions, tremors, and other movements, while behavioral states such as paralyses, anesthesias, dreamlike or amnesic states all serve to block emotional and physical stimuli, and thus could be manifestations of the sham-death reflex. Hysterical symptoms, according to Kretschmer, could also develop when a hysterical structure partakes of some essential biological drive or elaborates upon an organically based ailment. Ludwig also proposed that the hysterical symptom could be generated as a result of the biological tendency to react in progressively more primitive ways when confronted with a potentially dangerous but inescapable situation.

Ludwig pointed to a neurobiological basis for this pattern: corticofugal inhibition of afferent stimulation at the level of the brain stem reticular formation. The amount of incoming afferent stimuli or its conscious recognition could be influenced by attention regulated by efferent or corticofugal control. Ludwig attributed the hysteric's nonphysiologically based symptoms, the apparent lack of concern (*la belle indifférence*) about these symptoms, increased suggestibility, and propensity to a "field dependent" or psychologically undifferentiated global perceptual style (cf. Witkin, Dyk, Faterson, Goodenough, & Karp, 1962) to a subtle memory-attention dysfunction. Ludwig's theory of psychophysiological inhibition would predict that patients with hysterical conversion symptoms would be comparatively inattentive to stimulus input; thus, they would be more distractible, have higher recognition thresholds, low level sensory stimulation, and so on. This inattention should be correlated with a *decreased* somatosensory average-evoked response (AER: the average level of electrical discharge from certain areas of the brain which are measured on an electroencephalogram).

Moldofsky and England (1975) studied five patients with diagnosed symptoms of hysterical anesthesia and pain, and found that, contrary to the hypothesis of increased inhibition of AER habituation with tactile stimulation of the hysterical anesthetic region, responses contralateral to the affected side were *facilitated* with strong tactile stimuli. Consistent with these results are the findings by Lader and Sartorius (1968) comparing ten patients with conversion symptoms with a group of anxious-phobic patients. There was no GSR habituation in their patients with conversion symptoms. On both physiological measures of autonomic arousal and self-report measures of anxiety, the conversion patients showed significantly more arousal than patients with anxious states. The authors claimed that these results do not support the hypothesis derived from psychodynamic theory that conversion patients should be less anxious than anxiety patients (because the psychic energy has, presumably, been redirected into a symptom, and thus not experienced consciously as affect). It is interesting, however, that "overt anxiety," as measured by *observers'* ratings of patients' behavior, was significantly lower in hysterical than in anxious/phobic patients. While Lader and Sartorius distinguished this *appearance* of less anxiety than is reflected in physiological measures and self-ratings from *la belle indifférence*, it would seem that some explanation of this finding is in order before they fully reject all notions of psychological defense.

Moldofsky and England (1975) speculated that the tendency for localization of the facilitation phenomenon to the contralateral hemisphere might be explained by patients' relative vigilance to the hysterical anesthetic region. This produces increments of excitation transmitted by somatosensory pathways to the contralateral hemisphere, since normal habituation occurs when unaffected regions (to which the patients are less vigilant) are stimulated.

Another theory relevant to this hemispheric phenomenon was posed by Engel (1970), who, after Ferenczi's (1926) observations, asserted that conversion hemisensory disturbance is found more often to involve the left half of the body rather than the right. Galin, Diamond, and Branff (1977) tested this on a sample of 42 females and 10 males and found that for the female cases, conversion symptoms occurred more frequently on the left side of the body. These results cannot be directly compared with Moldofsky's findings because his subjects were male and had work-related symptoms. Even so, three of his five patients had symptoms on the left side. Galin et al. interpreted their findings in terms of the increasing number of observations of cerebral hemispheric specialization related to affect, personality organization, symptom formation, and defense process. In this view, unconscious processes mediated by the right hemisphere would be expressed, not through the main speech and motor channels "preempted" by the more consciously directed left hemisphere, but through somatic representation, such as a conversion symptom.

Behavioral theories of conversion. In the behavioral perspective, hysterical conversion symptoms, like all neurotic disorders, are acquired by a learning process. Dollard and Miller (1950) have argued that the symptom is acquired because it reduces the fear drive, which in turn reinforces the hysterical symptom. A major difficulty with this analysis—that such patients experience anxiety even after the onset of the hysterical symptoms—was cited by Eysenck and Rachman (1965). The notion that patients with hysterical conversion symptoms have *less* anxiety than other patients, whether the underlying theory is psychoanalytic or behavioral, has been seriously challenged, however, by recent neurophysiological findings, discussed in the previous section. Eysenck and Rachman also pointed out that Dollard and Miller's theory would not be able to explain why one patient would use symptom formation to reduce fear, while another patient would develop a compulsion or, indeed, any other neurotic disorder.

In Walter and Black's (1959) interpretation of the development of aphonia in their patient, the symptom began as an avoidance reaction to an anxiety-provoking situation. After the situation had passed, the aphonia persisted, autonomously, as a habit. Drawing upon this example, Eysenck and Rachman then theorized that extroverted personality types, who develop reactive inhibition quickly and dissipate it slowly, would be more predisposed to "block" under stress and then to develop conversion symptoms as a neurotic reaction.

How might this occur? According to Yates (1960), stimuli above a certain intensity cease to facilitate a response and begin to inhibit it; increased stress or anxiety in normal subjects will facilitate the speed of simple responses but have an opposite effect for complex tasks. If hysterics are already inclined to high inhibition (i.e., they are already on the inhibition side of a theoretical normal curve produced as a function of stimulus intensity), then they are constitutionally well on their way to accumulate reactive inhibition. Any increased intensity, whether produced by an external stimulus or by internal anxiety, will impede response in a complex task and produce "errors of inertia" (Davis, 1946); that is, blocking.

Psychodynamic theories of conversion. Distinct from the diagnostic category of Briquet's Syndrome in DSM-III is Conversion Disorder, which is the nosological heir of the conversion lineage. A Conversion Disorder usually features a single loss or alteration of physical functioning not explainable by any physical disorder. Usually, the symptom appears in temporal relation with extreme psychological stress. The definition of Conversion Disorder is unique in DSM-III because it posits a specific psychodynamic mechanism to account for the disturbance: (1) "primary gain" is achieved by keeping an internal conflict (often precipitated by a traumatic event) out of awareness, and (2) "secondary gain" is achieved by avoiding a particular noxious activity or by gaining environmental support. Another associated feature that links Conversion Disorder with its roots is the attitude toward the symptom of *la belle indifférence,* a relative lack of concern not consistent with the apparently severe affliction.

In DSM-II, Conversion Reaction was differentiated from Psychophysiologic Disorder (Code 316.00 in DSM-III: Psychological Factors Affecting Physical Condition), such as bronchial asthma, ulcerative colitis, or hypertension, which involve a recognized physical disorder with organic findings. In both conversion and psychophysiologic disorders, the symptom has symbolic meaning communicated through body language. The difference is that while both cases involve responses to psychological stimuli, a conversion symptom represents a covert attempt to express an emotion, while a psychophysiological disorder involves a physiologically adaptive (at least originally) response to constant or periodically recurring emotional states.

Unfortunately, much of the field has accepted Alexander's (1950) dictum that conversion symptoms involve neuromuscular or sensory perceptive systems, whose original functions are to register, express, or relieve emotional tension, in the voluntary rather than the autonomic nervous system. The "classical" conversion symptoms have always been suggestive of neurological disease: paralysis, aphonia, seizures, akinesia, dyskinesia, blindness, anesthesia, and paresthesia. However, some of the "classical" conversion symptoms such as fainting, nausea, and vomiting obviously involve the autonomic nervous system. Other tissue changes that may develop as complications at the site of the conversion are skin lesions and the development of lesions in the upper and lower gastrointestinal tract, respiratory passages, joints, and even parts of the vascular system. The distinction between voluntary and autonomic systems has also been blurred by research findings in biofeedback. For example, Barr and Abernathy (1972) demonstrated that visceral and glandular responses can be shaped through a process similar to the instrumental learning of voluntary behavior.

Engel and Schmale (1967), in a modern psychoanalytic interpretation, proposed that the capability of a body part to achieve mental representation is the crucial factor in conversion, not whether the body part is innervated through the ANS or CNS. If a body part can be engaged in relating to other people, and/or is involved in emotional discharge and expression, then physiological processes concomitant with these activities may achieve mental representation. Thus, physiological processes may acquire meanings that may be reactivated by symbolic stimuli. Conversion mechanisms may be involved in somatic disease to the extent that physiological processes can be linked with mental representations. In this view, local tissue lesions may develop as *complications* of bodily reactions to the conversion. While the lesion or disease itself does not have primary symbolic meaning nor serve a defensive function, it may be the result of a conversion process derived from meaningful mental representations that *did* serve such a purpose. Once such a pathway linking mental representations of body parts with psychic derivatives and physiological concomitants has been established, it is easier for stimuli with symbolic potential to set in motion a conversion process that can have physiological complications and for particular organs or functions to be involved in future conversions. Engel and Schmale's (1967) views are in accord with Freud's (1905a) concept of somatic compliance, the ability of the affected function or body part to be the locus of cathetic condensation (concentrated psychic energy) of the previously cathected but conflictual idea or impulse. The organ or disease may be chosen because it is the one under the highest tension at the moment or because it symbolizes the unconscious impulse or idea in question.

Historical psychoanalytic theories of conversion. Up until 1900, the study of hysteria was mainly concerned with hysterical symptoms from a medical, physiological, and neuroanatomical point of view. The French neurologist Charcot (1890) demonstrated that hysterical amnesic paralyses were different from organic paralyses and amnesias by using hypnotic suggestion to both reproduce and eradicate symptoms in hysterical patients. Breuer and Freud began using the hypnotic technique not only to remove symptoms but to explore their origins. In 1893 they proposed that hysterical symptoms were induced by a trauma, an accident or event made significant by the presence of an intense emotion such as fear, shame, or sexual arousal, or by a series of less intense traumas. According to Breuer, memories of such events, and their associated feelings, were not available to awareness because the experience took place during an abnormal state of consciousness—a hypnoid state, in which experiences could not be completely internalized. Freud thought that the memories and feelings were intentionally cut off from normal conscious thought because they were unacceptable to the patient. The concept of hypnoid state was deemphasized and finally abandoned, as Freud shifted from a physiological to a psychological theory of hysteria.

Both Freud and Breuer agreed that the hysterical symptom arose from the blocked flow of affect, stimulated by the traumatic event or emotional states. Such dammed-up feelings and energy were dynamically redirected into the soma and transformed into the hysterical symptom. Freud (1894) elaborated the notion of psychological conflict as the root of hysteria. Disturbing ideas incompatible with a person's moral and social codes were *repressed*, kept unconscious by the removal of affect from the ideas. This affect could be transformed into conversion, a somatic expression. Similar traumatic experiences later in life could stimulate the repressed idea, reconnecting it with affect. To prevent reappearance of the threatening idea, the patient could channel the affect into new conversions or discharge it through hysterical attacks or, in the therapeutic context, discharge it through abreaction or *catharsis*. Freud used catharsis and free association (1905a) to help patients overcome *resistance* to talking about the repressed ideas in treatment. What they eventually talked about—reports of childhood seduction—led Freud to develop a theory of hysteria in which a child is the passive participant in sexual activity. These traumatic events were repressed but later reactivated by the sexual drives of puberty and by later sexually tinged events. The traumatic reactivation led, Freud thought, to symptom formation as a symbolic substitute for the repressed conflict, which would allow the release of some affective tension, while not allowing the direct expression of the threatening idea.

Freud (1900, 1905b) revised his seduction theory when he realized that his patients were not reporting actual memories but *fantasies* and infantile wishes. He postulated that in the unconscious, it is impossible to distinguish fantasies from memories. Given this, the psychic reality of early childhood was more important in the etiology of hysteria than physical reality. In *Three Essays on Sexual Theory* (1905b), Freud elaborated his concepts of infantile sexuality, libido, the Oedipus complex, and character types. Freud described the greater predisposition of women than men to hysteria to their more complex course through psychosexual development. It was the golden age of hysteria for psychoanalysis.

Dissociative Disorders

Behavioral description. One of the biggest changes in DSM-III was the divorce of conversion and dissociative disorders, which had been married under the aegis of Hysterical Neuroses in DSM-II. Unifying the three adult and one nonadult form (sleep-walking) of Dissociative Disorder are the sudden, temporary alteration and loss in function of consciousness, identity, or motor behavior. *Psychogenic Amnesia*, a sudden inability to recall important personal information, may be (1) localized, in which only events in a circumscribed period of time, usually just after a stressful event, are forgotten; (2) selective, in which only some but not all events in a circumscribed period of time are forgotton; (3) generalized, in which an individual's entire life may be forgotten; or (4) continuous, in which the individual cannot recall events after a certain time up to and including the present. In *Psychogenic Fugue*, a person may suddenly assume a new identity, with no consciousness of the past, and travel or even construct a new life, for which there will be later amnesia if the old identity is recovered. A cycle of transitions from one whole personality, complete with memories, and particular social and behavior patterns, to one, two, or more distinct personalities defines the diagnosis of *Multiple Personality*.

The inclusion of *Depersonalization Disorder* with the more classical dissociative conditions is controversial. The overlap with the dissociative definition is in the loss of function of identity, a component of which is lost when the self is temporarily experienced as unreal. Depersonalization was previously classified as a separate neurosis in DSM-II. The term has been used over the years to refer to a diagnostic category, to various symptoms, and to a psychological defense used by both neurotics and psychotics. As a *symptom*, it has been associated with epilepsy, drug states, encephalitis, manic depression, and schizophrenia, and has been described in stressed normals (Brauer, Harrow, & Tucker, 1970).

Behavioral theories of dissociation. Behavioral formulations seem to be especially applicable to an understanding of combat neuroses. Dollard and Miller's (1950) learning theory predicts that the intense fear aroused by traumatic experiences such as war should motivate the victim to stop thinking about them. The inhibition of these terrifying memories should be reinforced by the relief that accompanies the removal of fear. A logical implication of this is that administration of a drug that reduces fear should facilitate recall of those experiences. In fact, this occurred when Grinker and Spiegel (1945) gave victims of combat amnesia an intravenous injection of sodium amobarbital.

According to Dollard and Miller (1950), other forms of repression could be motivated and reinforced in a similar manner. The consequences of motivated and reinforced repression could extend to the often noted cognitive style of the hysteric—the inability to remember and think about certain topics, to make accurate judgments, to problem-solve, to be creative—especially in areas touching on the repressed thoughts. This interpretation is also relevant to the discussion of Histrionic Personality Disorder above.

A brief history of psychiatric theories of dissociative phenomena. The history of psychoanalytic theorizing about dissociative disorders is nearly inextricable from that of conversion. Charcot, Breuer, Janet, and Freud all noted both dissociative and conversion symptoms in their patients. Revised conceptions of dissociative phenomena played a larger role than conversion, however, in the emergence of psychodynamic theory from a belief in possession and exorcism. Franz Mesmer believed that all illness was due to an imbalance, insufficient amount, or poor quality of a universal fluid. This condition could be rectified by *magnetic rapport,* in which his own stronger fluid would be transmitted to the patient. His disciple, the Marquis de Puységur altered the fluid theory of magnetism from one based on a pseudophysical to a psychological force and thereby made it more respectable. He used the "perfect crisis," which had the appearance of a waking state, to cure the ailing, who would be amnestic afterwards. This "perfect crisis" was soon called "artificial somnambulism" because of its similarity to natural somnambulism, and the whole curative procedure was called "mesmerising." Braid later renamed it "hypnosis." Charcot studied hypnosis using hysterical patients as subjects. He differentiated patients with "dynamic amnesia," who could recover their memories through hypnosis, from those with "organic amnesia." He also differentiated (Charcot, 1889) hysterical ambulatory automatism from fugue states precipitated by trauma or epilepsy (Ellenberger, 1970).

An increasing number of cases of multiple personality were documented and described in the eighteenth and nineteenth centuries. In 1887 Janet published a study showing that multiple subpersonalities could emerge through hypnosis. Ellenberger (1970) discussed the attempts made around the end of the nineteenth century to combine the prevailing sexual theory of hysteria with notions about dual personality. Certainly, observers had noticed that multiple personality occurred more frequently in hysterics, and that lethargy and similar states associated with hypnosis preceded the shift from one personality to the next. A theorist at that time might have argued that since hypnosis could produce hysterical symptoms, as well as such states as dual personality, lethargy, catalepsy, and somnambulism, then all these conditions must have something in common. Charcot made this grand synthesis and described hysteria as a permanent state of semisomnabulism. Adapting Briquet's theory of hysteria as a brain neurosis in constitutionally predisposed individuals, he viewed hypnosis as a pathological condition only when found in hysterics (Ellenberger, 1970).

Later, Janet (1889) conceived of hysteria as a permanent state of dual personality. Because of a "psychological weakness," hysterics manifested a narrowing of the field of consciousness. According to his theory, the hysterical personality maintained split parts existing in somnambulistic consciousness as fixed ideas (*idées fixes*) which originated in past traumatic events. Janet believed that these autonomously functioning fixed ideas in the subconscious gave rise to hysterical symptoms, while obsessive symptomatology derived from *conscious* fixed ideas.

In Breuer's view (Breuer & Freud, 1893–1895), dissociated ideas were originally registered during a "hypnoid" state. This was compatible with Janet's theory of the hysteric's constitutionally narrowed field of consciousness. It is well-known history, of course, that Freud rejected this idea and replaced it with his psychodynamic model, in which unacceptable ideas are repressed into the unconscious.

Apart from Morton Prince's (1926) famous publication of the case of Sally Beauchamps, psychiatry in the early decades of the twentieth century did not pay much attention to dissociative phenomena. Interest was rekindled, however, by the mid-1940s. Harriman (1943) used posthypnotic suggestion both directly (suggesting a second personality) and indirectly (suggesting that the subject had no close identity with his normal personality) to produce secondary personalities in normals. Basing their theory on a review of the literature, Taylor and Martin (1944) concluded that previous roleplaying, as in fantasy, and a dissociative mechanism are important in the genesis of multiple personality. In Fenichel's (1945) rendering of the traditional psychoanalytic theory of dissociation, disturbances in consciousness correspond to the repression of the sexual meaning of currently derivative Oedipal fantasies and of the affect connected with them. This double repression, as it were, functions to put the fantasies as far from awareness as possible, even into another personality. While Thigpen and Cleckley (1954) reported what is probably the most famous case of multiple personality of all time, which was even made into a movie (*The Three Faces of Eve*), they did not advance any new theory of dissociation.

Psychosocial theories of dissociation. Kirschner (1973) suggested that cases of war amnesia and dissociative states were crucial in demonstrating that such symptoms could occur in any diagnostic group and could be reactions of the normal personality to severe stress. Temoshok and Attkisson (1977) proposed that dissociative and conversion phenomena, whether they occur at the individual, group, or societal level, are forms of adaptation to psychosocial stress. The psychosocial perspective may be more clearly seen for dissociative rather than conversion phenomena, perhaps because (1) there have been so many cross-cultural reports of dissociative phenomena that "culture" has been rather permanently linked with them; (2) it is easier for Western commentators to understand and even to recognize societal dynamics in cultures other than our own; and (3) many of the observers of these phenomena have been anthropologists, who are more likely than psychoanalysts to entertain perspectives beyond the intrapsychic.

Temoshok and Attkisson (1977) argued that cultural contexts influence dissociative behaviors, first, by interpreting which behaviors are within the range of toleration and, second, by molding behavioral expression into culturally determined patterns. For example, altered states of consciousness are labeled psychiatric disorders when they occur in the Western world, but such kindred phenomena as trance or possession are appropriate and even desirable behaviors in certain non-Western societies. Some analogous Western forms of dissociation which are appropriate at certain times and in certain groups include the snake-handling cults of the southern United States and glossolalia, speaking in tongues.

Cultural contexts may in many instances *contribute to the etiology* of hysterical phenomena. While not an official psychiatric diagnosis, hysterical contagion (mass hysteria) has been described in at least 20 accounts (cf. Sirois, 1974); it is most simply defined as the dissemination through a defined group of a set of experiences or behaviors which are in some way connected with fear of a mysterious force (Kerckhoff & Bach, 1968). Temoshok and Attkisson (1977) noted the chronic stress or a conflictual event has been consistently associated with all groups that manifest hysterical contagion. Mass possessions, millenarian movements (Worsley, 1968), and cargo cults (La Barre, 1970) may be interpreted as group behaviors with a decided hysterical flavor. These phenomena seem to occur in societies undergoing rapid change. Spindler (1968) interpreted cargo cults as reactions to rapid social change occurring in the wake of confrontations between divergent cultural systems. In his view, the underlying dynamics of such cults are "the *search for identity* and the *attempt to reestablish cognitive control*" (p. 335). We would argue that if depersonalization can be included under Dissociative Disorders in DSM-III on the basis of its involving the loss of a function of an identity component, so these group phenomena, which involve loss of a function of a component of group identity, should also be considered dissociative phenomena. The theoretical overlap between this view of reactive movements and multiple personality is clear in Murphy's (1947) observations: "Most cases of multiple personality appear essentially to represent the organism's effort to live, at different times, in terms of different systems of values" (p. 450).

Cultural pathogenesis, as well as cultural patterning, was proposed by Temoshok and Attkisson (1977) to underlie such exotic psychiatric syndromes (cf. Abse, 1974) as *amok* (cf. Murphy, 1973), *latah, whitiko, susto,* and others. These syndromes have in common: (1) culturally defined stressed events which precipitate the disorder; (2) a brief dissociated period of stereotyped behaviors such as wild running, violence, shouting, seizures, and so forth, which occur in a distinctive pattern; (3) the possibility of contagion; and (4) a rich history and associated set of cultural meanings of the disorder. These acute psychotic-like reactions are strikingly suggestive of the persistent but officially unrecognized category of hysterical psychosis (cf. Hollender & Hirsch, 1972). It is interesting that, for the first time, DSM-III gives some recognition to this disorder, which was ignored by its predecessors, in the new category of Brief Reactive Psychosis, which is defined as always following a psychosocial stressor.

Temoshok and Attkisson (1977) suggested that so-called hysterical contagion and group dissociative reactions are transpositions to the scale of individual dissociative phenomena: hysterical psychosis, multiple personality, fugue, and "exotic psychiatric syndromes." While these disorders are not classified together (some do not even appear) in DSM-III, they are logically and phenomenologically related in terms of common etiology. Cultural change at the group level and stressors at the individual level are not the cause per se of distinctive behaviors which may be viewed in some instances as psychiatric disorders; rather, the crucial factor is whether and how societies and individuals *adapt* to these stressors. Group coherence may be maintained by various societal "defense mechanisms"—periodic cathartic rituals (e.g., Mardi Gras, *Oktoberfest, Walpurgisnacht*) which release destabilizing forces, or rituals of maintenance (e.g., *rites de passage*) which promote group identity. Similarly, the coherence of individual identity in the face of idiosyncratically interpreted stressors may be maintained by adaptive reactions that are manifested in culturally patterned behaviors. If extreme enough, these behaviors are called psychiatric disorders. It is hypothesized that hysterical phenomena, in particular, are understandable in terms of this psychosocial stress-adaptation-identity model.

Assessment

Projective Tests

Psychological testing attempts to obtain within a standardized situation a systematic sample of certain verbal, perceptual, and motor behavior. No one test in a battery is diagnostic in itself; it is the configuration of test results, as well as observations of interpersonal dynamics in the testing situation (cf. Schafer, 1954), that must be interpreted as a gestalt. In other words, a hypothesis may be in the process of formulation after the administration of one test, acquire more support after another, be in some doubt after a third; the doubt may be resolved as a more certain hypothesis emerges after the fourth, and so on.

Rapaport, Gill, and Schafer's (1968) classical text on diagnostic psychological testing discussed the use and interpretation of a battery of tests for several nosological groups, including 11 obvious cases of hysteria with conversion symptoms or conversion symptoms with phobic syndromes, and eight less clearly defined cases of "hysterical character formation with minor conversion symptoms and hysterical behavior." Care was taken to exclude medical and neurological problems, psychosomatic disorders, and somatic expressions of anxiety. The cornerstone of their psychodiagnostic approach to testing is that psychiatric disorders result largely from the encroachment of unconscious ideas upon consciousness, and/or as a defense against these ideas. Accordingly, the characteristic ego defenses of the hysteric—a generalized repressive strategy—would be manifested across a variety of situations and functioning.

For example, a repressive strategy would be expected to result in poor functioning on an information subtest of intelligence scales. More specifically, on the Wechsler-Bellevue scale, when Information is three or more points below the score on the Vocabulary subtest, hysteria should be entertained as a diagnostic hypothesis if psychosis has been ruled out, and particularly considered if the other verbal tests were consistent with Vocabulary. Other diagnostic suggestions by Rapaport and co-workers (1968) include the following:

- Hysterics, as well as obsessives (but for different reasons), may show impairment relative to Vocabulary and to the performance mean on the Picture Completion subtest.
- Hysterics are prone to produce distortions with affective elaboration on the Babcock Story Recall Test (a test of memory function), especially for the immediate recall.
- Intensely repressed hysterics may block or repeat the stimulus word on the Word Association Test, which assesses intellectual

functioning and concept formation. They may also have a few extremely long reaction times, especially to words with sexual connotations.

- On the Thematic Apperception Test (TAT), the hysteric's stories are likely to be shaped rather unreflectively around affect, rather than around a coherently organized plot. In telling the story, the hysteric may overemphasize emotions or mood and may even overreact affectively to the card, crying, expressing anger, or the like.
- On the most unstructured of the projective tests, the Rorschach, hysterics generally have a low average F% (responses determined only by the contour and articulation of the area chosen). They usually have a good F+%, which indicates a well-integrated, convincing fit of percepts to blots. This finding is consistent with clinical observations of minimally controlled intense affect and anxiety, which nevertheless do not impair perceptual organization and critical function.
- The incidence of Rorschach Movement responses (an impression of movement in the percept), indicative of the level of "natural endowment" and cultural interests, in the view of Rapaport et al., is rather low in hysterics, perhaps reflecting their use of repression and difficulty in controlling impulse.
- Hysterics tend to react strongly to color in the Rorschach cards and may be immediately attracted to the first hint of color in the test—the red areas on Card III. The use of color as a determinant in forming a percept may be interpreted as degree of affect tempered by critical awareness, depending on the concomitant integration of form as a determinant. Affectively labile hysterics would be expected to have more color responses.
- Popular responses have been considered as suggestive of social compliance and conventional thinking. Thus, naive hysterics may have a high P%.
- Symbolic, especially latently symbolic, responses (e.g., "an erect snake ready to strike") are frequent in hysterics' records, but are also seen in psychotics, whose responses may be overelaborated and more farfetched.
- Hysterics (as well as other diagnostic groups with anxiety and ideational lability) often verbalize affective reactions to the cards (e.g., "How scary!").

Smokler and Shevrin (1979) culled a list of defining projective characteristics for hysterical personality styles from Schafer (1948, 1954). These included expressive reactions (e.g., "Wow!"), phobic verbalizations (e.g., "Ugh!"), lack of specificity, naiveté, childlike manner of response, affectiveness (emotion coloring most responses, especially where not usual), tactile sensations (emphasis upon kinesthetic feelings), and repression.

Shapiro (1977) emphasized the predominance in hysterical and narcissistic Rorschach records of the CF response, a color-dominated form response which stands between the more immediate and passive pure C response and the more articulated FC response. In both diagnostic groups, there is an impairment of impulse and/or affect-organizing and expressive functions. Hysterics are characterized more by vivid and labile emotional reactions, narcissists more by impulsive action. Despite the hysteric's susceptibility to the immediate impression, thinking processes are not impaired, nor is the resulting percept distorted or diffuse.

It should be mentioned that the descriptions which Rapaport et al. (1968) found to be characteristic of conversion hysterics cannot be used to make a differential diagnosis from organic disease because medical and neurological groups were initially screened out. The descriptions may be useful, however, in differentiating hysterics from normals and, with more certainty, from other neurotic groups, particularly obsessive-compulsives. There is little applicability of the projective tests as they are currently used and scored for diagnosing many of the DSM-III categories: Somatization Disorder, Psychogenic Pain Disorder, Dissociative Disorders, and Brief Reactive Psychosis. They would be most appropriate for diagnosing Histrionic Personality Disorder. The limited diagnostic usefulness of projective tests may be attributed less to the tests' intrinsic value as clinical and research instruments than to the lack of adequate diagnostic criteria against which to validate possible indicators. DSM-III's Research Diagnostic Criteria may help remedy this situation. The most appropriate deployment of projective tests may be for assessing ego strengths, weaknesses, and cognitive/character style for the purposes of determining the appropriateness of individual patients for different modes of treatment and for suggesting therapeutic directions and strategies.

"Objective" Tests

The Hysteria (Hy) Scale 3 of the Minnesota Multiphasic Personality Inventory (MMPI) was developed to help identify patients using the neurotic defenses associated with conversion hysteria. The scale was intended to tap the personality predisposition of patients who, after breakdown, would use physical symptoms to resolve conflicts. As with most of the MMPI clinical scales, items for Hy were selected on the basis of their differentiation from normals of a group of patients demonstrating conversion reaction (Dahlstrom, Welsh, & Dahlstrom, 1972). The items for the scale contain two subtests: somatic and body reference items, and items relating to social facility and denial.

Scale 1 (Hs) attempts to measure personality characteristics associated with the neurotic pattern of hypochondriasis, an abnormal preoccupation with bodily function. Because items are not restricted to any particular part of the body, but cover digestion, breathing, thinking, vision, sensation, and sleep, a subject with real somatic illness might have an elevated score, but not as high as in psychiatric somatization cases, who would endorse a numerous variety of symptoms.

The "conversion valley" pattern refers to a configuration in which scales 1 and 3 are the highest, with Scale 2 (Depression) relatively lower. The pattern is more frequently found in women. It is not common in generally elevated profiles, but is typical of moderately elevated profiles or those within the normal range. Subjects with this pattern differ from normals in their denial of problems and/or inadequacies. A study by Black, reported by Dahlstrom et al. (1972), on normal college girls with the conversion V found that peers rated them on an adjective checklist as selfish, self-centered, having many physical complaints, neurotic, dependent, indecisive, high-strung, emotional, hostile, irritable, lacking in self-control, apathetic; and on the positive side: serious and idealistic (a short list). These adjectives are reminiscent of many similar lists generated by clinicians across the years to describe the hysterical/histrionic personality.

In terms of research bearing on the question of differential diagnosis, Gilberstadt and Jancis (1967) compared 13 MMPI patterns in psychiatric and medical settings. They concluded that the higher the elevation of Scales 1 and 3, the more likely the case is psychiatric rather than organic in nature.

Lair and Trapp (1962) concluded that hysterics could be differentiated from neurotics, those suffering psychophysiologic reactions, and physically ill persons by the MMPI when comparing patterns based on mean group scores. While this may be useful for research, there is too large an overlap of individual scores for the test to be used in medical settings to screen organic from functional disorders. A more recent article by Watson and Buranen (1979) found that the MMPI was not useful in separating true and false-positive conversion hysterics.

Regarding the MMPI's applicability to specific diagnostic categories other than conversion, there have been a few scattered, unreplicated, but very interesting studies. While the MMPI scales have never been standardized for patients with multiple personality, Brandsma and Ludwig (1974) showed that elevations in certain clinical scales were significantly related to pathological responses to items with content reflecting these unusual experiences. In another case study (Larmore, Ludwig, & Cain, 1977), the MMPI profile of four subpersonalities all suggested psychotic pictures, but there were certain significant differences (one standard deviation from the primary personality) *between* the profiles which were consistent with the clinical data on this case. Liskow, Clayton, Woodruff, Guze, and Cloninger (1977) compared the MMPI scores of 29 inpatients diagnosed with hysterical personality and 21 outpatients diagnosed with Briquet's Syndrome. Since the groups differed significantly in age (patients with hysterical personality were younger), the interpretation of the findings must be circumspect. The authors found that patients with Briquet's Syndrome had significantly higher T-corrected Hypochondriasis scores and a significantly higher Lie scale score. Since Hs items relate to a variety of overt bodily complaints, this finding is consistent with the definition of this syndrome as polysymptomatic. The authors suggested that the MMPI could be used to screen such patients, after further research to determine whether this difference would hold for comparisons with other psychiatric disorders.

Other objective measures. Bendefeldt, Miller, and Ludwig (1976) tested 17 hospitalized patients with hysterical conversion reaction and a control group of nonpsychotic patients, under stress and nonstress conditions, on various cognitive tests of memory, concentration-attention, and field dependence/independence. A discriminate analysis of the data was able to distinguish accurately 14 of 17 hysteric patients under nonstress conditions, and 16 of 17 in the stress condition. This impressive finding suggests that these tests or the best among them could form a diagnostic battery for conversion hysteria. Further research will be necessary to evaluate the battery's usefulness with the new DSM-III diagnostic categories.

Smokler and Shevrin (1979) compared subjects with hysterical and obsessive-compulsive styles (as determined by a modified Rorschach test and WAIS Comprehension subtest). There were significantly more lateral eye movements to the left for the hysterical group, and significantly more LEMs to the right for the obsessive group; these groups were significantly different from each other, and the hysterical group was significantly different from controls, who did not look in one direction more than the other. The authors suggested that LEMs could provide a way of assessing change in psychotherapy, as well as a way to explore individual differences in brain functioning (hemispheric laterality) that have implications for personality style.

Neuropsychological assessment. The general and more subtle manifestations of neurological disorders are likely to be confused with psychogenic symptoms. In Table 6.2, some neurological indicators cited by Small (1973) are compared with hysterical phenomena with which they may be confused. The striking degree of overlap illustrates the differential diagnostic problem.

In terms of neuropsychodiagnosis, Small (1973) advised the exa-

TABLE 6.2
Neuropsychological Assessment

Possible Neurological Manifestations	Possible Hysterical Phenomena
1. Alterations of consciousness	Multiple Personality Disorder
depersonalization perplexity, disorientation feelings of unreality	Depersonalization Disorder Psychogenic Amnesia and Fugue Other Dissociative Disorder (derealization)
2. Impairment of recall	Psychogenic Amnesia
3. Disorders of orientation	
(In space, time; disturbances of balance, left-right discrimination)	
4. Intellectual deficits	The lack of information and everyday knowledge, the lack of concern for careful analytic thinking in Histrionic Personality Disorder
5. Disturbance of drive	
6. Disorders of attention	The limited capacity for sustained intellectual achievement in Histrionic Personality Disorder
(Difficulty maintaining concentration, in sustaining an activity; susceptibility to distraction)	
7. Emotional disturbance	Intense emotional displays and excitability, irrational outbursts of anger, labile moods in Histrionic Personality Disorder
(Depression, elation, lability of mood, sensitivity, impulsiveness, easily exacerbated, anger)	

miner to use all available methods* to improve the probabilities of accurate diagnosis in individual cases. A contrary suggestion was made by Lezak (1976), who suggested that the neuropsychological exam should be tailored to the patient's needs, abilities, and limitations. Initial descriptive questions concerning the nature of the patient's condition as well as diagnostic questions can help narrow the field of inquiry and focus the exam around providing answers instead of just data. For example, if there is a question about the possibility of malingering, the examiner should be ready to improvise tests or situations which could reveal deliberate faking of poor performance. Lezak provided descriptions of the individually administered and paper-and-pencil neuropsychological batteries he has used. The interested reader is referred to his 1976 book for detailed lists and discussions of the tests. Another well-known battery is the Halstead-Reitan Battery (Reitan & Davison, 1974), which discriminates well between brain-damaged and neurologically intact groups and between patients with frontal-lobe lesions and patients with other kinds of lesions, as well as between normals and patients. When testing is primarily for screening purposes, the best diagnostic discriminations are made by including some tests sensitive to specific impairment and some sensitive to general impairment, according to Lezak (1976). Errors in diagnosis—false-positives and false-negatives—depend on where the cutting score is set to separate the hysteric from the organic groups. Such errors also are a function of the numbers and varieties of test used. Since most single tests have high misclassification rates, batteries are crucial.

Differential Diagnosis

The differential diagnosis of Somatoform Disorders and real physical illness is one of the most difficult but critical tasks facing both the medical and the psychiatric/psychological professions (see Table 6.3). In a seven- to 11-year follow-up of 85 patients diagnosed as having conversion disorders or hysterical personalities. Slater and Glithero (1965) discovered that 14 percent of their sample died and 48 percent more developed significant physical disorders. Watson and Buranen (1979) conducted a ten-year follow-up of 40 male veterans and estimated that 25 percent of the patients originally diagnosed with conversion were later found to have physical illness. The false-positives were associated

*Small (1973) thought the neuropsychological testing procedure should "encompass all significant sensory modalities, motor functions, manipulative and visuospatial tasks, concept formation, language and communication skills, alertness and memory, and, in addition, probe each of these at increasing levels of difficulty and complexity with requirements of intersensory integration, introduction of unfamiliar requirements in visuomotor tasks, comparison of the two sides of the body, and bilateral simultaneous sensory stimulation" (p. 262).

TABLE 6.3
Differential Diagnosis of Organic and Hysterical Symptoms

ORGANIC PROBLEM	HYSTERICAL PHENOMENON	NATURE OF DIAGNOSTIC PROBLEM	POSSIBLE DIFFERENTIAL CRITERIA
Head injury	Hypochondriasis Dissociative states	Head injury may precede or coexist with hysterical disorders in the majority of cases (cf. Whitlock, 1967).	Lishman's two basic "rules"
	Episodes of simple loss of consciousness or of disturbed behavior followed by amnesia, which may be due to epilepsy or hysteria or both.	Hysteria and epilepsy do not preclude each other.	See criteria listed below for seizures, temporal lobe epilepsy, and epileptic fugue.
Epileptic seizures	"Epileptiform seizures"	Both may be precipitated by shock, surprise, or distress. Psychogenic and physiological "predispositional" influences may jointly contribute to organic epilepsy, especially in stressful situations (cf. Krapf, 1957).	In contrast to epileptic attacks, hysterical fits do not conform to any recognized type of epilepsy, are variable across situations, lack a typical tonic-clonal phase, generate movements with a flavor of organized display in which self-injury is carefully avoided, lack cyanosis or pallor, and have unaltered reflexes during and immediately after an attack.

TABLE 6.3 (continued)

ORGANIC PROBLEM	HYSTERICAL PHENOMENON	NATURE OF DIAGNOSTIC PROBLEM	POSSIBLE DIFFERENTIAL CRITERIA
			True grand mal attacks are followed by slow EEG activity and respond to anticonvulsant medication.
Temporal lobe epilepsy	Bizarre hysterical behavior (brief reactive psychosis?)	Phenomenological similarity. Depressive and suicidal tendencies may be present in both.	Organic pathology is more likely if abnormal behavior occurs suddenly, is short-lived, is inconsistent in appearance, and is not characteristic for the individual (cf. Falconer & Taylor, 1970).
Epileptic fugue	Hysterical dissociation with amnesia	Phenomenological similarity	Hysteria is more likely if the fugue lasts several days or more, if there is no history of epileptic attacks, if the patient takes care of him/herself during the attack, and if legal, emotional factors and/or well-integrated behaviors are operative during the fugue.

(continued)

TABLE 6.3 (continued)

ORGANIC PROBLEM	HYSTERICAL PHENOMENON	NATURE OF DIAGNOSTIC PROBLEM	POSSIBLE DIFFERENTIAL CRITERIA
Memory failure from organic brain damage (epilepsy, head injury, neurosyphilis, increased cranial pressure, multiple sclerosis)	Hysterical amnesia	There may be psychological precipitants in cases of organic brain damage. Brain damage may predispose to more primitive means of escape or lower the threshold to stress which this mechanism then reacts against.	Consider all the criteria for specific organic problems listed.
Multiple sclerosis	Conversion disorder	At early stages of multiple sclerosis, differential diagnosis is especially difficult. Both multiple sclerosis and conversion disorder may coexist and/or share common mechanisms, characteristics, and symptoms, e.g., <u>la belle indifference</u>, mood inappropriate to the situation, relapse during emotional stress, precipitation by physical or emotional trauma.	Positive diagnosis of multiple sclerosis.
Stupor subsequent to organic brain damage	Hysterical stupor (schizophrenia, depression)	Phenomenological similarities	Hysterical stupors occur more in stressful situations, and symptoms wax and wane.

TABLE 6.3 (continued)

ORGANIC PROBLEM	HYSTERICAL PHENOMENON	NATURE OF DIAGNOSTIC PROBLEM	POSSIBLE DIFFERENTIAL CRITERIA
			Individuals with an organic condition show more passive dependence on others for basic daily functions.
Rheumatic encephalitis	Hysterical and/or schizophrenic features	Phenomenological similarities	Lishman's two basic "rules"
Potassium depletion	Conversion disorder	Tendon reflexes are preserved until very low potassium levels are reached.	
Narcolepsy	Hysterical "sleep"		The hysterical patient may have hypnogogic imagery, is actively withdrawing, and resists awakening from prolonged sleep.

with symptoms of degenerative diseases and structural failures affecting the spinal cord, peripheral nerves, bones, muscles, and connective tissues. A *concurrent* diagnosis of organic brain disease was found in 40 percent of a series of 50 British patients diagnosed with "hysterical neurosis" (DSM-II, 300.1) (Roy, 1980). Lesser and Fahn (1978) studied the records of 84 patients with idiopathic torsion dystonia (a disease characterized by sustained muscular contractions and twisting movements) and discovered that 37 cases had been given a prior diagnosis of hysteria. Because only one out of 85 cases was truly psychogenic, the authors concluded that psychiatrists should be alerted to recognize the disease as very probably an organic disorder.

DeJong (1967) wrote extensively about neurological examination in cases of suspected hysteria and malingering. Although hysteria and malingering can cover the entire gamut of medical disorder, the examiner should be alert for signs of dysfunction that do not fit organic patterns. If symptoms appear to follow stress or trauma, hysteria may be a possibility, whereas if they have medicolegal implications or are related to military service, malingering may be more suspected. DeJong cautioned that just as organic and nonorganic disease may exist simultaneously, hysteria and malingering may co-occur, requiring even greater diagnostic skill. Making the task even more difficult is the fact that the procedures to rule out organic disease do not distinguish hysteria from malingering. He then distinguished several levels of malingering: "pure" malingering, partial malingering or exaggeration of symptoms that already exist, and false imputation, a deliberate misattribution of cause of a real or fake disorder.

DeJong recommended a complete history which attempts to differentiate between organic and nonorganic factors for somatic symptoms in general. He offered detailed advice about examining the sensory system and discussed various indicators that can and cannot differentiate between organic and malingered pain. He also described examination of the motor system, which should include tests of muscle strength and power, as well as observations of muscle tone, volume, and coordination. In appraising motor function, the reflexes should also be examined. Hysterical and malingered visual problems may be detected by routine neurologic procedures, but a whole armamentarium of tests and ophthalmolgic instruments may be deployed, if necessary. Further, it may be useful to use some special diagnostic procedures which may contribute to the hysteria-malingerer distinction to aid in the final differentiation between organic and nonorganic disease. DeJong recommended: (1) tests of autonomic nervous system functioning, especially determinations of skin resistance, (2) electroencephalogram for the diagnosis of post-traumatic cerebral syndromes, (3) electromyogram for detecting peripheral nerve and nerve root lesions, and (4) hypnosis and interviews with sodium amobarbital or sodium thiopental. Peters (1975) suggested that a neurologist trying to make a differential diagnosis consider using the major tranquilizers to reduce hysterical symptomatology while conducting the neurologic exam.

Psychiatric criteria. Probably the best study testing the usefulness of psychiatric criteria to distinguish between conversion reactions and organic symptoms is a prediction study by Raskin, Talbott, and Myerson

(1966). Of the eight criteria tested, three were found most useful: (1) the patient's prior use of physical symptoms as a psychological defense, (2) the presence of a significant emotional stress prior to the onset of the symptom, and (3) evidence that the symptom was being used to solve a conflict brought about by the precipitating stress. When combined in a prediction index, conversion reactions were correctly diagnosed in 93 percent of the patients, while 29 percent of the patients with organic illness were incorrectly predicted to have conversion. The criterion of hysterical personality proved to be useless; 43 percent of patients in this study with organic illness had an hysterical personality. *La belle indifférence* was also useless in discriminating the groups.

Reveley, Woodruff, Robins, Taibleson, Reich, and Helzer (1977) reported on a short screening interview for Briquet's syndrome (which used the 1962 Perley–Guze criteria, not the abbreviated DSM-III criteria), which was fairly successful in discriminating the somatic symptoms associated with Briquet's syndrome from those attributable to physical illness. The authors suggested that the 14 percent false-positive rate found in this study could be reduced if the criterion of "no medical explanation," which requires a supplementary medical screening, is added.

The differential diagnosis of Malingering and Factitious Disorders is outlined in DSM-III, but there are no specific criteria, and certainly no researched ones. By definition, malingering is the simulation of physical disease symptoms for the purpose of achieving a specific and immediate goal (e.g., to avoid work, criminal prosecution, military service; to obtain drugs, financial compensation, etc.). Diagnosis is more certain in the presence of (1) a medicolegal context, (2) a discrepancy between claimed distress or disability and objective reality, (3) uncooperativeness with diagnostic evaluation, and (4) antisocial personality disorder. Malingering is differentiated from the Somatoform Disorders by the voluntary production of symptoms and by the more obviously recognizable goals. The more psychoanalytically inclined might pose the difference in terms of primary gain characterizing more those with hysterical conversions, and secondary gain more the malingerer. Eissler's work (1951) suggested that hysteria and malingering are not separate categories, but extremes on a continuum. Van Dyke (1982) discussed the close resemblance between Malingering and dissimulation for disability compensation (cf. Brodsky, 1978, for a summary of some issues involved in compensation cases).

The differential diagnosis of Somatoform and Factitious Disorders can be made on the basis of the more extreme medical course, mutilative (by self or through surgery) symptomatology, and the increased medical sophistication in the latter. More specifically, Munchausen's

Syndrome (Chronic Factitious Illness with Physical Symptoms, in DSM-III) is distinguished from malingering in the area of goals: while the goals in malingering are specific, recognizable, and understandable given the individual's circumstances, the goals in factitious illness are not time limited and suggest a lifelong pursuit of the patient role. Features associated with Munchausen's Syndrome include *pseudologica fantastica* (uncontrollable pathological lying about history and symptoms), dramatic presentation of story and symptomatology, and a past course of multiple hospitalizations and surgery (sometimes to the point of acquiring a "gridiron abdomen"). Predisposing factors could include a genuine past physical illness with treatment that might have been mismanaged, leaving the scar of a grudge against the medical profession, and an underlying masochistic character trait. Cramer, Gershberg, and Stern (1971) discussed the nature of the current patient–physician relationship in Munchausen's Syndrome, as well as the importance of early diagnosis to avoid unnecessary surgery and to make psychiatric referral.

The other large category of Factitious Disorders is Factitious Illness with Psychological Symptoms,* which includes the previous diagnosis of Ganser's Syndrome—the "nonsense syndrome" in which approximate answers are given to questions—and pseudopsychosis or pseudodementia ("pseudo" because there are no organic lesions to explain the bizarre behaviors and response to psychological tests).

Perhaps the main lesson to be learned from this discussion of the differential diagnosis conundrum is that there are numerous opportunities for making diagnostic mistakes—both Type 1 and Type 2 errors—and that the costs of making such mistakes are high. Multiple sclerosis, systemic lupus erythematosis, seizure disorders, and degenerative diseases of the central nervous system are all organic disorders which may mimic conversion, especially in their earlier phases, and which may have associated psychiatric symptoms (Van Dyke, in press). It should also be remembered that it is as difficult to make a negative diagnosis as it is to prove the null hypothesis in an experiment. Indications of a positive psychiatric picture should not remove a questionable case from further neurologic consideration. The converse is equally true; patients with positive psychiatric diagnoses may have—instead, prior, additional, or subsequently developed—physical illness. This situation demands that psychiatrists and psychologists should collaborate more with neurologists and other medical colleagues in the diagnosis and treatment of somatoform and factitious disorders. Finally, although DSM-III poses

*It should be mentioned that, in an otherwise excellent review of hysterical neurosis, McDaniel (1978) confused under the description "Hysterical (factitious) psychosis" Factitious Disorder with hysterical psychosis, which in DSM-III is classified as "Brief Reactive Psychosis." In Factitious Illness with Psychological Symptoms, psychotic symptoms may also appear following stress, but to be so diagnosed, it should be clear that the symptoms are under voluntary control.

diagnostic categories as separate entitites, there is evidence to suggest that somatoform, factitious disorders and malingering are all overlapping categories and that differential diagnosis is rightfully impossible in the areas of overlap.

Known Treatment Procedures

This section makes no claim to be comprehensive; rather it attempts to summarize and highlight main trends and significant developments in order to provide a coherent and suggestive overview.

Early Treatment Methods

The 4,000-year history of the treatment of hysteria (Veith, 1977) began, as did so many other things, in the fertile Nile Delta. Egyptian physicians, circa 1500 B.C., attributed hysterical character and symptomatology to the agency of the uterus, which was thought to become detached from its normal resting place and to wander about the interior of the body. This etiological conception held sway for, literally, millenia. Even today, it may be perceived in somewhat altered form in the psychoanalytic formulation that hysteria, and neuroses in general, arise from sexually based conflict. Egyptian treatment consisted in luring the womb back to its normal position by fumigating or anointing the vagina with sweet-smelling or precious substances, and/or pushing the womb back into place by inhalation or application at the distressed site of foul-smelling, noxious substances. Vaginal insertion was also practiced. Many of the herbs used in these procedures were still used in the early twentieth century as anti-hysterics (Veith, 1977).

The Greeks inherited Egyptian views and methods of treatment of hysteria, but added a more psychological turn to treatment and more extensive description of the syndrome, as well as providing it with a name, *hustera,* the Greek word for uterus. Two main schools of treatment existed in Greece: Hippocratic and Aesculapian. Hippocratic treatment was similar to the Egyptian, utilizing attention, strong stimuli, and genital insertions. Hysteria was considered a disease of women, a view which persists today, although men were also included by, among others, Plato and Galen. Hippocratic prescriptions often included marriage and the bearing of children, an exhortation that has often been expressed by physicians to their hysterical patients over the past two millenia. (Compare this injunction, for example, to the possibly apocryphal story that Breuer once joked that it was unfortunate he could not prescribe what his patient really needed: Rx—frequent insertion of normal penis!) Aesculapian tradition utilized a more psychotherapeutic approach, including fasting, rest, change of environment, ablutions, ritual, and dream interpretation as curative agents—even the couch was in evidence.

Many of these traditions continued well into medieval times, until they were replaced by theological doctrine that hysterical phenomena arose through witchcraft and bedevilment. Treatment was taken out of the hands of physicians and placed into the less gentle hands of priests and inquisitors, whose preferred methods involved exorcism and torture to rid the body of its evil possessions. Paracelsus (1493–1540) returned to a more naturalistic view of the etiology of hysterical symptoms, discounting theological dogma and spearheading a new current of rationalism. He offered, however, no new advances in either theory or treatment but, rather, reverted back to earlier conceptions for the most part. As centuries passed and therapeutic methods changed, hysterics were treated with whatever was fashionable; for example, circa 1700, cupping, bloodletting, change in environment, and horseback riding were often prescribed, as well as the sage advice to marry and bear children.

The nineteenth century current of rationalism provided the context for the birth of two trends in the conception and treatment of hysteria. Veith (1977) discussed how Von Feuchstenlaben in Germany and Mitchell in England, among others, discarded the notion of a floating or wandering uterus. They continued, at a more metaphorical level, to link hysterical symptomatology and sexual emotions, groping toward what would become the psychotherapeutic method. Briquet (1859) epitomized another view, however, which sought the etiology of hysteria in terms of brain lesions, discounting any connection between hysteria and sexuality. This view was challenged by Charcot (1890), whose demonstrations of the power of traumatic emotions to evoke hysterical symptoms and their elimination through suggestions under hypnosis were persuasive. Charcot used magnetism, change of environment, and massage in treatment, too. Liébeault and Bernheim of the rival Nancy school, also used suggestion and hypnosis, but eschewed (in fact condemned) the use of magnetism, as did Janet. Breuer and Freud (1893–1895) initially embraced suggestion and hypnotic anamnesis to promote abreaction. Soon, however, Freud discarded hypnosis and suggestion as therapeutic techniques, having become convinced of the greater efficacy of free association and interpretation.

Modern Treatment Methods

We will discuss two major categories of treatment methods. Nonbehavioral treatments include psychoanalysis and psychoanalytically oriented psychotherapy, hypnosis and hypnotherapy, somatic treatment, and psychopharmacologic treatment. Behavioral treatments include relaxation, systematic desensitization, aversive conditioning, massed practice, positive, negative, and differential reinforcement, extinction, shaping, and assertion training.

Most accounts of treatment are impressionistic, didactic, or anecdotal case reports, with at best pre–post measures and rather cursory follow-up data. Very few controlled studies exist. These are mostly reports of behavioral treatment, utilizing a single subject reversal or sequential treatment design, or reports of drug treatment utilizing a group contrast design. Moreover, given the crude state of diagnosis and outcome criteria, even the best of these studies would be difficult to replicate. A concerted effort to identify groups of "hysterics" in the many controlled or comparative psychotherapy outcome studies was abandoned when it became apparent that most studies did not specify their subject population by diagnosis or, if they did, did not report outcome or follow-up data in terms of diagnostic categories. A few studies meet these criteria, however, and these are discussed.

The state of the art of diagnosis and psychotherapy research in the area of hysteria reflects the embryonic level of psychotherapy research in general. It also emphasizes two very different and opposing theories of research, psychopathogenesis and therapeutic aim. One, exemplified by psychoanalysis, views symptoms as signs of underlying conflicts, which, if not addressed, will merely produce other symptoms if the first is removed (Fenichel, 1945; Freud, 1916–1917; White, 1963). For psychoanalysis, the exterior manifestations of psychopathology are epiphenomenal; the important phenomenon is the neurotic character structure itself. The other view, championed by behavior therapy, holds that the symptom is a functional and complete entity in itself—a learned association which has become habitual—whose removal does not necessarily, or usually, result in symptom recurrence or substitution (Eysenck, 1960; Walton & Black, 1959; Yates, 1960, 1970). Eysenck's behavioral formulation, that the sympton *is* the neurosis, may be contrasted with that of psychoanalysis, that the personality or character style, in this case the hysterical style, *is* the symptom (Allen, 1977, p. 323). Argument on both sides, however, still resides at the level of anecdotal report, rather than controlled experiment, with each side advancing nonempirical evidence for its point of view. Yates (1970) argued that the specific conditions under which symptom substitution will occur have not been rigorously specified and, therefore, that the psychoanalytic proposition cannot be empirically tested. It could also be argued, however, that behavioral reports of a lack of symptom substitution are not empirical tests of the proposition either.

Blanchard and Hersen (1976) proposed an explanation of the fact that psychoanalytically oriented therapists note symptom substitution in their cases, while behaviorally oriented therapists do not, as a rule. Basing their argument on distinctions made by Ullmann and Krasner (1969), they divided neurotic disorders into two classes, distinguished by the sets of conditions that promote or maintain maladaptive behaviors. In the first class, symptoms are maintained through avoidance of anxiety-producing situations. In the second class, they are maintained by social reinforcement or secondary gain. For individuals of the first class, subjective distress tends to be high; diagnostic categories include phobias (the prototype), obsessive-compulsive neuroses, anxiety neuroses, and some depressions. For individuals of the second class, subjective distress tends to be low (*la belle indifférence*); the prototypic diagnostic entity is hysterical conversion.

Blanchard and Hersen (1976) argued that the behavioral tradition has based its reports almost exclusively on work with the first class of patients, while the analytic tradition has focused on the second class. Since phobics would be *freed* through symptom relief to engage in a greater variety of more satisfying behaviors and their subjective distress therefore much reduced or eliminated, one would not expect symptom substitution to occur in this group. Here, the symptom truly is the neurosis, in their formulation. The second group, which includes hysterics, receive rewards from the environment for their behavior and therefore could be seen as more prone to develop new sypmtoms or relapse into old ones if environmental reinforcement contingencies remain the same. Blanchard and Hersen presented four cases of symptom substitution or return in patients with hysterical conversion symptoms and called for social skills training and environmental restructuring to prevent this.

While their argument is ingenious and their attempt to reconcile psychodynamic and behavioral views a worthy one, it fails for several reasons. First, as Blanchard and Hersen themselves pointed out, there are few pure types: most neurotic symptoms are maintained by both sets of conditions, in varying degrees. Added support for this notion comes from an empirical study that demonstrated at least as much self-reported anxiety and autonomic activity in conversion hysterics as in anxiety neurotics (Lader & Sartorius, 1968). Second, there are, of course, many reports of behavioral treatment of hysterical conversion, as well as analytic treatment of phobias, obsessive-compulsive neuroses, and the like. To dichotomize these treatments in this way is a violation of the data. Perhaps it is the case that behavior therapists are more aware of and focused upon work with phobics (and therefore miss symptom substitution in hysterics when it occurs), while analytic therapists are more aware of and focused upon their work with hysterics (and therefore fail to note a lack of symptom substitution in certain other diagnostic categories). Third, the conception of secondary gain is wedded to the conception of primary gain (the relief conferred by the symptom of intrapsychic anxiety); Blanchard and Hersen's logic confounds these two mechanisms. Finally, while conversion hysteria is extensively discussed, hysterical personality or other types of predisposing character structure are not mentioned. What is substituted instead is the doctrine of secondary gain through social reinforcement of maladaptive behavior. Were Blanchard and Hersen talking about conversion symptoms solely in terms of external reinforcers, or in the context of character structure? This was never made clear. Certainly, even Eysenck (1960) made this distinction, differentiating characterologic dimensions from environmental stimulation and reinforcement, as well as from neurotic symptomatology. Nevertheless, Blanchard and Hersen have made an important first step toward reconciling these two opposing points of view. More conceptual and empirical work needs to be done to settle this controversy, which has profound ramifications for the treatment of hysteria as well as psychopathologic conditions in general.

Psychoanalytic treatment. Many of Freud's early cases involved women suffering from conversion symptoms (Breuer & Freud, 1893, 1893–1895; Freud, 1905a, 1905b, 1909). It was on the basis of his therapeutic experience with these women that he developed the psychoanalytic method. As Fenichel (1945) observed:

> Conversion hysteria is the classical subject matter of psychoanalysis. As a matter of fact, the psychoanalytic method was discovered, tested, and perfected through the study of hysterical patients. . . . The technique of psychoanalysis still remains most easily applicable to cases of hysteria, and it is the psychoanalytic treatment of hysteria that has continued to yield the best therapeutic results [p. 230].

These latter claims of effectiveness have been attenuated by more recent and differentiated diagnostic formulations and by the growth of a panoply of different therapeutic methods, as well as by a lack of methodologically sound empirical research. The former claim seems self-evident, however; the psychoanalytic view of mental functioning and treatment of psychopathology certainly arose from Freud's early observations of hysteria.

Early analytic treatment of hysteria consisted of suggestion and hypnosis in order to facilitate anamnesis and promote abreaction, since it was believed that the discharge of conflictual, repressed, and specifically sexual emotions resulted in cure. Symptoms were attacked directly and at the outset of treatment. Later, Freud modified his method. He discarded hypnosis and suggestion, which he now felt impeded cure, since repressed contents were less easily integrated into the psychic structure as compared with the method of free association and interpretation in normal waking consciousness. Insight, in conjunction with abreaction, was sought and fostered by the interpretation of resistance and transference. Introducing the case of Dora, Freud (1905a) remarked that readers who were already familiar with his work from *Studies on Hysteria* (Breuer & Freud, 1893–1895) might be surprised that Dora's symptoms were not completely alleviated in three months of treatment. This, he explained, was the case because

> psychoanalytic technique has become completely revolutionized. At that time [i.e., 1893–95] the work of analysis started out from the symptoms and aimed at clearing them up one after the other. Since then I have abandoned that technique, because I find it totally inadequate for dealing with the finer structure of neurosis [i.e., the underlying character structure]. I now let the patient himself choose the subject of the day's work. . . . On this plan everything that has to do with the clearing up of a particular symptom emerges piecemeal, woven into various contexts, and distributed over widely separated periods of time. In spite of this apparent disadvantage, the new technique is far superior to the old [Freud, 1905a, p. 19].

Symptom removal was thought to impede analytic progress by diminishing motivation for cure (that is, character restructuring). Therefore, symptom removal alone was felt to be a useless expenditure of therapeutic energy.

Within the context of modern psychoanalytic theory and practice, Allen (1977) listed some basic treatment guidelines for the classical "phallic" hysteric. "Oral" hysterics, he cautioned, must be treated with methods more similar to those used for the borderline patient (cf. Kohut, 1971; Kernberg, 1967). Allen's guidelines are not very precise and could, in fact, be offered as general rules of psychoanalytic technique rather than as specific heuristics for the treatment of hysteria, phallic or oral. Perhaps, unfortunately, the very strength of psychoanalytic technique, that it is a treatment modality tailored—and in a very real sense, structured—by the individual patient, is also a source of vagueness and confusion in its more general explication. These guidelines are:

1. Don't attack the symptom first.

2. Develop a good working alliance with the patient before making interpretations.

3. Allow evidence to accumulate until conclusions are almost obvious before pointing them out.

4. Maintain an atmosphere in treatment that allows maximum working through of conflicts and transference issues while minimizing expectations of any other kind (such as mutual acting-out). (Adapted from Allen, 1977, p. 304.)

Horowitz (1977) presented a case report of a successful analysis of an hysterical personality with multiple conversion symptoms, whose presenting complaint was depression over her recent separation from her lover and her failure to develop enduring attachments to members of either sex. Horowitz provided two summaries of data, one of gains made during treatment and one of useful interventions in short-term therapy with hysterics, which may be generalized to long-term treatment as well. This particular analysis consisted of four years of four times a week treatment. A follow-up interview one year after termination indicated that gains made in treatment had not eroded.

Sperling (1973) presented two case reports of successful analyses of hysterics to illustrate her contention that conversion symptoms are the result of unresolved Oedipal conflicts, within the context of a personality structure with pre-Oedipal fixations at a symbiotic phase of mother–child relations. Sperling emphasized, as did Chodoff (1978), the importance of flexibility and the positive working alliance established between therapist and patient, especially with pre-Oedipally fixated oral hysterics. As with others within the psychoanalytic tradition, the restructuring of character, rather than relief of symptoms per se, is emphasized. Other case studies (Deutsch, 1959; Eichler, 1976; Rosenbaum, Friedlander, & Kaplan, 1956) also reported positive outcomes, though few included follow-up data. Knight (1941) provided a summary of an enormous number of cases (over a thousand), indicating that out of 156 patients who remained in analytic treatment for more than six months, 94 were cured or much improved at termination, as evaluated by their therapists. Criteria for improvement were quite strict, involving symptomatic relief as well as character change. There was, however, no follow-up data, nor, of course, any control condition.

In fact, while the treatment of hysteria has been characterized as the foundation of the psychoanalytic endeavor, few empirical, controlled studies, with either single-subject or group contrast designs, have been published. In part, this may be a function of psychoanalytic indifference or apathy to quantitative research; in part, this may be because analysis or psychoanalytically oriented psychotherapy does not lend itself to easy quantification. Treatment is typically long and involved, and criteria of change are difficult to specify or measure precisely, beyond the rather crude pre–post impressions presented in case reports. The original quantitative study of psychoanalysis and psychoanalytic psychotherapy, The Psychotherapy Research Project of the Menninger Foundation (Horwitz, 1974; Kernberg, Burstein, Coyne, Appelbaum, Horwitz, & Voth, 1972; Wallerstein, 1968) did not use patient diagnosis as a variable, finding other measures, such ego-strength and the like, more useful. This was the case for other psychoanalytic quantitative studies, as well as for more general comparative quantitative studies, such as Sloane, Staples, Christal, Yorkston, and Whipple (1975), DiLoreto

(1971), and Paul (1966), among others. The identification of patients according to diagnostic categories, based on specific, operational criteria, may be desirable for a more complete understanding of which patients may be most helped in what ways by various modes of treatment.

Hypnotherapeutic treatments. Hypnosis was very much a part of the early investigation of hysteria, as we have seen. Although Freud soon discarded hypnotic technique, later investigators, from within as well as from outside the psychoanalytic tradition, continued to use hypnotic techniques in their psychotherapeutic armamentarium.

Hypnosis may be thought of as a special relationship through which connection to earlier or dissociated ego-states, memories, fantasies, and the like may be fostered (Starker, 1973). It has also been recommended as a means of obtaining greater compliance to suggestion (Haley, 1973), and as a way of shortening the time needed for the therapeutic endeavor (Watkins, 1949). Also, Gill and Brenman (1959) note that hypnosis may perform a specific therapeutic function by lifting the amnesias that prevent access to repressed or unconscious contents, and Erickson and Kubie (1939) aver that with hypnosis they can:

> so motivate the total personality that there will be an increasing interplay of conscious and unconscious aspects of the personality so that the former gradually overcomes the resisting forces and acquires an understanding of the latter [p. 471].

The quality of the hypnotherapeutic relationship depends upon the style and intent (whether directive or nondirective) of the hypnotherapist. In many instances, hypnotherapy may be quite similar to psychoanalytically oriented psychotherapy (Lindner, 1945; Wolberg, 1945), while in other cases the technique may be much more directive (Haley, 1973; Rosen, 1952). Hypnotic *techniques*, as opposed to hypnosis per se, have also been found useful (Gruenewald, 1971; Haley, 1967). Hypnosis and hypnotic technique have been used to facilitate relaxation, free-association, and abreaction, to induce compliance and counter resistance, to achieve greater and quicker access to earlier or dissociated ego-states and mental contents, and to foster increased motivation for change, as well as insight. Hypnosis has been most frequently used to treat conversion and dissociative disorders and has been the prime method of treatment in cases of multiple personality. (But cf. Shreiber, 1974, for a case of multiple personality treated with psychoanalysis.)

During the Second World War, Watkins (1949) successfully used hypnosis to treat a wide variety of conversion symptoms and dissociative disorders experienced by American soldiers. Lindner (1945) and Wolberg (1945), utilizing a technique they called "hypnoanalysis," reported successful treatment of somnambulism and glove anesthesia, respectively. In each case, hypnosis was used to free up the flow of associations, to minimize resistance, and to promote recall of emotionally laden and painful memories and fantasies, facilitating abreaction and, finally, insight. Initially, post-hypnotic suggestions were given so that the material of each session remained outside normal consciousness. Gradually, as treatment progressed, the affects and images from the hypnotic anamnesis were integrated into normal waking consciousness as suggestions for post-hypnotic amnesia were lifted, and insight occurred.

Pelletier (1977) reported that eight weekly sessions of outpatient hypnotherapy effected the removal of an hysterical aphonia which had persisted for a year. Relaxation, speech modeling, assertive training, age regression, and ego-strengthening post-hypnotic suggestions were used. Kehoe (1967) relieved psychalgia in two cases of hysterical conversion with hypnosis. In one case, symptom removal and partial symptom substitution were accomplished; in the other, symptom amelioration with additional auto-hypnosis was achieved. Glenn and Simonds (1977) reported the successful treatment and two-year follow-up of an individual with psychogenic seizures and a variety of conversion symptoms. Here, ward milieu, individual psychoanalytically oriented psychotherapy, and hypnotherapy were utilized in concert. Wolpe (1958) utilized desensitization under hypnosis to successfully treat an hysterical arm paralysis.

Rosen (1952) reported seven cases of hysterical conversion in which hypnosis successfully effected cure by intensifying "the emotion of the moment." Hypnosis facilitated this intensification, allowing abreaction and insight to occur more quickly, Rosen claimed, than might otherwise have been possible. Moss, Thompson, and Nolte (1962) reported an unsuccessful course of treatment of a patient with multiple conversion and dissociative symptoms whose poor ego-strength and chaotic familial situation undermined their efforts.

In terms of multiple personality, the classic account is that of Prince's (1926) celebrated and apparently successful eight-year treatment of Miss Beauchamp. Thigpen and Cleckley's (1954) report of their treatment of the *Three Faces of Eve* is a more recent account, and Sybil, by Schreiber (1974), more recent still.

Accounts of this heretofore extremely rare phenomenon are markedly on the rise, particularly in the past ten years. Greaves (1980), in a well-organized review, suggested that diagnostic oversight has been the prime reason for the paucity of reports. With a better diagnostic handle on the attributes of multiple personality, greater numbers are reported.

Kaplan and Deabler (1975) applied age regression and ego-strengthening techniques under hypnosis during six of eight weekly outpatient therapy sessions to a dual personality disorder of five years' duration. No further dissociative episodes had occurred at the time of an eight-month follow-up. Gruenewald (1971) discusses a case of dual personality treated with hypnotic techniques without trance (since hypnosis per se has often been thought to exacerbate or even cause dissociative splitting). While success was achieved at termination, follow-up revealed some deterioration. Hodge (1959) reports a case of severe dissociative reaction in which a 19-year-old Marine suffered hysterical seizures during which time he acted the part of his own dog and often engaged in violent acts. Direct communication under hypnosis with the "dog" was helpful in predicting when seizures would occur, and then, utilizing hypnotic suggestion, in preventing their recurrence.

Brandsma and Ludwig (1974) effected the successful "fusion" of one patient's four personalities, utilizing suggestion, argument, and persuasion under hypnosis, of whatever personality was available. Allison (1974) used a similar technique in the successful treatment of a multiple personality, eventually enlisting the aid of one personality to help in the therapy by engaging in what he called "Internal Dialogue" with the rest.

Milieu psychotherapeutic treatments. Other psychotherapeutic approaches, including milieu (Cutler & Reed, 1975), milieu plus ECT (Noreik, 1970), milieu plus "social programming" (Brodsky & Fischer, 1964), milieu plus brief psychotherapy (Leaverton, Rupp, & Poff, 1977), and milieu plus group psychotherapy (Valko, 1976), have been used to treat hysterical neurosis, conversion symptoms, or dissociations. The reports of these procedures, however, are so vague that replication would be impossible.

Drug treatments. Psychopharmacologic treatment of hysteria is a relatively recent development. While reports detailing this approach usually lack follow-up data, they are among the most methodologically sophisticated, often employing controlled, double-blind group contrast or single-subject reversal designs.

Van Putten and Alban (1977) treated conversion symptoms, convulsions, and overemotionality in an inpatient population with lithium carbonate using a single-subject reversal design to evaluate effects. Using a group crossover design, Rifkin, Quitkin, and Carillo (1972) employed lithium to treat 21 inpatients who had overemotionality and conversion symptoms. Gomez-Lozano (1976) treated acute anxiety in seven inpatients suffering from hysterical neurosis with lorezapam, with improvement in five. Bacellar (1975) successfully treated acute anxiety in 19 patients diagnosed as hysterical neurotics utilizing a placebo-controlled double-blind group contrast design. Bottomly et al. (1967), using a double-blind group contrast design, tested the differential effects of pericyazine versus amylobarbitone sodium on acute anxiety in 24 inpatients diagnosed as hysterical neurotics. All improved, showing both drugs to be equally effective. Wheatley (1962) treated anxiety in 50 inpatient hysterics with phenobarbitone utilizing a placebo-controlled double-blind group contrast design. Peters (1975) compared the efficacy of chlordiazepoxide and chlorpromazine in alleviating headache or low back pain for 20 inpatient hysterics, utilizing a group contrast design, and found chlorpromazine far superior.

While, in general, the track record of psychopharmacologic interventions is good, it must be pointed out that many of these studies focused on anxiety, in inpatients, rather than the more "hard core" conversion symptoms or hysterical character structure. Therefore, these data may generalize poorly to outpatient hysterics. Moreover, the lack of follow-up data in any of these studies makes their initial outcome findings less impressive, in spite of their sophisticated designs.

Somatic treatments. Somatic interventions have had a somewhat longer history than drug treatments in the amelioration of hysterical symptomatology but cannot proclaim as many positive results. Electroconvulsive therapy (ECT) was used by Ingalls (1939) to successfully treat amnesia in an hysterical personality (without, however, any follow-up reported). Sands (1946), on the other hand, reported no success with ECT in the alleviation of depression and conversion symptoms in a number of hysterical neurotics. Feldman, Susselman, Lipetz, and Barrera (1945) used ECT and amytal interviews to successfully treat two individuals with hysterical paralysis, acute anxiety, and amnesia, although, again, without follow-up. In a study by Hearst, Cloninger, Crews, Remi, and Cadoret (1974) the technique of electrosleep could not alleviate depression, anxiety, or hypochondriasis in 11 inpatients diagnosed as hysterical neurotics.

Behavioral treatments. Behavioral treatments of hysteria have concentrated on the removal of symptomatology rather than, as the psychoanalytic tradition would prefer, on the restructuring of hysterical personality organization. While Yates (1970) supported this assessment, Wolpe (1973) disagreed, claiming that personality change does not occur when symptoms or maladaptive habits are removed, *if* "personality" is defined as the totality of a person's habits (a definition unacceptable to psychoanalytic theory). Moreover, he changed that psychoanalytic tradition has neither defined exactly what is meant by "personality change" nor specified under what conditions it should occur, nor how it should be measured, thus making research into the question problematic. It would seem that these two camps are talking from within two very different conceptual universes, with little common ground for research, much less discussion. We shall, however, make some suggestions for future research in a later section.

Both instrumental and operant methods have been utilized in the treatment of conversion symptoms and dissociative reactions. These include reinforcement, extinction, shaping, desensitization, massed practice, and a broad-spectrum approach combining a number of therapeutic strategies. Since a behavioral approach lends itself more readily to measurement, because outcome criteria are more easily operationalized and because experimentation is more within the behavioral (psychological) than psychoanalytic (psychiatric) tradition, a higher level of methodological sophistication is evident in the literature. As in the psychoanalytic corpus, however, the majority of behavioral reports consist of single case studies, although unlike most other approaches, there are established baselines, plots of symptomatic behavior over time, and follow-up data. A common design is the single-subject reversal, in which the subject serves as his own control. In the behavioral literature, hysterical symptoms are most frequently treated by reinforcement. Various kinds of reinforcement have been applied to hysterical blindness, psychalgia, aphonia, paralysis, gagging, chronic cough, and seizures. Desensitization, the technique next most widely used, has been applied to anesthesia, paresis, disturbed hearing, fugue, convulsions, aphonia, muscle spasms, hyperesthesia, paralysis, and psychalgia. Movement disorders have been treated almost entirely with massed or negative practice techniques.

Brady and Lind (1961) reported the first case of behavioral treatment of hysterical blindness. The patient had been functionally blind for two years and had been unsuccessfully treated by various other means, but regained his sight through an operant procedure that positively reinforced temporal, and then increasingly more difficult visual, discriminations. After 63 half-hour sessions, he was able to clinically see, and at a seven-month follow-up, he was described as being able to read fine print and to identify patterns and small objects. He was also holding a job. Several years later, however, Grosz and Zimmerman (1965) reported that this patient had failed to keep either his job or his sight, which raised the issue of malingering. In a series of experiments with operant procedures, Grosz and Zimmerman were able to influence this patient's performance, albeit in a negative way: he performed at a less than chance level during the experimental treatment condition (he "saw" worse than a blind man!). This confirmed, for Grosz and Zimmerman, his status as a malingerer, though maintaining his status, in their eyes, as "functionally" blind. After all, whether he could or could not actually see, the result was the same and, they reasoned, a product of reinforcement contingencies. Of course, this experiment does not resolve the question of whether this patient was, in fact, hysterically blind when he was examined by Brady and Lind, but it is suggestive. It also highlights the problems inherent in treating symptomatology without altering environmental (Blanchard & Hersen, 1976) and/or intrapsychic (White, 1963) response contingencies, whether or not this particular individual was a malingerer.

Parry-Jones, Sauter-Westrate, and Crawley (1970) report a case of hysterical blindness which they treated with a procedure similar to Brady and Lind's. After 127 sessions marked improvement was achieved. At a two-year follow-up vision had remained normal, and the patient was working as an orderly at a geriatric hospital, although her personal life remained as unstable as before her treatment.

Ohno, Sugita, Takeya, Akagi, Tanaka, and Ikemi (1974) treated three cases of hysterical blindness with a wide-ranging approach, comprising positive reinforcement, avoidance conditioning, desensitization, suggestion, placebo, environmental manipulation, and psychoactive drugs. While in each case vision was restored, in no case was restoration complete. Nevertheless, six month to two year follow-ups indicated that treatment gains had been maintained.

Stolz and Wolf (1969) used positive and differential reinforcement to successfully treat functional blindness and helplessness in a retarded male inpatient, employing a single-subject reversal design. No follow-up data are reported; however, the authors do comment that the target behaviors reappeared when reinforcement was absent, and so one might assume that this would continue to be the case in the future if no restructuring of environmental contingencies outside the ward was undertaken.

Fordyce, Fowler, and DeLateur (1968) applied differential reinforcement to a woman whose 18-year history of chronic pain included four spinal operations and five years of almost complete inactivity, although no neurological deficit was noted upon examination at referral. All treatment staff on the ward were neutral or socially unresponsive to the patient when she complained of pain and discomfort, but made positive efforts to be friendly and socially responsive when she was not complaining of pain. Her medications were administered on a time schedule, rather than on demand, to scotch this possible avenue of reinforcement for complaints of pain, and then were gradually discontinued. Plots of hour of nonreclining activity per week revealed marked improvement over the course of hospitalization. Upon discharge, however, amount of nonreclining activity per week plummeted precipitously, then returned to a somewhat higher level, but then continued to decline. No follow-up data are provided, but the authors' final comment is suggestive: "How long these new patterns will continue remains to be seen" (Fordyce et al., 1968, p. 107).

Liebson (1969) found positive reinforcement to ameliorate leg pain and weakness in a patient who had suffered chronically from this condition for five years, in spite of psychotherapy, milieu therapy, amytal interviews, and courses of over 50 different psychoactive drugs. At six-month follow-up he had returned to work, but still complained of pain occasionally.

Hersen, Gullick, Matherne, and Harbert (1972) tested the effects of instructions alone versus instructions plus positive reinforcement on a patient with lower back, hip, and leg pain and an inability to stand or walk, utilizing a single-subject reversal design. Instructions alone appeared to relieve symptomatology, but the most impressive gains were made when instructions and reinforcement were used conjointly. No follow-up is reported, although the importance of social contingencies in alleviating maladaptive behavior is clearly stressed.

Kallman, Hersen, and O'Toole (1975) replicated this approach with another similar patient. At admission to the ward, the patient was unable to stand or walk, was in much pain, and was bent over at a 45 degree angle. Successful treatment ensued, but four weeks after discharge symptoms recurred. During the patient's second admission, therefore, a family retraining program was instituted to encourage family members to praise positive behaviors and ignore complaints. At 12-week follow-up the patient continued to be free of symptomatology.

Turner and Hersen (1975) successfully utilized this procedure with a borderline mentally defective patient who was unable to walk. Five-month follow-up revealed that gains had been maintained.

Epstein and Hersen (1974) used positive reinforcement to eliminate hysterical gagging, although numerous medical interventions over a two-year period had been unable to alleviate this symptom. Onset had occurred after surgery had eliminated a gastrointestinal ulcer, which had been accompanied by frequent episodes of vomiting. A 12-week follow-up revealed only one episode of symptom recurrence, during a stressful Thanksgiving Day visit with the patient's family.

Working solely with the parents of a 10-year-old girl who suffered psychogenic seizures, Gardner (1967) applied a differential reinforcement paradigm with success. A 26-week follow-up revealed no sign of recurrence, although a planned removal of parental differential reinforcement resulted in an immediate reinstatement of seizures.

Walton and Black (1959) utilized avoidance conditioning, desensitization, and Dexedrine injections to successfully treat a case of aphonia of seven years' duration. During the two years preceding treatment, the patient had been completely mute, although examination of her vocal apparatus showed no physical abnormalities. Previous treatment had included intensive psychotherapy, hypnosis, modified insulin shock, ether and Methedrine abreactions, narco-analysis, and LSD therapy. Walton and Black report no recurrence of the aphonia and no symptom substitution at an 11-month follow-up, but they do report that the patient returned to the hospital eight months post-discharge for treatment of acute bronchitis, a suspiciously conversion-like ailment, especially since it involved that vocal apparatus. Further, a trend toward normalcy in her MMPI profile appeared to be reversing itself.

Avoidance conditioning was used by Alexander, Chai, Greer, Miltich, Renne, and Cardoso (1973), when punishment only exacerbated the symptom, to successfully treat a case of chronic coughing in a 15-year-old boy. Family therapy was also used to alter intrafamilial contingencies to prevent symptom return. At 18-month follow-up the patient was symptom free.

Bhattacharya and Singh (1971) used avoidance conditioning to successfully treat six individuals with hysterical seizure disorders. They remained unsymptomatic during a six-month follow-up. However, Singh (1975), comparing the effects of avoidance conditioning, attention withdrawal alone, and attention withdrawal plus positive reinforcement of non-fit behaviors, found the third condition most effective in alleviating hysterical fits and sustaining improvement over a 12-month follow-up.

Kohlenberg (1970) utilized avoidance conditioning to successfully control persistent vomiting. A one-year follow-up, however, revealed a return of this noxious symptom.

Munford, Reardon, Lieberman, and Allen (1976) were unsuccessful using aversive conditioning with a case of chronic hysterical coughing and mutism. Extinction and positive reinforcement shaping procedures were helpful, however, and the patient remained symptom free over a 20-month follow-up period. Erickson and Huber (1975) utilized a metronome as part of an operant shaping procedure to successfully eliminate hysterical torticollis in a schizophrenic patient. No return of symptoms at nine-month follow-up was noted.

Extinction was used by Alford, Blanchard, and Buckley (1972) to successfully alleviate hysterical vomiting of ten years' duration. The patient experienced some head and back pain briefly during a two-day period shortly after her vomiting had been extinguished, but she rallied and remained free of symptomatology during a seven-month follow-up.

Aversive conditioning was used by Brierly (1967) to relieve two cases of spasmodic torticollis. Six-month follow-up indicated no return of symptoms. Cleeland (1973) utilized an aversive conditioning procedure to evaluate the relative effectiveness of shock alone, feedback from a light that a spasm was occurring, and feedback and shock together, in the modification of spasmodic torticollis. The last condition was found most effective: nine of ten patients benefited, with four completely symptom free. At a one- to 40-month follow-up, six of eight had maintained their gains.

Systematic desensitization has been utilized a good deal in the treatment of hysterical symptoms. Wolpe (1958), as we mentioned before, successfully lifted an hysterical paralysis of the arm by repeated presentation of the precipitating event under hypnosis. Lazarus (1963) presented data on (mostly) desensitization treatment of 126 cases of severe, polysymptomatic neurosis, of which 27 were diagnosed "hysterical."

Nineteen of this group showed improvement at the end of therapy, and presumably at follow-up. (Of 20 cases in the total which were possible to contact after a mean 30 months for follow-up, only one had relapsed.) Clark (1963) utilized seven sessions of desensitization to successfully remove hysterical spasm and agoraphobia in a hysterical personality. Beyme (1964) used 12 sessions of desensitization to relieve hyperesthesia of taste and touch of two years' duration. One-year follow-up revealed no relapse or symptom substitution.

Negative or massed practice has often been utilized to treat movement disorders. Agras and Marshall (1965), for example, successfully treated a patient with spasmodic torticollis in this way and found no symptom recurrence over a seven-month follow-up. Tophoff (1973) utilized this technique in association with relaxation and assertion training to alleviate Gilles de la Tourette's syndrome in a 13-year-old boy who had been symptomatic for over two years. After 14 sessions no symptoms were observed, and a four-month follow-up showed the patient to be doing well in his social environment and asymptomatic.

Summary of Treatment Modalities

Let us briefly review the methods that have been used to treat hysterical personality and symptomatology.

Psychoanalysis and psychoanalytic psychotherapy are long-term treatments which operate within a framework of years, utilizing the free associations of the patient and the interpretations of resistance and transference by the therapist to effect character restructuring, usually eschewing direct attack on symptoms. Symptom removal is expected to occur when the conflicts that have given rise to these hypothesized symbolic expressions are resolved. Documentation of the effectiveness of analytically based methods in treating hysteria relies almost exclusively on anecdotal case reports, rather than on quantitative studies. This may be because the analytic (psychiatric) tradition has been indifferent to quantitative methods and because the kinds of changes analytic therapy seeks do not lend themselves to quantification.

Hypnosis is really a technique, rather than a therapeutic orientation, and has been utilized by various schools, from psychoanalytic to behavioral. It is often used to shorten or intensify therapy, operating within a time frame of months. The heightened response to suggestion and the lowering of defenses and inhibitions induced by hypnotic trance have typically been used to facilitate relaxation, abreaction, and insight. Effectiveness has been documented mostly by case reports. Hypnotherapy has been used most often, in hysteria, to treat dissociative phenomena.

Drugs treatments have utilized sophisticated research designs to test efficacy, but most lack follow-up. Therefore, while short-term effects may be positive, long-term effectiveness is unknown. Moreover, target symptoms have most often been anxiety and depression in hysterical personality, rather than the more central conversion symptoms or the hysterical character structure itself. Time frame may be brief or long term in actual practice and is often associated with another treatment modality, such as individual or milieu therapy.

Somatic treatment has demonstrated little effectiveness in treatment of hysteria. Time frame has typically been brief.

Milieu therapy has demonstrated some effectiveness in treatment, but documentation with case reports or grouped data is so imprecise that replication of treatment would be difficult.

Behavior therapists have utilized many approaches within both classical and operant paradigms to treat hysteria, concentrating on the amelioration or removal of symptomatology, rather than attempting to alter character structure, a concept which is not operationalizable in their view. Treatment is typically brief, often only weeks long. Quantitative research is part of the behaviorist (psychological) tradition, and therefore research designs are more adequate than in any other talking therapy. Nevertheless, our review noted a dearth of controlled group studies and few really excellent single case studies.

Table 6.4 outlines studies discussed in this section in terms of type of treatment, diagnosis, symptoms, initial outcome, follow-up, type of design, design quality rating (total score of 0–32, achieved on the basis of quality ratings of 13 design quality rating criteria, as modified from Gurman et al., in press), and specific study.

Conclusions and Prescription

Treating the hysteric, especially at the outset, is somewhat akin to the old American recipe for rabbit stew, which begins: "First catch a rabbit." One of the more difficult aspects of psychotherapy with the hysteric is, in fact, getting him or her to come into treatment! Ziegler, Imboden, and Meyer (1960) note that in their experience as psychiatric consultants on medical wards, patients with a clear diagnosis of conversion hysteria, for example (with or without hysterical personality structure), who had numerous physical complaints with little or no physical basis, often refused to accept a referral to psychotherapeutic treatment. They continued to maintain, instead, that their multiple symptoms were completely physically based, in spite of overwhelming evidence to the contrary. Those who did accept a referral, however, usually did quite well. In the case of our patient, who has already come to believe that

TABLE 6.4
Modern Treatment Methods for Hysteria

Treatment	Diagnosis	Symptoms	Initial Outcome	Follow-up	Design	DQR	Study
Hypnotic Treatments							
Hypnotherapy "Internal Dialogue"	Multiple personality	Dissociative episodes	++	++10 mos.	Case report	2	Allison, 1974
Hypnosis, Verbal Persuasion, and Argument	Multiple personality	Dissociation	++	++	Case report	18	Brandsma and Ludwig, 1974
Hypnoanalysis, Behavior Modification, Milieu, Drugs	Hysterical conversion	Psychogenic seizures, aphonia, bed-wetting, headache, nausea, fainting	++	++2 yrs.	Case report	6	Glenn and Simonds, 1977
Hypnotherapeutic Techniques	Dual personality	Dissociations	++	+-	Case report	2	Gruenwald, 1971
Hypnotherapy	Hysterical dissociation	Dissociative episodes, violence	++	lost to follow-up	Case report	1	Hodge, 1959
Hypnotherapy	Dissociative hysterical disorder	Dissociative episodes	++	++8 mos.	Case report	2	Kaplan and Deabler, 1975

TABLE 6.4 (continued)

Hypnotherapy	Hysterical conversion	Facial pain, anxiety, head-ache, dizziness	+ (N=2)	+-2 yrs.	Case report	2	Kehoe, 1967
Hypnoanalysis	Hysterical dissociation	Somnambulism	++	none	Case report	1	Lindner, 1945
Hypnoanalysis	Multiple personality	Dissociative episodes	+	+-1 yr.	Case report	2	Morton and Thomas, 1964
Hypnotherapy	Hysteria	Feelings of unreality, seizures, dissociations, frigidity	0	--6 mos.	Case report	2	Moss et al., 1962
Hypnotherapy	Hysterical conversion	Aphonia	++	++1 yr.	Case report	2	Pelletier, 1977
Hypnotherapy	Hysteria	Incapacitating back pain, frig-idity, anxiety, psychogenic asthma, bleeding, numbness and weakness of arms and legs, seizures	++ (N = 7)	++11-24 mos.	Case report	4	Rosen, 1952
Hypnotherapy	Hysterical conversion	Conversion symp-toms, dissocia-tions	++	++	Case report	2	Watkins, 1949

(continued)

TABLE 6.4 (continued)

Treatment	Diagnosis	Symptoms	Initial Outcome	Follow-up	Design	DQR	Study
Behavior Treatments							
Massed Negative Practice		Torticollis	++ (N=2)	++2 yrs. --5 wks.	Case study	6	Agras and Marshall, 1965
Avoidance Conditioning	Hysterical conversion	Chronic cough	++	++18 mos.	Case study	12	Alexander et al., 1973
Positive (shaping), Differential Reinforcement	Hysterical conversion	Vomiting, pain, weakness in legs, giddiness	++	++6 mos.	Sequential (ABAB-C) design	9	Alford et al., 1972
Desensiti-zation		Muscle cramp, hyperesthesia	++	++1 yr.	Case report	8	Beyme, 1964
Extinction, Punishment, Differential Reinforcement	Hysterical conversion	Fits	++ (N=8)	++6 mos.	Sequential treatment	12	Bhattacharya and Singh, 1971
Positive Reinforcement	Hysteria	Blindness, var-ied gastrointes-tinal symptoms	++	++1 yr.	Case study	14	Brady and Lind, 1961
Aversive Conditioning	Hysterical conversion	Torticollis	++ (N=2)	++6 mos.	Case report	6	Brierly, 1967

TABLE 6.4 (continued)

Desensitization	Hysterical personality	Muscle spasm, agoraphobia	++	NR	Case report	1	Clark, 1963
Aversive Conditioning	Hysterical conversion	Torticollis	++ (N=9/10)	++1-40 mos. (N=6/9)	Group contrast	21	Cleeland, 1973
Positive Reinforcement	Hysteria	Gagging	++	++3 mos.	Case study	11.5	Epstein and Hersen, 1974
Negative Shaping Reinforcement	Simple schizophrenia	Torticollis	++	++9 mos.	Case report	8	Erickson and Huber, 1975
Differential Reinforcement	Hysteria	Chronic low back pain precluding activity	++	none	Case report	11	Fordyce et al., 1968
Differential Reinforcement	Hysterical conversion	Seizures	++	++26 wks.	Case study with reversal	8	Gardner, 1967
Positive Reinforcement, Instructions	Hysterical conversion	Pain, astasia-abasia	++	NR	Sequential treatment of single case	11	Hersen et al., 1972
Positive Reinforcement	Hysterical conversion	Astasia-abasia	++	++3 mos.	Case study	11.5	Kallman et al., 1975
Milieu, Group, Various Other Treatments	Hysterical personality	Acting-out, histrionic, aggressive or seductive behavior	++ (N=4/5)	+	Case report	1.5	Kass et al., 1972

(continued)

TABLE 6.4 (continued)

Treatment	Diagnosis	Symptoms	Initial Outcome	Follow-up	Design	DQR	Study
Behavior Treatments (continued)							
Punishment	Hysterical conversion	Vomiting	++	--1 yr.	Case report	14	Kohlenberg, 1970
Desensitization	Hysteria	Multiple conversion symptoms	++ (N=19/26)	++2 yrs.	Case report	8	Lazarus, 1963
Positive Reinforcement	Hysterical conversion	Leg pain and weakness	++	+-6 mos.	Case report	3	Liebson, 1969
Aversion	Hysterical conversion	Writer's cramp	++	++	Case report	6	Liversledge and Sylvester, 1960
Positive (Shaping) Reinforcement, Extinction	Hysteria	Chronic cough, mutism	++	++22 mos.	Case report	17	Munford et al., 1976
Reinforcement, Desensitization, Suggestion, Placebo, Drugs	Hysterical conversion	Blindness, eye pain, photophobia, headache, nausea	++ (N=3)	++6-24 mos.	Case report	8	Ohno et al., 1974
Positive Reinforcement	Hysterical conversion	Blindness	++	++2 yrs.	Case report	11	Parry-Jones et al., 1970

TABLE 6.4 (continued)

Extinction, Punishment, Reinforcement	Hysteria	Seizures	++	++1 yr.	Case report	12	Singh, 1975
Positive Reinforcement, Extinction	Mental Re-tardation	Blindness, helplessness	++	--	Case report	13	Stolz and Wolf, 1969
Massed Practice, Relaxation, Assertion	Hysterical conversion	Gilles de la Tourette Syndrome	++	++4 mos.	Case report	12	Tophoff, 1973
Positive Reinforcement	Hysterical conversion	Astasia-abasia	++	++12 wks.	Case report	12	Turner and Hersen, 1975
Aversion	Hysterical conversion	Chronic aphonia	++	++1 yr.	Case report	10	Walton and Black, 1959
Desensiti-zation,plus Hypnosis	Hysterical conversion	Arm paralysis	++	++	Case report	8	Wolpe, 1958
<u>Milieu Psychotherapeutic Treatments</u>							
Milieu, Social Programming	Hysterical conversion Hysterical personality	Somatic com-plaints, act-ing-out be-havior	++ (N=35/47)	++2 yrs. (N=23/35)	Grouped case report	7	Brodsky and Fischer, 1964

(continued)

TABLE 6.4 (continued)

Treatment	Diagnosis	Symptoms	Initial Outcome	Follow-up	Design	DQR	Study
Milieu Psychotherapeutic Treatments (Continued)							
Milieu	Hysterical personality with disso-ciation	Dissociations, fugues, amnesias	++ -- (N=2)	++ --	Case report	2	Cutler and Reed, 1975
Milieu, Brief Therapy	Hysterical personality	Monocular hysterical blindness	++	NR	Case report	1	Leaverton et al., 1977
Milieu versus Milieu and ECT	Hysterical neurosis	Conversion symptoms	++ (N=11/16)	++5-15 yrs.	Group contrast	7	Noreik, 1970
Group Psychotherapy and Milieu	Briquet's Disorder	Emotionality, many somatic complaints	++ (N=6)	++ (N=4/6)	Grouped case report	2	Valko, 1976
Pharmacologic Treatment							
Lorazepam	Hysterical neurosis	Acute anxiety	++ (N=19)	NR	Placebo controlled double-blind group contrast	20	Bacellar, 1975

TABLE 6.4 (continued)

Pericyazine or Amylobar-bitone Sodium	Hysteria	Acute anxiety	++ (N=24)	NR	Double-blind group contrast	14	Bottomly et al., 1967
Lorazepam	Hysterical neurosis	Acute anxiety	++ (N=5/7)	NR	Pre-post group, no control	8	Gomez-Lozano, 1976
Lithium	Hysterical, explosive or anti-social personality	Over-emotion-ality, conver-sion symptoms, aggression, acting-out	++ (N=21)	NR	Double-blind contrast group crossover	14	Rifkin et al., 1972
Chlordiaze-poxide or Chlorpro-mazine	Hysteria	Headache, back pain	++ (N=20)	NR	Group contrast	10	Peters, 1975
Lithium	Hysteria and Munchausen Syndrome	Conversion symptoms, fits, impulsiveness, overemotionality	++	NR	Single-subject x2 reversal (ABAB)	7	Van Putten and Alban, 1977
Phenobarbitone	Hysterical personality Hysterical conversion	Anxiety	++ (N=50)	NR	Placebo controlled double-blind group	9	Wheatley, 1967
Metrazol	Hysterical neurosis	Depression, conversion symptoms	++	NR	Case report	2	Ingalls, 1939

(continued)

TABLE 6.4 (continued)

Treatment	Diagnosis	Symptoms	Initial Outcome	Follow-up	Design	DQR	Study
Somatic Treatments							
ECT and Amytal Therapy	Hysterical personality	Astasia-abasia, anxiety, amnesia	++ (N=2)	NR	Case report	2	Feldman et al., 1945
Electrosleep	Hysterical neurosis	Depression, anxiety, hypochondriasis	-- (N=11)	--2 wks.	Double-blind sham treatment control group contrast	24	Hearst et al., 1974
ECT	Hysterical neurosis	Depression, conversion symptoms	-- (N=29)	--1 yr. (N=20)	Grouped case reports	2	Sands, 1946
Psychoanalytic Treatments							
Psychoanalysis	Hysterical neurosis	Suicidal, poor interpersonal relationships, amenorrhea, vicarious menstruation	++ (N=2)	++27 yrs.	Case report	2	Deutsch, 1959
Psychoanalysis	Hysterical personality	Frigidity, poor interpersonal relationships, sadomasochism	++	NR	Case report	2	Eichler, 1976

TABLE 6.4 (continued)

Psychoanalysis	Hysterical personality	Conversion symptoms	++		Case report	2	Horowitz, 1977
Psychoanalysis	Anxiety and conversion Hysteria	Not stated	++ (N=94/156)	NR	Grouped case report data	7	Knight, 1941
Psychoanalytic Psychotherapy	Hysterical personality and Hysterical conversion	Conversion symptoms	++	none	Grouped case report data	7	Rosenbaum et al., 1956
Psychoanalysis	Conversion hysteria	Breathing difficulty, rapid heartbeat, dizziness, fainting spells, laryngitis, allergies, migraine headaches	++	++20 yrs.	Case report	2	Sperling, 1973

++, much improved
+, improved
−, deteriorated
+−, erosions of gains made

most or all of his difficulties are psychologically based, this problem did not exist. Moreover, his motivation for cure, as evidenced by his self-referral and initial contact with his therapist, augered well.

In any case, before treating the hysteric one must make a thorough diagnostic evaluation, such as is outlined above under Assessment. When this has been done, and any suspicious symptomatology has been checked out, one must choose a therapeutic method. As Scallet, Cloninger, and Othmer (1976) show, albeit with data that can be criticized on any number of methodological grounds, no demonstrable difference exists among the various treatments of hysteria. However, almost any treatment appears to be better than none at all; hysteria has a poor prognosis for improvement if left untreated (Guze & Perley, 1963; Saslow & Peters, 1956; Wheatley, 1962, 1967). This is, of course, just what the literature on psychotherapy outcome research has to tell us: that there is no significant difference among the various traditional therapies in terms of efficacy, but that therapy *is* significantly better than no treatment (Sloane et al., 1975). Of course, it may be that further investigations with more sophisticated methodology will begin to answer the magic question: "Which kind of treatment is best for which kind of patients treated by which kind of therapist?" For hysteria, however, this work has barely begun, since we are unable, really, even to specify what hysteria *is* conceptually or diagnostically. Thus, while psychotherapy research in general merely lumps all outpatient neurotics together in a treatment condition, research on hysteria must first specify sound, operational, generalizable criteria for the various syndromes associated with this term, *before* research can begin.

Nevertheless, as clinicians, we must deal with the real world of imperfect data and exquisite pain. Therefore, we shall propose a few basic guidelines which attempt to integrate and summarize what has already been presented above.

1. Whether one starts from symptoms or character structure, the treatment of the hysteric must take into account the interaction of symptoms, the response contingencies of the environment, and character structure.

2. For the hysteric, the relationship between therapist and patient is perhaps more salient than for any other class of person, save perhaps the borderline patient. Even in behavioral treatment, a goodly amount of warmth and empathy are necessary—if only to keep the patient from leaving the office! Sloane et al. (1975), for example, showed that behavior therapists were rated as warm and empathetic—and often more so than psychoanaytically oriented psychotherapists.

3. It is clinical practice, as we have seen, that behavior therapists treat symptomatology, while psychoanalytically oriented psychotherapists aim at character structure, and hypnotists focus on dissociative phenomena, for the most part. Let us assume that there is a kind of intuitive wisdom in this practice, and use it. Let us assess what kind of treatment might best fit the particular individual who comes in for therapy based on what kind of diagnostic category he or she fits, as well as what the individual wants. It may help, for example, for therapists to explain their theories of therapy, and to brief patients honestly on what they can expect from each approach. Does the patient expect, for example, symptomatic change or character change? Does the patient have the means and desire to essay long-term "restructuring" or does he or she want symptomatic relief quickly? Which treatment modality, then, is most congruent with this set of patient desires, expectations, and resources?

Case Study

This case is offered as a heuristic device by which the two major treatment approaches for hysteria, behavior therapy and psychoanalytically oriented psychotherapy, may be portrayed. The case is adapted from Kaminsky and Slavney (1976), who diagnose the patient to be suffering from Briquet's syndrome, a disorder which in their opinion, as well as ours, comprises both hysterical conversion symptoms and a specific underlying character structure. We have chosen a male oral hysteric to emphasize that many hysterics are neither women nor phallic (in a psychological sense), and that the interplay between symptomatology, character structure, and external environment must be taken into account in order for treatment to succeed. While Kaminsky and Slavney provide a history and mental status for their patient, they do not detail his treatment, except to say that he has done fairly well in supportive therapy. We have, therefore, fashioned the facts of this case into a plastic model, developing two alternate fantasies of treatment and this patient's response—fictions which we believe, however, to be psychologically valid.

The patient, Mr. Z, is a 31-year-old, divorced, unemployed but college-educated white male. His presenting complaints concerned episodic memory loss, depression, impotence, and a host of somatic symptoms for which no physical basis could be found. His amnesias, really fugue states, began in 1969 when his marriage collapsed. His somatic symptoms first began at 12 years of age, when he was hospitalized with suspected appendicitis but released without treatment. He was hospitalized at age 15 for an arm fracture, at age 17 for persistent, severe, and unexplained headaches, which still recur, at age 24, for diagnosed renal calculi, and at age 30 for severe abdominal pain, which also still recurs.

A cholecystectomy was performed at this time, but his gall bladder was found to be normal. Additionally, he has been evaluated for endocrin, respiratory, and gastrointestinal symptoms.

Mr. Z's birth and early developmental milestones were normal. As a child, he was prone to stuttering, sleepwaking, and night terrors and displayed "effeminate mannerisms," which still persist. He experienced a tumultuous childhood and adolescence, due to the "constant uproar" between him and his stepfather, a conservative and sometimes crude and boisterous lumbermill worker. His mother, who attempted to protect him from her husband, was an intellectual and strict public school teacher, to whom Mr. Z was close and looked for support. He was not close to his siblings. He completed public school uneventfully. Although bright, he was an average, though perhaps overly conscientious student. His work life, including a hitch in the army, was successful until interrupted by his hospitalization.

The patient was exclusively homosexual from the age of 16 to 21. In college he had a stormy long-term homosexual relationship, which ended when his lover permanently disabled himself in a suicide attempt. Acceding to maternal pressure, he began to date women and married at 22. His marriage, however, was also stormy, though not long-term, and marked as well by sexual indifference and impotence on his part. Divorce followed the miscarriage of a much-desired pregnancy.

Mental status examination revealed a stylishly dressed, well-groomed, muscular, friendly young man, whose manner was obsequious, sometimes flamboyant, and enthusiastic. His speech was prompt, though often garrulous and vague, but showed no signs of any formal thought disorder. Affect was labile. He was easily moved to tears or laughter, though he spoke of past fugues and depressions with little apparent distress. He denied hallucinations or delusions, but described bothersome obsessional doubting and a phobia of snakes.

Mr. Z described himself as quite dependent in relationships, disorganized by marked mood variations, and "very dramatic." On the other hand, he said, he was also fussy, self-critical, opinionated, and "very controlled." At present, he believes most or all of his problems are psychological in origin.

Behavioral Treatment

Mr. Z was admitted to the ward and observed for several days in order to develop baseline rates for his behaviors, as well as a treatment plan. Complaints of somatic symptoms, sleeplessness, and depression were noted. One dissociative fugue was observed, but the frequency of this behavior pattern was so low that no reliable baseline could be established. It was noted that Mr. Z spent his time either in the dayroom "playing therapist" or in his room alone. He was especially solicitous of the older women on the ward. He had several run-ins during the period with an older male alcoholic, who condemned his politics, criticized his effeminate mannerisms, and questioned his manhood, often in somewhat insulting terms. It was shortly after an extended and intense confrontation with this patient that Mr. Z experienced a fugue state. That night he complained of sleeplessness due to intrusive thoughts, and in the morning, of numerous somatic symptoms, including headache, abdominal pain, dizziness, and nausea. The elder women of the ward were particularly solicitous.

A multimodal behavioral intervention strategy was devised which incorporated differential social reinforcement, systematic desensitization, relaxation, assertion training, and social skills training. While he was routinely examined by a physcian periodically to make certain that he, in fact, had no physical problem, the ward staff was instructed to pay no attention to his complaints. On the other hand, it was suggested that they reinforce him with positive social attention whenever he participated in ward activities—*except* when he was speaking with older women. Instances of assertiveness and verbal expressions of feeling (that is, expressions of his own feeling experience) were also to be reinforced. In individual therapy, anxiety hierarchies were constructed to deal with two major areas: intimacy with women and conflict with male authority figures. After several sessions of relaxation training, desensitization procedures were commenced. Mr. Z proceeded up these hierarchies well, showing a high level of motivation. Assertiveness training and social skills training were also utilized well by him.

The number of hours that Mr. Z spent in the dayroom talking to older women, the number of hours he spent alone in his room between 9 A.M. and 9 P.M., and the number of complaints concerning sleeplessness, depression, or physical complaints, as well as any fugue states, were noted and plotted against the baseline for each behavior as established during the observation period.

Mr. Z was discharged in 12 weeks, much improved in mood, general outlook, and symptomatology, and referred to a private behavior therapist for continued treatment, both to solidify the gains he had made and to continue that process. A one-year follow-up revealed that he had a job, was dating women and enjoying it, was able to have satisfactory sexual relations most of the time and was less bothered when unable to, had few sexual desires, fantasies, or dreams concerning men, and had had no further episodes of fugue.

Psychoanalytically Oriented Psychotherapy

Mr. Z was admitted to the ward and initially observed for several days to better understand his ways of relating to the world and to himself. Preliminary impressions of his character style, object relations, typical defenses and conflicts, ego strengths and weaknesses, and general manner were noted. Based on these impressions, his presenting complaints, history, and associations during the intake interview, a psychodynamic formulation and treatment plan were devised. It was hypothesized that Mr. Z suffered from conflicts at the anal level of development; issues of control and aggressivity, as well as incorporation and dependency, were expected to be central in his treatment. Further interpretations were: that he had never really separated from his mother, that this pre-Oedipal fixation was translated into an Oedipal victory when she divorced his father, and that he felt betrayed when she remarried (precipitating a regression to earlier modes of defense). His various and multiform somatic symptoms were seen as ways to manipulate and maintain her attentiveness to him. Significantly, these symptoms began at puberty, when there is typically a resurgence of sexual drives and previously repressed feelings. His strong sense of morality, however, would not allow these sexual impulses to rise to consciousness. As a child, his love for his mother and fear that his father would punish him for his desires to have his mother for himself resulted in his stuttering, somnambulism, and night terrors. His effeminate manner and subsequent homosexual behavior could be interpreted as attempts to deny that he was interested in women (actually, his mother) and to become his mother, in a sense, by introjecting her. His fussiness, conscientiousness, and overcontrolling tendencies may also be seen as attempts at maternal identification. His stormy relationship with his stepfather may be seen in a similar light: his effeminacy was both assurance that he would not transgress against this authoritarian male by taking his woman, as well as passive-aggressively informing him of his (the patient's) connection with her.

His marriage (which occurred only with maternal pressure) was seen as unworkable because he still remained so strongly tied to his mother. Intercourse with any woman, especially one to whom he was in intimate relation, reverberated with thoughts of incest, punishment, and sin. In an attempt to remove himself from this incestuous situation, which his mother had, in fact, demanded, he became increasingly dissociated. When he was rejected by the wife/mother love object after the miscarriage, he entered the first of his fugues.

Individual treatment three times weekly initially consisted of the therapist listening with neutrality to the free associations of the patient, which were mostly self-deprecatory. Since the therapist was silent most of the time, this soon became an issue, the patient demanding that the therapist "give" him more. Various attempts at manipulation, either with obsequiousness or flamboyance were unsuccessful in altering the therapist's accepting, but neutral, silent style. When neither obsequious praise nor flamboyant hostility seemed to affect the therapist, the patient began to develop symptoms. When the therapist refused to "do" anything about these, but merely asked the patient if he thought they might have any meaning in the context of their relationship, the patient again became hostile and angry, accusing the therapist of not caring about him. This cycle of expressed anger, obsequious praise, and a resurgence of symptoms repeated itself several times with increasing intensity. To the outsider, the patient appeared to be becoming "worse." The therapist continued to be empathic but neutral and unmoved by these attempts at manipulation; he merely reflected back what the patient said to him and observed that perhaps these three kinds of behavior might mean something in the context of their relationship. Gradually, the patient began to feel that he could not manipulate the therapist, but that in spite of it all, the therapist remained present and attentive. This made him feel more comfortable, and as he became more at ease, he began to see that it was with these behaviors that he had attempted to deal with the world, and in particular, with his mother. "So in order for me to show that I like you, I must take care of you," the therapist said. This marked the watershed of the course of therapy. He began to become more relaxed and less anxious or symptomatic, as well as less obsequious or hostile.

During the rest of the course of therapy, the therapist continued to be reflective, neutral, and empathic. He asked for details to counter the patient's global, vague way of putting things. He asked for verbal labels when the patient expressed diffuse "feelings." He encouraged the patient to connect these islands of detailed and labeled thoughts, feelings, and images to discover what meanings might arise. He encouraged the patient to differentiate his feelings of self-deprecation from reality—that he was not, in fact, such a bad chap, after all. In an attempt to short-circuit the desire for instant cure through false insights or unusable (at this point) insights, the therapist kept subjects open, rather than seeking closure, by asking for more and more specific feelings, thoughts, and historical details.

The patient was discharged from the hospital after three months, feeling much improved in mood and self-image and free of most of his symptoms. He continued to see his therapist on an outpatient basis twice a week for the next four years. A one-year follow-up revealed the patient to be free of psychosomatic symptoms, dating women and enjoying it, and working with satisfaction and success.

Ethical Issues

Szasz (1961) questioned the causal-deterministic "medical" model of mental illness adopted by psychoanalytic theory. He argued that hysteria could be better conceptualized as:

1. a form of nonverbal communication, making use of a special set of signs;

2. a system of rule-following behavior, making use of the rules of illness, helplessness, and coercion; and

3. an interpersonal game characterized by, among other things, strategies of deceit to achieve the goal of domination and control (p. 10).

A problem for medicine is that hysterical or hypochondriacal bodily symptoms are often extremely difficult to distinguish from neurological disorders. The rules of the Medical Game are that a person goes to a physician because of a genuine physiological disorder or disability, and the physician will treat the person for an exchange of money. Even today, the typical response of a physician who discovers that an illness is not "real" is righteous indignation. Behaviors likely to elicit the wrath of physicians are factitious illnesses, with psychological or physical symptoms, and malingering.

Szasz maintained that Charcot and Freud changed the rules of the Medical Game by creating a new category—*mental* illness. Thus, instead of two categories, really ill people and malingerers, there were now three: physically ill people, who should be seen by medical doctors; mentally ill people, who should be seen by psychiatrists; and malingerers, who should be condemned by all. In a sense, this reclassification process is still going on, as more and more behaviors fall under the purview of mental disorders (DSM-III includes, for example, tobacco withdrawal and caffeine intoxication). While malingering is still differentiated as a condition not attributable to a mental disorder (although around the time of the Second World War, a number of psychiatrists were calling it a disease too, even more serious than a neurotic disorder because it indicated an earlier developmental arrest), there is a whole new section on Factitious Disorders, which are distinguishable from malingering, but which are characterized by "fake" physical or psychological symptoms that are under the individual's control.

Szasz argued that this reclassification process certainly functioned in the past to inflate the status and legitimacy of physicians. What does it do to people who have then been redefined as patients? One claim made to defend psychiatrists' embrace of the medical model has been that this allowed people with mental problems to be treated with concern and respect by the medical profession. But why, one might ask, cannot these problems be treated with concern and respect as genuine problems in living? By not recognizing them as such, psychiatry can be accused of creating and maintaining an iatrogenic disease; in the case of hysteria, one caused by the diagnosis of the physician. Let us suppose that a person wants help with a personal, interpersonal, or social problem, but the only sanctioned helpers are speaking some other language—the language of disease. The person, still desiring help, learns to express his or her problems in the language of physical complaint or mental *symptoms* (what behaviors become when seen from the perspective of the medical model). Now the medical establishment is able to deal with the help-seeker: if the complaint is phrased in the dialect of mental illness, a psychiatrist who has been trained to understand this language will catch the patient's message; if the complaint is phrased in somatic terms and brought to a hospital or neurology clinic, then an interpreter—a psychiatric consultant—may be called on to judge whether the person is truly speaking "psychologic" or "somatic" language, some strange patois ("psychosomatic"), or psychologic with a fake accent ("conversion"), or is pretending to be a native somatic speaker who is unable to comprehend psychologic ("malingering").

Szasz suggested that some people in the lower socioeconomic classes tend to consult medical rather than psychiatric specialists because being "sick" is acceptable in their subculture, while being crazy is not. These people are especially liable, therefore, to have their symptoms misdiagnosed as physical.

Another reason that someone eventually receives a diagnosis of emotional disturbance or medical disorder may be the strength of psychiatric influence within a medical setting. Rosen, Locke, Goldberg, and Babigan (1972) studied the extent to which physicians in five general-hospital clinics in Monroe County, New York, detected emotional problems among their patients. Of 1,413 patients over 15 years of age, 22 percent were judged to have an emotional disorder; but 27 percent were so judged at university-based clinics, contrasted with 10% at non-university clinics. The authors proposed that this difference reflects the strong psychiatric orientation in medical training at university-based clinics, rather than a difference in socioeconomic status or other characteristics of the populations served by university and non-university clinics. Contrary to Szasz' theory, the proportion of patients with emotional problems from the two lowest socioeconomic groups was similar to the proportion for purely medical problems—about 66 percent of the total clinic caseloads.

In his interpersonal approach to hysteria, Celani (1976) proposed that neurotics adopt certain roles that elicit the interpersonal confirmation (praise, rejection, nurturance, etc.) that they need. He concluded that the basis of this need to elicit a predictable response is a set of self-perceptions of powerlessness that were selectively reinforced by familial and wider societal influences. Szasz would probably agree with the observation that the hysteric may adopt an apparently helpless role in order to structure an interpersonal relationship, but he would probably emphasize the societally, rather than the intrapsychically, powerless position of the hysteric. Szasz has argued that people without power are more likely than those with it to express themselves in the language of hysteria. People without power in American society are those in the lower socioeconomic strata, blacks and other minorities, and women. The epidemiological evidence supporting this proposition in the case of women is especially strong (cf. Temoshok & Attkisson, 1977). A logical deduction from Szasz' assumption about power and hysteria is that conversions would be expected to increase for males who find themselves in powerless situations, such as being soldiers. The historical record confirms this (cf. Abse, 1974); hysterical conversions were often diagnosed in males during the war years of 1942–1945.

Temoshok and Attkisson (1977) interpreted the findings of an association between Briquet's Syndrome in daughters and sociopathy in their fathers (Cloninger & Guze, 1970), not in terms of a common genetic or psychogenic pathogenesis, but as two manifestations of problems arising from powerlessness in our society. Males have been socialized to express psychosocial stress in the language of physical action, which in the extreme becomes "acting out" and antisocial or criminal behavior. Females, on the other hand, have been taught the emotional, passive, and dependent language of the female sex role and have only to exaggerate some of these behaviors and traits to fall into the diagnosable range of hysterical disorders. Warner (1978) argued convincingly on the basis of MMPI data and psychophysiological evidence that antisocial and hysterical personalities are essentially sex-typed forms of a single behavioral dimension. As diagnoses, of course, these are separate personality disorders in DSM-III and have nonparallel diagnostic criteria. This raises the issue of whether a system based mainly on description obstructs insight into real connnections and etiology.

A Note on Ethics and Behavior Therapy

A series of four articles in the 1980 *Journal of Consulting and Clinical Psychology* approached the issue of ethical relativism and behavior therapy. Kitchener (1980) posed the following question: "If the behavior therapist is controlling the behavior of his or her client . . . then which behaviors should be changed? What moral and legal principles should be used to decide this question?" (p. 1).

If value judgments are relative to the culture, then should therapists reinforce behaviors that are consistent with a particular culture, subculture, or group? In the context of our previous discussion of the power dynamics of hysteria, would this translate into reinforcing traditional feminine role behavior, that is, a less extreme version of the Histrionic Personality Disorder?

Certainly, the case is more clear-cut with reference to conversion symptoms, whose removal would be conceded by most people to be "good" for all the concerned parties. If behavior therapists are going to move beyond concern with discrete target symptoms, however, to more complex behavior patterns, and to cognitive and personality styles, then the philosophical and pragmatic problems around values necessarily arise. Techniques of behavior modification and therapy are already being applied in the field of behavioral medicine (cf. Davidson & Davidson, 1980). Here, a relatively clear-cut stand may be taken on the basis of what we know is a medical risk and what changes in lifestyle will promote health. The issues are more complicated when they concern mental and social rather than biomedical phenomena. Certainly, the outcome criteria in biomedical, and by extension behavioral medical, research are both simpler and more "objective" than those in psychotherapy research. Bergin (1980) discussed research on psychotherapy outcome, which of necessity must consider goal definition, value judgments, and whether to define its methodology by "objective" or "subjective" measures. It is insufficient to say that there are no easy answers, but perhaps by posing some difficult questions, we may take an important first step.

Suggestions for Clinical and Experimental Research

Establishing the Reliability and Validity of the DSM-III Categories

1. There must be a series of studies to establish the reliability and validity of the diagnostic criteria, and of the diagnostics entities themselves, in DSM-III. It is especially important to determine whether the separate categories established by DSM-III are indeed substantially differentiable from each other and, if so, on the basis of which criteria.

2. Predictive research with long-term follow-up should be aimed at developing criteria to minimize the rates of false-positives and false-negatives in classifying different diagnostic groups.

3. Studies of diagnostic validity should not be limited to using the DSM-III research diagnostic criteria, which are based on clinicians' judgments. What tests of cognitive functioning, personality, or behavior patterns could theoretically be expected to converge with or diverge from diagnostic categories? The same question could be asked about physiological measures, and about epidemiologic, demographic, and life-event surveys, and so forth.

4. A uniform test battery should be selected by an interdisciplinary team of psychologists, psychiatrists, and neurologists and used in a series of collaborative studies with different diagnostic entities.

Assessing the Effectiveness of Interventions for Differentiated Diagnoses

5. Research criteria have to be established for each diagnostic entity, specifying the area of functioning with which interventions should be concerned and how improvement in these areas could be evaluated.

6. Psychological, psychiatric, and neurologic data should be systematically collected from patient and control groups and subjected to double-blind coding, evaluation, and analysis.

7. Empirical investigations of the prevalence of symptom substitution is essential to help resolve the controversy over whether psychotherapy should aim towards symptomatic relief or character restructuring. Longer periods of follow-up are needed to truly ascertain whether symptom return or substitution takes place.

8. Which kinds of people, suffering from which kinds of symptoms, treated by which methods are prone to symptom return or substitution?

9. Is there some reason other than historical precedence that behavior treatments have worked with discrete conversion symptoms, that psychoanalysis has dealt more with Histrionic Personality Disorder (or its predecessors under different names) and cases of multiple personality, while hypnotic techniques have been applied mainly to dissociative phenomena?

10. Can behavior therapists develop a treatment protocol for Histrionic Personality? How would outcome criteria be operationalized?

11. On the basis of systematic research crossing treatment modalities with diagnostic categories, can treatment differences be discriminated?

12. Single-subject design with time sampling could be used to elucidate the efficaciousness of *specific* techniques within various treatment modalities. In other words, what are the effective ingredients in behavior modification that produce favorable outcomes? What about other treatment modalities is specifically useful?

Research on Theoretical and Etiologic Issues

13. Very basically, what is the nature of "conversion"? Can a study be designed to test which metaphor of conversion captures reality better: Freud's model of repression and energy transformation, or Szasz' communication model of message translation?

14. Is there any similarity among patients in various diagnostic groups, including those outside the traditional boundaries of hysteria (e.g., schizophrenics, compulsives, etc.) who develop conversion symptoms?

15. Is there a difference between persons who develop conversion symptoms in the context of a histrionic personality and those who have the symptoms without the personality structure?

16. There should be a reconsideration of Engel's (1968) "Reconsideration of the role of conversion in somatic disease." Why might only some conversion processes eventuate in somatic complications? Why are some body parts more involved in conversion than others? Are certain diseases more associated with conversion than others? What is the nature of the relationship between conversion and psychophysiological disorders?

17. What is the basis for the associations found in some studies between Antisocial Personality Disorder and Histrionic Personality Disorder? Are these sex-typed manifestations of a single dimension, is there some genetic mechanism involved, or do they have a common psychological pathogenesis?

18. What exactly is the nature of repression if or as it occurs in hysterical phenomena? Is hysterical repression different from repression in, say compulsive personalities? *What* exactly is repressed? How can this be measured? It is strongly suggested that research into these questions employ a variety of measures and approaches (self-report, "objective" observational measures, clinicians' judgments, physiological concomitants, etc.)

19. Is there a relation between cognitive set and perception of pain? If so, can we assess the particular attitudes, expectations, and so forth of the person with Psychogenic Pain Disorder? This cognitive approach could be used with other diagnostic entities as well.

20. What is the relationship between different states of consciousness that are "voluntarily" produced, as through biofeedback, drugs, or hypnosis or during rituals (e.g., "trance states") and dissociated states that occur as part of a psychiatric disorder?

21. What are the mechanisms underlying conversion phenomena? Can these be understood in terms of the endocrine or immune systems, neurotransmitters, endorphins, or brain functions? Is there a "common denominator" to mental and somatic processes that figures in the conversion equation?

The question that worried Freud—the "mysterious leap" from mind to body in hysteria—is part of the more basic question about the relation of mind and body that has plagued philosophers and scientists for centuries. It is suggested that hysterical phenomena constitute a well-lit area of inquiry under the proverbial lamppost where the key may be found. It probably can be found, however, only if the area is crosscut by as many levels of collaborative investigation as possible, including biochemistry, endocrinology, neurology, psychology, psychiatry, anthropology, and sociology. The new findings in the area of mind–brain interactions should be extremely applicable to the subject. The nature of "hysteria" is a question whose time has come.

Summary

In its 4,000-year history, "hysteria" has been one of the most active and perplexing concepts challenging human description and understanding. The Egyptians thought that if the uterus were unmoored, it would wander about the body and finally lodge in a certain part, producing hysterical symptoms there. The etiologic theory of possession became popular in the Middle Ages. Toward the end of the nineteenth century, Charcot demonstrated the connection between hypnotic states and *la Grande Hystérie*. Janet thought that subconscious *idées fixes,* originating in past traumatic events, gave rise to hysterical symptoms. In Breuer and Freud's theory, dammed up affect produced by trauma was redirected into the soma to produce hysterical symptoms. Freud elaborated the notion of psychological conflict, that disturbing memories—later modified to fantasies—were repressed by the removal of affect from them, and that this affect was transformed into somatic expression. Eysenck constructed a theory of personality around an Introversion-Extroversion dimension; with the addition of an orthogonal dimension of Neuroticism, he had the structural basis of a theory of psychopathology. He thought that extroverted hysterics under stress would quickly generate strong reactive inhibition which would dissipate slowly; thus, in contrast to anxious, depressed, or obsessive-compulsive persons, hysterics (and antisocial personalities) would be less easily conditioned and, generalizing this idea, undersocialized. Consistent with Eysenck's concept of reactive inhibition, Ludwig's theory of inhibition of brain stem afferent stimulation predicts that hysterics would be relatively inattentive to stimulus input, which would have interesting implications for their cognitive performance on various tests.

Massive diagnostic revisions in the American Psychiatric Association's *Diagnostic and Statistical Manual*, especially in the third edition (DSM-III), have had a huge impact on the categorization of hysteria. Hysterical personality became Histrionic Personality Disorder, the name change reflecting the syndrome's defining characteristic. The conversion type of hysterical neurosis was split into symptomatically and behaviorally defined categories under the rubric of Somatoform Disorders. A new category, Factitious Disorders, was distinguished from Malingering in terms of the nature of the goals pursued. The dissociative type of hysterical neurosis was similarly split into distinct diagnoses under a separate heading, Dissociative Disorders. The old designation "hysterical psychosis" was officially resurrected under the category Brief Reactive Psychosis. Assessment has not kept up with these diagnostic changes. Projective tests may be more appropriately used to assess psychological strengths and weaknesses, or the relative appropriateness of different treatments and strategies, rather than for diagnostic purposes except for evaluating Histrionic Personality Disorder. The MMPI has not been useful in differentiating conversion from organic cases. For making differential diagnoses, batteries of neuropsychological tests are more successful in reducing misclassification rates. It was suggested that neurologists and psychologists/psychiatrists must work together in developing better criteria for making the differential diagnoses among somatoform, factitious, and physical disorders, and malingering.

In terms of interventions used with various hysterical phenomena, no one treatment emerges as the overall best choice, but it is difficult to prove anything on the basis of the psychotherapy research record. Documentation of analytically based methods rely almost exclusively on anecdotal case reports, rather than on quantitative studies. Case reports constitute the bulk of the documentation of the effectiveness of hypnotic techniques as well. Hypnotherapy has been used most often to treat dissociative phenomena. Drug treatments have utilized sophisticated research designs, but most lack follow-up, so that long-term effectiveness is unknown. Moreover, target symptoms have been anxiety and depression rather than the more central conversion symptoms or character structure. Somatic treatments have demonstrated little effectiveness in the treatment of hysteria. Behavior therapists have utilized many approaches within both classical and operant paradigms to treat hysteria, concentrating on the amelioration or removal of symptomatology, rather than attempting to alter character structure. Research designs for this modality are more adequate than for the other psychotherapies, but there are few controlled studies.

Ethical issues about the diagnosis and conceptualization of hysterical phenomena were stimulated by Szasz' commentary on the creation of hysteria by psychiatrists in the image of the medical model. Specific suggestions for research were headed by the need to validate the new diagnostic criteria and categories in DSM-III. This will provide a basis for studies on diagnostically specific outcome criteria and on which treatments affect these criteria. There was a final call for collaborative basic research into the age-old question of mind–body/brain interactions in the development of "hysterical" symptomatology.

References

*Abse, D. W. Hysterical conversion and dissociative syndromes and the hysterical character. In S. Arieti & E. B. Brody (Eds.), *American handbook of psychiatry* (Vol. 3, 2nd ed.). New York: Basic Books, 1974.

Agras, S., & Marshall, C. The application of negative practice to spasmodic torticollis. *American Journal of Psychiatry*, 1965, *122*, 579–582.

Alexander, F. *Psychosomatic medicine*. New York: Norton, 1950.

Alexander, A. B., Chai, H., Greer, T., Miltich, D., Renne, C., & Cardoso, R. The elimination of chronic cough by response suppression shaping. *Journal of Behavior Therapy and Experimental Psychiatry*, 1973, *4*, 75–80.

Alford, G. S., Blanchard, E. B., & Buckley, T. M. Treatment of hysterical vomiting by modification of social contingencies: A case study. *Journal of Behavior Therapy and Experimental Psychiatry*, 1972, *3*, 209–212.

Allen, D.W. Basic treatment issues. In M. Horowitz (Ed.), *Hysterical personality*. New York: Jason Aronson, 1977.

Allison, R.B. A new treatment approach for multiple personalities. *American Journal of Clinical Hypnosis*, 1974, *17*, 15–32.

American Psychiatric Association. *Diagnostic and statistical manual of mental disorders* (1st ed.). Washington, D.C.: APA, 1952.

American Psychiatric Association. *Diagnostic and statistical manual of mental disorders* (2nd ed.). Washington, D.C.: APA, 1968.

*American Psychiatric Association. *Diagnostic and statistical manual of mental disorders* (3rd ed.). Washington, D.C.: APA, 1980.

Ascher, E. Psychodynamic considerations in Gilles de la Tourette's disease (*maladie des tics*). *American Journal of Psychiatry*, 1948, *105*, 267–276.

Ascher, E. Motor syndromes of functional or undetermined origin: Tics, cramps, Gilles de la Tourette's disease, and others. In S. Arieti & E.B. Brody (Eds.), *American handbook of psychiatry* (Vol. 3, 2nd ed.). New York: Basic Books, 1974.

Asher, R. Munchausen's syndrome. *Lancet*, 1951, *1*, 339.

Bacellar, B. B. The treatment of acute anxiety states in neurotic patients with intravenous lorezepam. *Current Medical Research and Opinion*, 1975, *3*, 16–21.

Barr, R., & Abernathy, V. Conversion reaction: Differential diagnosis in the light of biofeedback research. *Journal of Nervous and Mental Disease*, 1977, *164*, 287–292.

Baumbacher, G., & Amini, F. The hysterical personality disorder: A proposed clarification of a diagnostic dilemma. *International Journal of Psychoanalytic Psychotherapy*, 1980–81, *8*, 501–532.

Bendefeldt, F., Miller, L. M., & Ludwig, A. M. Cognitive performance in conversion hysteria. *Archives of General Psychiatry*, 1976, *33*, 1250–1254.

Bergin, A.E. Behavior therapy and ethical relativism: Time for clarity. *Journal of Consulting and Clinical Psychology*, 1980, *48*, 11–13.

*Denotes especially recommended publications.

Beyme, F. Hyperesthesia of taste and touch treated by reciprocal inhibition. *Behavior Research and Therapy*, 1964, *2*, 7–14.

Bhattacharya, D.D., & Singh, R. Behavior therapy of hysterical fits. *American Journal of Psychiatry*, 1971, *128*, 602–606.

Binet, A. *On double consciousness: Experimental psychological studies*. Chicago: Open Court Publishing Company, 1889–1890.

Bishop, E.R. & Torch, E.M. Dividing 'hysteria': A preliminary investigation of conversion disorder and psychalgia. *Journal of Nervous and Mental Diseases*, 1979, *167*, 348–356.

*Blanchard, E.B., & Hersen, M. Behavioral treatment of hysterical neurosis: Symptom substitution and symptom return reconsidered. *Psychiatry*, 1976, *39*, 118–129.

Bottomly, M.B., Clyne, M.B., Cronk, P.G., Hopkins, P., Jessup, G., Johnston, E.M., Mallett, C.F.R., Russell, L., & Whitelaw, J.D.A. General practitioner clinical trials: Two new psychotropic drugs (2) A new antianxiety drug. *The Practitioner*, 1967, *198*, 139–141.

*Brady, J. P., & Lind, D. L. Experimental analysis of hysterical blindness. *Archives of General Psychiatry*, 1961, *4*, 331–339.

Brandsma, J. M., & Ludwig, A. M. A case of multiple personality: Diagnosis and therapy. *International Journal of Clinical and Experimental Hypnosis*, 1974, 22, 216–233.

Brauer, R., Harrow, M., & Tucker, G.J. Depersonalization phenomena in psychiatric patients. *British Journal of Psychiatry*, 1970, *117*, 509–515.

Breuer, J., & Freud, S. On the psychical mechanism of hysterical phenomena: Preliminary communication. *Standard edition* (Vol. 2). London: Hogarth Press, 1955. (Originally published 1893.)

Breuer, J., & Freud, S. Studies on hysteria. *Standard edition* (Vol. 2). London: Hogarth Press, 1955. (Originally published 1893–1895.)

Brierly, H. The treatment of hysterical spasmodic torticollis by behavior therapy. *Behavior Research and Therapy*, 1967, 5, 139–142.

Briquet, P. *Traite clinique et thérapeutique de l'hystérie*. Paris: Ballière, 1859.

Brodsky, C.M. The genesis of a problem population. In P.F. Ostwald (Ed.), *Communication and social interaction*. New York: Grune and Stratton, 1978.

Brodsky, C.M., & Fischer, A. Therapeutic programming for the nonpsychotic patient. *American Journal of Psychiatry*, 1964, *120*, 793–797.

Cameron, N. *The psychology of behavior disorder*. Boston: Houghton-Mifflin, 1947.

Celani, D. An interpersonal approach to hysteria. *American Journal of Psychiatry*, 1976, *133*, 1414–1418.

Charcot, J. M. *Leçons du mardi à la Salpêtrière*. Paris: Progrès Médical, 1889.

Charcot, J. M. *Leçons sur les maladies du système nerveux: Oeuvres complètes*. Paris: Progrès Médical, 1890.

Chodoff, P. Psychotherapy of the hysterical personality disorder. *Journal of the American Academy of Psychoanalysis*, 1978, *6*, 497–510.

Chodoff, P., & Lyons, H. Hysteria, the hysterical personality and "hysterical" conversion. *American Journal of Psychiatry*, 1958, *114, 734–740*.

Clark, D. F. The treatment of hysterical spasm and agoraphobia by behavior therapy. *Behavior Research and Therapy*, 1963, *1*, 245–250.

Cleeland, C. S. Behavior techniques in the modification of spasmodic torticollis. *Neurology*, 1973, *23*, 1241–1247.

Cloninger, C.R., & Guze, S.B. Hysteria and parental psychiatric illness. *Psychological Medicine*, 1975, *5*, 27–31.

Cramer, B., Gershberg, M.R., & Stern, M. Munchausen syndrome: Its relationship to malingering, hysteria, and the physician–patient relationship. *Archives of General Psychiatry*, 1971, *24*, 573–578.

Cutler, B., & Reed, J. Multiple personality: A single case study with a 15 year follow-up. *Psychological Medicine*, 1975, *5*, 18–26.

Dahlstrom, W., Welsh, G., & Dahlstrom, L. *An MMPI handbook* (Vol. 1). *Clinical interpretation* (Rev. ed.). Minneapolis: University of Minnesota Press, 1972.

Davidson, P. O., & Davidson, S. M. *Behavioral medicine: Changing health lifestyles*. New York: Bruner/Mazel, 1980.

Davis, D. R. The disorganization of behavior in fatigue. *Journal of Neurological Psychiatry*, 1946, *9*, 23–29.

*DeJong, R. N. Examination in cases of suspected hysteria and malingering. In *The neurological examination* (3rd ed.). Hagerstown, Md.: Harper and Row, 1967.

Deutsch, H. Psychoanalytic therapy in the light of follow-up. *Journal of the American Psychoanalytic Association*, 1959, *7*, 445–458.

DiLoreto, A. G. *Comparative psychotherapy*. Chicago: Aldine-Atherton, 1971.

Dollard, J., & Miller, N.E. *Personality and psychotherapy*. New York: McGraw-Hill, 1950.

Easser, B.R. & Lesser, S.R. Hysterical personality: A reevaluation. *Psychoanalytic Quarterly*, 1965, *34*, 390–405.

Eichler, M. The psychoanalytic treatment of an hysterical character with special emphasis on problems of aggression. *International Journal of Psychoanalysis*, 1976, *57*, 37–44.

Eissler, K. R. Malingering. In G.B. Wilbur & W. Muensterberger (Eds.), *Psychoanalysis and culture: Essays in honor of Geza Roheim*. New York: International Universities Press, 1951.

Ellenberger, H. *The discovery of the unconscious: The History and evaluation of dynamic psychiatry*. New York: Basic Books, 1970.

*Engel, G.L. A reconsideration of the role of conversion in somatic disease. *Comprehensive Psychiatry*, 1968, *9*, 316–326.

Engel, G.L. Conversion symptoms. In C.M. MacBride & R.S. Blacklon (Eds.), *Applied pathologic physiology and clinical interpretation* (5th ed.). Philadelphia: J.B. Lippincott, 1970.

Engel, G.L., & Schmale, A.M. Psychoanalytic theory of somatic disorder: Conversion, specificity, and the disease onset situation. *Journal of the American Psychoanalytic Association*, 1967, *15*, 344–365.

Epstein, L. A., & Hersen, M. Behavioral control of hysterical gagging. *Journal of Clinical Psychology*, 1974, *30*, 102–104.

Erickson, M. H., & Kubie, L. S. The permanent relief of an obsessional phobia by means of communication with an unsuspected dual personality. *Psychoanalytic Quarterly*, 1939, *8*, 471–509.

Erickson, R. A., & Huber, H. Elimination of hysterical torticollis through the use of a metronome in an operant conditioning paradigm. *Behavior Therapy*, 1975, *6*, 405–406.

Eysenck, H. J. *Dimensions of personality*. London: Kegan Paul, 1947.

Eysenck, H.J. *The scientific study of personality*. London: Routledge and Kegan Paul, 1952.

Eysenck, H.J. *The structure of human personality*. London: Methuen, 1953.

*Eysenck, H.J. A dynamic theory of anxiety and hysteria. *Journal of Mental Science*, 1955, *101*, 28–51.

Eysenck, H.J. (Ed.) *Behavioral therapy and the neuroses*. Oxford: Pergamon Press, 1960.

Eysenck, H.J., & Rachman, S. (Eds.). *Causes and cures of neurosis*. San Diego: Knapp, 1965.

Falconer, M. A., & Taylor, D. C. Temporal lobe epilepsy: Clinical features, pathology, diagnosis, and treatment. In J. H. Price (Ed.), *Modern trends in psychological medicine* (Vol. 2). London: J. H. Butterworth, 1970.

Feldman, F., Susselman, S., Lipetz, B., Barrera, S.E. Electroconvulsive therapy of acute hysteria. *Journal of Nervous and Mental Disease*, 1945, *102*, 498–503.

Fenichel, O. *The psychoanalytic theory of neurosis*. New York: Norton, 1945.

Ferenczi, S. *Further contributions to the theory and technique of psychoanalysis*. London: Hogarth Press, 1926.

Fordyce, W. E., Fowler, R. S., & DeLateur, B. An application of behavior modification techniques to a problem of chronic pain. *Behavior Research and Therapy*, 1968, *6*, 105–107.

Freud, S. The neuro-psychoses of defence. *Standard edition* (Vol. 3). London: Hogarth Press, 1962, pp. 45–61. (Originally published 1894.)

Freud, S. The interpretation of dreams. *Standard edition* (Vols. 4 & 5). London: Hogarth Press, 1953. (Originally published 1900.)

Freud, S. Fragment of an analysis of a case of hysteria. *Standard edition* (Vol. 7). London: Hogarth Press, 1953, pp. 7–122. (Originally published 1905.)(a)

Freud, S. Three essays on the theory of sexuality. *Standard edition* (Vol. 9). London: Hogarth Press, 1953, pp. 159–166. (Originally published 1905.) (b)

Freud, S. Analysis of a phobia in a five-year-old boy. *Standard edition* (Vol. 10). London: Hogarth Press, 1955, pp. 5–149. (Originally published 1909.)

Freud, S. Introductory lectures on psycho-analysis. *Standard edition* (Vols. 15 & 16). London: Hogarth Press, 1963. (Originally published 1916–1917.)

Freud, S. From the history of an infantile neurosis. *Standard edition* (Vol. 18). London: Hogarth Press, 1955, pp. 7–64. (Originally published 1918.)

Freud, S. The ego and the id. *Standard edition* (Vol. 19). London: Hogarth Press, 1961, pp. 2–66. (Originally published 1923.)

*Galin, D., Diamond, R., Branff, D. Lateralization of conversion symptoms: More frequent on the left. *American Journal of Psychiatry*. 1977, *134*, 578–580.

Gardner, J. E. Behavior therapy treatment approach to a psychogenic seizure.

Journal of Consulting Psychology, 1967, *31*, 209–212.

Gilberstadt, H., & Jancis, M. "Organic" versus "functional" diagnoses from 1-3 MMPI profiles. *Journal of Clinical Psychology*, 1967, *23*, 480–483.

Gill, M. M., & Brenman, M. *Hypnosis and related states*. New York: International Universities Press, 1959.

Glenn, T. J., & Simonds, J. F. Hypnotherapy of a psychogenic seizure in an adolescent. *The American Journal of Hypnosis*, 1977, *19*, 245–250.

Gomez-Lozano, P. Intravenous lorazepam in the acute anxiety crisis: A preliminary report on 60 cases. *Current Therapeutic Research*, 1976, *19*, 469–474.

Gray, J.A. Relation between stimulus intensity and operant response rate as a function of discrimination training and drive. *Journal of Experimental Psychology*, 1964, *69*, 9–24.

Greaves, G. B. Multiple personality. 165 years after Mary Reynolds. *The Journal of Nervous and Mental Disease*, 1980, *168*, 577–596.

Grinker, R.R. & Spiegel, J.P. *Men under stress*. N.Y.: McGraw-Hill, 1945. (reprinted, N.Y.: Irvington Pub., 1978.)

Grosz, H.J., & Zimmerman, J. Experimental analysis of hysterical blindness. *Archives of General Psychiatry*, 1965, *13*, 255–260.

Gruenwald, P. Hypnotic techniques without hypnosis in the treatment of dual personality. *Journal of Nervous and Mental Disease*, 1971, *153*, 41–46.

Guze, S.B., & Perley, M.J. Observations on the natural history of hysteria. *American Journal of Psychiatry*, 1963, *119*, 960–965.

Haley, J. *Advanced techniques of hypnosis and therapy: Selected papers of Milton H. Erickson, M.D*. New York: Grune & Stratton, 1967.

Haley, J. *Uncommon therapy: The psychiatric techniques of Milton H. Erickson, M.D*. New York: Ballantine, 1973.

Harriman, P.L. A new approach to multiple personality. *American Journal of Orthopsychiatry*, 1943, *13*, 638–643.

Hearst, E.D., Cloninger, C.R., Crews, E.L., & Cadoret, R.J. Electrosleep therapy: A double-blind trial. *Archives of General Psychiatry*, 1974, *30*, 463–466.

Hersen, M., Gullick, E.L., Matherne, P.M., & Harbert, T.L. Instructions and reinforcement in the modification of a conversion reaction. *Psychological Reports*, 1972, *31*, 719–722.

Hodge, J. R. The management of dissociative reactions with hypnosis. *International Journal of Clinical and Experimental Hypnosis*, 1959, *4*, 217–222.

Hollender, M. H. & Hirsch, S. J. Hysterical psychosis. *American Journal of Psychiatry*, 1972, *26*, 311–314.

Horwitz, L. *Clinical prediction in psychotherapy*. New York: Aronson, 1974.

Horowitz, M. J. Structure and the process of change. In M.J. Horowitz (Ed.), *Hysterical Personality*. New York: Aronson, 1977.

Ingalls, G.S. Hysterical amnesia relieved by induced convulsions. *Journal of Nervous and Mental Disease*, 1939, *90*, 453.

Janet, P. L'Anesthesie systematisée et la dissociation des phenomènes psychologiques. *Révue Philosophique*, 1887, *23*, 449–472.

Janet, P. *L'Automatisme psychologique*. Paris: Alcan, 1889.

Kallman, W., Hersen, M., & O'Toole, D. The use of social reinforcement in a case of conversion reaction. *Behavior Therapy*, 1975, *6*, 411–413.

Kaminsky, M., & Slavney, P. Methodology and personality in Briquet's Syndrome: A reappraisal. *American Journal of Psychiatry,* 1976, *133,* 85–88.

Kaplan, J.M., & Deabler, H.L. Hypnotherapy with a severe dissociative hysterical disorder. *American Journal of Clinical Hypnosis,* 1975, *18,* 83–89.

Kass, D.J., Silvers, F.M., & Abroms, G.M. Behavioral group treatment of hysteria. *Archives of General Psychiatry,* 1972, 26, 42–50.

Kehoe, M.J. Facial pain: Hypnotic suggestion as a method of treatment. *American Journal of Psychiatry,* 1967, *123,* 1577–1581.

Kerckhoff, A.C. & Bach, K.W. *The June Bug: A study of hysterical contagion.* New York: Appleton-Century-Crofts, 1968.

Kernberg, O. Borderline personality organization. *Journal of the American Psychoanalytic Association,* 1967, *15,* 641–685.

Kernberg, O., Burstein, E., Coyne, L., Appelbaum, A., Horwitz, L., & Voth, H. Psychotherapy and psychoanalysis: Final report of the Menninger foundation's psychotherapy research project. *Bulletin of the Menninger Clinic,* 1972, *36,* 1–275.

*Kirshner, L. A. Dissociative reactions: An historical review and clinical study. *Acta Psychiatrica Scandanavica,* 1973, *49,* 698–711.

Kitchener, R. F. Ethical relativism and behavior therapy. *Journal of Consulting and Clinical Psychology,* 1980, *48,* 1–7.

Knight, R. P. Evaluation of the results of psychoanalytic therapy. *American Journal of Psychiatry,* 1941, *98,* 434–446.

Kohlenberg, R. J. The punishment of persistent vomiting: A case study. *Journal of Applied Behavior Analysis,* 1970, *3,* 241–245.

Kohut, H. *Analysis of the self.* New York: International Universities Press, 1971.

Krapf, E. E. On the pathogenesis of epileptic and hysterical seizures. *Bulletin of the World Health Organization,* 1957, *16,* 749–762.

Kretschmer, E. *Hysteria.* New York: Nervous and Mental Disease Publishing Co., 1926.

Kroll, P., Chamberlain, K.R., & Halpern, J. The diagnosis of Briquet's Syndrome in a male population: The Veteran's Administration revisited. *Journal of Nervous and Mental Disease,* 1979, *167,* 171–174.

La Barre, W. *The Ghost Dance: The origins of religion.* Garden City: Doubleday, 1970.

Lader, M., & Sartorius, N. Anxiety in patients with hysterical conversion symptoms. *Journal of Neurology, Neurosurgery, and Psychiatry,* 1968, *31,* 490–495.

Lair, C. V., & Trapp, P. The differential diagnostic value of the MMPI with somatically disturbed patients. *Journal of Clinical Psychology,* 1962, *18,* 147.

Larmore, K., Ludwig, A. M., & Cain, R. L. Multiple personality—An objective case study. *British Journal of Psychiatry,* 1977, *131,* 35–40.

Lazare, A., Klerman, G. L., & Armor, D. J. Oral, obsessive and hysterical personality patterns. *Archives of General Psychiatry,* 1966, *14,* 624–630.

Lazarus, A.A. The results of behavior therapy in 126 cases of severe neurosis. *Behavior Research and Therapy,* 1963, *1,* 69–79.

Leaverton, D.R., Rupp, J.W., & Poff, M.G. *Child psychiatry and human development,* 1977, *7,* 255–261.

Lesser, R., & Fahn, S. Dystonia: A disorder often misdiagnosed as a conversion reaction. *American Journal of Psychiatry*, 1978, *135*, 349.

Lezak, M. *Neuropsychological assessment*. New York: Oxford University Press, 1976.

Liebson, I. Conversion reaction: A learning theory approach. *Behavior Research and Therapy*, 1969, *7*, 217–218.

Lindner, R.M. Hypnoanalysis in a case of hysterical somnambulism. *Psychoanalytic Review*, 1945, *32*, 325–339.

Lishman, W. A. *Organic psychiatry: The psychological consequences of cerebral disorder*. Oxford: Blackwell, 1980.

Liskow, B., Clayton, P., Woodruff, R., Guze, S.B., & Cloninger, R. Briquet's syndrome, hysterical personality, and the MMPI. *American Journal of Psychiatry*, 1977, *134*, 1137–1139.

Liversledge, L.A. & Sylvester, J.D. Conditioning techniques in the treatment of writer's cramp. In H.J. Eysenck (Ed.), *Behavior therapy and the neuroses*. Oxford: Pergamon Press, 1960.

*Ludwig, A.M. Hysteria: A neurobiological theory. *Archives of General Psychiatry*, 1972, *27*, 771–777.

Luisada, P. V., Peele, R., & Pittard, E. A. The hysterical personality in men. *American Journal of Psychiatry*, 1974, *131*, 518–522.

Mahler, M., & Rangell, L. A psychosomatic study of *Maladie des Tics* (Gilles de la Tourette's Disease). *Psychiatric Quarterly*, 1943, *17*, 519.

Marmor, J. Orality in the hysterical personality. *Journal of the American Psychoanalytic Association*, 1953, *1*, 656–671.

Martin, P. A. Dynamic considerations of the hysterical psychosis. *American Journal of Psychiatry*, 1971, *128*, 745–748.

McDaniel, E. Hysterical neurosis. In G. Balis, L. Wurmser, & E. McDaniel (Eds.), *Clinical psychopathology: The psychiatric foundations of medicine*. Boston: Butterworth Publishers, Inc., 1978.

Moldofsky, A. & England, R. S. Facilitation of somatosensory average-evoked potentials in hysterical anesthesia and pain. *Archives of General Psychiatry*, 1975, *32*, 193–197.

Morton, J.H. & Thomas, E. A case of multiple personality. *American Journal of Clinical Hypnosis*, 1964, *6*, 216–225.

Moss, C.S., Thompson, M.M. & Nolte, J. An additional study in hysteria: The case of Alice M. *Clinical and Experimental Hypnosis*, 1962, *10*, 59–74.

Mowrer, O.H. *Learning theory and personality dynamics*. New York: Ronald Press, 1950.

Munford, P.R., Reardon, D., Lieberman, R.P., & Allen, L. Behavioral treatment of hysterical coughing and mutism: A case study. *Journal of Consulting and Clinical Psychology*, 1976, *44*, 1008–1014.

Murphy, G. *Personality*. New York: Harper & Row, 1947.

Murphy, H. B. M. History and evolution of syndromes: The striking case of *latah* and *amok*. In M. Hammer, K. Salzinger, & S. Sutton (Eds.), *Psychopathology: Contributions from the social, behavioral, and biological sciences*. New York: Wiley, 1973.

Noreik, K. A follow-up examination of neuroses. *Acta Psychiatrica Scandanavica* 1970, *46*, 81–95.

Ohno, Y., Sugita, M., Takeya, T., Akagi, M., Tanaka, Y., & Ikemi, Y. The treatment of hysterical blindness by behavior therapy. *Psychosomatics*, 1974, *15*, 79–82.

Parry-Jones, W. L., Sauter-Westrate, H. C., & Crawley, R. C. Behavior therapy in a case of hysterical blindness. *Behavior Research and Therapy*, 1970, *8*, 79–85.

Paul, G. L. *Insight vs. desensitization in psychotherapy*. Stanford: Stanford University Press, 1966.

Pelletier, A.M. Hysterical aphonia: A case report. *American Journal of Clinical Hypnosis*, 1977, *20*, 149–153.

Perley, M.J., & Guze, S.B. Hysteria—the stability and usefulness of clinical criteria: A quantitative study based on a follow-up period of six to eight years in 39 patients. *New England Journal of Medicine*, 1962, *266*, 421–426.

Peters, J. The neurologist's use of rating scales, EEG, and tranquilizers in dealing with hysterical symptoms. *Behavioral Neuropsychiatry*, 1975, *6*, 85–86.

Prince, M. *The dissociation of a personality*. New York: Longmans, Green, 1926.

Rapaport, D., Gill, M. M., & Schafer, R. *Diagnostic psychological testing*. New York: International Universities Press, 1968.

*Raskin, M., Talbott, J., & Meyerson, A. Diagnosis of conversion reactions: Predictive value of psychiatric criteria. *Journal of the American Medical Association*, 1966, *197*, 530–534.

Reich, W. *Character analysis*. New York: Farrar, Straus, & Giroux, 1972. (Originally published 1933.)

Reitan, R., & Davison, L. *Clinical neuropsychology: Current status and applications*. New York: Winston/Wiley, 1974.

Reveley, M., Woodruff, R., Robins, L., Taibleson, M., Reich, T., & Helzer, J. Evaluation of a screening interview for Briquet Syndrome (hysteria) by the study of medically ill women. *Archives of General Psychiatry*, 1977, *34*, 145–149.

Rice, D. G., & Greenfield, N. S. Psychophysiological correlates of *la belle indifférence*. *Archives of General Psychiatry*, 1969, *20*, 239–245.

Richer, P. *Études cliniques sur l'hystéro-epilepsie ou Grande Hystérie*. Paris: Delahaye et Lecrosnier, 1881.

Rifkin, A., Quitkin, F., & Carillo, C. Lithium carbonate in emotionally unstable character disorders. *Archives of General Psychiatry*, 1972, *27*, 519–523.

Rosen, B.M., Locke, B.Z., Goldberg, I.D. Identification of emotional disturbance in patients seen in general medical clinics. *Hospital and Community Psychiatry*, 1972, *23*, 364–370.

Rosen, H. The hypnotic and hypnotherapeutic unmasking: Intensification and recognition of an emotion. *American Journal of Psychiatry*, 1952, *109*, 120–127.

Rosenbaum, M., Friedlander, J., & Kaplan, S.M. Evaluation of results of psychotherapy. *Psychosomatic Medicine*, 1956, *18*, 113–132.

Roy, A. Hysteria. *Journal of Psychosomatic Research*, 1980, *24*, 53–56.

Sands, D.E. Electro-convulsion therapy in 301 patients in a general hospital. *British Medical Journal*, 1946, *2*, 289–293.

Saslow, G., & Peters, A. D. A follow-up study of "untreated" patients with various behavior disorders. *Psychiatric Quarterly*, 1956, *30*, 283–302.

*Scallet, A., Cloninger, C. R., & Othmer, E. The management of chronic hysteria: A review and double-blind trial of electrosleep and other relaxation methods. *Diseases of the Nervous System*, 1976, July, 347–353.

Shafer, R. *The clinical application of psychological tests*. New York: International Universities Press, 1948.

Schafer, R. *Psychoanalytic interpretation in Rorschach testing: Theory and application*. New York: Grune and Stratton, 1954.

Schreiber, F.R. *Sybil*. New York: Warner Paperback Library, 1974.

*Shapiro, D. *Neurotic styles*. New York: Basic Books, 1965.

Shapiro, D. A perceptual understanding of color response. In M. A. Rickers-Ovsiankina (Ed.), *Rorschach psychology*. Huntington, N.Y.: Krieger Publishing Co., 1977.

Singh, R. Experiments in two cases of hysterical fits. *Journal of Behavior Therapy and Experimental Psychiatry*, 1975, *6*, 351–353.

Sirois, F. Epidemic hysteria. *Acta Psychiatrica Scandinavica (Suppl.)*, 1974, *252*, 11–46.

Slater, J.E., & Glithero, E. A follow-up of patients diagnosed as suffering from hysteria. *Journal of Psychosomatic Research*, 1965, *9*, 9–13.

Slavney, P.R. The diagnosis of hysterical personality disorder: A study of attitudes. *Comprehensive Psychiatry*, 1978, *19*, 501–507.

Slavney, P. R., & McHugh, P. R. The hysterical personality. *Archives of General Psychiatry*, 1974, *30*, 325–332.

Sloane, R. B., Staples, F. R., Christal, A. H., Yorkston, N.J., & Whipple, K. *Psychotherapy and behavior therapy*. Cambridge: Harvard University Press, 1975.

Small, L. *Neuropsychodiagnosis in psychotherapy*. New York: Bruner/Mazel, 1973.

Smokler, I., & Shevrin, H. Cerebral lateralization and personality style. *Archives of General Psychiatry*, 1979, *36*, 949–954.

Sperling, M. Conversion hysteria and conversion symptoms: A revision of classification and concepts. *Journal of the American Psychoanalytic Association*, 1973, *21*, 745–771.

Spindler, G.D. Psychocultural adaption. In E. Norbeck (Ed.), *The study of personality: An interdisciplinary approach*. New York: Holt, Rinehart and Winston, 1968.

Starker, S. Hysterical reactions to hypnotic inductions. *Psychotherapy: Theory, research, and practice*, 1973, *10*, 141–144.

Stolz, S.B., & Wolf, M.M. Visually discriminated behavior in a "blind" adolescent retardate. *Journal of Applied Behavior Analysis*, 1969, *2*, 65–77.

*Szasz, T. *The myth of mental illness: Foundations of a theory of personal conduct*. New York: Hoeber-Harper, 1961.

Taylor, W.S., & Martin, M.F. Multiple personality. *Journal of Abnormal and Social Psychology*, 1944, *39*, 281–300.

*Temoshok, L., & Attkisson, C.C. An epidemiological approach to hysteria. In M. Horowitz (Ed.), *Hysterical personality*. New York: Jason Aronson, 1977.

Thigpen, C. H., & Cleckley, H. A case of multiple personality. *Journal of Abnormal and Social Psychology*, 1954, *49*, 135–151.

Tomkins, S. S. *Affect, imagery, consciousness* (Vol. 1). *The positive emotions*. New York: Springer, 1962.

Tophoff, M. Massed practice, relaxation, and assertion training in the treatment of Gilles de la Tourette's syndrome. *Journal of Behavior Therapy and Experimental Psychiatry*, 1973, *4*, 71–73.

Tourette, Gilles de la. Étude sur une affection nerveuse, caracterisée par de l'incoordination motrice, accompagnée d'écholalie et la coprolalie. *Archives de Neurologie*, 1885, 9, 159.

Turner, S. M., & Hersen, M. Instructions and reinforcement in the modification of a case of astasia-abasia. *Psychological Reports*, 1975, *36*, 607–612.

Ullmann, L.P., & Krasner, L.A. *A psychological approach to abnormal behavior*. Englewood Cliffs, N.J.: Prentice-Hall, 1969.

Valko, R.J. Group therapy for patients with hysteria (Briquet's disorder). *Diseases of the Nervous System*, 1976, *37*, 484–487.

*Van Dyke, C. Hysteria and hypochondriasis. In H. Leigh (Ed.), *Psychiatry in primary care medicine*. New York: Addison-Wesley, 1982.

Van Putten, T., & Alban, J. Lithium carbonate in personality disorders: A case of hysteria. *Journal of Nervous and Mental Disease*, 1977, *164*, 218–222.

*Veith, I. Four thousand years of hysteria. In M. Horowitz (Ed.), *Hysterical personality*. New York: Jason Aronson, 1977.

Wallerstein, R.S. The psychotherapy research project of the Menninger foundation. In J. Shlein (Ed.), *Research in psychotherapy* (Vol. III). Washington, D.C.: American Psychological Association, 1968.

Walton, D., & Black, O. The application of modern learning theory to the treatment of chronic hysterical aphonia. *Journal of Psychosomatic Research*, 1959, *3*, 303–311.

Warner, R. The diagnosis of antisocial and hysterical personality disorders: An example of sex bias. *Journal of Nervous and Mental Diseases*, 1978, *166*, 839–845.

Watkins, J.G. *Hypnotherapy of war neuroses*. New York: Ronald Press, 1949.

*Watson, C., & Buranen, C. The frequency and identification of false positive conversion reaction. *The Journal of Nervous and Mental Disease*, 1979, *167*, 243–247.

Wheatley, D. Evaluation of psychotherapeutic drugs in general practice. *Psychopharmacology Bulletin*, 1962, *2*, 25–32.

Wheatley, D. General practitioner clinical trials. Two new psychotropic drugs. *Practitioner*, 1967, *198*, 135–141.

White, R.W. Ego and reality in psychoanalytic theory. *Psychological Issues*, 1963, *3*, 1–210.

Witkin, H. A., Dyk, R. B., Faterson, H. F., Goodenough, D. R. & Karp, S. A. *Psychological differentiation: Studies of development*. New York: John Wiley, 1962.

Wittels, F. The hysterical character. *Medical Review of Reviews*, 1930, *36*, 186–190.

Wolberg, L.R. A mechanism of hysteria elucidation during hypnoanalysis. *Psychoanalytic Quarterly*, 1945, *14*, 528–534.

Wolpe, J. *Psychotherapy by reciprocal inhibition*. Stanford: Stanford University Press, 1958.

Wolpe, J. *The practice of behavior therapy*. New York: Pergamon, 1973.

*Woodruff, R. A., Clayton, P. J., & Guze, S. B. Hysteria: Studies of diagnosis, outcome, and prevalence. *Journal of the American Medical Association*, 1971, *215*, 425–428.

Worsley, P. *The trumpet shall sound*. New York: Schocken, 1968.

*Yates, A. Symptoms and symptom substitution. In H. J. Eysenck (Ed.), *Behavior therapy and the neuroses*. Oxford: Pergamon, 1960.

*Yates, A. *Behavior therapy*. New York: Wiley, 1970.

Zetzel, E. The so-called good hysteric. *International Journal of Psycho-analysis*, 1968, *49*, 256–260.

Ziegler, F.J., Imboden, J.B., & Meyer, E. Contemporary conversion reactions: A clinical study. *American Journal of Psychiatry*, 1960, *116*, 901–909.

Suggested Readings

Asher, R. Malingering. In F. A. Jones (Ed.), *Richard Asher talking sense*. Baltimore: University Park Press, 1972.

Griest, J. H., Jefferson, J., & Spitzer, R. (Eds.). *Treatment for DSM-III disorders*. New York: Oxford University Press, 1980.

Hyler, S. E., & Spitzer, R. L. Hysteria split asunder. *American Journal of Psychiatry*, 1978, *135*, 1500.

Jones, M. M. Conversion reaction: Anachronism or evolutionary form? A review of the neurology, behavioral, and psychoanalytic literature. *Psychological Bulletin*, 1980, *87*, 427–441.

Krohn, A. *Hysteria: The elusive neurosis*. New York: International Universities Press, 1978.

Lewis, A. The survival of hysteria. *Psychological Medicine*, 1975, 5, 9–12.

Lewis, W. C. Hysteria: The consultant's dilemma. *Archives of General Psychiatry*, 1974, *30*, 145–151.

Index